Around Parliament
Pages 108–123

HUNGÁRIA KÖRÚT
KÓS KÁROLY SÉTÁNY
THÖKÖLY ÚT
TERÉZ KÖRÚT
ANDRÁSSY ÚT
BAJCSY-ZSILINSZKY ÚT
AROUND VÁROSLIGET
ANDRÁSSY ÚT
ERZSÉBET KÖRÚT
THÖKÖLY ÚT
RÁKÓCZI ÚT
CENTRAL PEST
RÁKÓCZI ÚT
JÓZSEF KÖRÚT
BAROSS U.
VÁMHÁZ KRT
ÜLLŐI ÚT

Around Városliget
Pages 144–155

Central Pest
Pages 124–143

EYEWITNESS TRAVEL

BUDAPEST

EYEWITNESS TRAVEL

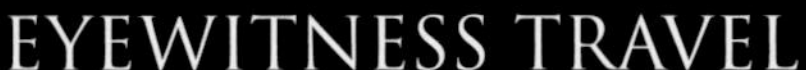

BUDAPEST

Main Contributors **Barbara Olszańska, Tadeusz Olszański**

DK

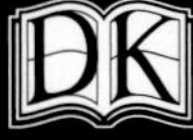

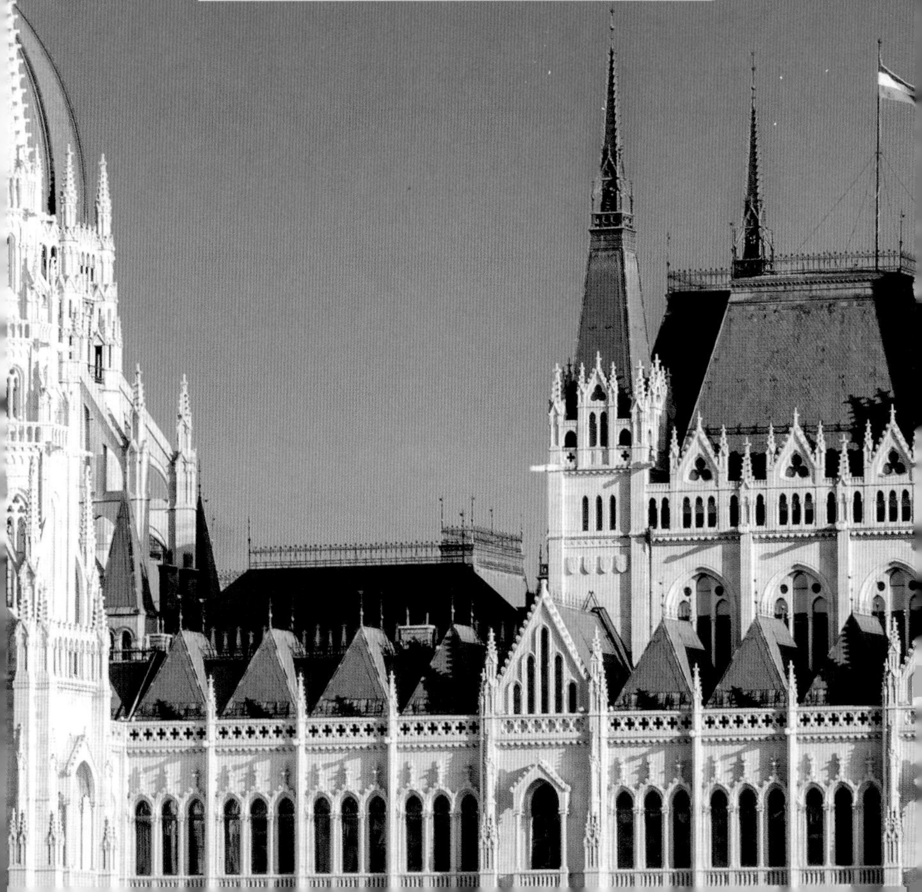

LONDON, NEW YORK,
MELBOURNE, MUNICH AND DELHI
www.dk.com

Produced by Wydawnictwo Wiedza i Życie, Warsaw

Series Editor Ewa Szwagrzyk

Consultants András Hadik, Małgorzata Omilanowska, Katalin Szokolay

Editors Joanna Egert, Anna Kożurno-Królikowska, Bożena Leszkowicz

Designer Paweł Pasternak

Dorling Kindersley Ltd

Project Editor Jane Oliver

Editors Felicity Crowe, Nancy Jones

Translators Magda Hannay, Anna Johnson, Ian Wisniewski

Photographers Gábor Barka, Dorota and Mariusz Jarymowiczowie

Illustrators Paweł Mistewicz, Piotr Zubrzycki

Printed and bound by South China Printing Co. Ltd., China

First American edition, 1999
14 15 16 17 10 9 8 7 6 5 4 3 2 1

Published in the United States by
DK Publishing, 345 Hudson Street,
New York, New York 10014

Reprinted with revisions 2000, 2001, 2004, 2007, 2009, 2011, 2013, 2015

A catalog record for this book is available from
the Library of Congress

ISSN 1542-1554

ISBN 978-1-46542-568-3

Floors are referred to throughout in accordance with European usage; ie the "first floor" is the floor above ground level.

MIX
Paper from responsible sources
FSC™ C018179

The information in this DK Eyewitness Travel Guide is checked regularly.

Every effort has been made to ensure that this book is as up-to-date as possible at the time of going to press. Some details, however, are liable to change. The publishers cannot accept responsibility for any consequences arising from the use of this book, nor for any material on third party websites, and cannot guarantee that any website address in this book will be a suitable source of travel information. We value the views and suggestions of our readers very highly. Please write to: Publisher, DK Eyewitness Travel Guides, Dorling Kindersley, 80 Strand, London WC2R 0RL, UK, or email: travelguides@dk.com.

Front cover main image: Chain Bridge, Gresham Palace and St Stephen's Basilica at dusk

◀ Hungary's Neo-Gothic Parliament building, with the central point marked by a dome

Contents

Statue in Batthyány Square *(see p104)*

Introducing Budapest

Hungarian crest adorning a wall close to the Tunnel *(see p104)*

Budapest Area by Area

Barrel-organ player in the historic Castle District *(see pp72–89)*

The Hungarian National Gallery *(see pp78–81)*, in the former Royal Palace

Travellers' Needs

Survival Guide

The elaborate exterior of the Parliament building *(see pp112–13)*

Porcelain in the Museum of Applied Arts *(see pp140–41)*

The landmark domes and towers of four of Budapest's most striking places of worship

HOW TO USE THIS GUIDE

This Eyewitness Travel Guide helps you get the most from your stay in Budapest with the minimum of difficulty. The opening section, *Introducing Budapest*, locates the city geographically, sets modern Budapest in its historical context and describes events through the entire year. *Budapest at a Glance* is an overview of the city's main attractions. *Budapest Area by Area* starts on page 70. This is the main sightseeing section, which covers all of the important sights, with photographs, maps and illustrations. It also includes day trips from Budapest and three walks around the city. Information about hotels, restaurants, shops and markets, entertainment and sports is found in *Travellers' Needs*. The *Survival Guide* has advice on everything from using the postal service and telephones to Budapest's public transport system and medical services.

Finding Your Way Around the Sightseeing Section

Each of six sightseeing areas in Budapest is colour-coded for easy reference. Every chapter opens with an introduction to the area of the city it covers, describing its history and character, and has one or two *Street-by-Street* maps illustrating typical parts of that area. Finding your way around the chapter is made simple by the numbering system used throughout. The most important sights are covered in detail in two or more full pages.

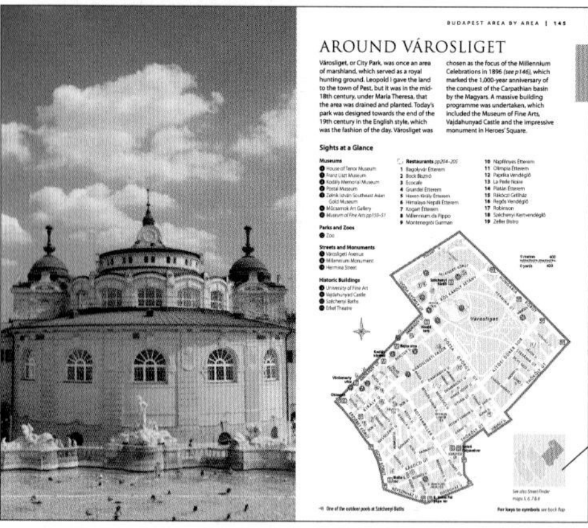

1 Introduction to the area
For easy reference, the sights in each area are numbered and plotted on an area map. To help the visitor, this map also shows underground stations, main bus and tram stops and parking areas. The area's key sights are listed by category: Museums and Galleries; Churches; Historic Streets and Squares; Palaces and Historic Buildings; Hotels and Baths; and Parks and Gardens.

A locator map shows where you are in relation to the other areas in the city centre.

2 Street-by-Street map
This gives a bird's-eye view of interesting and important parts of each sightseeing area. The numbering of the sights ties up with the area map and the fuller description on the pages that follow.

Each area has colour-coded thumb tabs.

A suggested route takes in some of the most interesting and attractive streets in the area.

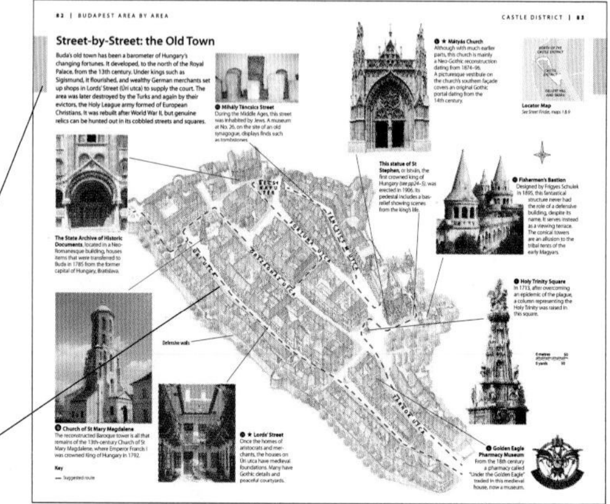

Budapest Area Map

The coloured areas shown on this map *(see inside front cover)* are the six main sightseeing areas used in this guide. Each is covered in a full chapter in *Budapest Area by Area (pp70–171)*. They are highlighted on other maps throughout the book. In *Budapest at a Glance*, for example, they help you locate the top sights. They are also used to help you find the position of the three walks *(pp172–9)*.

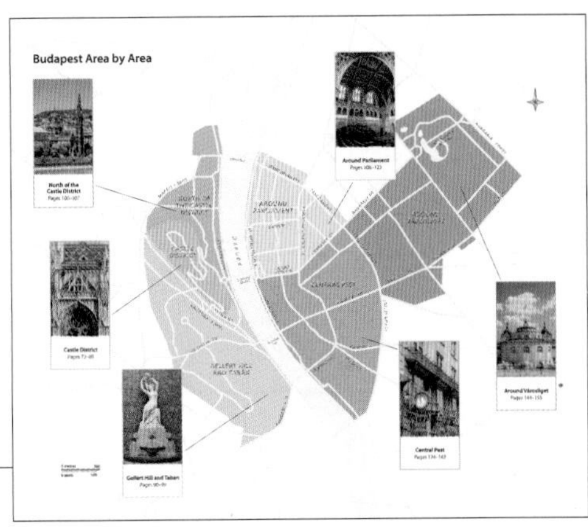

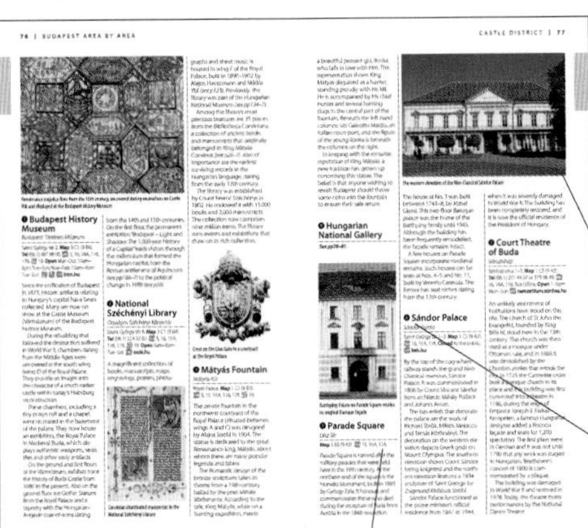

3 Detailed information on each sight

All the important sights in Budapest are described individually. They are listed in order following the numbering on the area map at the start of the section. Practical information includes a map reference, opening hours, telephone numbers and admission charges. The key to the symbols used is on the back flap.

Façades of important buildings are often shown to help you recognize them quickly.

Numbers refer to each sight's position on the area map and its place in the chapter.

Practical information provides everything you need to know to visit each sight. Map references pinpoint the sight's location on the Street Finder maps *(pp242–53)*.

4 Budapest's major sights

Historic buildings are dissected to reveal their interiors; museums and galleries have colour-coded floorplans to help you find important exhibits.

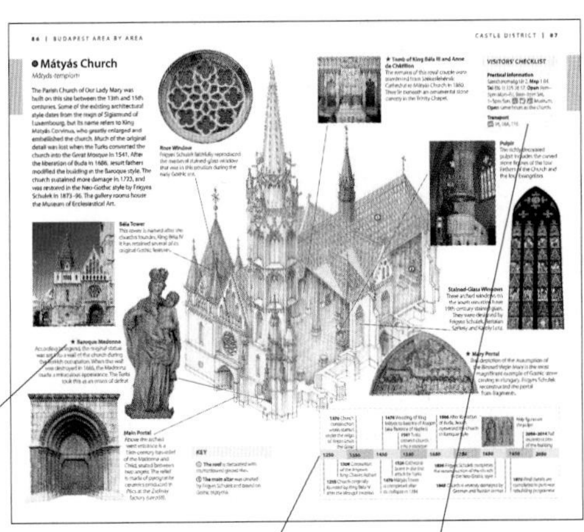

Stars indicate the features no visitor should miss.

A timeline charts the key events in the history of the building.

The visitors' checklist provides all the practical information needed to plan your visit.

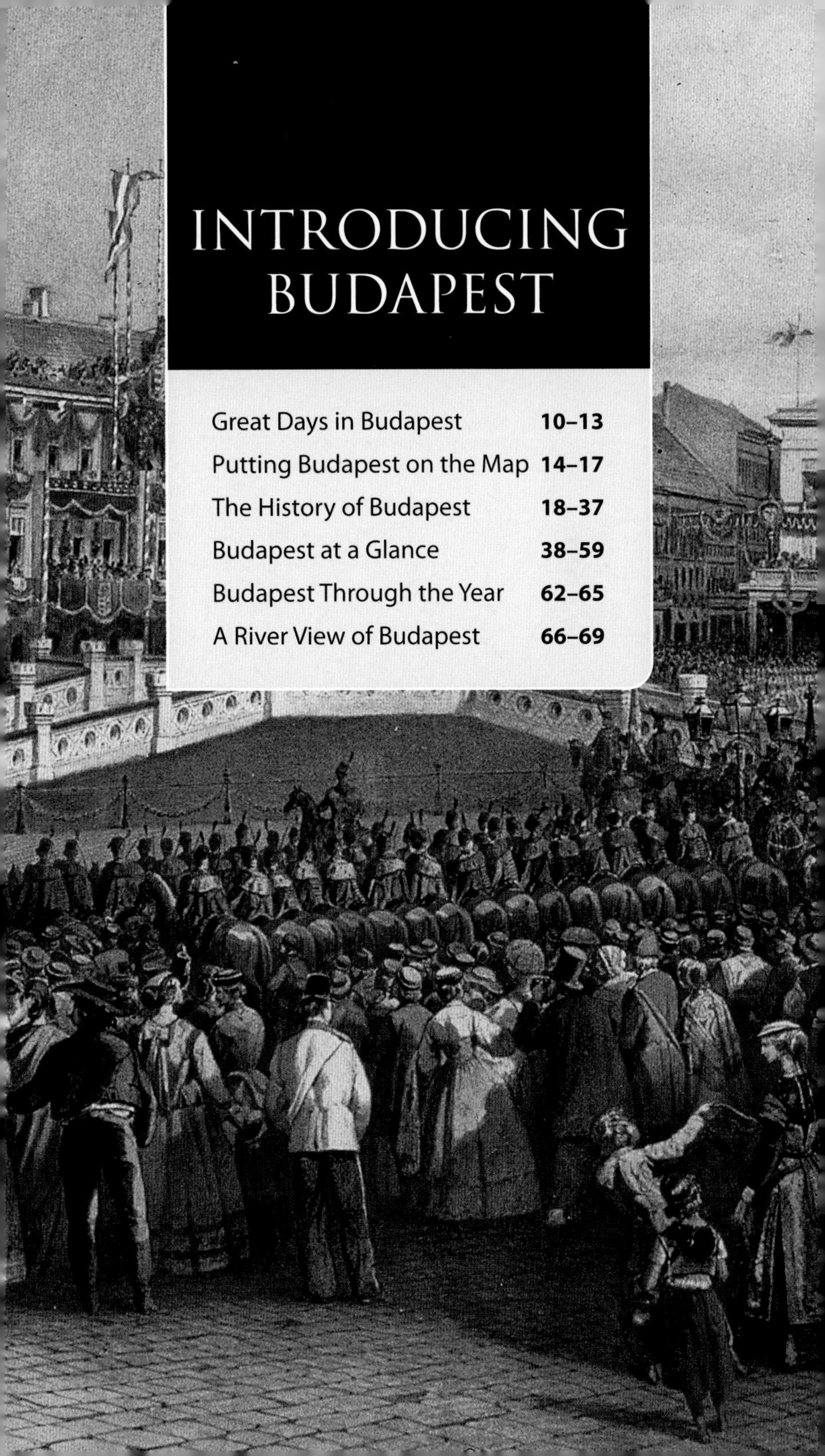

INTRODUCING BUDAPEST

GREAT DAYS IN BUDAPEST

This historic, sprawling city has so much to offer it can be difficult to decide how best to spend your time. Whether you are here for several days, or just wanting a flavour of this great city, you'll find itineraries for some of the best of Budapest's attractions on the following pages, arranged first under themes and then by length of stay. Sightseers should manage everything on these itineraries, but the selections can also be dipped into for ideas. All routes are reachable by public transport. Price guides on pages 10 and 11 are for two adults or for a family of two adults and two children, including lunch.

Passengers ride the antique Sikló funicular railway up Castle Hill

A Day on Castle Hill

Two adults allow 25,000–30,000 HUF

- **Art at the Royal Palace**
- **Lunch in a Castle courtyard**
- **Concert at Mátyás Church**
- **A subterranean Labyrinth**

Morning

Buda's **Castle District** *(see pp72–89)* towers over Pest. Winding paths lead up Castle Hill from Clark Adám tér, but the traditional way up is by the **Sikló** *(see p239)*, a 100-year-old funicular railway. Start the day with a tour of the grounds of the **Royal Palace** *(see pp74–5)*. Take time to admire the Romantic design of **Mátyás Fountain** *(see pp76–7)*, and to visit the wonderful collection of 19th-century Hungarian paintings at the **National Gallery** *(see pp78–81)*. Leave the Palace area through the ornamental Habsburg Gate, then stop at **Rivalda** *(see p196)* for a splendid *al fresco* lunch.

Afternoon

A short walk along Tárnok utca into central Buda, past myriad souvenir shops, leads to **Fishermen's Bastion** *(see p84)*. From here there are glorious views of Pest, especially **Parliament** *(see pp112–13)* and **Chain Bridge** *(see p66)*, almost directly below. Do not fail to visit ancient **Mátyás Church** *(see pp86–7)* – where there are organ concerts some summer evenings – before walking along the wonderfully preserved streets of Buda's Old Town. Follow Fortuna utca round to Kapisztran tér and the lone, ruined tower of **St Mary Magdalene** *(see p88)*.

Peerless **Lords' Street** *(see p89)*, with its Gothic details and peaceful courtyards, leads to the bizarre subterranean **Labyrinth** *(see p89)*. Nearby **Alabárdos** *(see p196)* is the perfect place for an early dinner in a medieval setting.

The Finer Side of Life

Two adults allow at least 35,000 HUF

- **A morning at the spa baths**
- **The Museum of Fine Arts**
- **A walk to the Opera House**
- **Dinner at Gresham Kávéház**

Morning

Start with coffee in **Gerbeaud** *(see p201)*, the city's most famous café. Then ride the beautifully preserved **Millennium Line** *(see p238)* to **Széchenyi Baths** *(see p155)*, and spend at least three hours indulging in bathing, sauna, massage and other treatments in glorious imperial surroundings. Stop for lunch at **Gundel Étterem** *(see p205)*.

One of three outdoor pools at Széchenyi Baths, the deepest in Budapest

◀ The coronation of Franz Joseph I by Ede Heinrich (1819–1885)

Afternoon
Walk off the effects of lunch in the **Museum of Fine Arts** *(see pp150–53)*, which houses Hungary's finest collection of foreign art in a monumental building facing **Heroes' Square** *(see pp146–7)*.

On leaving the museum, walk past the **Millennium Monument** *(see p149)* and down Andrássy út – a superb avenue of embassies and consulates, giving way to restaurants and shops – and stop at one of the many cafés on **Liszt Ferenc tér** *(see pp202, 203)*. The highlight of Andrássy út is No. 22, the **Hungarian State Opera** *(see pp122–3)*, which offers guided tours in the late afternoon. From here, walk along lower Andrássy út, over Erzsébet tér, to the **Gresham Palace** hotel *(see p118)*, facing Chain Bridge. Finally, spend the evening dining at the informal **Gresham Restaurant** *(see p199)*, famous for its *"Three Foie Gras"*, a Hungarian speciality.

Family Fun al Fresco

Family of 4 allow at least 30,000 HUF

- **A tour of the Buda Hills on the Children's Railway**
- **A walking safari round Budakeszi Wildlife Park**
- **Supper and folk music**

Morning
Head for the **Buda Hills** *(see p165)* by means of the Széchenyi Hill cog railway *(5am–11pm; Tel (06 1) 355 41 67)*, which begins at Szilágyi Erzsébet fasor, just north of Széll Kálmán tér metro station. At the top, a short walk leads to the TV tower (closed) and the terminus of the **Children's Railway** *(open May–Aug: 10am–5pm)*. The steam engine departs on the hour and meanders through the Buda hills to Hűvösvölgy, passing the **Erzsébet Look-Out Tower**. Disembark at Szép Juhászné station for lunch at the outdoor café.

Children relax at Budakeszi Wildlife Park in the Buda Hills

Afternoon
A well-marked path runs from the café to **Budakeszi Wildlife Park** *(open 9am–5pm Mon–Fri, 9am–6pm Sat & Sun; Tel (06 1) 23 451 783)*. The park is set over 3 sq km (1 sq mile) and contains a wide variety of animals, from wild boar (which also roam the surrounding countryside), to wolves. There is a separate reserve for plants and flora. A walking safari tours the best of both areas. The on-site restaurant is a great place for supper, and offers folk music after 6pm. At going-home time the Children's Railway will be closed, but metro Line 1 takes you back to Deák Ferenc utca.

History and Shopping

Two adults allow at least 20,000 HUF (plus shopping)

- **The surviving monuments of the Jewish Quarter**
- **A traditional Jewish lunch**
- **Shopping on Váci utca and in Central Market**

Morning
Start at the **Hungarian National Museum** *(see pp134–7)*, where Sándor Petőfi read his *National Song* in 1848 *(see p33)*. Spend an hour amongst the treasures of Hungary's turbulent past, then go to another historic location – the **Jewish Quarter** *(see p138)*. The **Great Synagogue** *(p138)* on Dohány utca is a splendid Byzantine-style building, attached to which is the **Jewish Museum**. The **Holocaust Memorial** is found behind the synagogue's courtyard. The rest of the quarter is known for its gift shops and book stores, and the less ostentatious synagogues on Rumbach S. utca and Kazinczy utca. On the same street, stop for a kosher lunch at **Carmel Étterem** *(see p203)*.

Afternoon
Váci utca *(see p131)* offers great shopping at its northern end – for souvenirs, fashion and fine Hungarian porcelain at Goda (No. 9). Visit the **Inner City Parish Church** *(see pp128–9)*, then cross Kossuth Lajos út, and head south past the **Klotild Palaces** *(see p131)* and more shops, to Fővám tér. Rest here in a café. Across the road is the final retail challenge of the day – the huge food market at **Central Market Hall** *(see p211)*.

One of the many busy terrace cafés that line Váci utca

2 Days in Budapest

- **Explore Castle Hill, the historic heart of Buda**
- **Hop aboard the city's century-old funicular**
- **Browse amongst the colourful food stalls at the Central Market Hall**

Day 1

Morning Explore the historic heart of Buda, **Castle Hill** *(pp72–89)*. Admire the fine 13th-century **Mátyás Church** *(pp86–7)* before taking in the superlative views across the Danube from the **Fishermen's Bastion** *(p84)*. Enjoy lunch in one of the area's many classy restaurants.

Afternoon Carry on down to the **Royal Palace** *(pp74–5)*, which houses the engrossing **Hungarian National Gallery** *(pp78–81)*. Then jump aboard the **Sikló** *(p239)*, the funicular that transports you down to the majestic **Chain Bridge** *(p66)*. End the day by taking a stroll along the banks of the Danube through the **Víziváros** district *(pp102–103)*, perhaps ending the day in a local café.

Day 2

Morning Devote the morning to discovering the historic **Parliament** *(pp112–13)*, with its iconic red dome, and then **St Stephen's Basilica** *(pp120–21)*, in which the Holy Right Hand of the eponymous saint resides. Enjoy lunch in the buzzy area of **Vörösmarty tér** *(p130)*.

Afternoon Resume with a leisurely walk down touristy, but entertaining, **Váci utca** *(p131)*. Eventually you'll reach the elegantly designed **Central Market Hall** *(p211)*, where you can enjoy the dazzling array of fresh produce and other edible goodies. A host of marvellous treasures can then be admired at the **Hungarian National Museum** *(pp134–7)*.

3 Days in Budapest

- **Take a dip in Budapest's most historic bath house**
- **Marvel at the Great Synagogue, the largest in Europe**
- **Stretch your legs in Városliget before tucking into a lakeside lunch**

Day 1

Morning Begin the day in style by hopping aboard the antique **Sikló** funicular railway *(p239)* up to **Castle Hill** *(pp72–89)*, where the **Royal Palace** *(pp74–5)*, housing the wonderful **Hungarian National Gallery** *(pp78–81)* and **National Széchényi Library** *(p76)*, awaits. Walk along **Fishermen's Bastion** *(p84)* for unrivalled river views.

Afternoon Admire the beautifully asymmetrical, diamond-patterned roofs of the **Mátyás Church** *(pp86–7)*, followed by a gentle wander through the area's ancient cobbled streets, notably **Lords' Street** *(p89)*, awash with Gothic details. Wallow for a couple of relaxing hours at the magnificent **Gellért Hotel and Baths Complex** *(pp94–5)*.

Boating lake at Városliget, Budapest's largest city park

Day 2

Morning Immerse yourself in the **Jewish Quarter** *(p138)*, dominated by the **Great Synagogue** *(p138)*, the largest in Europe, before moving on to the **Hungarian National Museum** *(pp134–7)*, which is packed with terrific art and artifacts. As the morning ends, treat yourself to a few goodies at the **Central Market Hall** *(p211)*. You can even lunch here.

Afternoon Hop aboard the scenic no. 2 tram along the Pest embankment up to **Parliament** *(pp112–13)* for a tour of the city's landmark building. From here, it's a pleasant walk down to **St Stephen's Basilica** *(pp120–21)*, Budapest's most important ecclesiastical building. Have a peek inside the opulent **Gresham Palace Hotel** *(p118)*, before enjoying refreshments in one of the many grand coffee houses hereabouts.

Day 3

Morning Walk up **Andrássy út** to view the opulent **Hungarian State Opera** *(pp122–3)* and the striking eight-sided Oktogon square, beyond which lies the absorbing, if sobering, **House of Terror Museum** *(p148)*. Continue along the upper stretch of Andrássy út to Pest's green oasis, the **Városliget** or City Park *(p145)*, and take lunch at one of the park's many lakeside restaurants.

Széhenyi Chain Bridge with Buda Castle in the background

One of the stone lions on Széchenyi Chain Bridge with the Fishermen's Bastion behind

Afternoon Head to **Budapest Zoo** *(pp154–5)*, as famous for its fantastic Secessionist enclosures as its animals – don't miss the beautifully designed Elephant House. Make your way round to the opposite side of the park for a nose around the fairytale **Vajdahunyad Castle** *(p154)*, then, if there's time, round the day off with a leisurely boat ride.

5 Days in Budapest

- **Make a beeline for the shops and stalls on bustling Váci utca**
- **Enjoy great views from the Buda Hills**
- **Explore Margaret Island, the city's green lungs**

Day 1

Morning Start the day by delving into the country's turbulent past at the **Hungarian National Museum** *(pp134–7)*. Then head to another historic location – the **Jewish Quarter** *(p138)*, taking in the Byzantine-inspired **Great Synagogue** *(p138)* and the striking **Holocaust Memorial** *(p138)*.

Afternoon Peruse the souvenir and fashion shops along pedestrianized **Váci utca** *(p131)*, before making a beeline for **Andrássy út** and a backstage tour of the Miklós Ybl-designed **Hungarian State Opera** *(pp122–3)*. Further along Andrássy út, visit the **House of Terror Museum** *(p148)*, which powerfully documents previous terror regimes.

Day 2

Morning Jump aboard the **Sikló** funicular *(p239)* for splendid head-on views of the iconic **Chain Bridge** *(p66)*. Once on **Castle Hill** *(pp72–89)*, head to the **Royal Palace** *(pp74–5)* where you can spend the morning poring over native masters like Csontváry and Munkácsy inside the **Hungarian National Gallery** *(pp78–81)*.

Afternoon After a glimpse inside the **Mátyás Church** *(pp86–7)* and a short ramble along **Fishermen's Bastion** *(p84)*, wander across to **Gellért Hill** *(pp92–3)*, crowned by the formidable bulk of the **Citadel** *(p92)* and the imposing **Liberation Monument** *(p92)*.

Day 3

Morning Stimulate your senses at the **Central Market Hall** *(p211)*, before enjoying close-up views of the Danube with a walk across **Liberty Bridge** *(p69)*. Now on the Buda side, round off the morning with a soak at the historic **Gellért Hotel and Baths Complex** *(pp94–5)*.

Afternoon Head for the **Buda Hills** *(p165)* by means of the **Cogwheel Railway** *(p165)*, a 3km- (2-mile) long stretch of track built in 1874. Take in the views before returning to **Víziváros** *(pp102–103)*, the old fishermen's district, for light refreshments.

Day 4

Morning Ride the beautifully preserved **Millennium Line** *(p238)* to **Heroes' Square** *(pp146–7)*, pausing to look at the **Millennium Monument** *(p149)* before visiting the **Museum of Fine Arts** *(pp150–53)*, housing Hungary's finest collection of foreign art. Enjoy lunch at one of the lakeside restaurants in **Városliget** *(p145)*.

Afternoon Take a stroll through the park to **Vajdahunyad Castle** *(p154)*, where you can visit the **Museum of Hungarian Agriculture** *(p154)* and, across the way, the beautiful little **Ják Church** *(p147)*. Amble between the lakes to **Budapest Zoo** *(pp154–5)*, whose animal enclosures are perhaps the most striking feature of the entire complex.

Day 5

Morning Catch the no. 2 tram along the Pest embankment to view the peerless **Parliament** *(pp112–13)*. Continue north to **Margaret Island** *(pp176–7)*, walking from the **Centenary Monument** at its southern tip, past the **Franciscan ruins** and **Water Tower**, before reaching the **Grand Hotel Margitsziget** *(p177)* for refreshment.

Afternoon Now on the Buda side, take the hév train to **Aquincum** *(pp166–7)*, the old Roman town, where you can pick your way through the extensive remains, including ancient streets, temples, baths and houses. Return to the heart of **Buda** for a bite to eat.

Guests enjoying one of the indoor pools at the Géllert Hotel and Baths Complex

Putting Budapest on the Map

The capital of Hungary, Budapest has over 1.8 million inhabitants, a fifth of the country's total population. The city is situated on the Danube and covers an area of 525 sq km (200 sq miles). One third of the city is taken up by hilly Buda and Óbuda, on the western bank of the Danube, and the remaining two thirds by flat Pest, on the eastern bank. Budapest has a pivotal location at the heart of central Europe. From here one can easily reach other major cities such as Vienna, Zagreb, Bratislava, Belgrade, Bucharest and Prague.

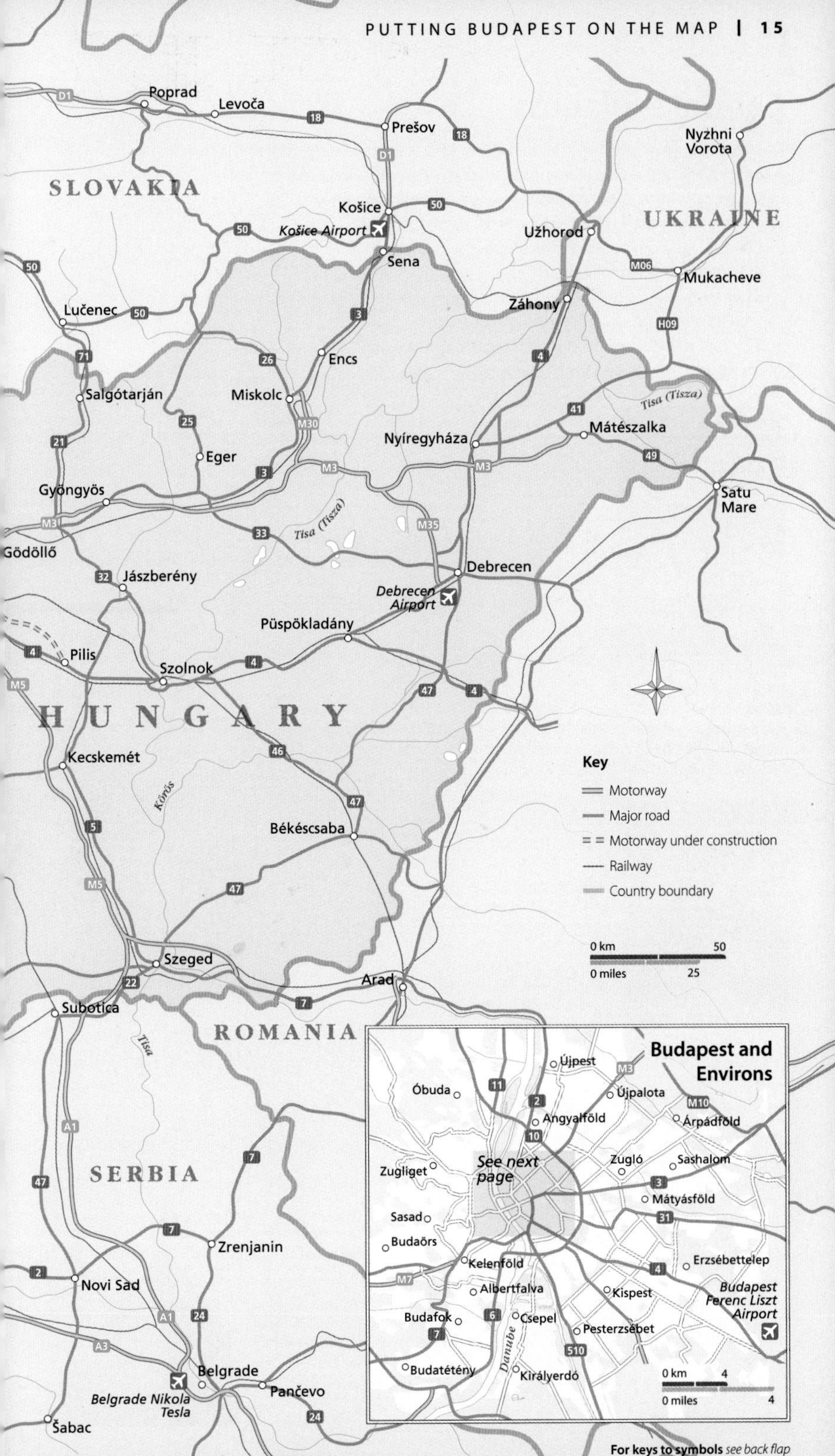

For keys to symbols see back flap

Central Budapest

The centre of town includes Castle Hill (district I), parts of districts II and XI on the western bank of the Danube and districts V, VI, VII, VIII and IX of Pest on the river's eastern bank, bounded by the city's original tram line. The Roman numerals denote the official administrative districts. For the purposes of this guide, the centre is divided into six areas. Each area has its own chapter containing a selection of sights that convey its character and history. Sights on the outskirts of the city, and suggested day trips and walks, are covered in separate chapters.

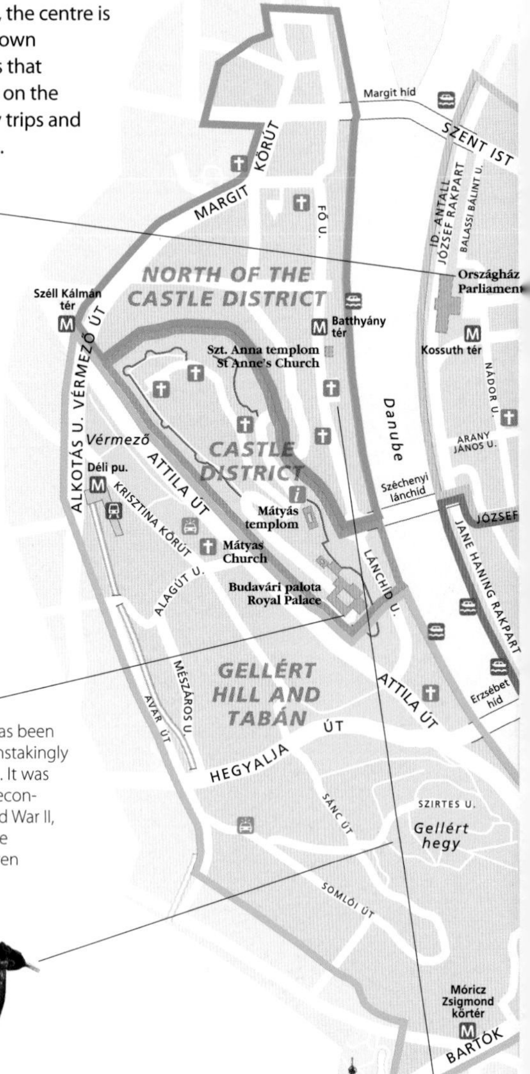

Parliament
This magnificent building hosts the sessions of the National Assembly. It is also the location of Hungary's most important government offices, including those of the prime minister *(see pp112–13)*.

Royal Palace
The Royal Palace has been destroyed and painstakingly rebuilt many times. It was last meticulously reconstructed after World War II, to the form that the Habsburgs had given it *(see pp74–5)*.

Liberation Monument
This statue of a woman holding aloft the palm of victory was created by the Hungarian sculptor Zsigmond Kisfaludi Stróbl. Situated in a park on Gellért Hill, the monument is visible from all over the city. It is now one of the symbols of Budapest *(see p96)*.

Calvinist Church
Situated close to the Danube, this church is distinguished by its eye-catching, polychromatic roof *(see p104)*.

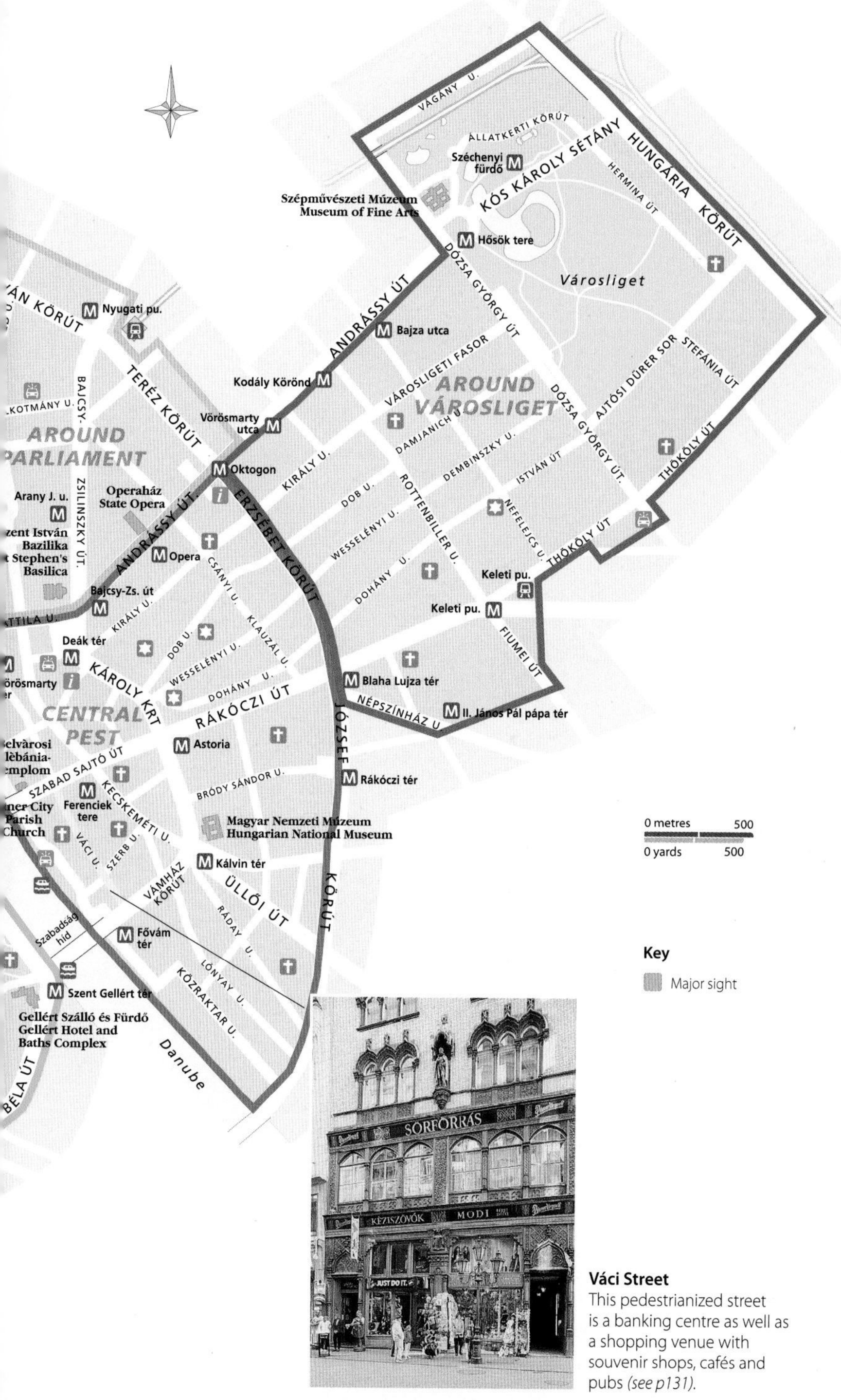

Váci Street
This pedestrianized street is a banking centre as well as a shopping venue with souvenir shops, cafés and pubs *(see p131)*.

For keys to symbols *see back flap*

HISTORY OF BUDAPEST

As early as the Palaeolithic era, there were settlements in the area of Budapest: the narrowing of the Danube made the crossing of the river easy at this particular spot. In around AD 100, the Romans established the town of Aquincum here. Their rule lasted until the early 5th century AD, when the region fell to Attila the Hun. It was subsequently ruled by the Goths, the Longobards and, for nearly 300 years, by the Avars.

The ancestors of modern Hungarians, the Magyars, migrated from the Urals and arrived in the Budapest region in 896. They were led by Prince Árpád, whose dynasty ruled until the 13th century. At the turn of the first millennium, St István, whose heathen name was Vajk, accepted Christianity for the Hungarians. As their first crowned king, István I also laid the basis of the modern Hungarian state.

It was Béla IV who, in 1247, after the Mongol invasion, moved the capital to Buda. Much of the expansion of Buda took place under kings from the dynasty of the Angevins. Buda reached a zenith during the reign of Mátyás Corvinus in the 15th century, but further development was hindered by the advancing Turks, who took the region and ruled Buda for 150 years. Liberation by the Christian armies resulted in the submission of the country as a whole to the Habsburgs. They suppressed all nationalist rebellions, but at the same time took care of economic development. Empress Maria Theresa and Archduke Joseph, the emperor's governor, made particular contributions to the modernization of both Buda and Pest. Yet, the slow pace of reforms led to an uprising in 1848, which was brutally crushed by Franz Joseph I. Compromise in 1867 and the creation of an Austro-Hungarian Empire stimulated economic and cultural life once more. Soon after, in 1873, Buda and Pest were united to create the city of Budapest.

Following World War I, the monarchy fell and Hungary lost two thirds of its territory. The desire to regain this contributed to its support of Germany in World War II. However, Budapest was taken by Soviet troops in 1945 and became a territory within the Soviet sphere of interest. Under the subsequent Communist rule, the popular uprising of 1956 was ruthlessly suppressed by Soviet tanks but it initiated a crisis that shook the regime. Free elections took place in 1990, resulting in the victory of the democratic opposition, and the emergence of a new bourgeoisie.

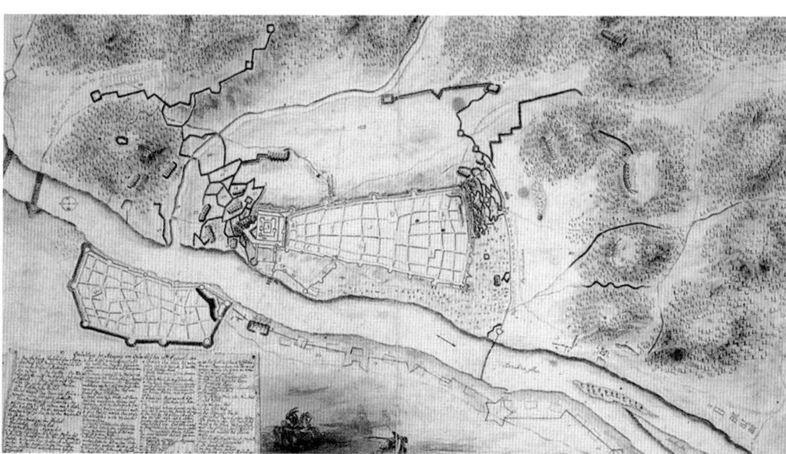

Dating from 1686, when the Turks were expelled, this map shows the fortified towns of Pest and Buda

◀ Gyula Benczúr's *The Baptism of Vajk*, displayed in the Hungarian National Gallery *(see pp78–81)*

The City's Rulers

In the 13th century, Béla IV built a castle in Buda and designated the town as his new capital. Until that time, the Árpád dynasty, the first family of Hungarian kings, had ruled their domain from elsewhere. When, at the beginning of the 14th century, there were no male heirs to the Árpád throne, Hungary began a long period during which it was mainly ruled by foreign kings including the French Angevins and the Polish Jagiellonian dynasty. Under Mátyás Corvinus, a great Hungarian king, Buda became one of Europe's most impressive cities. The Habsburgs, while suppressing national insurrections, rebuilt Buda and Pest after the devastation left by the Turks, adding fine pieces of architecture.

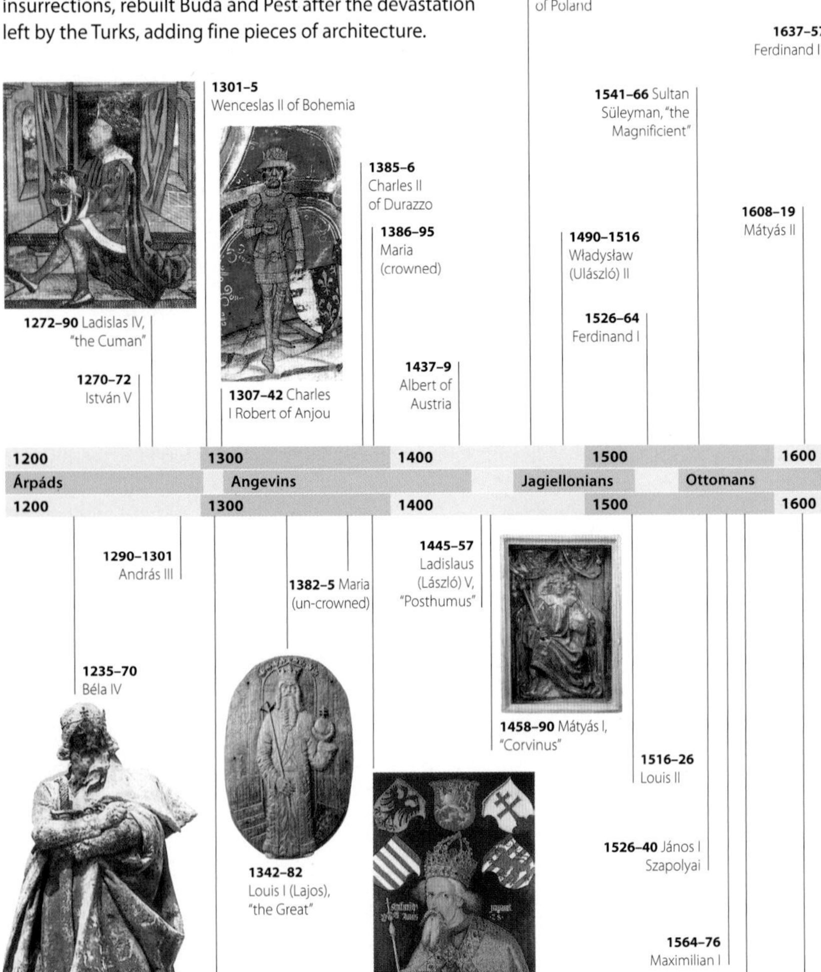

1235–70 Béla IV

1270–72 István V

1272–90 Ladislas IV, "the Cuman"

1290–1301 András III

1301–5 Wenceslas II of Bohemia

1305–7 Otto Wittelsbach of Bavaria

1307–42 Charles I Robert of Anjou

1342–82 Louis I (Lajos), "the Great"

1382–5 Maria (un-crowned)

1385–6 Charles II of Durazzo

1386–95 Maria (crowned)

1387–1437 Sigismund of Luxembourg (initially as Maria's consort)

1437–9 Albert of Austria

1440–44 Władysław (Ulászló) I of Poland

1445–57 Ladislaus (László) V, "Posthumus"

1458–90 Mátyás I, "Corvinus"

1490–1516 Władysław (Ulászló) II

1516–26 Louis II

1526–40 János I Szapolyai

1526–64 Ferdinand I

1541–66 Sultan Süleyman, "the Magnificient"

1564–76 Maximilian I

1576–1608 Rudolf I

1608–19 Mátyás II

1619–37 Ferdinand II

1637–57 Ferdinand III

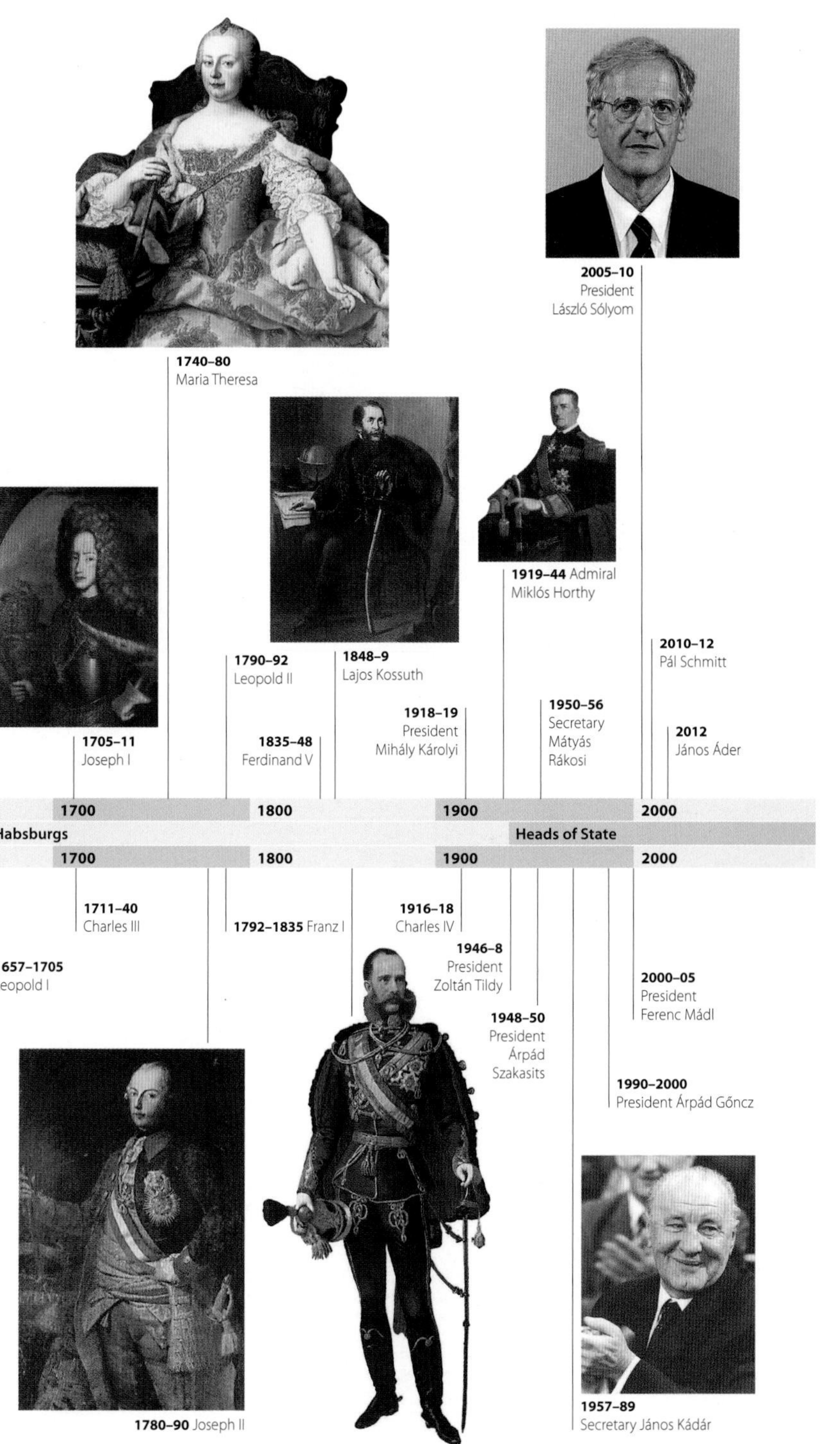
1740–80
Maria Theresa
2005–10
President
László Sólyom
1919–44 Admiral
Miklós Horthy
1790–92
Leopold II
1848–9
Lajos Kossuth
2010–12
Pál Schmitt
1918–19
President
Mihály Károlyi
1950–56
Secretary
Mátyás
Rákosi
1705–11
Joseph I
1835–48
Ferdinand V
2012
János Áder
1700
1800
1900
2000
Habsburgs
Heads of State
1700
1800
1900
2000
1711–40
Charles III
1792–1835 Franz I
1916–18
Charles IV
1946–8
President
Zoltán Tildy
1657–1705
Leopold I
2000–05
President
Ferenc Mádl
1948–50
President
Árpád
Szakasits
1990–2000
President Árpád Göncz
1780–90 Joseph II
1957–89
Secretary János Kádár
1848–1916
Franz Joseph I

Early Settlers

Traces of settlements in the region by the Scythians and the Celtic Eravi date from around 400 BC onwards. In the 1st century AD, the Romans conquered the area as their province of Pannonia and soon established Aquincum *(see pp166–7)* within the limits of the modern city. Little evidence remains of the next rulers, the Huns, who were followed by the Goths and the Longobards. For nearly three centuries, starting in around AD 600, the Avars were pre-eminent. In 896, the Magyars swept into the region and laid claim to what would later become the Hungarian state.

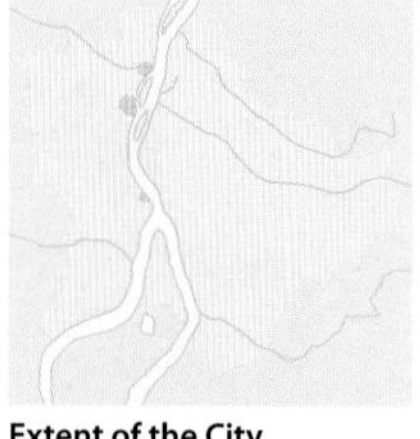

Extent of the City

AD 300 Today

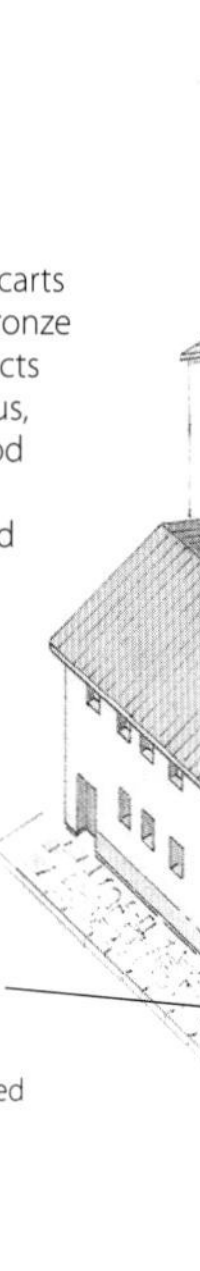

Bronze Decorations
In the 2nd century AD, Roman carts were often decorated with bronze plaques. This example depicts (from left): a satyr, Bacchus, god of wine and Pan, god of shepherds, under a palm frond. It was found in Somodor.

Workshops and shops, known as *tabernae*, were enclosed and faced onto the street.

The Sun God Mithras
The Persian god Mithras was adopted by the Eravi and his cult survived into the Roman period. This bronze image dates from 2nd–3rd centuries AD.

Reconstruction of the Macellum

This solidly built, square market hall was the focus for trade in the Roman town of Aquincum. At its centre was a courtyard with stalls, shops and workshops built around.

10,000 BC Remains dating from the Palaeolithic era indicate the existence of a settlement in the Remeda Cave in Buda.

Silver Celtic coin dating from the 4th century BC

800 BC Tombs with Iron Age urns at Pünkösdfürdő.

c. 50 BC Celtic Eravi settlement on Gellért Hill *(see pp92–3)*

400 BC Scythians in the region

c. AD 100 The town of Aquincum is established by the Romans

10,000 | **5000** | **1000** | **AD 1**

5000 BC Stone Age settlements in Talxina and along the Danube

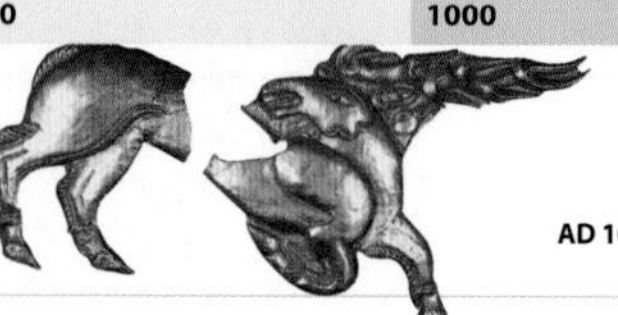

Scythian ornamental gold stag

AD 89 Romans establish a permanent army camp in modern-day Óbuda

AD 106 Aquincum becomes the capital of the Roman province of Lower Pannonia

Sacrificial Altar
This altar, decorated with rams' heads, dates from the Neolithic era. It was found in Szeged.

Shell Necklace
Dating from the Neolithic era, some 5,000 years ago, this necklace was found in Kisköre. It provides evidence of the early migration of tribes and their developed trade activities.

Butchers' stalls faced onto the courtyard.

The rotunda housed the weights and measures.

Silver Augur's Rod
This instrument was used by Roman priests for divination purposes. This one was found near Komárom, the site of a 3rd-century Roman town.

Where to See the Early City

Some quite considerable relics of the Roman legions that were once stationed here can be seen in modern Óbuda. The remains of an amphitheatre are near an unusual underground museum *(see p174)*, while magnificent mosaics adorn the Hercules Villa *(p175)*. Further up the Danube are the ruins of Aquincum itself *(pp166–7)*. Here visitors can wander around the remains of various buildings and enter a museum. On the Pest side of the river, just to the north of the Inner City Parish Church, there is a small, open-air section of remains from Contra Aquincum *(p126)*.

This Roman amphitheatre, one of two in Aquincum, indicates the status of the town.

The mosaic of Hercules and Diana, which survives at the Hercules Villa, was probably imported from Alexandria during the 2nd or 3rd century AD.

c. 140–60 Two amphitheatres are built to serve Aquincum's growing population

409 The Huns, under Attila, conquer Aquincum

c. 600–896 The Avars rule the region

Ornate earring from the 7th century AD

200 | 400 | 600 | 800

194 Aquincum is promoted to the status of a Roman colony

294 Contra Aquincum is founded on the eastern bank of the Danube

453 Collapse of the Huns' domination

Carving of the Sun God Mithras

896 Magyar (Hungarian) tribes take over Pannonia

The Árpád Dynasty

After a long journey beginning in the Urals region in Russia, nomadic tribes of Magyars eventually settled in Pannonia in AD 896. Following a period of internal disputes, the tribes made a blood-bonded alliance and chose one leader, Árpád. While Géza the Grand Prince of the Hungarians made contact with missionaries, it was his son, István I, who accepted Christianity for his people. Their first crowned king, István organized the state according to the European, feudal model. Initially under the Árpáds, Esztergom *(see p168)* was the country's capital and later Székesfehérvár. The development of Buda, Pest and Óbuda began in the second half of the 12th century, but was interrupted by the Mongol invasion of 1241.

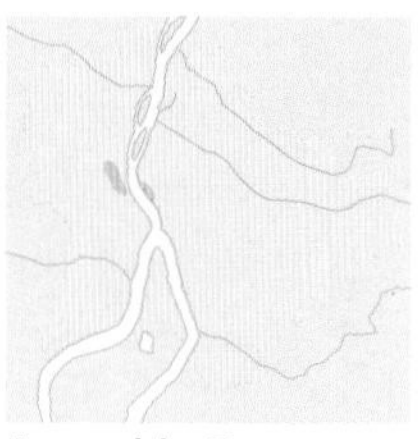

Extent of the City
1300 Today

Trinity of Hungarian Saints
The figures of three saints, King István, his son Imre and Bishop Gellért, are presented on this colourful triptych in the Chapel of St Imre in Mátyás Church *(see pp86–7)*.

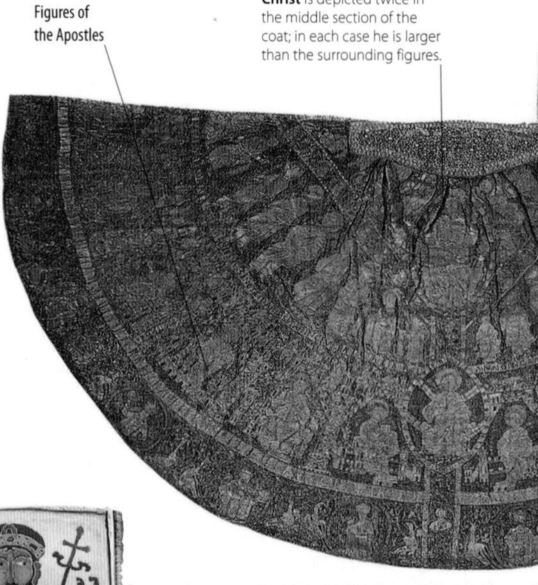

Figures of the Apostles

Christ is depicted twice in the middle section of the coat; in each case he is larger than the surrounding figures.

King Géza I
Géza I (1074–77), the father of Kálmán the Book-Lover, is represented on an enamel plaque on the Crown of the Árpáds.

Coronation Mantle

This silk coronation coat was made in 1031 for the Árpád kings. It has a pearl-beaded collar and is embroidered with the figures of Christ, Mary, the Apostles and the Prophets.

Sculpture of King István I by Imre Varga

c.900 Árpád settles on Csepel Island (in modern-day Budapest) and his brother Kurszán in Óbuda

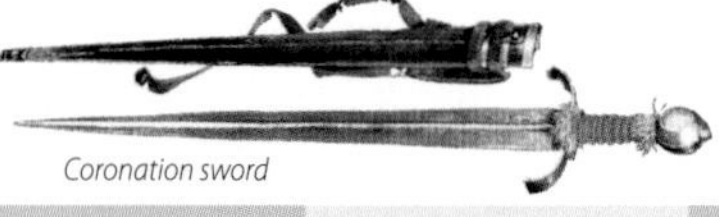

Coronation sword

850 | 900 | 950 | 1000 | 1050

973 Prince Géza invites missionaries into the region

1001 Coronation of István (Stephen) I

1046 Revolt by pagans and the martyr's death of Bishop Gellért, thrown in a barrel into the Danube

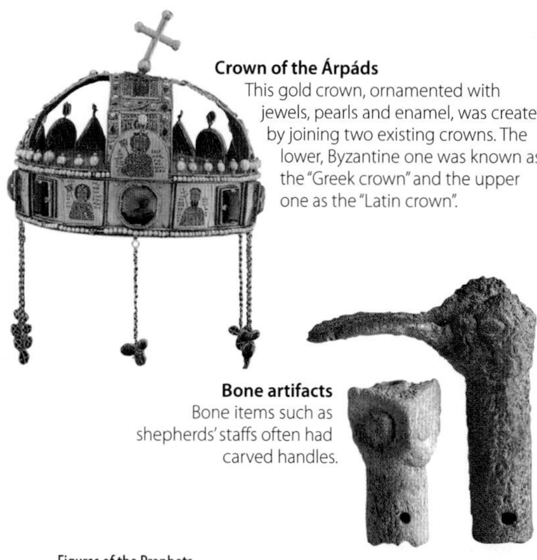

Crown of the Árpáds
This gold crown, ornamented with jewels, pearls and enamel, was created by joining two existing crowns. The lower, Byzantine one was known as the "Greek crown" and the upper one as the "Latin crown".

Bone artifacts
Bone items such as shepherds' staffs often had carved handles.

King István's coin
The first Hungarian coin, the denar, was produced soon after AD 1000, during King István's reign.

Tympanum
This 11th-century church tympanum, from Gyulafehérvár in modern Romania, is in the Hungarian National Gallery *(see pp78–81)*.

Where to See the Medieval City

Only a few monuments survive from the Middle Ages. Among the notable ones that still remain are the crypts in Mátyás Church *(see pp86–7)*, and the elevations and cellars of some historic houses in the Castle District (a few of which are now converted into wine bars). The reconstructed lower chambers of the Royal Palace *(pp74–5)* and parts of its fortifications also date from the medieval era.

This 19th-century copy of the Romanesque Ják Church *(see p147)* reveals how the Árpáds adopted European styles.

Gothic niches can be seen by the entrances to many houses in the Old Town *(see pp82–3)*.

1188 Béla III moves his headquarters to Óbuda and sets out on Frederick Barbarossa's crusade

1222 "Golden Bull" grants nobility privileges including tax exemption

1241 Mongol invasion

1244 The citizens of Pest are granted civic rights

1247 Béla IV builds castle in Buda, which becomes capital of Hungary

1255 The citizens of Buda get civic rights

1267 Béla IV announces new "Golden Bull"

1301 Death of King András III, last king of the Árpád dynasty

1100 | 1150 | 1200 | 1250 | 1300

Magyar belt buckle dating from the 10th century

Gothic and Renaissance Eras

As a result of the efforts of the Angevins and Sigismund of Luxembourg, the Gothic style reached Buda in the 14th century. Buda's palace and the summer palace in Visegrád were both extensively rebuilt. Shortly after defeat by the Turks at Varna, Hungary regained control of Belgrade and, for a while at least, halted their invasion. Mátyás Corvinus, the son of General János Hunyadi, the victor of Belgrade, became king. Under Mátyás's rule Hungary was turned into the greatest monarchy of Middle Europe, and, as a result of his marriage to Beatrice, a Neapolitan princess, the Renaissance began to blossom in the country.

Extent of the City

c 1480 Today

Illuminated letter from the Philostratus Codex
This letter depicts the son of King Mátyás I, Johannus Corvinus, after he took Vienna. It is housed in the National Széchényi Library *(see p76)*.

Castellan Ferenc Sárffy was the commander of Győr Castle.

Hungarian soldier

Ulrik Czettrich, an officer of the royal household, discovered the body of Louis II on the marshy bank of the Csele river.

Royal Medallion
An unknown master from Lombardy commemorated King Mátyás I in this marble silhouette dating from the 1480s.

Gold Seal
This gold seal, which belonged to King Mátyás I, is indicative of the affluence enjoyed by Hungary while he was on the throne.

Ciborium dating from the 14th century

1335 Treaty on co-operation and succession signed by the kings of Hungary, Poland and Bohemia in Visegrád

1342 Louis I, "the Great", becomes king

1350

1355 Óbuda's citizens gain civic rights

1370 Louis I enters a political union and becomes king of Poland

1375

1382 After death of Louis I, one daughter, Maria, becomes queen of Hungary and another, Jadwiga, queen of Poland

1385 Sigismund of Luxembourg marries Maria

1387–1437 Rule of Sigismund of Luxembourg. He enlarges the Royal Palace *(see pp74–5)*

1395 University established in Óbuda

1400

1425

Wine Cups
This pair of elaborate Renaissance wine cups, dating from the 16th century, is designed to fit together to form a covered receptacle.

Crest of King Mátyás Corvinus
Inscribed with the date 1470, this crest commemorates the building of significant additions to Mátyás Church *(see pp86–7)*, which was then renamed after the king.

Where to See the Gothic and Renaissance City

The full bloom of the Gothic period took place in Hungary in the 14th century. Mátyás Church *(see pp86–7)* has portals that survive from this era. Renaissance art reached Hungary thanks to Italian masters brought by Mátyás's second wife, Beatrice. Both the Royal Palace *(pp74–5)* and the summer palace at Visegrád *(p168)* were outstanding pieces of Renaissance architecture. Since the storming of Buda by the Turks, only a few remnants of the former splendour have remained.

A chapel of the Royal Palace from the period of Angevin rule can be seen in the basement of the Budapest History Museum *(see p76)*.

This portal of Mátyás Church dates from the 14th century. In the 19th century, a Neo-Gothic porch was built around it.

The Discovery of Louis II's Body

At the Battle of Mohács, on 29 August 1526, King Louis II lost his life together with thousands of Hungarian and Polish knights. The tragic scene of the finding of his body was recreated by Bertalan Székely in 1859.

1440 Władysław III of Poland is Ulászló I of Hungary

1444 Ulászló I I is killed during the Battle of Varna

1450

1456 Victory over Turks at the Battle of Belgrade

1458–1490 Reign of Mátyás Corvinus

1473 Chronica Hungarorum, the first book to be published in Hungary, is printed by András Hess

1475

1478 Law is passed threatening landlords who fail to maintain their buildings with dispossession

1500

1514 Peasant revolt under György Dózsa

Shield of soldier in the army of Mátyás Corvinus

Ulászló I I (ruled 1490–1516)

1525

1526 Defeat by the Turks at the Battle of Mohács. King Louis II perishes during the fighting

1550

The Turkish Occupation

After the battle of Mohács, the Turks razed Buda, but they temporarily turned their attention elsewhere and did not return to occupy it until 1541. When they then moved into the Royal Palace *(see pp74–5)*, Buda became the capital of Ottoman Hungary, while eastern Hungary and Transylvania were feudal suzerains. The Ottomans soon converted the city's churches, including Mátyás Church, into mosques and also built numerous Turkish baths *(see pp52–5)*. The Habsburgs tried relentlessly to recover Buda during this period. Their sieges destroyed the city progressively and when, in 1686, the Christian armies eventually recovered it the scene was one of devastation.

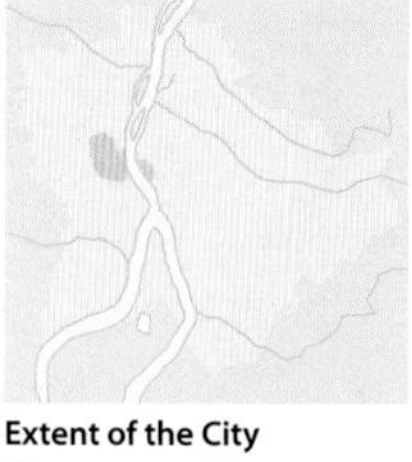

Extent of the City

1630 Today

The Liberation of Buda in 1686
After a bloody siege, the Christian army, led by Prince Charles of Lorraine, entered Buda and liberated it from the Turks. This painting by Gyula Benczúr, dating from 1896, depicts the event.

Turkish fortress on Gellért Hill

The Rudas and Rác Baths

Pest and Buda in 1617
Georgius Hurnagel's copperplate print shows the heavily-fortified towns of Pest and Buda in a period when much of Hungary was firmly under Turkish rule.

Ottoman Tombstones
A few inscribed Ottoman tombstones, topped by distinctive turbans, remain to this day in Tabán *(see p98)*.

1526–41 Turks conquer Buda on three occasions

1529 János I Szapolyai, the Hungarian monarch, pays homage to Sultan Süleyman I

1541–66 Reign of Sultan Süleyman I, "the Magnificent", who considered himself the Turkish king of Hungary

1602–3 Austrians, led by General Herman Russworm, fail in attempts to storm Pest and Buda

1525 | 1545 | 1565 | 1585 | 1605

1530–40 János I Szapolyai rebuilds Buda

1542 The Austrians lay siege to Buda

Austrian siege of Buda

1594 Bálint Balassi, Hungary's first great lyric poet, is killed taking part in a battle against the Turks at Esztergom *(see p168)*

Campaign Tent
This Turkish leader's tent, decorated with appliqué work, was used during the siege of Vienna in 1683.

Ottoman Coat
This 16th-century leather coat was supposedly taken from the battlefield of Mohács *(see p27)*.

Mátyás Church *(see pp86–7)* was converted into a mosque.

Ottoman Jug
Dating from the 17th century, this copper vessel was found in Buda during the reconstruction of the Royal Palace *(see pp74–5)*.

Where to See the Turkish City

Almost all Turkish buildings were razed by their successors, the Habsburgs, during or after the recapture of the city. Churches which the Turks had used as mosques were converted back again, although some *mihrabs*, the niches pointing towards Mecca, were left. These can be seen in the Inner City Parish Church *(see pp128–9)* and in the Capuchin Church *(p104)*. Among the few wonderful examples of classical Ottoman architecture to survive are the Rudas, Rácz *(p99)* and Király Baths, and the Tomb of Gül Baba, a Turkish dervish *(p105)*.

The Király Baths, built in the 16th century by Arshlan Pasha, remain an impressive Ottoman monument *(see p105)*.

The Rudas Baths, dating from 1550, have an original Turkish dome covering their central chamber *(see p97)*.

Ottoman tablet with calligraphy

1624 Signing of the Treaty of Vienna

1625

1634 György I Rákóczi, prince of Transylvania, joins an anti-Habsburg alliance with France and Sweden

1645

1648 Death of György I Rákóczi

Gold five-ducat coin from 1603, showing the prince of Transylvania's crest

1665

1684 Start of ultimately successful siege of Buda by the Austrians

1685

1686 Christian troops enter Buda. The end of Turkish rule in Hungary

Viennese sword dating from the 17th century

Habsburg Rule

In order to gain control of Hungary, the Habsburgs encouraged foreign settlers, particularly Germans, to move into the country. This policy led to a national uprising in 1703–11, led by the prince of Transylvania, Ferenc II Rákóczi. Only in the second half of the 18th century, particularly under Empress Maria Theresa, did the reconstruction of Buda, Óbuda and Pest begin in earnest. This was accompanied by economic development and a further increase in the country's population. The university at Nagyszombat (now Trnava in the Slovak Republic) moved to Buda in 1777, and subsequently to Pest in 1784, and was an important factor in their expansion.

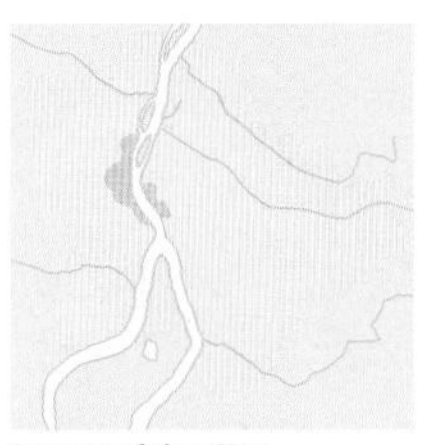

Extent of the City

1770 Today

The Return of the Crown to Buda (1790)
A vast ceremonial procession of commissioners marked the arrival in Hungary of royal insignias from Vienna, a sign of peace between the two countries.

Maria Theresa holds the infant Joseph, the successor to her throne.

"Vitam et Sanguinem"
In 1741, the Hungarian states swore on "life and blood" their loyalty to the Habsburg Empress Maria Theresa. This copperplate print by Joseph Szentpétery depicts the scene of the oath-taking.

Ferenc II Rákóczi
This fine portrait by Ádám Mányoki depicts Ferenc II Rákóczi, the leader of the national uprising of 1703–11 and a figure much loved by the Hungarian people.

1687 Under Austrian pressure, the Hungarian parliament gives up its right to elect a king and accedes to the inheritance of the throne by the Habsburgs

1689 Bubonic plague devastates the population of Buda and Pest

1690

1702 The Jesuits open a college and theological seminary

1703 The Prince of Transylvania, Ferenc II Rákóczi, leads a rebellion by the Hungarians against the Habsburgs

1705 First Hungarian newspaper, *Mercurius Hungaricus*, is printed in Latin

1705

1711 Suppression of Rákóczi's rebellion; a second bubonic plague decimates the city

1720

1723 Great Fire of Buda

1724 The population of Buda and Pest reaches 12,000 people

1729 The start of the reconstruction of Pest's suburbs

1735

Triple-jug of the Andrássy family These silver jugs are joined by a miniature of the castle belonging to the Andrássy family, at what is now Krásna Hôrka in the Slovak Republic.

Hungarian aristocrats swear on their lives to protect Maria Theresa's throne.

Dress (c. 1750) This dress, typical of Hungarian style with its corset which was tightened by golden cords, was worn by a lady from the noble Majtényi family.

Ferenc II Rákóczi's Chair Richly upholstered, this graceful 18th-century chair from Regéc Castle is typical of the style of the period.

Where to See the Habsburg City

Having taken Buda and Pest from the Turks in the late 17th century, the Habsburgs set about rebuilding them in the 18th century, mainly in the Baroque style. Famous buildings from this era include the Municipal Council Offices, St Anne's Church *(see pp106–7)*, St Elizabeth's Church *(p105)* and the University Church *(p143)*.

St Anne's Church, which was built between 1740–1805, astonishes visitors with its magnificent Baroque interior.

The Municipal Council Offices in the heart of Pest have a portico decorated with allegorical figures by Johann Christoph Mader *(see p131)*.

745–71 Building of the absburg Royal Palace

The magnificent Habsburg Royal Palace

1778 Roman remains are discovered in Óbuda

1780 *Magyar Hírmondó*, the first Hungarian language newspaper, begins printing

A hussar, or soldier

1750 | 1765 | 1780 | 1795

1752 A regular postal service operates between Buda and Vienna

1746–57 Construction of the Zichy Palace in Óbuda *(see p175)*

1766 A floating bridge links Buda and Pest

1777 University moves from Nagyszombat to Buda; later relocates to Pest

1792 Convocation of parliament and the coronation of Franz I

1784 Establishment of Ferenc Goldberger's textile factory in Óbuda

National Revival and the "Springtime of Revolutions"

The dynamic economic development of Buda and Pest began at the start of the 19th century. Pest, in particular, benefited from favourable circumstances for the grain trade and became, in the Napoleonic Wars, an important centre for the Habsburg monarchy. A national revival and rekindling of cultural life took place after the Napoleonic Wars. The Hungarian National Museum and many other public and private buildings were built at this time. Yet, Hungarian reformers were hampered by the Viennese royal court and an uprising erupted in the spring of 1848. This rebellion was suppressed by the Habsburgs, with the help of the Russian army, and a period of absolutism followed.

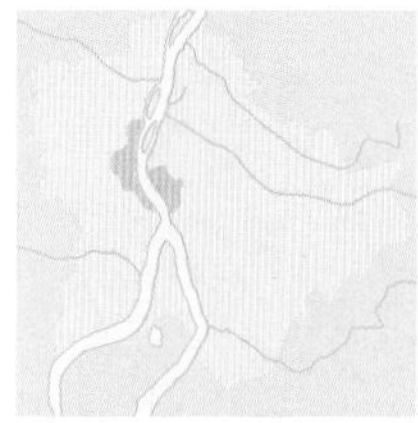

Extent of the City

1848 Today

Count György Andrássy, offered 10,000 forints towards the building of the Hungarian Academy of Sciences.

The Advance of the Hussars
In this watercolour, painted in 1850, Mór Than depicts fighting in the Battle of Tápióbicske of 1849. The Hungarian side was led by a Polish general, Henryk Dembiński.

The Founding of the Academy
In 1825, István Széchenyi put up 60,000 forints towards the building of Hungarian Academy of Sciences (see p118)*, a move which led to a national effort to collect funds for it. Barnabás Holló created this bas-relief depicting the major donors.*

The Great Flood
This bas-relief, made by Barnabás Holló in 1905, shows a heroic rescue by Count Miklós Wesselényi during the Great Flood of 1838.

1802 Count Ferenc Széchényi donates collections which will form the basis for National Széchényi Library *(see p76)* and Hungarian National Museum *(see pp134–7)*

1809 Royal court moves from Vienna to Buda as Napoleon advances. Despite his offer of Hungarian independence, the Hungarians back the Habsburgs

1817 First steamboat sails on Danube in the environs of Buda and Pest

1800 **1805** **1810** **1815** **1820**

1808 Establishment of the Embellishment Commission, led by Governor Archduke Joseph

Boats on the Danube

Lajos Batthyány Eternal Flame
This lamp, designed by Móric Pogány, has burnt since 1926 in Liberty Square (see p114). It was there that the Austrians shot Lajos Batthyány, the first prime minister of liberated Hungary, on 6 October 1849.

National Song
The 1848 uprising was sparked on 15 March when Sándor Petőfi recited his poem, *Nemzeti Dal* (National Song), outside the Hungarian National Museum.

Count István Széchenyi, an energetic force for change, is regarded as the one of the greatest Hungarians.

György Károlyi

Buda and Pest in 1838
Seen here in the year before the construction of the Chain Bridge, the Danube was an important means of transport.

Where to See the Neo-Classical City

In the early 19th century, the Embellishment Commission, set up by Archduke Joseph and led by architect József Hild, prepared a plan for the development of Pest in which its centre was redesigned on a pattern of concentric streets. Monumental Neo-Classical buildings were built here and to this day they form the heart and the character of this area. Structures to look for in particular include the Hungarian National Museum, the Chain Bridge and several houses located on József Nádor Square *(see p130)*.

The Hungarian National Museum, which was built in 1837, is among Hungary's finest examples of Neo-Classical architecture *(see pp134–5)*.

The Chain Bridge, the first permanent bridge over the Danube, was built by Adam Clark in 1839–49 *(see p67)*.

1825–48 Period of major projects: establishment of the Hungarian Academy of Sciences, Hungarian National Museum and National Theatre

Poet Sándor Petőfi (1823–49)

1836 Language Act: Hungarian becomes an official language

15 March 1848 Uprising begins

1847 Death of Archduke Joseph, emperor's governor

1825 | 1830 | 1835 | 1840 | 1845

The Great Flood

1830 István Széchenyi publishes his book, On Credit. It is seen as the manifesto for the fight for modern Hungary

1838 Catastrophic Great Flood results in destruction of half of Pest's buildings

1846 First railway line in the city, linking Pest and Vác

1849 After stout resistance, the Russian army, under the command of General Ivan Paskevich, suppresses uprising

Compromise and the Unification of Budapest

After suffering a defeat by Prussia in 1866, the Habsburgs realized the necessity of reaching an agreement with Hungary and the Compromise brokered in 1867 proved to be of tremendous importance for the future of Buda, Óbuda and Pest, as it created political stability and prosperity and marked the beginning of rapid industrialization in the country. The option of uniting the three cities had been considered since the opening of the Chain Bridge in 1849. It eventually came about in 1873 and Budapest soon found itself among Europe's fastest growing metropolises. In 1896, Városliget was the focal point for Hungary's Millennium Celebrations *(see p146)*.

Extent of the City

1873 Today

Hungarian Wine Cup
This 19th-century wine cup is embellished with the Hungarian crest, which incorporates the Crown of the Árpáds *(see p25)*.

Ferenc Deák (1803–76)
A great statesman, Deák was an advocate of moderate reforms. He argued persuasively in favour of accepting the Compromise reached with the Habsburgs in 1867.

The Citadel *(see p96)* on Gellért Hill

Castle District

Today's Boráros tér, where goods were once traded.

Decorative Pipe (1896)
Made in the year of Hungary's Millennium Celebrations, this pipe of "heavenly peace" includes figures of the Árpád kings and Emperor Franz Joseph.

1854 Martial law ends five years after 1848–9 uprising

1857 Tunnel built by Adam Clark under Castle Hill opened

Entrance to the Tunnel

1875 Opening of the Franz Liszt Academy of Music *(see p133)*, with the composer as its principal

1850 **1860** **1870** **1880**

1859 Synagogue on Dohány utca *(see p138)* completed

1873 The unification of Buda, Óbuda and Pest as one city, with a total of 300,000 inhabitants

1867 Compromise with Austria, giving Hungary independence in its internal affairs. Creation of the Dual Monarchy; Emperor Franz Joseph accepts the Hungarian crown

Monument to Hungarian Soldiers Killed in World War I
This bas-relief, by János Istók, commemorates the dead of World War I, in which Hungary fought on the German side. It is located next to the main entrance to the Servite Church *(see p132)*.

"Handcuff" Bracelet
Following the defeat of the national uprising of 1848–9, Hungarians sought to symbolize their oppression even in pieces of jewellery.

Trading on the Pest Embankment

Completed in 1887, this painting by Antal Ligeti shows the Pest embankment at a time when the city was booming. Manufactured goods and grain were sent along the Danube for sale in Germany and the Balkans.

Where to See the Historicist City

Historicism had a profound influence on the form of the rapidly developing metropolis at this time. A wonderful example of the style is the Hungarian Academy of Sciences. Among others are Parliament *(see pp112–13)*, St Stephen's Basilica *(pp120–21)*, the Museum of Fine Arts *(pp150–51)*, the New York Palace *(p133)* and many of the buildings that stand on Andrássy Street *(p148)*.

The Hungarian Academy of Sciences is housed in this fine Neo-Renaissance palace built between 1862–5 *(see p118)*.

St Stephen's Basilica was built over a period of 60 years by three architects. It was finished in 1905 *(see pp120–21)*.

1894 Body of Lajos Kossuth *(see p110)* is returned from Turin

1904 Grand opening of Parliament *(see pp112–13)*

Old Upper House Hall in Parliament

1916 Franz Joseph dies and Charles IV becomes king of Hungary

1890 | 1900 | 1910 | 1920

1896 First metro line and several museums opened

1897 Opening of the Great Market Hall *(see p211)*

1909 Airport opened in Rákos, now Kőbánya

1900 With a population of 773,000, Budapest is Europe's fastest growing city

1914 Hungary enters World War I on the German side

1918 Abdication of Charles IV marks end of the Austro-Hungarian Empire

Modern Budapest

Hungary paid a high price for its one-state union with Austria and its later alliance with Nazi Germany. Following defeat in both World Wars, the country had lost a large portion of its territory. As a result of the Yalta Agreement of 1945, it then found itself within the Soviet-controlled zone of Europe. Stalinism took on a particularly ruthless form here and led to the 1956 Uprising, which was brutally put down by Soviet tanks on the streets of Budapest. Efforts towards reform, undertaken by János Kádár, brought some changes but political opposition was not tolerated. In 1989, the Communists were ousted and Hungary at last regained control of its own affairs.

1960–66 Rebuilding of Castle District *(see pp72–89)*, including Royal Palace, and the Danube bridges

1919 Communists take over government and declare the Hungarian Soviet Republic

1928 Budapest is a free port on Danube

1937 Sixth and last visit of author Thomas Mann

1939 Hungary neutral at beginning of World War II. Accepts refugees after capitulation of Poland

1941 Hungary enters World War II on Germany's side

1945 After a siege lasting six weeks, the Soviet army takes Budapest

1946 Proclamation of Republic of Hungary. Smallholders' Party wins election

1949 Stalinist terror prevails. Cardinal Mindszenty *(see p115)* goes on trial. László Rajk, secret police chief, sentenced to death by Moscow loyalists

1920 | 1930 | 1940 | 1950 | 1960

1920 | 1930 | 1940 | 1950 | 1960

1918 Democratic revolution; Hungary declared a republic. Mihály Károlyi selected as the country's first president

1919 Admiral Miklós Horthy enters Budapest; many killed in the period of "White Terror". Horthy becomes regent

1925 Radio Budapest broadcasts its first programme

1933–6 Tabán *(see p98)* levelled (it was turned into a park in the 1960s)

1938 Eucharistic World Congress

1945–1 August 1946 Banknotes valued at one billion pengő are printed during rampant inflation. There is not enough room for all the zeros on the notes. As part of monetary reform, the new currency, Forint was introduced

1944 Efforts to withdraw from World War II end with German troops entering the country. A ghetto is established in Budapest and the extermination of Hungarian Jews begins

1947 After falsification of election results, Communists control the whole country

1948 Mátyás Rákosi leads Hungarian Workers' Party, run by Communists

1953 The national football team beats England 6–3 at Wembley

1958 The leader of the 1956 Uprising, Prime Minister Imre Nagy, is executed

1964 The Elizabeth Bridge *(see p67)* reopens, having been totally rebuilt

1968 Introduction of new economic system known as "goulash-Communism"

970 Opening of a new metro line

October 1989 Republic of Hungary is proclaimed once more. The national emblem is changed

1981 Director István Szabó receives an Oscar for his film *Mephisto*

February 1989 Round-table talks between opposition parties and ruling socialist government

1990 Hungarian coat of arms, adopted on 3 July 1990

1991 Warsaw Pact is dissolved. Russian army leaves Hungary

1994 Election won by the Hungarian Socialist Party

1998 Election won by the centre-right Fidesz party, first premiership of Viktor Orbán

2002 Election won by the Hungarian Socialist Party. Imre Kertész receives the Nobel prize for Literature

2007 Hungary joins the Schengen open-borders agreement

2010 Fidesz party wins landslide majority in elections. Viktor Orbán is elected prime minister for his second term

2012 New Constitution adopted. The official name of the country is shortened to Magyarország (Hungary)

2014 Fidesz is re-elected with a landslide majority

70 | 1980 | 1990 | 2000 | 2010 | 2020

70 | 1980 | 1990 | 2000 | 2010 | 2020

1987 UNESCO places the historic Castle District and the Banks of the Danube on its list of world heritage sights

June 1989 Ceremonial funeral for Imre Nagy and rehabilitation for other leaders of 1956 Uprising

September 1989 Hungary opens its borders to allow refugees to flee from East Germany to the West

1990 The Democratic Hungarian Forum wins free elections. József Antall becomes the first prime minister to be elected in a democratic process; Árpád Göncz is elected president

1993 Pope John Paul II visits Hungary

2004 Hungary becomes a member of the EU

2005 László Sólyom becomes president of Hungary

1991 Václav Havel, József Antall and Lech Walesa sign an agreement in Visegrád *(see p168)* between Czechoslovakia, Hungary and Poland

BUDAPEST AT A GLANCE

Often described as the "Little Paris of Middle Europe", Budapest is famous not only for the monuments reflecting its own 1,000-year-old culture, but also for the relics of others who settled here. Remains from both Roman occupation, and, much later, rule by the Turks can still be seen in the city. After Turkish rule, union with Austria had a particular influence on the city's form and style. Descriptions of nearly 150 places of interest can be found in the *Area by Area* section of the book. However, to help you make the most of your stay, the following 20 pages are a guide to the best Budapest has to offer. Museums and galleries, churches and synagogues, palaces and historic buildings, baths and pools are presented, together with the influence of Secession in the city. Each sight is cross-referenced to its main entry. Below are the sights not to be missed.

Budapest's Top Ten Sights

Váci Street
See p131.

Gellért Monument
See p97.

Gellért Baths
See pp94–5.

Parliament
See pp112–13.

National Museum
See pp134–7.

Hungarian State Opera
See pp122–3.

Margaret Island
See pp176–7.

Danube and Chain Bridge
See p66.

Mátyás Church
See pp86–7.

National Gallery
See pp78–81.

◀ Statues of the guardians in the walls of Buda

Budapest's Best: Museums and Galleries

Unlike many other European cities – such as Paris with the Louvre and Madrid with the Prado – Budapest does not have a museum founded from a royal treasury because Hungary was for so long ruled by foreign powers. In the early 19th century, however, the modern aristocracy, backed by an increasingly affluent middle class, began to take an interest in preserving historic objects for the nation. Today, there are over 60 museums and galleries in Budapest, ranging from those with collections of international significance to others of much more local interest. For more information on museums and galleries see pages 42–3.

Museum of Military History
This museum has interesting displays illustrating the history of Hungarian weaponry.

Margit híd
SZENT ISTVÁN K
MARGIT KÖRÚT
AROUND PARLIAMENT
NORTH OF THE CASTLE DISTRICT
BÁTHORY
CASTLE DISTRICT
FŐ U.
Danube
ID. ANTALL JÓZSEF R.
JÓZSEF ATTILA U.
ATTILA ÚT
KRISZTINA KÖRÚT
Széchenyi lánchíd
JANE HANING R
Erzsébet híd
HEGYALJA ÚT
GELLÉRT HILL AND TABÁN
BARTÓK BÉLA ÚT

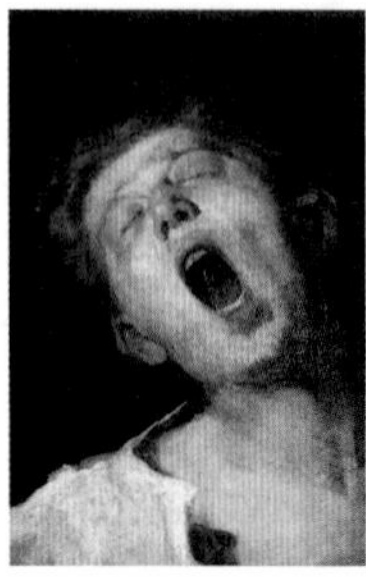

Hungarian National Gallery
The Hungarian art displayed here dates from the Middle Ages right through to the 20th century. *The Yawning Apprentice* (1868), by the great Mihály Munkácsy, is among the highlights of the collection.

Budapest History Museum
This Gothic work is one of the medieval treasures of the Budapest History Museum. The oldest exhibits are located in the original, lower-floor rooms of the Renaissance Royal Palace.

Semmelweis Museum of Medical History
Doctor Ignác Semmelweis, famous for his discovery of how to prevent puerperal fever, was born in 1818 in the house where the museum is now situated.

Museum of Ethnography
Among the exhibits at this museum illustrating the material culture of the Hungarians, including textiles, ceramics, artifacts and furniture, is this jug, dating from 1864, made by György Mantl.

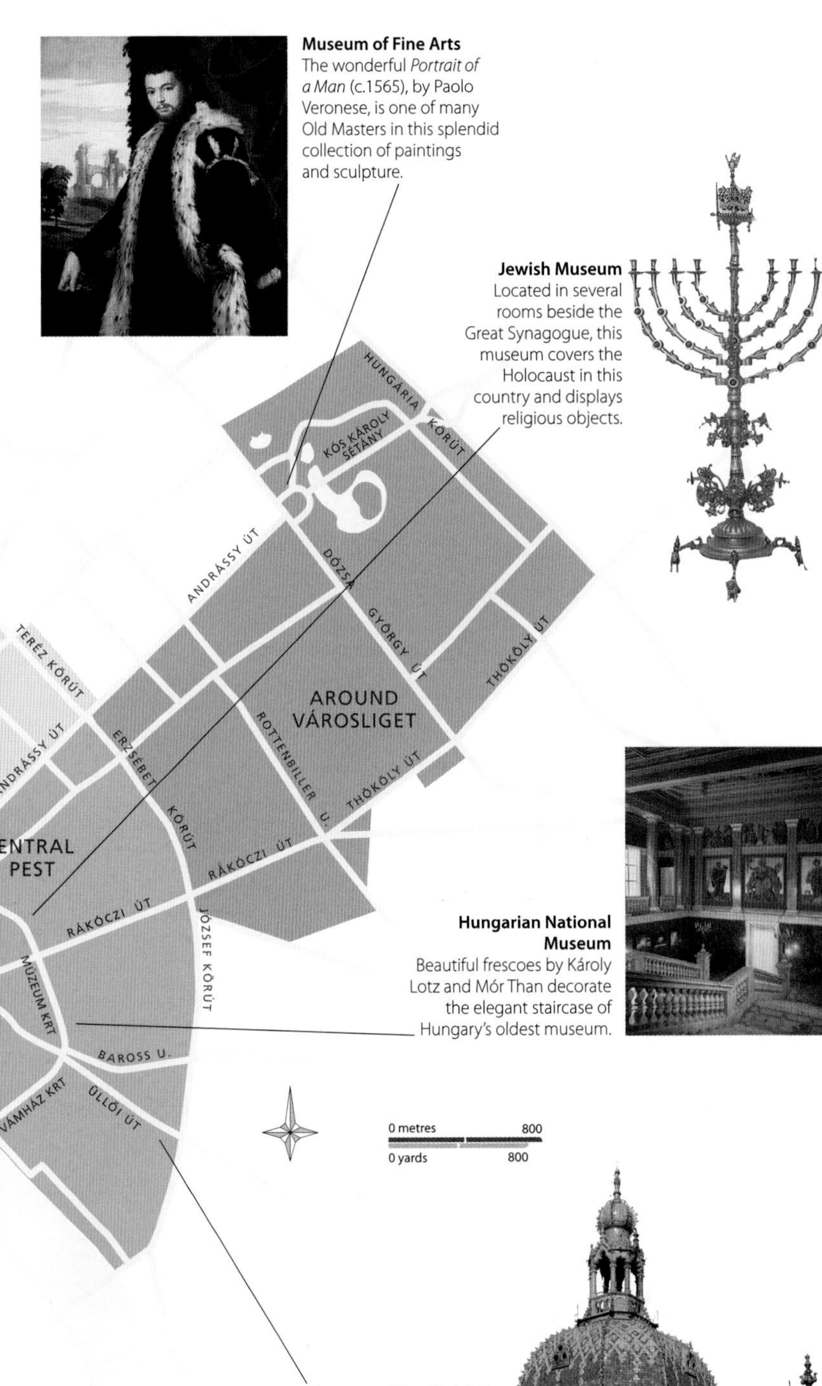

Museum of Fine Arts
The wonderful *Portrait of a Man* (c.1565), by Paolo Veronese, is one of many Old Masters in this splendid collection of paintings and sculpture.

Jewish Museum
Located in several rooms beside the Great Synagogue, this museum covers the Holocaust in this country and displays religious objects.

Hungarian National Museum
Beautiful frescoes by Károly Lotz and Mór Than decorate the elegant staircase of Hungary's oldest museum.

Museum of Applied Arts
Precious ceramics, porcelain and furnishings are housed in a building that is itself a work of art, surmounted by a magnificent, oriental-style dome.

Exploring the Museums and Galleries

Most of the city's museums and galleries are located in historic buildings. These include the spacious chambers of the restored Royal Palace, which in the 1970s and 1980s were designated as the premises of several museums, including the Hungarian National Gallery. Many museums – including the Hungarian National Museum and Budapest History Museum – also stage temporary exhibitions that are popular with both locals and tourists.

Sculpture of Imre Varga at the gallery named after him *(see p175)*

Hungarian Paintings and Sculpture

There are two important venues that should be on the itinerary of anyone interested in viewing the finest examples of Hungarian art.

At the **Hungarian National Gallery**, seven chronological sections present paintings and sculpture dating from the Middle Ages up until modern times. The sequence begins in the Lapidarium, where fragments of recovered medieval stone sculptures from the castles of the first Hungarian kings are exhibited.

As a rule, very few examples of Gothic and Renaissance art survive in Budapest because of the pillage inflicted by the Turks during their rule. However, a fine collection of altar retables from the 15th and 16th centuries are on display in the Hungarian National Gallery. In the 19th century, Hungarian painting developed and flourished, at the same time reflecting all the major international modern art movements. The Hungarian style can be seen particularly in the works of Pál Szinyei-Merse, Mihály Munkácsy and László Paál. For sculpture, meanwhile, the main names to look out for are István Ferenczy, Zsigmond Kisfaludi Stróbl and Imre Varga.

It is portraits, rather than paintings and sculpture, that are shown at the **Hungarian National Museum**. These provide a fascinating insight into the country's history.

The **Vasarely Museum** has a collection of 300 works by Hungarian-born artist Victor Vasarely. He moved to Paris in 1930 and became famous as one of the main exponents of the Op Art movement.

European Paintings and Sculpture

Masterpieces by the finest European artists, from medieval times to the modern day, are also divided between two museums in Budapest.

The **Museum of Fine Arts** has a magnificent collection of Italian paintings, dating from the 14th century up to the Baroque period, by masters such as Titian, Antonio da Correggio, Paolo Veronese, Giambattista Tiepolo and Jacopo Tintoretto. However, it is the *Esterházy Madonna* (1508) by Raphael, that is the jewel of the Italian collection. Equally splendid is the exhibition of Spanish paintings, which is one of the largest in the world. Works by Goya include *The Water Carrier* (c.1810). There are seven canvases by El Greco and others by Francisco de Zurbarán and Bartolomé Esteban Murillo. Other galleries within the museum represent artists of the Netherlands and Germany, as well as British, French and Flemish masters. The museum also owns more than 100,000 drawings and engravings by the Old Masters, while its modern art collection includes some notable works.

Modern European paintings can also be viewed in the **Ludwig Museum of Contemporary Art**. All the canvases belong to the Peter Ludwig Foundation of Germany. Highly prized works here include two paintings by Pablo Picasso, *Mother and Child* and *Musketeer*.

Pablo Picasso's *Musketeer* (1967), in the Ludwig Collection

The Jewish Museum, located beside the Great Synagogue

History

The history of Budapest, and that of Hungary as a whole, is illustrated in several museums. Relics from the Roman era can be found at the **Aquincum Museum** and at a handful of museums, including the **Roman Baths Museum**, in Óbuda.

The most important national historic treasures are housed in the **Hungarian National Museum**. The Coronation Mantle, dating back to the 11th century, is included in this collection.

Medieval seals and Gothic statuary are among the exhibits at **Budapest History Museum**. At the **Museum of Military History**, displays chart various Hungarian struggles for liberty, including the 1956 Uprising *(see p36)*.

The **Jewish Museum** has a room covering the Holocaust, as well as many ritual objects. The collection of the **Lutheran Museum**, situated next to the Lutheran Church, includes a copy of Martin Luther's will.

Music

Two of the museums featured in this book, the **Franz Liszt Museum** and the **Zoltán Kodály Museum**, are dedicated to internationally renowned composers. In each case, the setting is the apartment where the composer lived and worked, and on display are the instruments they played, musical scores and photographs. A more general view of Hungarian music is on offer at the **Museum of Musical History**, located in a Baroque palace on Mihály Táncsics Street. Displays feature the development of instruments and music in the 18th and 19th centuries; a special section is dedicated to Béla Bartók.

Ethnography and Oriental Crafts

Lavish folk costumes, as well as many other everyday items that belonged to the people of the region, can be viewed in the beautiful interiors of the **Museum of Ethnography**. Ethnic items from North and South America, Africa, Asia and Australia can also be seen here.

Chinese and Japanese artworks, porcelain, ceramics and textiles are displayed alongside pieces from Indonesia, India and Tibet at the **Ferenc Hopp Museum of Eastern Asian Art** (run by the Museum of Fine Arts) and the **Ráth György Museum**. The wonderful private collection of the **Zelnik István Southeast Asian Gold Museum** displays Southeast Asian art pieces.

Decorative Arts

Housed in an extraordinary building designed by Ödön Lechner *(see p58)*, the **Museum of Applied Arts** gives an impressive overview of the development of crafts from the Middle Ages onwards. Meissen porcelain is exhibited alongside oriental carpets and Hungarian pieces. The display relating to Art Nouveau *(see pp56–9)* is striking. The museum's permanent collection was founded in 1872. Major exhibitions tend to change each year, while smaller national and foreign displays change monthly.

Stained-glass window at the Museum of Applied Arts

Specialist Museums

The **Semmelweis Museum of Medical History** explores the work of a doctor called Ignác Semmelweis, who discovered how to prevent puerperal fever. This affliction had previously been a serious threat for women who had recently given birth. The **Golden Eagle Pharmacy Museum** is situated in a building that first opened as a pharmacy in 1681. Many original fixtures are intact and pharmaceutical exhibits are displayed.

Railway enthusiasts of all ages will appreciate the **Transport Museum** on Hermina Street, with its enormous collection of model trains and exhibits on the evolution of air, sea, road and rail transport.

Where to Find the Museums and Galleries

Budapest's Best: Churches and Synagogues

There are very few medieval and Renaissance churches still standing in Budapest. This is mainly due to the fact that the Turks, during their 150-year rule, turned all churches into mosques, which were later destroyed or converted by the Christians. The reconstruction of old churches and the building of new ones started in the late 17th century, hence the prevalence of Baroque and Neo-Classical styles.

Capuchin Church
Two Turkish windows remain from the time when this church was used as a mosque, alongside fragments of its medieval walls.

St Anne's Church
Built in the mid-18th century, this is one of the most beautiful Baroque churches in the city. The joined figures of St Anne and Mary decorate the centre of its façade.

Mátyás Church
Romanesque and Gothic styles are both evident in the coronation church of the Hungarian kings. The Neo-Gothic altar dates from the 19th century.

Cave Church
In the rocky interior of St Ivan's Cave, on the south side of Gellért Hill, the priests of the Pauline order established a church in 1926. It was designed to imitate the holy grotto at Lourdes.

St Stephen's Basilica
A bas-relief by Leó Feszler, representing the Virgin Mary surrounded by Hungarian saints, decorates the main tympanum of St Stephen's Basilica. This imposing church was built between 1851–1905.

Lutheran Church
This Neo-Classical church was completed by Mihály Pollack in 1808. The impressive façade was added half a century later by József Hild.

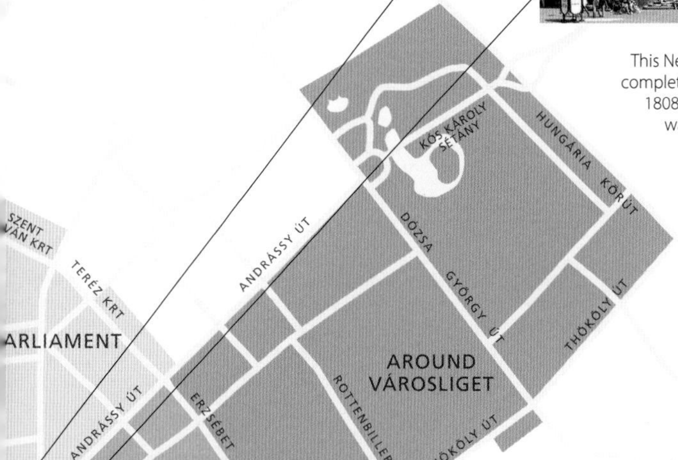

Great Synagogue
Two Moorish-style minarets, each topped by an onion-shaped dome, dominate the exterior of the largest synagogue in Europe.

Franciscan Church
The magnificent 19th-century paintings that decorate the interior of this Baroque church are by Károly Lotz.

Inner City Parish Church
Dating from 1046, this church is Pest's oldest building. A figure of St Florian, the patron saint of fire fighters, was placed on the wall beside the altar after the church survived the great fire of 1723.

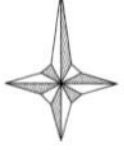

Exploring the Churches and Synagogues

Most of the city's churches are found around the centres of Buda and Pest. Only a few sacred buildings of architectural interest are situated on the outskirts of the city. The greatest period of construction took place in the 18th century, after the final expulsion of the Turks. Another phase occurred in the second half of the 19th century, producing two of Budapest's grandest places of worship: St Stephen's Basilica and the Great Synagogue. Religious buildings were neglected after World War II, but thanks to restoration some have now regained their former splendour.

Reconstructed Gothic window of the Church of St Mary Magdalene

Medieval

Both **Mátyás Church** and the **Inner City Parish Church** date originally from the reign of Béla IV in the 13th century. Glimpses of their original Romanesque style can be seen, although each church was subsequently rebuilt in the Gothic style. After being sacked by the Turks in 1526, Mátyás Church was given a Baroque interior by the Jesuits who had at that time taken it over. Finally, the church was returned to a likeness of its medieval character between 1874–96, when all Baroque elements were systematically removed and it was given a Neo-Gothic shape.

The **Church of St Mary Magdalene**, built in 1274 in the Gothic style, was almost completely destroyed in 1945. All that remains intact today is the 15th-century tower with its two chapels. A Gothic window has also been rebuilt.

St Michael's Church, founded in the 12th century on Margaret Island, was completely destroyed by the Turks. However, in 1932 it was reconstructed from its original Romanesque plans.

Baroque

In the 18th century, 17 churches were built in Pest, Buda and Óbuda, all of them in the Baroque style. The influence of the Italian architectural school is visible in many of them, although only **University Church** was built by an Italian architect, Donato Allio. Under Habsburg rule, the leading architects working in the city, András Meyerhoffer, Mátyás Nepauer and Kristóf Hamon, often chose to follow Austrian examples.

University Church and **St Anne's Church** are generally considered to be the most beautiful buildings in the city dating from this era. The former astonishes visitors with its beautifully carved stalls and pulpit, and with the paintings by Johann Bergl adorning its vaults. St Anne's Church has a magnificent Baroque façade and reveals the influence of southern German Baroque in its oval floor plan. Inside, there is a lavish altar and pulpit designed by Károly Bebó.

The **Franciscan Church**, which is situated in the centre of Budapest and dates from 1758, has a wide Baroque nave and a main altar created by Antal Grassalkovich.

The interior of the Servite Church (1725), with its Baroque altar

Spires and Domes

The Gothic spire belonging to the Church of St Mary Magdalene and the Neo-Gothic spire of Mátyás Church are among Budapest's main landmarks. The twin Baroque towers of St Anne's Church and the soaring spire of the Calvinist Church rise above the Danube in Buda. On the Pest side, the dome of St Stephen's Basilica and the minarets of the Great Synagogue dominate.

Gothic spire of the Church of St Mary Magdalene

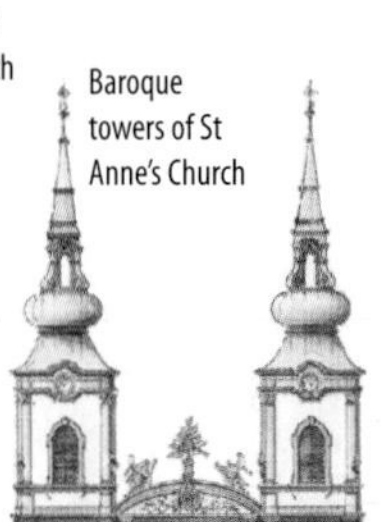

Baroque towers of St Anne's Church

Neo-Gothic spire of the Calvinist Church

Neo-Classical and Historicist

In 1781, Joseph II passed an edict permitting the building of Protestant churches. The city already had many Catholic churches and Protestant communities now started to build their own places of worship in the prevailing style of the time, Neo-Classicism.

One of the first to go up was the **Lutheran Church**, on Deák Ferenc tér, completed in 1808 by Mihály Pollack, a gifted master of Neo-Classical architecture. The white, ascetic interior of the church, with its two-floor gallery, was ideally suited to the nature of this place of worship. The majesty and simplicity of the Neo-Classical style corresponded with the more austere nature of Protestant belief. József Hild, another master of the style, later extended the church. He added the portico with its Doric columns, linking the church with the presbytery and a school. The complex as a whole is one of the best examples of Neo-Classical architecture in Budapest.

On a more modest scale is the **Calvinist Church**, built in the Neo-Gothic style between 1893–6.

Baptismal font at the Lutheran Church

When plans for it were drawn up by József Hild in 1845, **St Stephen's Basilica** was intended to be the pinnacle of Neo-Classical architecture. However, several delays, including the collapse of its dome at one point, meant that the realization of the original design was impossible. Following Hild's death in 1867, Miklós Ybl continued the project. He departed from Hild's plan, incorporating Renaissance-style features. The Basilica was finally completed by a third architect, József Kauser, in 1905.

Late 19th- and 20th-Century

The two most stunning synagogues in Budapest were designed by Viennese architects in the second half of the 19th century.

Ludwig Förster constructed the **Great Synagogue** in Byzantine-Moorish style in 1859 and Otto Wagner, an important Secession architect *(see pp56–9)*, realized one of his first projects in 1872. This was the **Orthodox Synagogue** on Rumbach utca, which also incorporated Moorish ideas.

Closely linked to the Secession style is the Hungarian National Style, based on an idiosyncratic combination of ethnic motifs and elements from folk art. This style is most visible in two churches by Hungarian architects. Ödön Lechner, the originator of the Hungarian National Style, completed **Kőbánya Parish Church**, on the outskirts of Budapest, in 1900. Meanwhile, Aladár Árkay built **Városliget Calvinist Church** in 1913. These two churches display a striking combination of colourful ceramics, Eastern-style ornamentation and also Neo-Gothic elements.

The Byzantine-Moorish interior of the Great Synagogue

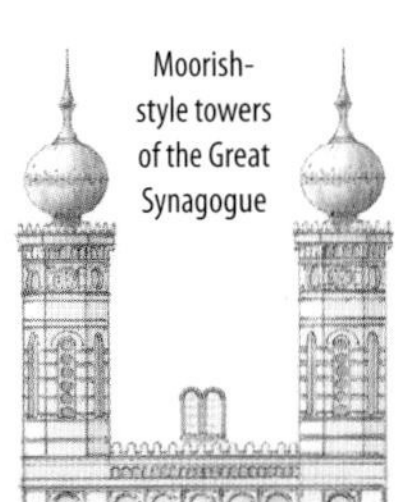

Moorish-style towers of the Great Synagogue

Dome of the eclectic St Stephen's Basilica

Where to Find the Churches and Synagogues

Buda Lutheran Church *p88*
Calvinist Church *p104*
Capuchin Church *p104*
Cave Church *p96*
Chapel of St Roch *p139*
Church of St Mary Magdalene *p89*
Cistercian Church of St Imre *p161*
Franciscan Church *p143*
Great Synagogue *pp138–9*
Inner City Parish Church *pp128–9*
Józsefváros Parish Church *p159*
Kőbánya Parish Church *p160*
Lutheran Church *p132*
Mátyás Church *pp86–7*
Orthodox Synagogue, Jewish Quarter *p138*
St Anne's Church *pp106–107*
St Elizabeth's Church *p105*
St Michael's Church, Margaret Island *p177*
St Stephen's Basilica *pp120–21*
Serbian Church *p142*
Servite Church *p132*
Tabán Parish Church *p99*
Újlak Parish Church *p158*
University Church *p143*
Városliget Calvinist Church, Városligeti Avenue *p148*

Budapest's Best: Palaces and Historic Buildings

Budapest boasts historic buildings and palaces in a broad range of architectural styles. The majority represent the Neo-Classicism, Historicism and Secession of the 19th and early 20th centuries, when a dynamic development of the capital took place. All but a few Gothic and Renaissance details were lost in the destruction of Buda and Pest by Christian troops in 1686, but some examples of its Baroque heritage remain. This map gives some highlights, with a more detailed look on pages 50–51.

Royal Palace
This palace has a turbulent history dating back to the 13th century. Its present form, however, reflects the opulence of the 19th century. Today the palace houses some of the city's finest museums.

MARGIT KÖRÚT

NORTH OF THE CASTLE DISTRICT

FŐ U.

CASTLE DISTRICT

Danube

ATTILA ÚT

KRISZTINA KÖRÚT

Houses on Vienna Gate Square
This charming row of four houses was built in the late 18th and early 19th centuries on the ruins of medieval dwellings. The houses are adorned with decorative motifs in the Baroque, Rococo and Neo-Classical styles.

Sándor Palace
The original friezes that decorated this 19th-century palace were recreated by Hungarian artists as part of its restoration. The palace is now the headquarters of the President of Hungary.

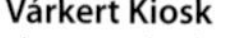

Várkert Kiosk
This Neo-Renaissance pavilion was built by Miklós Ybl *(see p123)* as a pump house for the Royal Palace. It now operates as a venue for events.

Hungarian Academy of Science
The façade of the academy is adorned with statues by Emil Wolf and Miklós Izsó, symbolizing major fields of knowledge: law, natural history, mathematics, philosophy, linguistics and history.

Gresham Palace
Now housing a Four Seasons Hotel, this splendid example of Secession design was built in 1905–7 by Zsigmond Quittner.

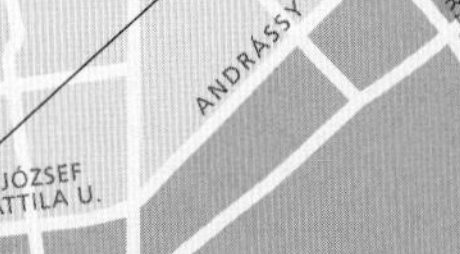

Pallavicini Palace
Gustáv Petschacher built this Neo-Renaissance mansion on Kodály körönd in 1882. The inner courtyard was copied from the Palazzo Marini in Milan.

Ervin Szabó Library
The grand, Neo-Baroque palace that now houses this library was originally built in 1887 for the Wenckheims, a family of rich industrialists.

Péterffy Palace
This plaque, commemorating a flood of 1838, was placed on one of the few Baroque mansions that remain in Pest. The house was built in 1756.

Exploring the Palaces and Historic Buildings

Little more than fragments remain of Budapest's Gothic and Renaissance past. However, some Baroque buildings have survived in Buda's Castle District and Víziváros. Neo-Classicism, on the other hand, has a much wider presence; there are many apartment buildings, palaces and secular monuments built in this style, especially around the old fortification walls of Pest on the eastern side of the Danube. Historicism dominated the architecture of the second half of the 19th century. It played a vital role in the enlargement of the city as it expressed and celebrated the optimism of the era.

Façade of the Gross Palace, built by József Hild in 1824

Baroque Palaces and Buildings

Many buildings in the Castle District and neighbouring Víziváros, around Fő utca, have retained their original Baroque façades. The main entrance of the **Hilton Hotel**, formerly a 17th-century Jesuit college, is a fine example.

Other outstanding instances of this style are the four houses on **Vienna Gate Square, the Batthyány Palace** on Parade Square and the **Erdődy Palace** on Mihály Táncsics Street, now the Museum of Musical History.

The **Zichy Palace** in Óbuda is a splendid Baroque edifice, and the buildings of the former **Trinitarian Monastery**, now the Kiscelli Museum, stand as significant models of the style.

There are only two Baroque monuments remaining in Pest. The **Péterffy Palace**, a mansion that stands below the current street level, dates from 1755. Pest's other Baroque edifice was, however, the first to be built in either Buda or Pest. The huge complex of the **Municipal Council Offices**, formerly a hospital for veterans of the Turkish wars, was constructed by the Italian master Anton Erhard Martinelli. It was greatly admired by Empress Maria Theresa, who declared it to be more beautiful than the Schönbrunn Palace in Vienna.

The outstanding Baroque façade of Erdődy Palace, Museum of Musical History

Neo-Classical Palaces and Buildings

Neo-Classicism, influenced by ancient Greco-Roman design, was popular in the first half of the 19th century as it reflected the confidence of this period of national awakening and social reform. Many monumental Neo-Classical structures were produced, including the **Chain Bridge**, built in 1839–49. The leading Neo-Classical architect was Mihály Pollack, who built the **Hungarian National Museum**.

Two stunning Neo-Classical palaces deserve particular mention – **Sándor Palace** in Buda and **Károlyi Palace** in Pest. The first stands on Castle Hill, by the top of the funicular railway, and impresses visitors with its harmonious elegance. The second, now housing the Petőfi Literary Museum, gained its present form in 1834 after considerable reconstruction.

A group of particularly attractive Neo-Classical houses is situated on **József Nádor Square**. Some of their features, such as the pillars, projections and tympanums, merit individual attention.

In 1808, the Embellishment Commission was set up by the Austrian architect János Hild to develop Pest. He and his son, József Hild, who built the **Gross Palace** in 1824, were both involved in the general restoration of the city. Having studied architecture in Rome, they created many splendid Italianate buildings.

Historicist Palaces and Buildings

In the second half of the 19th century, Historicism took precedence over Neo-Classicism. After the unification of Buda, Óbuda and Pest in 1873, Historicism had a significant influence on the city's architectural development. In this period Budapest gained an eclectic mix of new apartment buildings and palaces, as Historicist architects sourced different genres for inspiration. Miklós Ybl, whose work includes the **Hungarian State Opera** and the expansion of the **Royal Palace**, looked to the Renaissance, while Imre Steindl designed a Neo-Gothic **Parliament** (to which a Neo-Renaissance dome was added).

Sculptures on the Vigadó façade

Frigyes Schulek's **Fishermen's Bastion** features Neo-Gothic and Neo-Romanesque designs.

The **Vigadó**, a concert hall built by Frigyes Feszl between 1859 and 1864, is often thought of as the most magnificent Historicist building, with its façade richly decorated with relief sculptures and busts of the great Hungarians. However, the complex of three French-style, Neo-Renaissance palaces, Festetics, Károly and Esterházy, in **Mihály Pollack Square**, is also considered by many to be a fine example.

The **Drechsler Palace** in Andrássy út is a marvellous model of Neo-Renaissance design, while Páris Nagyáház (Paris department store) features Lotz's Hall, decorated with paintings and gold. The twin apartment buildings known as the **Klotild Palaces** incorporate Spanish-Baroque motifs and can be admired near the Elizabeth Bridge. Perhaps one of the most extravagant examples of Historicism is the Neo-Baroque **New York Palace** by Alajos Hauszmann, which has a luxurious interior of marble columns and rich colour.

Beautiful Neo-Baroque interior of the New York Palace

Decorative Features

The façades of many palaces and buildings still display the rich sculptural decoration characteristic of the various styles of architecture prevalent in the city. These features include coves, cartouches, finials, relief sculptures and ornamental window frames.

Regrettably, almost no original Gothic detail remains in Budapest, but niches or pointed arches decorating old apartment buildings can be spotted in the Old Town.

Baroque elements are still evident in fine buildings such as the Zichy Palace and the Erdődy Palace. Decorative Neo-Classical features, such as borders and tympanums, are visible on many buildings from the first half of the 19th century.

A finial with cartouche on the Neo-Classical Károlyi Palace

Relief on the Hungarian National Bank (1905)

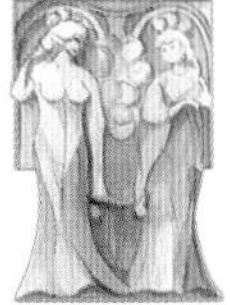

Cove detail on the façade of the Staffenberg House

Ornate window frame adorning the house at 21 József Nádor utca

Where to Find the Palaces and Historic Buildings

Budapest's Best: Baths and Pools

Budapest is one of the great spa cities of Europe. Numerous natural hot springs pour out over 80 million litres (18 million gal) of richly mineralized water every day. The greatest concentrations of natural springs are situated in Óbuda, near Gellért Hill, on the Buda embankment near Margaret Bridge and on Margaret Island itself. Baths have existed here since Roman times, but it was the Turks who best exploited Budapest's natural resources. Today there is a wide choice of therapeutic and recreational baths and pools.

Palatinus Strand
With ten swimming pools, hot springs, water slides and a restful location on Margaret Island, this spa is perhaps the most beautiful in Europe.

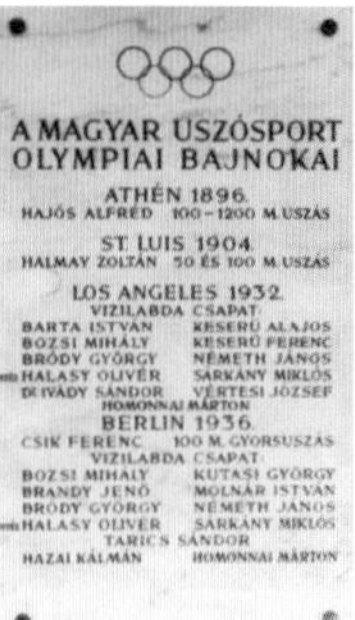

Hajós Olympic Pool
The pool was designed by Alfréd Hajós, who won Hungary's first Olympic gold medal for swimming in 1896, and on the walls of the swimming hall hang gold-engraved marble plaques citing Hungary's numerous Olympic champions.

Lukács Baths
These 19th-century thermal pools are open all year round, and attract both tourists and the locals of Budapest.

Király Baths
Dating from 1566, these baths were built by the Turks and have many authentic Ottoman features.

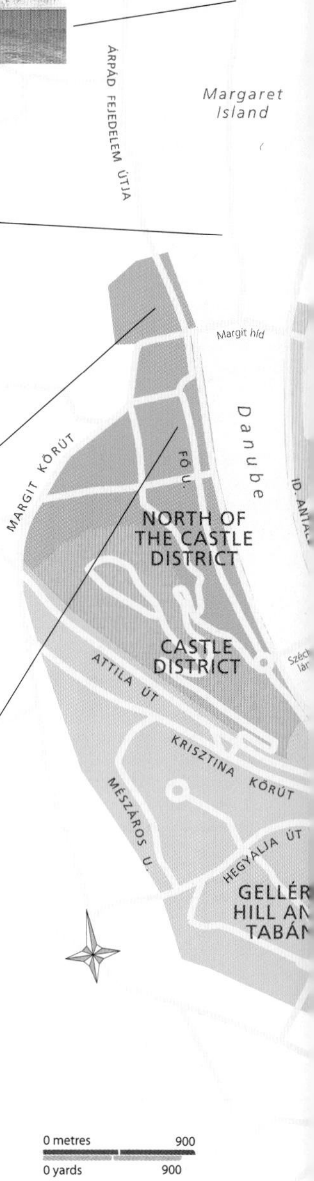

Árpád
ÁRPÁD FEJEDELEM ÚTJA
Margaret Island
Margit híd
MARGIT KÖRÚT
FŐ U.
Danube
NORTH OF THE CASTLE DISTRICT
CASTLE DISTRICT
ATTILA ÚT
KRISZTINA KÖRÚT
MÉSZÁROS U.
HEGYALJA ÚT
GELLÉR HILL AN TABÁN

0 metres 900
0 yards 900

Dagály Strand
Half a century ago, it was discovered that the water in a pond on this site was beneficial to health. Now a huge open-air complex of swimming pools, children's pools and a hydrotherapy and fitness centre is located here.

Széchenyi Baths
This spa has the deepest thermal baths in Budapest and the added attraction of magnificent Neo-Baroque architecture. The warmth of the water is such that these baths are popular even during the winter season.

Rácz Hotel & Thermal Spa
The original Ottoman pool and cupola are hidden behind a 19th-century façade, and adjacent to a luxury hotel.

Rudas Baths
The most famous of the Turkish baths were constructed during the 16th century. They still have an original Ottoman cupola and octagonal pool.

Gellért Baths
The main indoor swimming pool of this popular Buda spa delights bathers with its beautiful Secession interior, marble columns and colourful mosaics.

Exploring Budapest's Baths and Pools

Heated deep inside the earth, the waters of the mineral-rich hot springs which bubble up through fractures in the rocky hills of Buda and Óbuda have given the city a Turkish-influenced bathing culture which has survived even the rigours of Communism. A total of 31 spa-water pools and thermal baths, including both indoor and outdoor options, make taking the waters an unmissable treat for visitors to Budapest.

The Turkish Influence

Although the ruins of Roman thermal baths dating from the 2nd century AD have been found in Óbuda, it was only under the Ottoman occupation of the 16th–17th centuries *(see pp28–9)*, that the bathing culture really took hold in Budapest.

Four stunning Turkish-built baths, some of the few remaining examples of Ottoman architecture in Budapest, are still in operation. The **Rudas**, the **Rácz Hotel & Thermal Spa**, the **Király** and the **Veli Bej Bath** (formerly known as Császár) were all built in the 16th century, and are constructed on a single model. A marble staircase leads into a chamber containing a dome-topped, octagonal thermal pool, which is surrounded by smaller dome-covered pools at temperatures ranging from icily cold to roastingly hot. The most beautiful are almost certainly the Rudas Baths, followed closely by the Király Baths. The Rácz Baths have been extended and facilities improved to include a thermal spa and hotel complex. The Veli Bej Bath is now part of the Lukács Baths complex *(see below)*.

Many of the city's newer baths and almost all the Turkish baths are for both men and women. The Rudas Baths are the exception; they are open to men only on weekdays, except Tuesdays when they accept only women. At weekends they are open to both men and women, when bathing suits are obligatory. On single-sex days a small apron is provided.

After the Turks

The late 19th and early 20th century was a new golden age for Budapest *(see pp34–5)*, and saw the building of a number of splendid baths. Many have spring-water swimming pools attached.

Opened in 1894 the Neo-Classical **Lukács Baths** offer two outdoor swimming pools as well as the 16th-century Császár thermal pool. The **Széchenyi Baths**, opened 20 years later on the Pest side of the river, make up the biggest bathing complex in Europe. In addition to the usual indoor thermal pools, they also boast outdoor thermal and swimming pools, complete with sun terraces. With the hottest spa-water in the city, the outdoor thermal pool is popular even in the depths of winter.

As well as the thermal pools, Budapest's bathing establishments also include a steam room and sauna. Professional massages are almost always available for a small fee. Some places offer medicinal mud baths. You will be invited to take a shower, and indulge in a short nap in the rest room before you leave.

Outdoor pool at the Gellért Hotel and Baths Complex

Swim in style at the Rudas Baths

Spa Hotels

Nestling at the foot of Gellért Hill, the beautiful **Gellért Hotel and Baths Complex** is the oldest and most famous of a handful of luxury hotels in Budapest offering swimming and thermal pools, steam rooms, sauna and massage. The renowned Gellért Baths were opened to the general public in 1918, and include a fabulous, marble-columned indoor swimming pool, a labyrinth of thermal baths that can be used by both sexes, single-sex nudist sun-bathing areas and an outdoor swimming pool. A hugely popular wave machine is switched on in the latter for 10 minutes in every hour.

A second wave of spa-hotels were built in the 1970s and '80s. Set on Margaret Island, the modern, squeaky-clean and extremely luxurious **Danubius Health Spa Resort Margitsziget**, is linked by an underground passage to the older **Danubius Grand Hotel Margitsziget**. In addition to the usual range of baths and pools, treatments include manicure, pedicure and a solarium. The late 1980s saw the arrival of two new spa hotels, the **Danubius Health Spa Resort Helia** not far from the Pest riverbank and, on the Buda side, the **Aquincum Hotel**. Both hotels offer a huge range of fitness and wellness facilities, including gym equipment, pools, steam baths and a sauna, as well as a wide variety of treatments.

The Healing Waters

The citizens of Budapest are great believers in the social, psychological and medical benefits of the thermal baths. Office workers will often visit the public baths as early as 6am, to prepare for the day. Others like to visit at the end of the day, at 6pm, to relax, recharge and work up an appetite. Most of the baths employ staff who can offer advice on the most appropriate pools and special treatments for a particular ailment. The warm, mineral-rich spa waters are extremely good for general relaxation. They can also be helpful in the relief of a number of specific complaints, including post-traumatic stress, joint and muscle damage, rheumatism and menstrual pain. Prices vary greatly at Budapest's public baths and are no longer subsidised. Admission is usually around 3,000–6,000 forints, and a 15-minute massage costs about the same. All baths employ expert masseurs.

An ornamental tap, typical of the architectural detail found in Budapest's historic baths

Széchenyi Baths, the biggest bathing complex in Europe

Swimming as Sport

Many Hungarians are excellent swimmers, and the country has achieved great success in competitive water sports. In addition to Budapest's many recreational pools, sports pools include the **Hajós Olympic Pool** complex on Margaret Island. The complex consists of three sports pools, two outdoor, including one at full Olympic size, and one indoor. The pools are used for professional training, but are also open to the public. Together with the Komjádi Béla Swimming Stadium on Árpád Fejedelem útja, the Hajós Olympic Pool is the place to go to see professional swimming, diving or water polo.

A Day at the Strand

Designed as a complete bathing day out, the strands of Budapest are a phenomenon not to be missed. A total of 12 strands in the city testifies to their popularity. Outdoor swimming and thermal pools are surrounded by grassy sun-bathing areas. Trampolines and ping-pong and pool tables offer a change from the water, while ice creams, beers and hot dogs add to the summer-holiday atmosphere.

The lovely **Palatinus Strand**, set in a large area of parkland on Margaret Island, boasts seven outdoor pools, some thermal and some for swimming, complete with water slides and wave machines. Just east of the Pest river bank is the vast, modern **Dagály Strand** complex. Built after World War II, it includes 12 pools, with space for up to 12,000 people. Other strands worth visiting include **Római Strand** in Óbuda in the north of the city. Three pools have been carefully rebuilt here, on the site of some Roman baths, together with a not-so-Roman water chute.

Sculpture at the Római Strand

To the north of the city at Csillaghegy on the hév suburban train line, **Csillaghegy Strand** consists of four pools set in picturesque grounds, and includes a popular south-facing nudist beach.

Where to Find the Baths and Pools

Aquincum Hotel *p187*
Danubius Grand Hotel Margitsziget *pp177*
Danubius Health Spa Resort Helia *p188*
Danubius Health Spa Resort Margitszieget *pp177, 188*
Gellért Hotel and Baths Complex *pp94–5*
Hajós Olympic Pool *p176*
Király Baths *p105*
Lukács Baths *p105*
Palatinus Strand *p176*
Rácz Hotel & Thermal Spa *p99*
Rudas Baths *p97*
Széchenyi Baths *p155*
Veli Bej Baths *p105*

Budapest's Best: the Secession

Visitors to Budapest are often impressed by its wonderful late 19th and early 20th century buildings. The majority of these are found in central Pest and around Városliget; Buda was already developed at this stage and so boasts few examples. The movement started among groups of avant-garde artists in Paris and Vienna, from where the term Secession comes. In Budapest, the Secession style was also the inspiration for the development of the Hungarian National Style. Further details are given on pages 58–9.

The School on Rose Hill
Dezső Zrumeczky , a student of the renowned architect Károly Kós, used motifs from village houses in Transylvania to give this building on Áldás utca its character.

Woman with a Birdcage (1892)
This painting by József Rippl-Rónai has an atmosphere of mystery and intimacy typical of Hungarian art of the period. It hangs in the Hungarian National Gallery *(see p81)* today.

Margit híd
MARGIT KÖRÚT
NORTH OF THE CASTLE DISTRICT
FŐ U.
CASTLE DISTRICT
Danube
ID. ANTALL JÓZSEF R.
Széchenyi lánchíd
ATTILA ÚT
KRISZTINA KÖRÚT
HEGYALJA ÚT
GELLÉRT HILL AND TABÁN

Ironwork Gates of Gresham Palace
Two peacocks, a classic Secession motif, decorate the wrought-iron gates of the Four Seasons Gresham Palace hotel. The building was built by Zsigmond Quittner and the Vágó brothers between 1905–6.

Lechner House on Bartók Béla út
Ödön Lechner was the leading exponent of the Hungarian National Style. He built this apartment block for his brother Gyula, with a studio for himself on the fourth floor, in 1899. The block is at 40 Bartók Béla út.

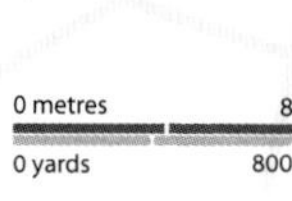

Post Office Savings Bank
The main staircase of this building by Ödön Lechner is embellished by fine fretted balusters, rounded lamps and decorative windows.

Entrance to the Zoo
Kornél Neuschloss made ingenious use of elements of Hindu architecture when he created this amusing gate guarded by two elephants.

Sipeky Balázs Villa
Built between 1905–6, this fanciful villa is perhaps the most representative example of the Secession style in Budapest. It was designed by Ödön Lechner.

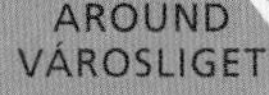

Philanthia Florist's
This extraordinary florist's is on Váci utca. The interior of the shop is in the Secession style, while the building itself is Neo-Classical.

Gellért Hotel and Baths Complex
Supported by flattened arches, a glass roof adds to the tranquil appeal of this hall in the famous spa at the Gellért Hotel. The Secession interiors created here are among the most splendid to be found in Budapest.

Exploring Secession Budapest

The Secession movement crossed artistic boundaries, influencing painting and the decorative arts as well as architecture. Colourful, sometimes fantastical designs are instantly recognizable hallmarks of the style. The Hungarian National Style drew heavily on this general trend, incorporating motifs from old Hungarian architecture, particularly that of Transylvania, folk art and even oriental features.

Vase designed by István Sovának, in the Museum of Applied Arts

József Rippl-Rónai's *Woman in White-Spotted Dress* (1889), in the Hungarian National Gallery

Paintings and Drawings

The main exponents of Secession art in Hungary were József Rippl-Rónai, János Vaszary and Lajos Gulácsy.

Rippl-Ránai spent many years in Paris, at the time when the Art Nouveau movement was beginning to flourish. *Lady in Red*, which he painted in 1899, was the first Hungarian painting in the Secession style. Many of Rippl-Rónai's works are on show in the **Hungarian National Gallery**. There is also a tapestry version of *Lady in Red* in the **Museum of Applied Arts**.

The work of János Vaszary was heavily influenced by both German and English art. His finest pictures, which include *Golden Age* and the mysterious *Adam and Eve*, can be admired in the Hungarian National Gallery. Lajos Gulácsy was influenced by the Pre-Raphaelite and expressionist movements and his pictures are often symbolic. Many of his paintings, too, can now be viewed in the Hungarian National Gallery.

The artists' colony based at Gödöllő was an important centre for painters working in the new Secession style. Its founder, Aladár Körösfői-Kriesch, created numerous works, including a fresco entitled *The Fount of Youth* which decorates the **Liszt Ferenc Academy of Music**.

Decorative Arts

New ideas in the decorative arts at this time were closely related to architectural developments. Ödön Lechner began to make use of colourful ceramic tiles, acquired from his father-in-law's brickyard in Pécs in southern Hungary, not only to cover roofs but also as a decorative element.

The owner of this brickyard, Vilmos Zsolnay, discovered an innovative method of glazing tiles and ceramics. This proved so successful that the brickyard was turned into a factory specializing in their production. Zsolnay's factory eventually made most of the vivid and distinctive pyrogranite ceramic tiles covering the Secession buildings in the city.

Zsolnay also employed leading designers to create ranges of dinner services, vases and candlesticks. For these he was awarded the Gold Medal of the Legion of Honour at the World Fair in Paris. And at an exhibition organized in 1896, to mark the millennial anniversary of the Hungarian Kingdom, the factory introduced its most beautiful pieces.

Ödön Lechner (1845–1914)

The most influential architect of the Hungarian Secession, Ödön Lechner trained in Berlin before completing his apprenticeship by working in both Italy and France. His quest was to create an identifiable Hungarian National Style, by combining Secession motifs with elements from Hungarian folk art and Hindu designs. The colourful ceramics that he often used became his signature. Among the buildings that Budapest owes to him are the Museum of Applied Arts, the Post Office Savings Bank and the Institute of Geology. Behind the ingenious and fantastical exteriors, Lechner's buildings have wonderfully simple, functional and superbly lit interiors.

Portrait of Lechner

Gresham Palace and the **Gellért Hotel and Baths Complex** are among the many buildings in the city that are embellished by ornamental wrought-iron gates, gratings and banisters that incorporate Secession motifs.

Interior Decoration

Among the interiors of the era, those of the **New York Palace** are a real jewel. Decked out in the best materials, including bronze and marble, they retain the splendour of their original, Neo-Baroque form.

Also worth visiting are the **Hungarian National Bank** and the **Post Office Savings Bank**, with their furnished secure rooms and ornate door and window frames. The interior of **Philanthia Florist's**, is another wonderfully preserved example of decor from the Secession.

A Secession cabinet, displayed in the Museum of Applied Arts

Window created by Miksa Róth, at the Hungarian National Bank

Exhibitions of attractive Secession furniture are a feature of both the Museum of Applied Arts and also the **Nagytétényi Palace**.

Architecture

Hungarian architecture of the *fin de siècle* is characterized not only by decorative forms using glazed ceramics, but, more fundamentally, by the implementation of modern technical solutions. Reinforced concrete, steel and glass were used together, and large, light-filled interiors were often achieved. The central hall of the Museum of Applied Arts is a fine example of this.

Aside from Ödön Lechner, the most important of the Hungarian Secession architects, others who contributed significant buildings in the prevailing style included Béla Lajta, Aladár Árkay, Károly Kós and István Medgyaszay. Béla Lajta, a pupil of Lechner, designed the **Rózsavölgyi Building**, with its distinctive geometrical ornamentation, on Szervita tér. Also among his buildings is the extra-ordinary former **Jewish Old People's Home**, at Nos. 53–5 Amerikai út. With sophisticated ornamental details based on folk designs, **Városliget Calvinist Church** was the creation of Aladár Árkay.

Károly Kós was a highly original member of this set. Fascinated by the traditional architecture of Transylvania, he trawled the whole of that region, making drawings of the village churches and manor houses he encountered. Motifs from these buildings were later transferred to the aviary at Budapest's **Zoo** and the houses of the **Wekerle Estate**.

Frieze on the Rózsavölgyi Building

Where to Find Secession Budapest

Gellért Hotel and Baths Complex *pp94–5*
Gresham Palace *p118*
Hungarian National Bank, Liberty Square *p114*
Hungarian National Gallery *pp78–81*
Institute of Geology *p158*
Liszt Ferenc Academy of Music *p133*
Museum of Applied Arts *pp140–41*
Nagytétényi Palace *p165*
New York Palace *p133*
Philanthia Florist's *p57*
Post Office Savings Bank *p115*
Turkish Bank *p132*
Városliget Calvinist Church *p148*
Wekerle Estate *p161*
Zoo *p154*

Decorative Motifs

Stylized folk motifs derived from embroidery and also oriental patterns were often employed in Budapest's decorative arts during this period. Secession motifs such as feline forms, based on Viennese and Parisian examples, also feature.

Secession lettering on the sign of Philanthia Florist's

Sunflower motif adorning the Post Office Savings Bank

Colourful mosaic at No. 3 Aulich utca

BUDAPEST THROUGH THE YEAR

Set in the middle of Hungary, Budapest enjoys a continental climate with sharply defined seasons, each of which brings its own attractions, from traditional feast days to cultural and sporting events. Historically a centre of cultural, and especially musical, activity, Budapest continues the tradition with many musical events including the Spring Festival, an international celebration of classical music and ballet, and the Budapest Autumn Festival, devoted to contemporary classical arts. Many hotels and tourist offices provide a programme of the events taking place in the city, as do the festivals' websites which are usually available in English.

Spring

Spring makes a welcome return to the city in March, with sunshine and fresh, warm days. Budapest turns green and the Spring Festival sees the arrival of some of the year's first tourists.

March

The Spring Uprising *(15 Mar)*. A public holiday marks the day in 1848 when the youth of Pest, led by the poet Sándor Petőfi, rebelled against the Habsburg occupation of Hungary *(see pp32–3)*. Thousands of people take to the streets to lay wreaths and light eternal flames, wearing the national colours of red, white and green. There are speeches and street theatre, especially in front of the Hungarian National Museum *(see pp134–5)*.

Spring Festival *(the last two weeks of Mar–mid-Apr)*. Top national and international musicians gather for several weeks of music and dance in churches and concert halls all over the city. The emphasis of the festival is on the classical tradition, but also in evidence are folk music and dance, as well as pop and jazz. *(www.festivalcity.hu)*

Parade in the Castle District during the Spring Festival

April

Easter is an important religious event in Hungary and the Easter service is well worth attending in one of the city's many churches. On the morning of Easter Monday young men spray their female friends and relatives with perfume or water, a ritual which is said to keep the recipients beautiful until the following year. Painted eggs are given in return.

Festival Celebrating the Day of Dance *(end Apr)*. The National Dance Theatre and the Association of Hungarian Dance Artists organize this festival every year, with participation from top Hungarian dance groups and foreign guest artists. *(www.nemzetitancszinhaz.hu)*

Horse Racing *(Sun, Apr–Oct)*. April sees the beginning of the flat-racing season. Place your bets at the busy and charmingly down-at-heel Kincsem Park race course on Albertirsai út.

Budapest International Book Festival. Organized in co-operation with the Frankfurt Book Fair, this festival is the most important event in Hungary's publishing year, both for the publishing industry and for the general public. It is held at a modern venue in the Millenáris Park. *(www.bookfestival.hu)*

Springtime magnolia blossom on Margaret Island

May

May Day *(1 May)*. No longer a compulsory display of patriotism, May Day celebrations take place in public parks all over the city and involve craft markets, street performers and sausage and beer tents. A dip in the local thermal bath or swimming pool *(see pp52–5)*, is another popular May Day activity.

◀ Folk dancers at the Budapest Wine Festival

Average Daily Hours of Sunshine

Hours

12
9
6
3
0

Jan Feb Mar Apr May Jun Jul Aug Sep Oct Nov Dec

Sunshine Chart
Budapest enjoys some of the sunniest weather in Europe, with an average of 8 hours of sunshine each day from April to September. During the sticky months of high summer (June, July and August), the Buda hills provide a welcome refuge from the heat of the city.

Summer

The long hot days of summer are made for relaxing on Margaret Island or sun-bathing at the city's open-air pools.

June

Budapest Summer Festival *(Jun–Aug)*. Margaret Island provides one of the major venues for this summer-long, open-air festival. The Margaret Island open-air theatre is the largest in Budapest and hosts excellent Hungarian and international performances of grand operas, ballets and concerts. *(www.eng.szabadter.hu)*

Danube Carnival International Multicultural Festival
Various venues host music and dance events. *(www.dunakarneval.hu)*

Formula One racing in the Hungarian Grand Prix

July

Hungarian Formula One Grand Prix *(end Jul)*. The biggest event in the Hungarian sporting calendar takes place at Mogyoród. *(www.hungaroring.hu)*

Concerts in St Stephen's Basilica *(Jul–Aug)*. Organ and choir concerts in the city's largest church *(see pp120–21)* provide a perfect opportunity to study the lavish interior decoration of this extraordinary building.

The Vajdahunyad Castle Summer Music Festival *(mid-Jul–Aug)*. This open-air festival features excellent classical as well as jazz, ragtime and gypsy music. *(www.vajdahunyad.hu)*

August

St István's Day *(20 Aug)*. St István, the patron saint of Hungary, is celebrated with mass in St Stephen's Basilica followed by a huge procession. The day ends with fireworks along the Danube.

Festival of Folk Arts *(around 20 Aug)*. Masters of Hungarian folk art set up at Buda Castle, offering workshops and selling their crafted items. *(http://mestersegekunnepe.hu)*

Sziget Festival *(Aug)*. Several stages and a camp site are set up on Óbuda Island for this popular week-long festival of rock, folk and jazz, which features top bands such as The Kooks and Iron Maiden. *(www.sziget.hu)*

Fireworks to celebrate St István's Day

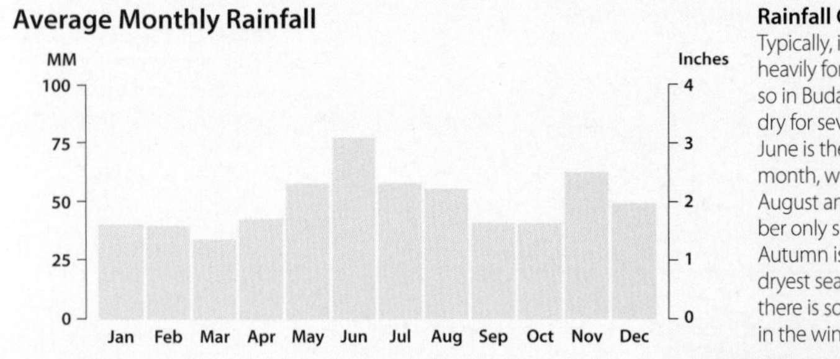

Rainfall Chart
Typically, it rains very heavily for two days or so in Budapest, then is dry for several weeks. June is the wettest month, with May, July, August and November only slightly dryer. Autumn is usually the dryest season, while there is some snowfall in the winter months.

Autumn

Budapest becomes an array of colour in Autumn and the summer crowds leave the city. Fruit and vegetable markets have vast displays of jewel-coloured produce and several festivals and events take place. Highlights of the season include the Wine and Autumn Festivals.

September

Jewish Summer Cultural Festival *(end Aug–beg Sep).* This multicultural festival includes a Jewish book fair, an Israeli film festival, art exhibitions, and cuisine presentations. *(www.zsidonyarifesztival.hu)*

Budapest Wine Festival *(2nd week of Sep).* Wine makers set up stalls for wine tastings and folk dancing on Buda's Castle Hill *(see p73).* *(www.aborfesztival.hu)*

Nemzeti Vágta (National Gallop) *(mid-Sep).* This horse race is held annually on a special course built around Heroes' Square for the event.

October

Budapest International Marathon and Running Festival *(Oct).* There is a marathon, a relay race, a mini-marathon and a family running competition. Concerts and events are held for spectators.

Performers take part in the Open-Air Theatre Festival

A colourful food stall in one of Budapest's covered markets

Autumn Festival *(mid-Oct).* Contemporary film, dance and theatre at venues across the city.

Vienna-Bratislava-Budapest Super Marathon Running Competition. This competition aims to strengthen ties between central European countries, particularly Austria, Slovakia and Hungary, and celebrates open European borders. *(www.bbu.hu)*

Remembrance Day *(23 Oct).* This is a national day of mourning to remember the 1956 Uprising, when 2,500 people were killed by Soviet tanks and 200,000 fled the country. Wreaths are laid in Municipal Cemetery *(see pp162–3)*, on the grave of the executed leader Imre Nagy *(see p36).*

November

Budapest Christmas Fair *(26 Nov–24 Dec).* The Budapest Christmas Market transforms Vörösmarty Square into a festive marketplace, where Hungarian artisans display their work and national dishes are served. *(www.budapestinfo.hu)*

Average Monthly Temperature

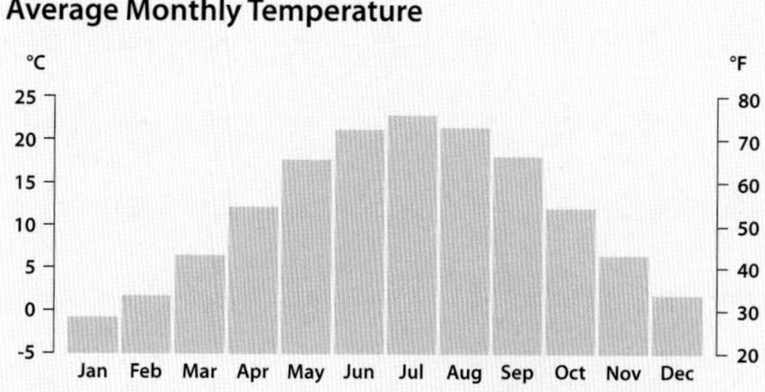

Temperature Chart
Seasons in Budapest are sharply defined. Day time temperatures rise rapidly from March onwards. By June, the thermometer often reaches 30°C (90°F) and more. September sees cooler weather, with temperatures falling rapidly to lows of well below freezing in January.

Winter

Despite the cold weather, winter can be an exciting time to visit Budapest. Open-air ice-skating takes place from November, roast-chestnut sellers appear on the streets and a Christmas tree is erected in Vörösmarty Square.

December

Budapest Christmas Fair *(26 Nov–24 Dec)* continues.

Silver and Gold Sunday *(2nd-to-last Sunday before Christmas)*. All the city's shops stay open for this Sunday of serious Christmas shopping.

Mikulás *(6 Dec)*. On *Mikulás*, or St Nicholas Day, children leave their shoes on the window sill for Santa Claus to fill.

Christmas *(24–26 Dec)*. The city shuts down for three days on 24 Dec. Although it is not an official public holiday, shops and offices close early. For the majority of Hungarians, the most important and sacred event is the family meal on the evening of 24 Dec. This is also when Christmas presents are brought by Little Jesus.

Seeing in the New Year, a stylish affair in Budapest

Colourfully decorated Christmas tree in Vörösmarty Square

Szilveszter *(31 Dec)*. Budapest celebrates in style on New Year's Eve, with music in Vörösmarty and Nyugati Squares until dawn, street parties, and fireworks. Public transport runs all through the night.

January

New Year's Gala Concert *(1 Jan)*. This occasion is an excellent way to start the new year. Outstanding Hungarian and foreign artists perform excerpts from European opera and musicals, providing a lively evening of music at the Hungarian State Opera. *(www.viparts.hu)*

February

Masked-Ball Season *(Feb)*. Budapest forgets the cold weather to welcome the coming of spring, and the arrival of the *farsang*, or fancy dress masked-ball season. The climax of the season is the spectacular Opera Ball and a masked procession, on the last Saturday and Sunday before Lent, respectively. *(www.operabal.com)*

Winter ice skating in City Park

Public Holidays

Public holidays mainly follow the Christian calendar. Two days mark cataclysmic events in Magyar history.

New Year (1 Jan)
Spring Uprising (15 Mar)
Easter Sunday (Mar/Apr)
Easter Monday (Mar/Apr)
Whit Monday (May/Jun)
May Day (1 May)
St István's Day (20 Aug)
Remembrance Day (23 Oct)
All Saints' Day (1 Nov)
Christmas Day (25 Dec)
Boxing Day (26 Dec)

Margaret Bridge to Elizabeth Bridge

A trip on a river boat along the Danube provides a unique panorama of the city. Most major cities have a river at their heart, however, the Danube historically played an interesting role in this case, for centuries dividing the separate towns of Buda and Pest. Today, several road bridges link the two halves of the modern city; they were all reconstructed after being destroyed by the retreating Nazi army towards the end of World War II.

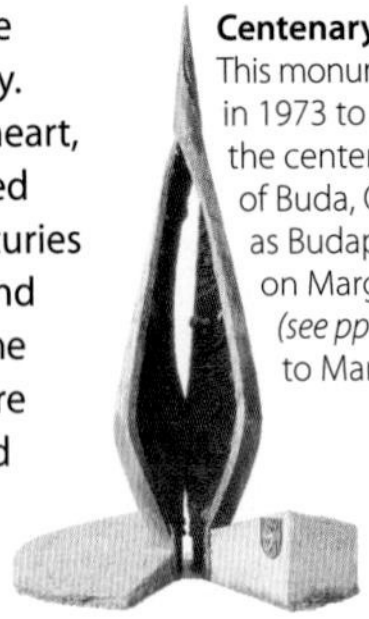

Centenary Monument
This monument was erected in 1973 to commemorate the centenary of the joining of Buda, Óbuda and Pest as Budapest. It stands on Margaret Island *(see pp176–7)*, close to Margaret Bridge.

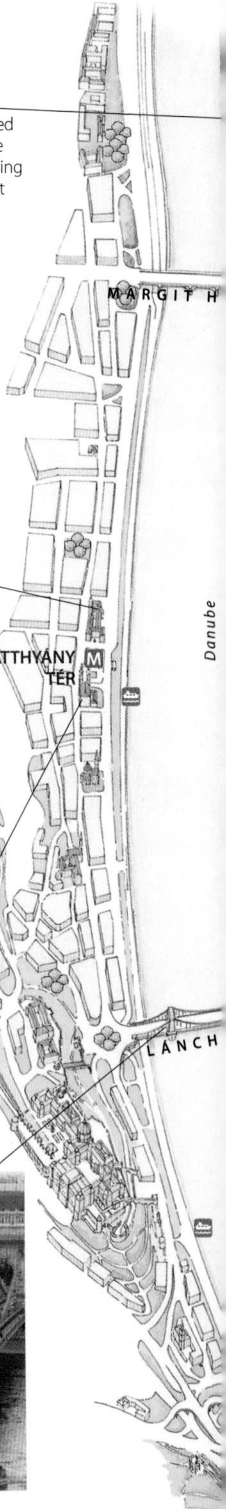

St Francis's Wounds Church
This Baroque church, built for an order of nuns, has its front facing away from the Danube. The hospital and shelter run by the sisters face the river *(see p105)*.

Mátyás Church
With medieval origins, the tower of this church has been rebuilt several times. It overlooks the Hilton Hotel and the Fishermen's Bastion *(see pp86–7)*.

St Anne's Church can be recognized by its twin, slender Baroque towers.

MARGIT H

BATTHYÁNY TÉR

Danube

LÁNCH

Chain Bridge was built between 1839–49 at the inititiative of Count István Széchenyi *(see p33)*. It was designed by Englishman William Tierney Clark and built by the (unrelated) Scot, Adam Clark. The bridge extends for 380 m (1,250 ft), supported by two towers – a major feat of engineering for the time.

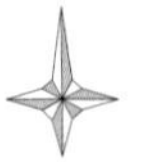

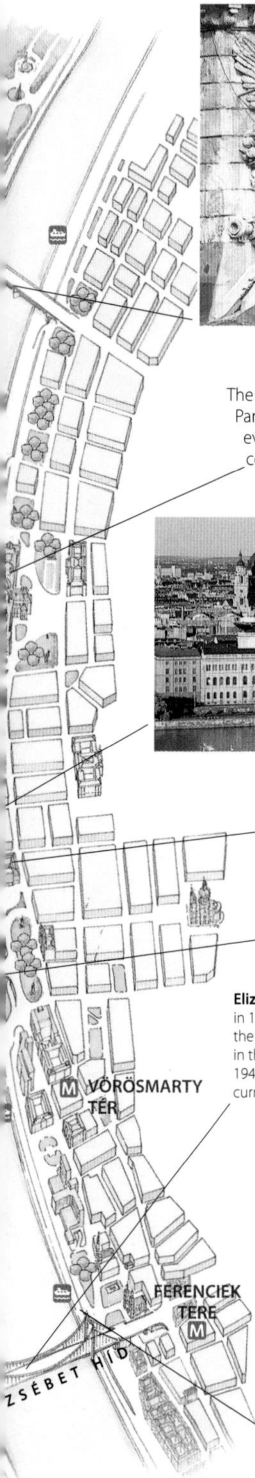

Margaret Bridge was built by the French engineer Ernest Gouin, at the point where the Danube becomes a single body once more after dividing to flow around Margaret Island. The bridge is distinguished by its unusual chevron shape. It was erected in 1872–6, and between 1899–1900 access from the bridge onto the island was added. Sculptures by Adolphe Thabart decorate its columns.

Parliament
The magnificent, high dome of the Parliament building is visible from every point along the Danube in central Budapest *(see pp112–13)*.

Much of the eastern bank of the river is characterized by fairly uniform architecture. Variation is provided here by the dome and towers of St Stephen's Basilica *(see pp120–21)*.

Hungarian Academy of Sciences

Elizabeth Bridge, constructed in 1897–1903, was at that time the longest suspension bridge in the world. Destroyed in 1945, it was rebuilt in its current form by Pál Sávolya.

VÖRÖSMARTY TÉR

The bridgehead of Chain Bridge is guarded by two vast stone lions sculpted by János Marschalkó. According to an anecdote János was heartbroken because he forgot to give the lions any tongues, so he drowned himself in the river. In fact the lions do have tongues, but they are not easy to see.

FERENCIEK TERE

ZSÉBET HÍD

Piers, from which passenger cruises operate daily in summer, are spaced frequently along the Danube in central Budapest.

Elizabeth Bridge to Rákóczi Bridge

Like Paris, Budapest has fully exploited the opportunities given by its river. The most important and beautiful buildings of Buda and Pest crowd along the banks of the Danube. These include the Royal Palace, churches, historic palaces and the Gellért Hotel and Baths Complex.

Royal Palace
The monumental Habsburg Royal Palace that once occupied this spot was destroyed during World War II, then reconstructed to reveal defensive walls and royal chambers that date from the Middle Ages *(see pp74–5)*.

Inner City Parish Church
This church *(see pp128–9)* was built in the 12th century on the ruins of Roman Contra Aquincum's walls. The spot was, from early times, an important place for crossing the river.

Gellért Hotel and Baths Complex
The architects of this hotel maximized its river façade to make it as imposing as possible *(see pp94–5)*.

Technical University
The university campus *(see p161)* occupies almost the entire space between Liberty Bridge *(Szabadság híd)* and Lágymányosi híd.

The embankment walk near Petőfi Bridge extends along the length of the Danube on the Pest side. It is a favourite place to meet or to go for a stroll, and is lined by smart hotels and restaurants.

Little Princess (1989), perched by the tram rails on the Pest side of the Danube, was so liked by Charles, Prince of Wales, on his visit here that he invited its designer, László Marton, to exhibit in London.

Liberty Bridge was built between 1894–9 by Hungarian engineer János Feketeházy. Opened by Emperor Franz Joseph, it initially took his name. All its original features were retained when it was rebuilt after World War II: on top of the bridge there are legendary Hungarian turul birds and royal crests.

Corvinus University
Formerly a customs' headquarters, this building has an elegant façade decorated with ten allegorical figures. These are the work of German sculptor August Sommer.

Rákóczi Bridge
Budapest's most modern and southernmost bridge was built in 1995 for a planned world exhibition that never happened. It carries traffic on a ring road bypassing the city centre.

Interior of St Stephen's Basilica, Budapest ▶

STEPHANE INTERCEDE

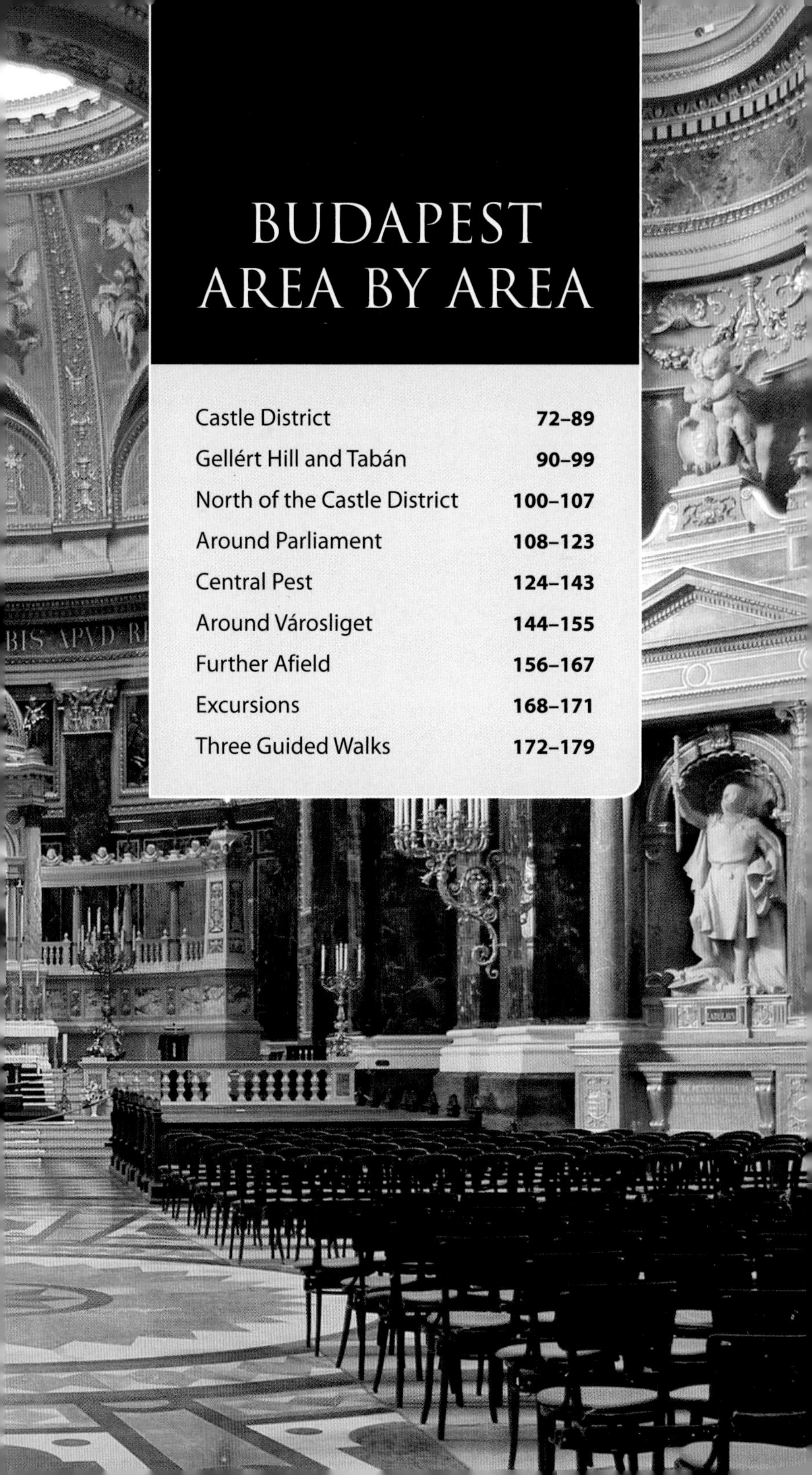

BUDAPEST AREA BY AREA

CASTLE DISTRICT

The hill town of Buda grew up around its castle and Mátyás Church from the 13th century onwards. At 60 m (197 ft) above the Danube, the hill's good strategic position and natural resources made it a prize site for its earliest inhabitants. In the 13th century, a large settlement arose when, after a Tartar invasion, King Béla IV decided to build his own defensive castle and establish his capital here. The reign of King Mátyás Corvinus in the 15th century was an important period in the evolution of Buda, but it suffered neglect under Turkish rule during the next century and was then destroyed by Christian troops. The town was reborn, however, and assumed an important role during the 18th and 19th centuries under the Habsburgs. By the end of World War II, the Old Town had been almost completely destroyed and the Royal Palace burnt to the ground. Since the war the Royal Palace and Old Town have been reconstructed, restoring the original appeal of this part of the city.

Sights at a Glance

Churches

- 11 *Mátyás Church pp86–7*
- 17 Buda Lutheran Church
- 18 Church of St Mary Magdalene

Museums and Galleries

- 1 Budapest History Museum
- 2 National Széchényi Library
- 4 *Hungarian National Gallery pp78–81*
- 8 Golden Eagle Pharmacy Museum
- 10 Hospital in the Rock
- 20 Museum of Military History
- 22 Labyrinth in the Buda Castle

Historic Streets and Squares

- 5 Parade Square
- 9 Holy Trinity Square
- 14 András Hess Square
- 15 Mihály Táncsics Street
- 16 Vienna Gate Square
- 19 Parliament Street
- 21 Lords' Street

Palaces, Historic Buildings and Monuments

- 3 Mátyás Fountain
- 6 Sándor Palace
- 7 Court Theatre of Buda
- 12 Fishermen's Bastion
- 13 Hilton Hotel

Restaurants *p196*

1. 21 – Magyar Vendéglő
2. Alabárdos
3. Café Miró
4. Café Pierrot
5. Fekete Holló Vendéglő
6. Halászbástya
7. Pest-Buda Bistro
8. Rivalda Café & Restaurant
9. Ruszwurm Cukrászda
10. Vár: a Speiz Étterem
11. Zóna Budapest

See also Street Finder maps 1, 3 & 9

◀ Ornate architectural details of the Mátyás Church in Budapest's Castle District

For keys to symbols *see back flap*

Street-by-Street: The Royal Palace

The Royal Palace has borne many incarnations during its long life. Even now it is not known exactly where King Béla IV began building his castle, though it is thought to be nearer the site of Mátyás Church *(see pp86–7)*. The Holy Roman Emperor Sigismund of Luxembourg built a Gothic palace on the present site, from which today's castle began to evolve. In the 18th century, the Habsburgs built their monumental palace here. The current form dates from the rebuilding of the 19th-century palace after its destruction in February 1945. During this work, remains of the 15th-century Gothic palace were uncovered. Hungarian archeologists decided to reveal the recovered defensive walls and royal chambers in the reconstruction.

SZÍNHÁZ U

SZT GYÖRGY U

An ornamental gateway, dating from 1903, leads from the Habsburg Steps to the Royal Palace. Nearby, a bronze sculpture of the mythical turul bird guards the palace. This statue marks the millennium anniversary of the Magyar conquest in 896.

❸ ★ Mátyás Fountain
In the northwest courtyard of the Royal Palace stands the Mátyás Fountain. It was designed by Alajos Stróbl in 1904 and depicts King Mátyás Corvinus and his beloved Ilonka.

Lion Gate, leading to a rear courtyard of the Royal Palace, gets its name from the four lions that watch over it. These sculptures were designed by János Fadrusz in 1901.

1200 | **1400** | **1600** | **1800**

1255 First written document, a letter by King Béla IV, refers to building a fortified castle

c.1356 Louis I builds a royal castle on the southern slopes of Castle Hill

c.1400 Sigismund of Luxembourg builds an ambitious Gothic palace on this site

1458 A Renaissance palace evolves under King Mátyás

1541 After capturing Buda, the Turks use the Royal Palace to stable horses and store gunpowder

1686 The assault by Christian soldiers leaves the palace completely razed to the ground

1719 The building of a small palace begins on the ruins of the old palace, to a design by Hölbling and Fortunato de Prati

1749 Maria Theresa builds a vast palace comprising 203 chambers

1849 Royal Palace is destroyed again, during an unsuccessful attack by Hungarian insurgents

1881 Miklós Ybl *(see p123)* begins programme to re-build and expand the Royal Palace

Turul bird

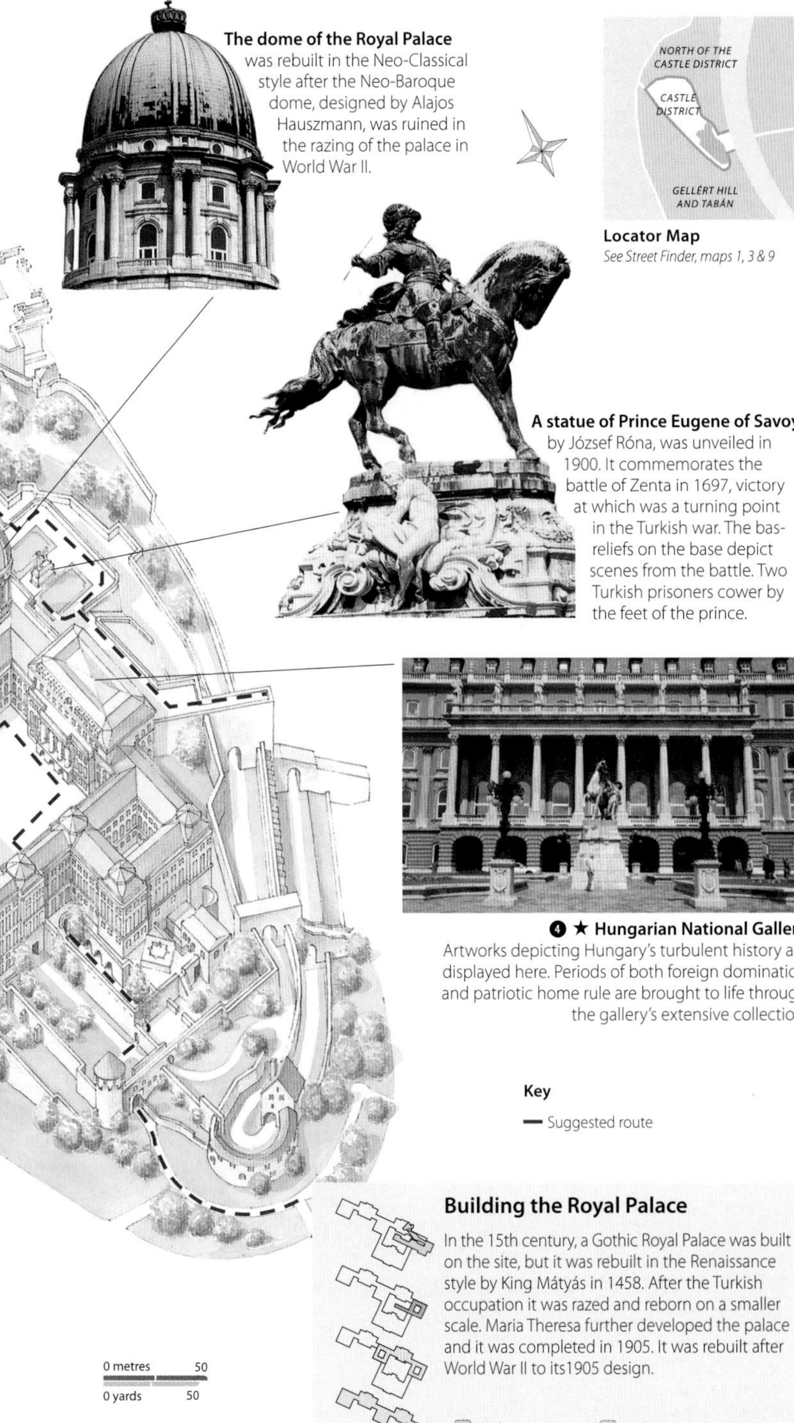

The dome of the Royal Palace was rebuilt in the Neo-Classical style after the Neo-Baroque dome, designed by Alajos Hauszmann, was ruined in the razing of the palace in World War II.

Locator Map
See Street Finder, maps 1, 3 & 9

A statue of Prince Eugene of Savoy, by József Róna, was unveiled in 1900. It commemorates the battle of Zenta in 1697, victory at which was a turning point in the Turkish war. The bas-reliefs on the base depict scenes from the battle. Two Turkish prisoners cower by the feet of the prince.

❹ ★ Hungarian National Gallery
Artworks depicting Hungary's turbulent history are displayed here. Periods of both foreign domination and patriotic home rule are brought to life through the gallery's extensive collection.

Key

— Suggested route

Building the Royal Palace

In the 15th century, a Gothic Royal Palace was built on the site, but it was rebuilt in the Renaissance style by King Mátyás in 1458. After the Turkish occupation it was razed and reborn on a smaller scale. Maria Theresa further developed the palace and it was completed in 1905. It was rebuilt after World War II to its1905 design.

15th century
1719
1749
1905

Renaissance majolica floor from the 15th century, uncovered during excavations on Castle Hill and displayed at the Budapest History Museum

❶ Budapest History Museum

Budapesti Történeti Múzeum

Szent György tér 2. **Map** 3 C1 (9 B4). **Tel** (06 1) 487 88 00. 5, 16, 16A, 116, 178. 18. **Open** Mar–Oct: 10am–6pm Tue–Sun; Nov–Feb: 10am–4pm Tue–Sun. **btm.hu**

Since the unification of Budapest in 1873, historic artifacts relating to Hungary's capital have been collected. Many are now on show at the Castle Museum (Vármúzeum) of the Budapest History Museum.

During the rebuilding that followed the destruction suffered in World War II, chambers dating from the Middle Ages were uncovered in the south wing (wing E) of the Royal Palace. They provide an insight into the character of a much earlier castle within today's Habsburg reconstruction.

These chambers, including a tiny prison cell and a chapel, were recreated in the basement of the palace. They now house an exhibition, the Royal Palace in Medieval Buda, which displays authentic weapons, seals, tiles and other early artifacts.

On the ground and first floors of the Vármúzeum, exhibits trace the history of Buda Castle from 1686 to the present. Also on the ground floor are Gothic Statues from the Royal Palace and a tapestry with the Hungarian-Angevin coat-of-arms dating from the 14th and 15th centuries. On the first floor, the permanent exhibition "Budapest – Light and Shadow: The 1,000-year History of a Capital" leads visitors through the millennium that formed the Hungarian capital, from the Roman settlement of Aquincum *(see pp166–7)* to the political change in 1989 *(see p36)*.

❷ National Széchényi Library

Országos Széchényi Könyvtár

Szent György tér 6. **Map** 3 C1 (9 B4). **Tel** (06 1) 224 37 00. 5, 16, 16A, 116, 178. 18. **Open** 9am–8pm Tue–Sat. **oszk.hu**

A magnificent collection of books, manuscripts, maps, engravings, posters, photographs and sheet music is housed in wing F of the Royal Palace, built in 1890–1902 by Alajos Hauszmann and Miklós Ybl *(see p123)*. Previously, the library was part of the Hungarian National Museum *(see pp134–7)*.

Corvinian illuminated manuscript in the National Széchényi Library

Among the library's most precious treasures are 35 pieces from the Bibliotheca Corviniana, a collection of ancient books and manuscripts that originally belonged to King Mátyás Corvinus *(see p26–7)*. Also of importance are the earliest surviving records in the Hungarian language, dating from the early 13th century.

The library was established by Count Ferenc Széchényi in 1802. He endowed it with 15,000 books and 2,000 manuscripts. The collection now comprises nine million items. The library runs events and exhibitions that draw on its rich collection.

Crest on the Lion Gate in a courtyard at the Royal Palace

❸ Mátyás Fountain

Mátyás Kút

Royal Palace. **Map** 1 C5 (9 B3). 5, 16, 16A, 116, 178. 18.

The ornate fountain in the northwest courtyard of the Royal Palace (situated between wings A and C) was designed by Alajos Stróbl in 1904. The statue is dedicated to the great Renaissance king, Mátyás, about whom there are many popular legends and fables.

The Romantic design of the bronze sculptures takes its theme from a 19th-century ballad by the poet Mihály Vörösmarty. According to the tale, King Mátyás, while on a hunting expedition, meets a beautiful peasant girl, Ilonka, who falls in love with him. This representation shows King Mátyás disguised as a hunter, standing proudly with his kill. He is accompanied by his chief hunter and several hunting dogs in the central part of the fountain. Beneath the left-hand columns sits Galeotto Marzio, an Italian court poet, and the figure of the young Ilonka is beneath the columns on the right.

In keeping with the romantic reputation of King Mátyás, a new tradition has grown up concerning this statue. The belief is that anyone wishing to revisit Budapest should throw some coins into the fountain to ensure their safe return.

❹ Hungarian National Gallery

See pp78–81.

Batthyány Palace on Parade Square retains its original Baroque façade

❺ Parade Square

Dísz Tér

Map 1 B5 (9 A3). 🚌 16, 16A, 116.

Parade Square is named after the military parades that were held here in the 19th century. At the northern end of the square is the Honvéd Monument, built in 1893 by György Zala. It honours and commemorates those who died during the recapture of Buda from Austria in the 1848 revolution.

The western elevation of the Neo-Classical Sándor Palace

The house at No. 3 was built between 1743–8, by József Giessl. This two-floor Baroque palace was the home of the Batthyány family until 1945. Although the building has been frequently remodelled, the façade remains intact.

A few houses on Parade Square incorporate medieval remains. Such houses can be seen at Nos. 4–5 and No. 11, built by Venerio Ceresola. The former has seat niches dating from the 13th century.

❻ Sándor Palace

Sándor Palota

Szent György tér 1–3. **Map** 1 C5 (9 A3). 🚌 16, 16A, 116. **Closed** to the public. **W keh.hu**

By the top of the cog-wheel railway stands the grand Neo-Classical mansion, Sándor Palace. It was commissioned in 1806 by Count Vincent Sándor from architects Mihály Pollack and Johann Aman.

The bas-reliefs that decorate the palace are the work of Richárd Török, Miklós Melocco and Tamás Kőrössényi. The decoration on the western elevation depicts Greek gods on Mount Olympus. The southern elevation shows Count Sándor being knighted and the northern elevation features a 1934 sculpture of Saint George by Zsigmond Kisfaludi Stróbl.

Sándor Palace functioned as the prime minister's official residence from 1867 to 1944, when it was severely damaged in World War II. The building has been completely restored, and it is now the official residence of the President of Hungary.

❼ Court Theatre of Buda

Várszínház

Színház utca 1–3. **Map** 1 C5 (9 A3). **Tel** (06 1) 201 44 07 or 375 86 49. 🚌 16, 16A, 116. Box Office: **Open** 1–6pm Mon–Sun. **W nemzetitancszinhaz.hu**

An unlikely assortment of institutions have stood on this site. The church of St John the Evangelist, founded by King Béla IV, stood here in the 13th century. This church was then used as a mosque under Ottoman rule, and in 1686 it was demolished by the Christian armies that retook the city. In 1725 the Carmelite order built a Baroque church in its place and this building was first converted into a theatre in 1786, during the reign of Emperor Joseph II. Farkas Kempelen, a famous Hungarian designer added a Rococo façade and seats for 1,200 spectators. The first plays were in German and it was not until 1790 that any work was staged in Hungarian. Beethoven's concert of 1800 is commemorated by a plaque.

The building was damaged in World War II and restored in 1978. Today, the theatre hosts performances by the National Dance Theatre.

4 Hungarian National Gallery

Magyar Nemzeti Galéria

Established in 1957, the Hungarian National Gallery houses a comprehensive collection of Hungarian art from medieval times to the 20th century. Gathered by various groups and institutions since 1839, these works had previously been exhibited at the Hungarian National Museum *(see pp134–7)* and the Museum of Fine Arts *(see pp150–53)*. The collection was moved to the Royal Palace in 1975 and today occupies four wings. There are now six permanent exhibitions, presenting the most valuable and critically acclaimed Hungarian art in the world.

St Anne Altarpiece (c.1520)
Elaborately decorated, this folding altarpiece from Kisszeben is one of the Gothic highlights in the gallery.

Madonna of Toporc (c. 1420)
This is a captivating example of medieval wood sculpture in the Gothic style. It was originally crafted for a church in Spiz (now part of Slovakia).

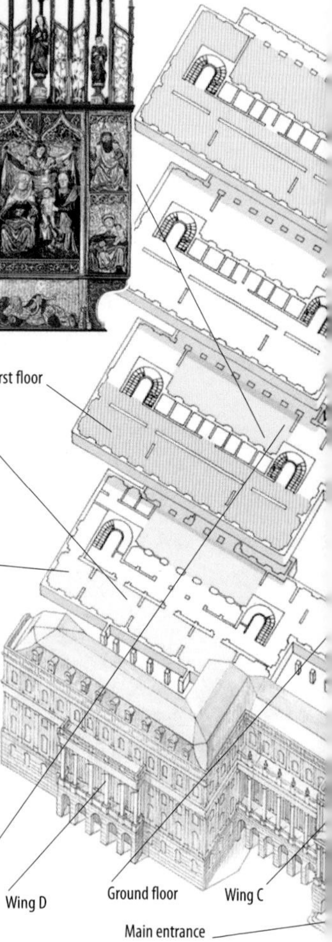

First floor

Madonna of Bártfa (1465–70)
This painting of a Madonna and Child is from a church in Bártfa (now in Slovakia). It is thought to have been painted in Cracow, Poland.

★ The Visitation (1506)
This painting by Master MS is a delightful example of late Gothic Hungarian art. It is a fragment of a folding altarpiece from a church in Selmecbánya in modern-day Slovakia.

Wing D

Ground floor

Wing C

Main entrance

Key

- Stone sculptures and artifacts
- Gothic works
- Late-Gothic altarpieces
- Renaissance and Baroque works
- 19th-Century works
- 20th-Century works
- Hungarian works post 1945
- Temporary exhibitions

Luischen (1884)
One of the earliest works by the sculptor Alajos Stróbl is this marble bust of Luischen on display on the first floor.

Second floor

Third floor

Wing B

Wing A

VISITORS' CHECKLIST

Practical Information
A, B, C and D wings in the Royal Palace. **Map** 3 C1 (9 B4).
Tel (06 1) 3620 201 9082, 3620 439 7325 or 3620 439 7331. **Open** 10am–6pm Tue–Sun. to arrange for an English-speaking guide call (06 1) 201 90 82. **mng.hu**

Transport
16, 16A, 116.

Woman Bathing (1901)
This painting by Károly Lotz is the best example of Neo-Classical painting in Hungary. It reflects his fascination for the work of the French painter, Ingres.

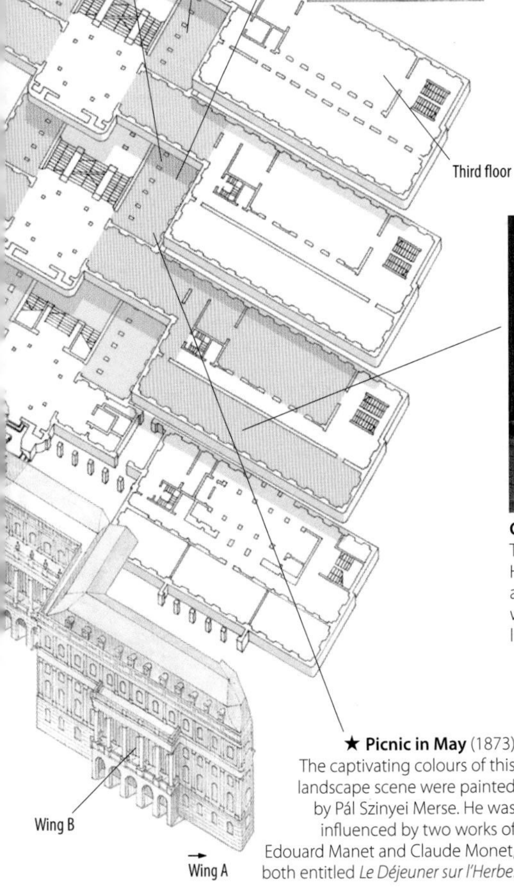

Gallery Guide

The gallery's permanent exhibitions are housed in wings B, C and D. Early stone and Gothic exhibits are on the ground floor. Late Gothic, Renaissance and Baroque works and 19th-century works share the first floor. Works from the 20th century are on the second floor, and Hungarian works post 1945 are on the top floor. Temporary exhibits are displayed in wing A, as well as on the ground floor of wing C and the third floors of wings C and D.

Churning Woman (1872–73)
This painting is by Mihály Munkácsy, Hungary's most internationally celebrated artist. The tiredness of the woman's features with her worn hands show the reality of a life of poverty.

★ **Picnic in May** (1873)
The captivating colours of this landscape scene were painted by Pál Szinyei Merse. He was influenced by two works of Edouard Manet and Claude Monet, both entitled *Le Déjeuner sur l'Herbe*.

Exploring the Hungarian National Gallery

The works are displayed in six permanent exhibitions and give a thorough insight into Hungarian art from the early Middle Ages to the present day. Although one-and-a-half centuries of Turkish occupation and wartime destruction interrupted the development of Hungarian art, the birth of national pride in the 19th century allowed a new indigenous style to develop. Among the most interesting exhibits are the Hungarian paintings of the late 19th century, when a greater diversity of styles came to the fore. The collection of 20th-century works includes paintings, prints, drawings and sculptures.

The Habsburg Crypt, with the sarcophagus of Palatine Archduke Joseph

The Lapidarium

On the ground floor, to the left of the main entrance, is a display of stone objects discovered during the reconstruction of the Royal Palace *(see p74)*. Situated on the ground floor, under the southern yard of the main building is the Lapidarium, which includes sculptures and fragments of architectural features, such as balustrades and windows, that decorated the royal chambers during the Angevin and Jagiełło eras *(see p20)*. It also displays Renaissance relics. The most valuable exhibit, however, is a sculpture of King Béla III's head, which dates from around 1200.

Also in this first section are two marble bas-reliefs of King Matthias and his wife Beatrice, by an unknown Renaissance master from Lombardy.

The second section exhibits late Gothic and Renaissance artifacts from other palaces in Hungary. There are pillars and balustrades from the palace at Visegrád and bas-reliefs from a chapel in Esztergom.

Gothic Works

A superb collection of painted panels, sculptures and fragments of altar decoration is opposite the Lapidarium. Note, however, the image of the *Madonna of Bártfa*, which is a rare complete example from the Gothic period.

The sculptures of the "Beautiful Madonnas" are executed in the Soft Style. This style is characterized, as its name suggests, by the sentimental and gentle imagery of the Madonna playing with the Christ child.

The Visitation, a magnificent late Gothic work by Master MS, is, in fact, only the main section of an altar; the other pieces are now in the city of Esztergom *(see p168)*.

Renaissance and Baroque Works

The exhibition begins with a still life by Jakab Bogdány (1660–1724) and portraits by Ádám Mányoki (1673–1757) *(see p28)*, who actually settled outside Hungary. As a result of the powerful influence of the Habsburgs during this period *(see pp30–31)*, Baroque art was overwhelmingly dominated by Austrian artists. Painters such as Joseph Dorfmeister and Franz Anton Maulbertsch and sculptors Georg Raphael Donner and Philipp Jakob Straub were the acknowledged masters of the style. Jan Kupetzky's portraits are also exemplary models of this era.

The wooden sculptures by Donner and the sacred paintings of Dorfmeister conclude this section of the gallery.

Late-Gothic Altarpieces

One of the star exhibits of this collection is the imposing late Gothic altarpiece. Arranged in the Great Throne Room, the majority of these vast altarpieces date from the 15th and early 16th centuries. Architecturally these altarpieces are pure Gothic,

The Great Throne Room, displaying the collection of folding altarpieces

while adorned with sculptures and paintings revealing a Renaissance influence. This is evident in the altars of St Anne and St John the Baptist from a church in Kisszeben (now Sabinov in Slovakia), which date from 1510–16. The most recent altarpiece dates from 1643 and is from the church of Our Lady Mary in Csíkmenaság.

Bertalan Székely's *Women of Eger* (1867), depicting the Turkish wars

19th-Century Works

The wonderful collection of works from this period reflects the rise of fine art in Hungary in the 19th century.

Historicist art developed during this period. Among those distinguishing themselves in particular were Gyula Benczúr and Bertalan Székely, who produced the epic works *The Recapture of Buda in 1686* (1896) and *Women of Eger* (1867) respectively. The latter depicts the women of the town defending the Castle of Eger against the Turks.

Viktor Madarász's work *The Mourning of László Hunyadi* (1859) refers to the execution of László Hunyadi by the Habsburgs in 1457. It alludes, too, to the execution of many Hungarians after the crushing of the uprising against Austria in 1849 *(see pp32–3)*.

European developments in fine art can also be seen in Hungarian painting from the late-19th century. The influence of Impressionism, for example, is best seen in Pál Szinyei Merse's *Picnic in May* (1873). Hungarian Realism is expressed in the work of László Paál and Mihály Munkácsy, the latter being widely regarded as the country's greatest artist. Paintings by Munkácsy which deserve particular attention are *The Yawning Apprentice* (1869), *Dusty Road* (1874), the still life *Flowers* (1881), and – most notably – *Woman Carrying Brushwood* (1870), which was painted at the zenith of his career.

Christmas (1903) by Jozsef Rippl-Ronai, a leading Hungarian artist

It is also worth spending a few moments seeing the paintings of the Neo-Classical artists. The work of Károly Lotz, who is perhaps better known for his frescoes that can be seen on walls and ceilings around Budapest, is exhibited here.

20th-Century Works

Examples of work from the Secession era through to Expressionism and Surrealism, and even contemporary art are exhibited here. They provide a comprehensive review of 20th-century Hungarian art.

József Rippl-Rónai studied in France with Gaugin and Toulouse-Lautrec. His work shows the influence of the Secession style in *The Palace in Körtyvélyes* and *Woman with a Birdcage*. But one of the most engaging artists from the early-20th century is Károly Ferenczy whose *The Paintress* (1903) exemplifies the serene qualities of his work.

Tivadar Kosztka Csontváry is an artist whose work did not follow any conventional style but was greatly admired, even by Pablo Picasso. One of his paintings in particular, the *Ruins of the Greek Amphitheatre in Taormina* (1905), captures his abstract interpretation of the world.

The Eight, a group of artists who set up the first Hungarian avant-garde school, were active between the two world wars. Notable examples of their work are *Young Girl with a Bow* by Béla Czóbel, *Woman Playing a Doublebass* by Róbert Berény, *The Oarsmen* by Ödön Marffy, *Landscape* by Lajos Tihanyi and *Riders at the Edge* by Károly Kernstok.

The best works of Hungarian Expressionism can be seen in the paintings *Along the Tracks, For Bread* and *Generations*, by Gyula Derkovits.

Among the sculptures on display, the most interesting are *Raising Oneself* and *The Sower*, by Ferenc Medgyessy, and *Standing Girl*, by Béni Ferenczy.

The exhibition is completed by a section featuring contemporary artists.

The Paintress by Károly Ferenczy (1903), a typically peaceful work

Street-by-Street: the Old Town

Buda's old town has been a barometer of Hungary's changing fortunes. It developed, to the north of the Royal Palace, from the 13th century. Under kings such as Sigismund, it flourished, and wealthy German merchants set up shops in Lords' Street (Úri utca) to supply the court. The area was later destroyed by the Turks and again by their evictors, the Holy League army formed of European Christians. It was rebuilt after World War II, but genuine relics can be hunted out in its cobbled streets and squares.

⑮ Mihály Táncsics Street
During the Middle Ages, this street was inhabited by Jews. A museum at No. 26, on the site of an old synagogue, displays finds such as tombstones.

The State Archive of Historic Documents, located in a Neo-Romanesque building, houses items that were transferred to Buda in 1785 from the former capital of Hungary, Bratislava.

BÉCSI KAPU TÉR

FORTUN

ORSZÁGHÁZ UTCA

ÚRI UTCA

Defensive walls

⑱ Church of St Mary Magdalene
The reconstructed Baroque tower is all that remains of the 13th-century Church of St Mary Magdalene, where Emperor Francis I was crowned King of Hungary in 1792.

Key

— Suggested route

㉑ ★ Lords' Street
Once the homes of aristocrats and merchants, the houses on Úri utca have medieval foundations. Many have Gothic details and peaceful courtyards.

⓫ ★ Mátyás Church
Although with much earlier parts, this church is mainly a Neo-Gothic reconstruction dating from 1874–96. A picturesque vestibule on the church's southern façade covers an original Gothic portal dating from the 14th century.

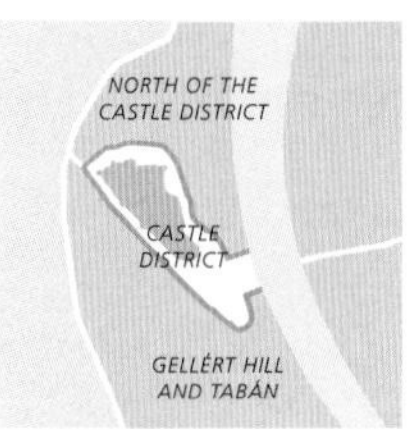

Locator Map
See Street Finder, maps 1 & 9

This statue of St Stephen, or István, the first crowned king of Hungary *(see pp24–5)*, was erected in 1906. Its pedestal includes a bas-relief showing scenes from the king's life.

⓬ Fishermen's Bastion
Designed by Frigyes Schulek in 1895, this fantastical structure never had the role of a defensive building, despite its name. It serves instead as a viewing terrace. The conical towers are an allusion to the tribal tents of the early Magyars.

❾ Holy Trinity Square
In 1713, after overcoming an epidemic of the plague, a column representing the Holy Trinity was raised in this square.

0 metres 50
0 yards 50

❽ Golden Eagle Pharmacy Museum
From the 18th century a pharmacy called "Under the Golden Eagle" traded in this medieval house, now a museum.

❽ Golden Eagle Pharmacy Museum

Aranysas Patikamúzeum

Tárnok utca 18. **Map** 1 B5 (9 A2). **Tel** (06 1) 375 97 72. 16, 16A, 116. **Open** Mar–Oct: 10am–5:30pm Tue–Sun; Nov–Feb: 10am–3:30pm Tue–Fri, 10am–5:30pm Sat, Sun. **semmelweismuseum.hu**

This pharmacy was opened in 1688 by Ferenc Ignác Bösinger and traded under the name the "Golden Eagle" from 1740. It moved to this originally Gothic building, with its Baroque interior and Neo-Classical façade, in the 18th century. The museum opened here in 1974. It displays pharmaceutical items from the Renaissance and Baroque eras.

❾ Holy Trinity Square

Szentháromság Tér

Map 1 B4 (9 A3). 16, 16A, 116.

This square is the central point of the Old Town. It takes its name from the Baroque Holy Trinity Column, originally sculpted by Philipp Ungleich in 1710–13, and restored in 1967. The column commemorates the dead of two outbreaks of the plague, which struck the inhabitants of Buda in 1691 and 1709.

The pedestal of the column is decorated with bas-reliefs by Anton Hörger. Further up are statues of holy figures and at the summit is a magnificent composition of the figures of the Holy Trinity. The central section of the column is decorated with angelic figures surrounded by clouds.

Buda's Old Town Hall, a large Baroque building with two courtyards, was also built on the square at the beginning of the 18th century. It was designed by the imperial court architect, Venerio Ceresola, whose architectural scheme incorporated the remains of medieval houses. In 1770–74 an east wing was built, and bay windows and a stone balustrade with Rococo urns, by Mátyás Nepauer, were added. The corner niche, opposite Mátyás Church, houses a small statue by Carlo Adami of Pallas Athene.

❿ Hospital in the Rock

Sziklakórház

Lovas út 4/c. **Map** 1 A4. **Tel** (07 0) 701 01 01. 16, 16A, 116. **Open** 10am–8pm daily (last entry 7pm). **sziklakorhaz.eu**

The huge system of caves and cellars under Buda Castle served as a shelter for thousands of people during World War II. An emergency surgery also operated here from 1944–5, saving thousands of lives. After the war, the Communist government classified the institution as top secret, and extended the hospital with a new ward and additional equipment. From the late 1960s to 2004, the hospital was used for civil defense training. Visitors can now tour the eerie operating rooms and wards peopled by wax figures.

⓫ Mátyás Church

See pp86–7.

A statue of St István stands in front of the Fishermen's Bastion

⓬ Fishermen's Bastion

Halászbástya

Szentháromsag tér. **Map** 1 B4 (9 A2). 16, 16A, 116. **Open** mid-Mar–Apr: 9am–7pm daily; May–mid-Oct: 9am–8pm daily.

Frigyes Schulek designed this Neo-Romanesque monument to the Guild of Fishermen in 1895. It occupies the site of Buda's old defensive walls and a medieval square where fish was once sold. The bastion is a purely aesthetic addition to Castle Hill and boasts beautiful views of the Danube and Pest. In front of it stands a statue of St István, the king who introduced Christianity to Hungary.

Buda's Old Town Hall, its clocktower crowned with an onion-shaped dome, on Holy Trinity Square

Bas-relief depicting King Mátyás on the façade of the Hilton Hotel

⓭ Hilton Hotel

Hilton Szálló

Hess András tér 1–2. **Map** 1 B4 (9 A2). **Tel** (06 1) 889 66 00. 16, 16A, 116. **hilton.com**

Built in 1976, the Hilton Hotel is a rare example of modern architecture in the Old Town. Controversial from the outset, the design by the Hungarian architect Béla Pintér combines the historic remains of the site with contemporary materials and methods.

From 1254 a Dominican church, to which a tower was later added, stood on this site, followed by a late-Baroque Jesuit monastery. The remains of both these buildings are incorporated into the design. For example, the remains of the medieval church, uncovered during excavations in 1902, form part of the Dominican Courtyard, where concerts and operettas are staged during the summer season.

The main façade comprises part of the façade of the Jesuit monastery. To the left of the entrance is St Nicholas's Tower. In 1930, a replica of the 15th-century German bas-relief of King Mátyás, considered to be his most authentic likeness, was added to this tower.

⓮ András Hess Square

Hess András Tér

Map 1 B4 (9 A2). 16, 16A, 116.

This square is named after the Italian-trained printer who printed the first Hungarian book, *Chronica Hungarorum*, in a printing works at No. 4 in 1473. The house was rebuilt at the end of the 17th century as an amalgamation of three medieval houses, with quadruple seat niches, barrel-vaulted cellars and ornamental gates.

The former inn at No. 3 was named the Red Hedgehog in 1696. This one-floor building has surviving Gothic and Baroque elements.

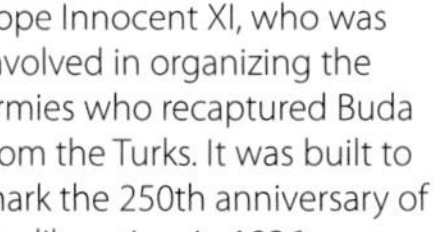

Hedgehog on the façade of No. 3 András Hess Square

The square also features a statue by József Damkó of Pope Innocent XI, who was involved in organizing the armies who recaptured Buda from the Turks. It was built to mark the 250th anniversary of the liberation, in 1936.

⓯ Mihály Táncsics Street

Táncsics Mihály Utca

Map 1 B4 (9 A2). 16, 16A, 116. Museum of Musical History: **Tel** (06 1) 214 67 70. **Open** 10am–4pm Tue–Sun.

Standing at No. 7 is Erdődy Palace, built in 1750–69 for the Erdődy family by Mátyás Nepauer, the leading architect of the day. It features outstanding Baroque façades. Like many houses on this street, it was erected on the ruins of medieval houses.

In 1800, Ludwig van Beethoven, who was then giving concerts in Budapest, resided here for a short period.

The palace now houses the Museum of Musical History and the Béla Bartók archives. A permanent exhibition illustrates musical life in Budapest from the 18th to 20th centuries, and includes the oldest surviving Hungarian musical instruments.

The Royal Mint stood on the site of No. 9 during the Middle Ages, and, in 1810, the Joseph Barracks were built here. These were later used by the Habsburgs to imprison leaders of the 1848–9 uprising, including Mihály Táncsics himself.

An original mural has survived on the façade of the house at No. 16, which dates from around 1700. It depicts Christ and the Virgin Mary surrounded by saints. The bas-reliefs on the gateway are, however, from a Venetian church.

Relics of Buda's Jewish heritage can be found at Nos. 23 and 26. The remains of a 15th-century synagogue stand in the garden of the mansion at No. 23. During archeological excavations, tombs and religious items were also found in the courtyard of No. 26.

The Museum of Musical History on Mihály Táncsics Street

⓫ Mátyás Church

Mátyás-templom

The Parish Church of Our Lady Mary was built on this site between the 13th and 15th centuries. Some of the existing architectural style dates from the reign of Sigismund of Luxembourg, but its name refers to King Mátyás Corvinus, who greatly enlarged and embellished the church. Much of the original detail was lost when the Turks converted the church into the Great Mosque in 1541. After the liberation of Buda in 1686, Jesuit fathers modified the building in the Baroque style. The church sustained more damage in 1723, and was restored in the Neo-Gothic style by Frigyes Schulek in 1873–96. The gallery rooms house the Museum of Ecclesiastical Art.

Rose Window
Frigyes Schulek faithfully reproduced the medieval stained-glass window that was in this position during the early Gothic era.

Béla Tower
This tower is named after the church's founder, King Béla IV. It has retained several of its original Gothic features.

★ Baroque Madonna
According to legend, the original statue was set into a wall of the church during the Turkish occupation. When this wall was destroyed in 1686, the Madonna made a miraculous appearance. The Turks took this as an omen of defeat.

Main Portal
Above the arched west entrance is a 19th-century bas-relief of the Madonna and Child, seated between two angels. The relief is made of pyrogranite ceramics produced in Pécs at the Zsolnay factory *(see p58)*.

KEY

① **The roof** is decorated with multicoloured glazed tiles.

② **The main altar** was created by Frigyes Schulek and based on Gothic triptychs.

★ Tomb of King Béla III and Anne de Châtillon
The remains of this royal couple were transferred from Székesfehérvár Cathedral to Mátyás Church in 1860. They lie beneath an ornamental stone canopy in the Trinity Chapel.

VISITORS' CHECKLIST

Practical Information
Szentháromság tér 2. **Map** 1 B4. **Tel** (06 1) 355 56 57. **Open** 9am–5pm Mon–Fri, 9am–1pm Sat, 1–5pm Sun. Museum: **Open** same hours as the church.

Transport
16, 16A, 116.

Pulpit
The richly decorated pulpit includes the carved stone figures of the four Fathers of the Church and the four Evangelists.

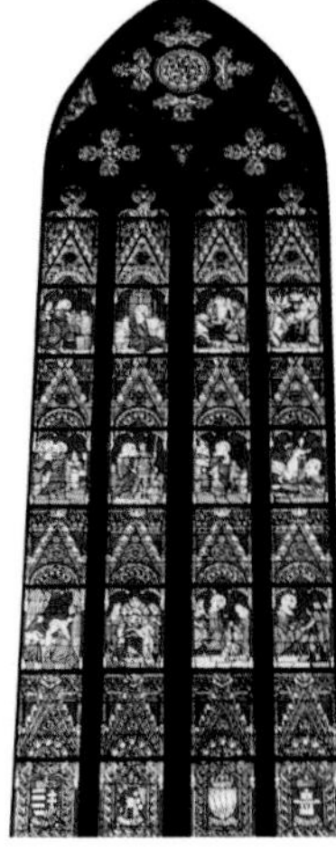

Stained-Glass Windows
Three arched windows on the south elevation have 19th-century stained glass. They were designed by Frigyes Schulek, Bertalan Székely and Károly Lotz.

★ Mary Portal
This depiction of the Assumption of the Blessed Virgin Mary is the most magnificent example of Gothic stone carving in Hungary. Frigyes Schulek reconstructed the portal from fragments.

1255 Church originally founded by King Béla IV after the Mongol invasion

1309 Coronation of the Angevin king Charles Robert

1370 Church construction works started under the reign of Anjou Louis the Great

1470 Mátyás Tower is completed after its collapse in 1384

1476 Wedding of King Mátyás to Beatrice of Aragon (aka Beatrice of Naples)

1526 Cathedral burnt in the first attack by Turks

1541 Turks convert church into a mosque

1686 After liberation of Buda, Jesuits converted the church in Baroque style

1896 Frigyes Schulek completes the reconstruction of the church in the Neo-Gothic style

1945 Church is severely damaged by German and Russian armies

1970 Final details are completed in post-war rebuilding programme

2004–2014 Full reconstruction of the building

1250 | 1350 | 1450 | 1550 | 1650 | 1750 | 1850 | 1950 | 2050

Holy figures on the pulpit

Vienna Gate, rebuilt in 1936, commemorating the liberation of Buda

⓰ Vienna Gate Square

Bécsi Kapu Tér

Map 1 B4. 16, 16A, 116.

The square takes its name from the gate that once led from the walled town of Buda towards Vienna. After being damaged several times, the old gate was demolished in 1896. The current gate, based on a historic design, was erected in 1936 on the 250th anniversary of the liberation of Buda from the Turks.

The square has a number of interesting houses. Those at Nos. 5, 6, 7 and 8 were built on the ruins of medieval dwellings. They are Baroque and Rococo in design and feature sculptures and bas-reliefs. The façade of No. 7 has medallions with the portraits of Classical philosophers and poets; Thomas Mann, the German novelist, lodged here between 1935–6. No. 8, meanwhile, is differentiated by its bay windows, attics and the restored medieval murals on its façade.

On the left-hand side of the square is a vast Neo-Romanesque building with a beautiful multicoloured roof, built in 1913–20 by Samu Pecz. This building houses the National Archive, which holds documents dating from before the battle of Mohács in 1526 and others connected with the Rákóczi uprising and the 1848 rebellion *(see pp27, 30 and 32–3)*.

Behind the Vienna Gate Square is a monument built in honour of Mihály Táncsics, the leader of the Autumn Uprising. It was unveiled in 1970.

⓱ Buda Lutheran Church

Budavári Evangélikus Templom

Bécsi kapu tér. **Map** 1 B4. **Tel** (06 1) 356 97 36. 16, 16A, 116.

Facing the Vienna Gate is the Neo-Classical Lutheran church, built in 1896 by Mór Kallina. A plaque commemorates pastor Gábor Sztehlo, who saved 2,000 children during World War II.

At one time, a painting by Bertalan Székely, called *Christ Blessing the Bread*, adorned the altar, but it was unfortunately destroyed during the war.

⓲ Church of St Mary Magdalene

Mária Magdolna Templom Tornya

Kapisztrán tér 6. **Map** 1 A4. 16, 16A, 116.

Now in ruins, this church was built in the mid-13th century. During the Middle Ages, Hungarian Christians worshipped here because Mátyás Church was only for use by the town's German population. The church did not become a mosque until the second half of the Turkish occupation, but it was severely damaged in 1686, during the liberation of Buda from the Turks. An order of Franciscan monks subsequently took possession and added a Baroque church and tower.

After World War II, all but the tower and the gate were pulled down. These now stand in a garden, together with the reconstructed Gothic window.

The reconstructed Baroque tower of the Church of St Mary Magdalene

⓳ Parliament Street

Országház Utca

Map 1 A4 & 1 B4.

This street was once inhabited by the Florentine artisans and craftsmen who were working on King Mátyás' Royal Palace *(see pp74–5)*, and it was known for a time as Italian Street. Its present name comes from the building at No. 28, where the Hungarian parliament met from 1790–1807. This building was designed in the 18th century by the architect Franz Anton Hillebrandt as a convent for the Poor Clares. However, Emperor Joseph II dissolved the order before the building was completed.

Numerous houses on Parliament Street have retained attractive Gothic and Baroque features. No. 2, now with a Neo-Classical façade, is the site of the Alabárdos *(see p196)*, but its history dates back to the late 13th century. In the 15th century, Sigismund of Luxembourg built a Gothic mansion here and some details, such as the colonnade around the courtyard and the murals on the second floor, have survived until the present day. The entrance to No. 9 features the Gothic traceried seat niches that were popular in Buda at this time. In front of the Neo-Classical house at No. 21 is a statue of Márton Lendvay (1807–58), who was a famous Hungarian actor and member of the National Theatre.

⑳ Museum of Military History

Hadtörténeti Múzeum

Tóth Árpád sétány 40. **Map** 1 A4. **Tel** (06 1) 325 16 00. 16, 16A, 116. **Open** Apr–Sep: 10am–6pm Tue–Sun; Oct–Mar: 10am–4pm Tue–Sun.

The museum is located in a wing of the former Palatine barracks. It houses a wide range of military items relating to the skirmishes and wars that have afflicted Budapest from before the Turkish occupation to the 20th century. Uniforms, flags, weapons, maps and ammunition from as far back as the 11th century give an insight into the long, turbulent history of Budapest.

Of particular interest is the exhibit concerning the 1956 Uprising. Photographs illustrate the 13 days of demonstrations that ended in a Soviet invasion. and a huge civilian death toll.

㉑ Lords' Street

Úri Utca

Map 1 A4, 1 B4 and 1 B5 (9 A2). 16, 16A, 116. Telephone Museum: **Open** 10am–4pm Tue–Sun. **W** **postamuzeum.hu**

The buildings in Lords' Street were destroyed first in 1686 and again in 1944. Reconstruction in 1950–60 restored much of their original medieval character. Almost all have some remnant of a Gothic gateway or hall, while the façade is Baroque or Neo-Classical.

An excellent example of a Gothic façade can be seen on Hölbling House at No. 31. Enough of its original features survived the various wars and renovations to enable architects to reconstruct the façade in considerable detail. The first-floor window is a particularly splendid Gothic feature. The houses opposite are also examples of this restoration work.

The building at No. 53 was rebuilt between 1701–22 as a Franciscan monastery, but in 1789 it was restyled for use by Emperor Joseph II. In 1795, Hungarian Jacobites, led by Ignác Martinovics, were imprisoned here; a plaque records this event. A well featuring a copy of a sculpture of Artemis, the Greek goddess of hunting, by Praxiteles, was set in front of the house in 1873.

There are two museums on Lords' Street. The Telephone Museum, at No. 49, is a former telephone exchange and one of the most fun and interactive museums in the city. At No. 9 is the entrance to the Labyrinth, one of the seven underground wonders of the world.

㉒ Labyrinth in the Buda Castle

Budavári Labirintus

Úri utca 9. **Map** 1 B5. **Tel** (06 1) 212 02 07. 16, 16A, 116. **Open** 10am–7pm daily. 6pm daily. **W** **labirintusbudapest.hu**

The haunt of prehistoric man some half a million years ago, the Labyrinth in the Buda Castle comprises a 1,200-metre (1,000-yard) section of the impressive complex of caves, cellars, dungeons and springs that run beneath Castle Hill at about 10–15 metres (33–50 ft) below ground level.

The complex has been used variously as wine vaults, torture chambers, a prison, a hideaway and also served as a shelter during World War II. Vlad Tepes, also known as Dracula, was imprisoned here. The Hungarian King Matthias captured Dracula in Transylvania in 1462 and had him taken to Buda, where he was sentenced to ten years in the Labyrinth's prison. Visitors can explore the torture chamber, red marmor tombstone, medieval handcuffs and manequins of Dracula's victims.

From 6pm, oil lamps are lit. Visitors can then tour the caves by the eerie light of lanterns. In the "Maze of Darkness" section, there is complete darkness and only a thread to hold on to.

One of many caves in the ancient, subterranean Labyrinth

Lords' Street, which runs the full length of the Old Town

GELLÉRT HILL AND TABÁN

Rising steeply beside the Danube, Gellért Hill is one of the city's most attractive areas. From the top, at a height of 140 m (460 ft), a beautiful view of the whole of Budapest unfolds. The Celtic Eravi, who preceded the Romans, formed their settlement on the hill's northern slope *(see p98)*. Once called simply Old Hill, many superstitions and tales are connected with it. In 1046, heathen citizens threw a sealed barrel containing Bishop Gellért, who was trying to convert them to Christianity, from the hill to his death. Afterwards, the hill was named after this martyr. Gellért Hill bulges out slightly into the Danube, which narrows at this point. This made the base of the hill a favoured crossing place, and the settlement of Tabán evolved as a result.

Sights at a Glance

Museums

12 Semmelweis Museum of Medical History

Churches

2 Cave Church
10 Tabán Parish Church

Historic Buildings

4 Citadel
13 Golden Stag House

Hotels and Baths

1 *Gellért Hotel and Baths Complex pp94–5*
6 Rudas Baths
9 Rácz Hotel & Thermal Spa

Districts, Squares and Monuments

3 Liberation Monument
5 Statue of St Gellért
7 Queen Elizabeth Monument
8 Tabán
11 Miklós Ybl Square

Restaurants *pp196–7*

1 Aranyszarvas Vendéglő
2 Búsuló Juhász Étterem
3 Café Déryné
4 Gellért Espresso
5 Hadik Kávéház Café
6 Hemingway
7 János Étterem
8 Marcello
9 Márványmenyasszony Étterem
10 Szeged Vendéglő
11 Tabáni Gösser Restaurant
12 Vinopolis Naphegy

See also Street Finder maps 1, 3, 4, 9 & 10

◀ Fountain with an intricate mosaic background, Gellért Hotel and Baths Complex

For keys to symbols *see back flap*

Street-by-Street: Gellért Hill

The hill to the south of Castle Hill was long regarded as a notorious spot. In the 11th century, Prince Vata, brother of King István, incited a heathen rebellion here that resulted in the death of Bishop Gellért. During the Middle Ages, witches were reputed to celebrate their sabbath here. Under the Turks, a small stronghold was first built on the hill to protect Buda. In 1851, the Austrians placed their own bleak and intimidating Citadel at the summit. Not until the end of the 19th century did the popular image of Gellért Hill begin to change, when it became a venue for picnicking parties. In 1967, the area around the Citadel was made into an attractive park.

7 Queen Elizabeth Monument
Close to the entrance to Elizabeth Bridge stands this statue of Emperor Franz Joseph's wife, who was popular with the Hungarians.

5 ★ Statue of St Gellért
Blessing the city with his uplifted cross, the martyred Bishop Gellért is regarded as the patron saint of Budapest.

HEGYALJA ÚT

4 Citadel
Once a place to inspire terror, visitors now come to the Citadel to explore the old defensive walls and enjoy the fantastic view of the city.

Key

 Suggested route

3 Liberation Monument
At the foot of the Liberation Monument, towering above the city, are two sculptures, one representing the battle with evil.

0 metres 500
0 yards 500

6 Rudas Baths
These famous Turkish baths, which date from the 16th century, have a characteristic Ottoman cupola.

The observation terraces on Gellért Hill provide those who climb up to them with a beautiful panorama over the southern part of Buda and the whole of Pest.

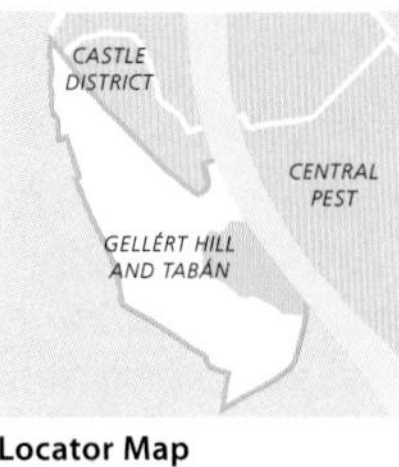

Locator Map
See Street Finder, maps 3, 4 & 9

The Reservoir

In 1978, a reservoir for drinking water was established close to the Uránia Observatory on Gellért Hill. The surface of the reservoir is covered over and provides a point from which to observe the Royal Palace *(see pp74–5)* to the north. A sculpture by Márta Lessenyei, representing the union of Buda and Pest, decorates the structure.

Márta Lessenyei's sculpture on Gellért Hill's reservoir

2 ★ Cave Church
This church was established in 1926 in a holy grotto. Under the Communists, the Pauline order of monks was forced to abandon the church, but it was reopened in 1989.

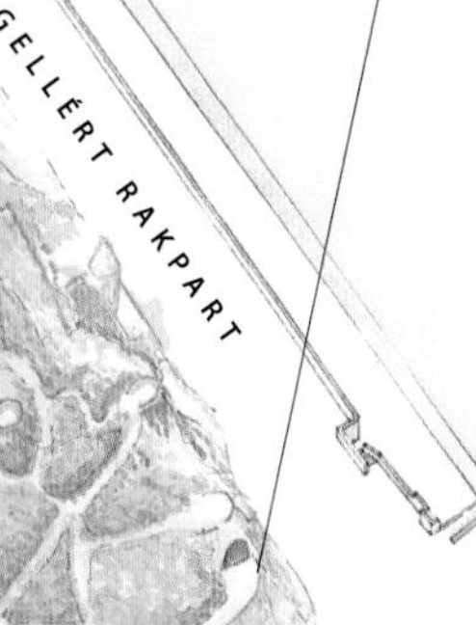

1 Gellért Hotel and Baths Complex
One of a number of bath complexes built at the beginning of the 20th century, this magnificent spa hotel was erected here to exploit the natural hot springs.

❶ Gellért Hotel and Baths Complex

Gellért Szálló és Fürdő

Between 1912–18, this hotel and spa was built in the modernist Secession style *(see pp56–9)* at the foot of Gellért Hill. The earliest reference to the existence of healing waters at this spot dates from the 13th century, during the reign of King András II and in the Middle Ages a hospital stood on the site. Baths built here by the Ottomans were referred to by the renowned Turkish travel writer of the day, Evliya Çelebi. The architects of the hotel were Ármin Hegedűs, Artúr Sebestyén and Izidor Sterk. It was destroyed in 1945, but then rebuilt and modernized. The hotel has several restaurants and cafés. The baths include an institute of water therapy, set within Secession interiors, but with modern facilities.

Outdoor Wave Pool
An early swimming pool with a wave mechanism, built in 1927, is situated at the back of the complex, looking towards Gellért Hill behind.

★ Baths
Two separate baths, one for men and one for women, are identically arranged. In each there are three plunge pools, with water at different temperatures, a sauna and a steam bath.

Balconies
The balconies fronting the hotel's rooms have fanciful Secession balustrades that are decorated with lyre and bird motifs.

★ Entrance Hall
The interiors of the hotel, like the baths, have kept their original Secession decor, with elaborate mosaics, stained-glass windows and statues.

Sun Terraces
Situated in the sunniest spot, these terraces are a popular place for drying off in the summer.

VISITORS' CHECKLIST

Practical Information
Szent Gellért tér. **Map** 4 E3.
Tel (06 1) 466 61 66.
Baths: Kelenhegyi út 4.
Open 6am–8pm daily.
spabudapest.hu

Transport
7, 86. 18, 19, 47, 49.
M Szent Gellért tér.

Hot pool with medicinal spa water

Eastern-Style Towers
The architects who designed the hotel gave its towers and turrets a characteristically oriental, cylindrical form.

Main Staircase
The landings of the main staircase have stained-glass windows by Bózó Stanisits, added in 1933. They illustrate an ancient Hungarian legend about a magic stag, recorded in the poetry of János Arany.

Restaurant Terrace
From this first-floor terrace, diners can appreciate a fine view of Budapest. On the ground and first floors of the hotel there are a total of four cafés and restaurants.

★ Main Façade
Behind the hotel's imposing façade are attractive recreational facilities and a health spa that is also open to non-guests. The entrance to the baths is around to the right from the main entrance, on Kelenhegyi út.

❷ Cave Church

Sziklatemplom

Gellért rakpart 1a. **Map** 4 E3. **Tel** (06 2) 077 52 472. **Open** 9:30am–7:30pm Mon–Sat. 7, 86. 18, 19, 47, 49. M Szent Gellért tér.

On the southern slope of Gellért Hill, the entrance to this grotto church is a short walk from the Gellért Hotel and Baths Complex. Based on the shrine at Lourdes, the church, designed by Kálmán Lux, was established in 1926.

The church was intended for the Pauline order of monks, which was founded in the 13th century by Eusebius of Esztergom. In 1934, 150 years after Joseph II had dissolved the order in Hungary,15 friars arrived back in the city from exile in Poland. However, their residence lasted only until the late 1950s, when the Communist authorities suspended the activities of the church, accusing the monks of treasonable acts, and sealed the entrance to the grotto.

The church and adjoining monastery were reopened in 1989, when a papal blessing was conferred on its beautiful new altar, designed by Győző Sikota. To the left within the grotto is a copy of the *Black Madonna of Czestochowa* and a depiction of a Polish eagle. Visitors will also see a painting of St Kolbe, a Polish monk who gave his life to protect other inmates at Auschwitz concentration camp.

At the entrance to the church stands a statue of St István, the first Hungarian king and founder of Christianity in the country. Inside the Chapel of St István, it is worth pausing to look at the exquisite wood carvings by Béla Ferencz. The Cave Church can be reached through the Pauline Welcome Center in the outer cave. The entrance fee includes an audio guide and a short film. The monastery is closed to tourists.

Entrance to the Cave Church, run by the Pauline order of monks

❸ Liberation Monument

Felszabadulási Emlékmű

Map 4 D3. 27.

Positioned high on Gellért Hill, this imposing monument towers over the rest of the city. It was designed by the outstanding Hungarian sculptor Zsigmond Kisfaludi Stróbl and set up here to commemorate the liberation of Budapest by the Russian army in 1945 *(see p36)*. The monument was originally intended to honour the memory of István, son of the Hungarian Regent Miklós Horthy, who disappeared in 1943 on the eastern front. However, after the liberation of the city by Russian troops, Marshal Kliment Voroshilov spotted it in the sculptor's workshop and reassigned it to this purpose.

The central figure on the monument is a woman holding aloft a palm leaf. Standing on its pedestal, this reaches a height of 14 m (46 ft). At the base of the monument there are two allegorical compositions, representing progress and the battle with evil.

The Liberation Monument, standing at the top of Gellért Hill

The arrival of the Russians in Budapest was a liberation but also the beginning of Soviet rule. After Communism's fall, a figure of a Russian soldier was removed from the monument to Statue Park *(see p164)*.

❹ Citadel

Citadella

Map 4 D3. 27. Citadel: **Open** daily.

After the suppression of the uprising of 1848–9 *(see pp32–3)*, the Habsburgs decided to build a fortification on this strategically important site. Constructed in 1850–54, the Citadel housed 60 cannons, which could, in theory, fire on the city at any time. In reality, from its very inception the Citadel did not fulfil any real military requirements, but served rather as a means of intimidating the population.

The Citadel is some 220 m (720 ft) long by 60 m (200 ft) wide, and has walls 4 m (12 ft) high. After peace was agreed with the Habsburgs, Hungarian society continually demanded the destruction of the Citadel, but it was not until 1897 that the Austrian soldiers left their barracks here. A section of its entrance gateway was then symbolically ripped out.

After much discussion in the early 1960s, the Citadel

was converted into a leisure complex. Although the complex is currently closed due to a legal dispute, the Citadel and the path to the Liberation Monument remain open to the public. From the old defensive walls of the Citadel there is a spectacular panorama of the city below.

❺ Statue of St Gellért

Szent Gellért Emlékmű

Map 4 D2. 27. (And a long walk. Go via the steps by Elizabeth Bridge.)

In 1904 a vast monument was established on the spot where Bishop Gellért was supposedly murdered in the 11th century. It is said the bishop was thrown into the Danube in a barrel, by a mob opposed to the adoption of Christianity. St Gellért holds a cross in his outstretched hand and a Hungarian convert to Christianity kneels at his feet.

The statue was designed by Gyula Jankovits; the semi-circular collonade behind it is by Imre Francsek. A spring that bubbles up here was used to create the fountain.

Overlooking the Elizabeth Bridge, the monument can be seen from throughout the city.

The main plunge pool at the Rudas Baths, covered by a Turkish cupola

The landmark Gellért Monument overlooking the Elizabeth Bridge

❻ Rudas Baths

Rudas Gyógyfürdő

Döbrentei tér 9. **Map** 4 D2 (9 C5). 18, 19. **Tel** (06 1) 356 13 22. Spa Baths: **Open** 6am–8pm daily, 10pm–4am Fri & Sat. Swimming pool: **Open** 6am–6pm Mon–Wed, 6am–8pm Thu & Sun, 10pm–4am Fri & Sat. **budapestspas.hu**

Dating originally from 1550, these baths were extended in 1566 by Sokoli Mustafa, an Ottoman pasha. The main part of the baths, dating from this period, have an octagonal plunge pool and four small corner pools with water of varying temperatures.

The baths now include a mixed swimming pool. The spa pools are mixed on weekends, but Tuesdays are reserved for women and the rest of the week for men.

❼ Queen Elizabeth Monument

Erzsébet Királyné Szobra

Döbrentei tér. **Map** 4 D2 (9 C5).

This monument to Queen Elizabeth, wife of Habsburg Emperor Franz Joseph, was created by György Zala.

The statue was erected in its present location in 1986. It stands close to the Elizabeth Bridge *(see p67)*, which was also named after the empress, who showed great friendship to the Hungarians. The statue stood on the opposite side of the river from 1932 until 1947, when the Communists ordered it to be taken down.

❽ Tabán

Map 3 C1, C2, C3 (9B5). 🚌 5, 112, 178. 🚋 18, 19.

The Tabán now consists of a pleasant park and a few historic buildings, but was once very different. In the early 20th century this district, nestling in between Castle Hill and Gellért Hill, was a slum which was cleared as part of a programme to improve the city. Only a few buildings, including Tabán Parish Church, escaped the demolition.

Natural conditions ensured that this was one of the first places in the area where people chose to live. The Celtic Eravi were the first to make a settlement here, while the Romans later built a watchtower from which they could observe people using a nearby crossing point over the river. The first reference to bathing in thermal waters in Tabán dates from the 15th century. The Turks took advantage of this natural asset and built two magnificent baths here, the Rácz Baths and the Rudas Baths *(see pp 53 and 97)*, around which a blossoming town was established. Apart from the baths, virtually everything was destroyed in the recapture of Buda in 1686 *(see p28)*.

In the late 17th century, a large number of Serbs, referred to in Hungarian as Rács, moved into the Tabán after fleeing from the Turks. They were joined by Greeks and Gypsies. Many of the inhabitants of the Tabán at this stage were tanners or made their living on the river. On the hillside above grapevines were cultivated. By the early 20th century, though picturesque, the district was still without proper sanitation.

The old, decaying Tabán, with its numerous bars and gambling dens, was demolished and the present green space established in its place.

A statue of Miklós Ybl, the 19th-century architect, was erected here in 1894. It was designed by Ede Mayer.

Gardens with terraces, decorative stairways and arcades designed by Miklós Ybl were established here to connect the Royal Palace *(see pp74–5)* with the banks of the Danube.

Several Ottoman tombstones stand here. They are the remnants of a cemetery in which the Turks who died defending Buda in 1686 were buried.

⑨ Rácz Hotel & Thermal Spa

Rácz szálloda és Gyógyfürdő

Hadnagy utca 8–10. **Map** 4 D2 (9 B5). **Tel** (06 1) 487 03 13. 5, 178. 18, 19. **Open** 7am–10pm daily.

Taking their name from the Serbian, or Rác, people who once lived here, the baths date back to the Turkish era *(see pp28–9)*. This is not clear from the outside, as the baths were redeveloped in 1869 to a design by Miklós Ybl. Inside, however, original Ottoman features include an octagonal pool and cupola. The hotel complex includes 21 treatment rooms, 13 pools, a relaxation area and saunas.

Interior of the Rácz Hotel & Thermal Spa

⑩ Tabán Parish Church

Tabáni Plébániatemplom

Attila út 11. **Map** 4 D1 (9 C5). **Tel** (06 1) 375 54 91. 18, 19.

A temple is thought to have stood on this site even in the reign of Prince Árpád. In the Middle Ages a church was built here, which was converted into a mosque by the Turks and subsequently destroyed. In 1728–36, after the Habsburgs had taken control of the city, a second church was erected to a design by Keresztély Obergruber. Mátyás Nepauer added the tower in the mid-18th century. In 1881 the façade was extended and the tower crowned by a Neo-Baroque dome.

Inside the church, on the right-hand side under the choir gallery, is a copy of a

Tabán Parish Church, with its Neo-Baroque domed tower

12th-century carving entitled *Christ of Tabán*; the original is now in the collection of the Budapest History Museum *(see p76)*. The altar, pulpit and several paintings adorning the walls of the church all date from the 19th century.

⑪ Miklós Ybl Square

Ybl Miklós Tér

Map 4 D1 (9 C4). 19.

It is no coincidence that the important architect Miklós Ybl *(see p123)* is commemorated by a statue in this square, close to many of his buildings. Among Ybl's most monumental projects were the State Opera House *(see pp122–3)*, St Stephen's Basilica *(see pp120–21)* and also a large-scale rebuilding of the Royal Palace *(see pp74–5)*.

The Várkert Kiosk, on the square, was also built by Ybl. Initially it pumped water up to the Royal Palace, but in 1903 it was converted into a café. It is now used as an event venue available for hire.

⑫ Semmelweis Museum of Medical History

Semmelweis Orvostörténeti Múzeum

Apród utca 1–3. **Map** 4 D1 (9 B4). **Tel** (06 1) 375 35 33. 18, 19. **Open** Mar–Oct: 10:30am–6pm daily; Nov–Feb 10:30am–4pm.
semmelweismuseum.hu

This museum is located in the 18th-century house where Dr Ignáz Semmelweis was born in 1818. He is renowned for his discovery of an antiseptic-based prevention for puerperal fever, a fatal condition common among women who had recently given birth.

The history of medicine from ancient Egypt onwards is portrayed, and there is a replica 19th-century pharmacy. Semmelweis's surgery can also be seen with its original furniture. In the courtyard is a monument called *Motherhood* by Miklós Borsos.

⑬ Golden Stag House

Szarvas Ház

Szarvas tér 1. **Map** 3 C1 (9 B4). **Tel** (06 1) 375 64 51. 18, 19.
aranyszarvas.hu

Standing at the foot of Castle Hill is this distinctive early 19th-century house. It received its name from the inn that opened here called "Under the Golden Stag" – above the entrance you will see a bas-relief depicting a golden stag pursued by two hunting dogs. The building still accommodates a restaurant of that name, Aranyszarvas *(see p197)*, offering international cuisine, and some game dishes.

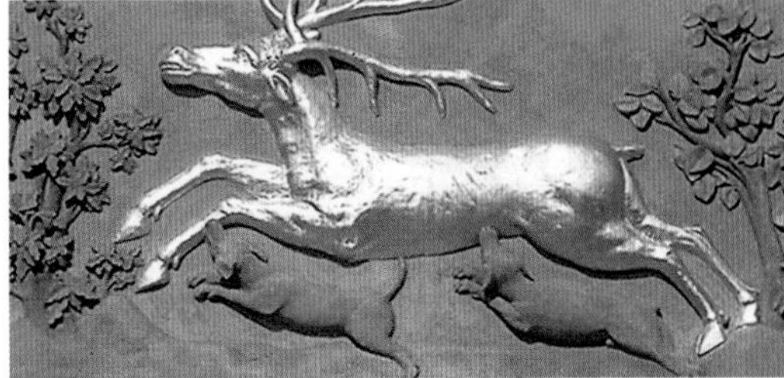

Bas-relief above the entrance to Golden Stag House

NORTH OF THE CASTLE DISTRICT

Between Castle Hill and the western bank of the Danube, extending north from the Chain Bridge towards Margit körút, is the area known as Víziváros or Water Town. This area gained its name in the Middle Ages due to constant flooding. It was originally an area inhabited by artisans and fishermen who, consequently, remained poorer than their neighbours on Castle Hill. Today, the church towers of Víziváros create a wonderful vista along the western bank of the Danube.

In the Middle Ages and during the 150 years of Turkish occupation this area north of Castle Hill was fortified by a system of walls. A short section of these walls still exists by No. 66 Margit körút, and is commemorated by a plaque. The tomb of Gül Baba, a Turkish dervish, is in the north of the area. It is one of the few surviving Ottoman monuments.

Sights at a Glance

Churches

2 Capuchin Church
3 Calvinist Church
4 *St Anne's Church pp106–7*
6 St Francis's Wounds Church

Historic Buildings and Monuments

1 Tunnel
8 Tomb of Gül Baba

Squares

5 Batthyány Square

Baths

7 Király Baths
9 Lukács Baths

Restaurants *pp197–8*

1 Arany Kaviár Étterem
2 Arriba
3 Carne di Hall
4 Csalogány utca 26
5 Dunaparti Matróz Kocsma
6 Gusto Café
7 Horgásztanya Vendéglő
8 Kacsa Vendéglő
9 Mandragóra
10 Nagyi Palacsintázója
11 Pavillion de Paris
12 Róma Ételbár
13 Trófea Grill
14 Vigadó Söröző

0 metres 300
0 yards 300

See also Street Finder maps 1 & 9

◀ The Calvinist Church with its roof of colourful ceramic tiles

For keys to symbols *see back flap*

Street-by-Street: Víziváros

Fő utca, the main street of Víziváros (Water Town), runs the length of the neighbourhood. Numerous cafés and restaurants, spectacular Baroque monuments, and a promenade along the Danube give this area a charming atmosphere. A fine array of churches, in an interesting assortment of architectural styles, reflect the history of the area as far back as the Middle Ages. From the Danube promenade the panorama of Pest opposite, with Parliament *(see pp112–13)* in the foreground, can best be viewed.

6 ★ St Francis's Wounds Church
The Baroque pulpit in this church was carved by the Franciscans, for whom the church was built in the mid-18th century.

The Hikisch House was built on top of medieval walls. The façade, dating from 1795, features bas-reliefs of cherubs carrying out different tasks. Other reliefs depict allegories of the four seasons.

The White Cross Inn, one of Budapest's earliest inns, was established in 1770. Its asymmetrical façade was created by joining two houses together. Among those reputed to have stayed here are Emperor Joseph II and also Casanova.

5 ★ Batthyány Square
A monument to Ferenc Kölcsey (1790–1838) overlooks this square. He was a literary critic and political commentator of the early 19th century, and also wrote the prayer Lord, Bless Hungary, which is used as the lyrics for the Hungarian national anthem.

0 metres 100

0 yards 100

Key

 Suggested route

4 ★ St Anne's Church
Characteristic of the late Baroque period, the interior of this church is quite stunning. The main portal is decorated with allegorical sculptures of Faith, Hope and Charity.

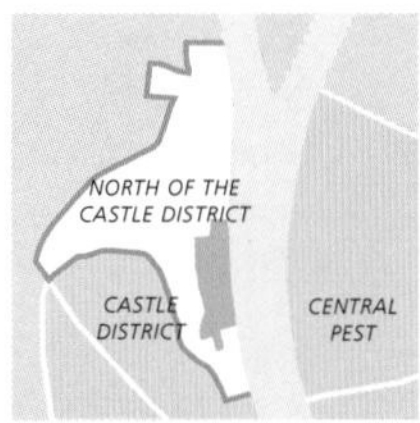

Locator Map
See Street Finder, maps 1 & 9

3 Calvinist Church
The roof of this church, built in 1893–6, is covered with colourful ceramic tiles from the Zsolnay factory *(see p58)*. They are an attractive focal point in the panorama of Buda.

STEHLO GÁBOR RAKPART

A Monument to Samu Pecz stands beside one of his most important buildings, the Calvinist Church. Pecz was a follower of the Neo-Gothic movement and constructed many other important buildings in the city.

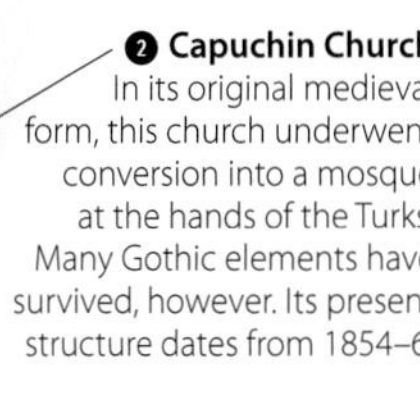

2 Capuchin Church
In its original medieval form, this church underwent conversion into a mosque at the hands of the Turks. Many Gothic elements have survived, however. Its present structure dates from 1854–6.

FŐ UTCA

↓ To Clark Ádám tér and the Chain Bridge

Kapisztory House, at No. 20 Fő utca, was built in 1811 for the Greek merchant, Joseph Kapisztory. Its unusual turretted cylindrical window is an attractive feature of this street.

The imposing entrance to the Tunnel on Clark Ádám tér

❶ Tunnel

Alagút

Clark Ádám tér. **Map** 1 C5 (9 B3). 16, 105, 116.

The Scottish engineer Adam Clark settled in Hungary after completing the Chain Bridge *(see p66)*. One of his later projects, in 1853–7, was building the Tunnel that runs right through Castle Hill, from Clark Ádám tér to Krisztinaváros. The Tunnel is 350 m (1,150 ft) long, 9 m (30 ft) wide and 11 m (36 ft) in height.

The entrance on Clark Ádám tér is flanked by two pairs of Doric columns. This square is the city's official centre because of the location here of the Zero Kilometre Stone, from which all distances from Budapest are calculated.

The Tunnel's western entrance was originally ornamented with Egyptian motifs. However, it was rebuilt without these details after it was damaged in World War II.

❷ Capuchin Church

Kapucinus Templom

Fő utca 32. **Map** 1 C4 (9 B2). **Tel** (06 1) 201 47 25. by arrangement.

The origins of this church date from the 14th century, when the mother of Louis I, Queen Elizabeth, decided to establish a church here. Fragments of walls on the northern façade survive from this time.

During the Turkish occupation *(see pp28–9)*, the church was converted into a mosque. Features from this period, such as the window openings and the doorway on the southern façade, have remained. Between 1703–15 the church was rebuilt, following a Baroque design created by one of the Capuchin Fathers.

In 1856 the church was again restyled, by Ferenc Reitter and Pál Zsumrák, who linked the differently styled façades harmoniously together. The statue of St Elizabeth on the mid-19th-century Romantic façade also dates from 1856.

The altar of the Capuchin Church

❸ Calvinist Church

Református Templom

Szilágyi Dezső tér 3. **Map** 1 C4 (9 B2). **Tel** (06 1) 457 01 09.

One of Budapest's more unusual churches, the Calvinist Church was built by Samu Pecz between 1893–6 on the site of a former medieval market. It is one of the major examples of his work.

Despite the use of modern tiles on the roof, the church is Neo-Gothic in style. It is also interesting to note that Pecz used this traditional design of medieval Catholic churches for a Calvinist church, which has very different liturgical and ecclesiastical needs.

❹ St Anne's Church

See pp106–7.

❺ Batthyány Square

Batthyány Tér

Map 1 C3 (9 B1). H5. 11. 19. Batthyány tér.

Batthyány Square is one of the most interesting squares on the Danube's western bank. Beautiful views of Parliament and Pest on the opposite bank unfold from here.

In 1905, the square was renamed after Count Lajos Batthyány, the prime minister during the Hungarian uprising of 1848–9 *(see pp32–3)*, who was shot by the Austrian army.

The square features buildings in many different styles. The Hikisch House, at No. 3, dating from the late 18th century, is late Baroque. It is notable for the bas-reliefs on its façade depicting the four seasons. The White Cross Inn, at No. 4, also late Baroque, features Rococo decoration. On the western side of the square is the first covered market in Buda, dating from 1902. Though damaged in World War II, it is now fully restored.

The Hikisch House, with bas-reliefs representing the four seasons

❻ St Francis's Wounds Church

Szent Ferenc sebei-templom

Fő utca 41–43. **Map** 1 C3 (9 B1). **Tel** (06 1) 201 80 91. H5. 11. 19. Batthyány tér.

In 1731–57 a church was built for the Franciscan order on the ruins of a former mosque, to a design by Hans Jakab. In 1785, after he had dissolved the Franciscan order, Emperor Joseph II gave the church to St Elizabeth's Convent.

The Baroque interior is adorned with late 19th-century frescoes, including one of St Florian protecting Christians from a fire in 1810. Their resonance is due to their skilful restoration. The original pulpit and pews have remained intact. In the early 19th century, a hospital and hostel were built adjacent to the church. These were run by the Elizabeth Sisters.

❼ Király Baths

Király Gyógyfürdő

Fő utca 84. **Map** 1 C2. **Tel** (06 1) 202 36 88. Batthyány tér. **Open** 9am–9pm daily. **budapestspas.hu**

The Ottoman Király Baths are one of the city's four remaining Turkish baths *(see pp52–5)*. Built from 1566–70, with 19th-century Neo-Classical additions, they retain many original features, the most beautiful being the central cupola hall with its octagonal pool. From here radiate out the smaller pools of different temperatures, the steam rooms and saunas. The baths are now open to men and women.

At the end of Fő utca, in the square that bears his name is the monument to the Polish general József Bem. The hero of the 1848–9 uprisings, he is depicted with his arm in a sling. It was in this state, in the front line of the Battle of Pisk, that he inspired the Hungarian troops to attack the bridge and achieve victory over the Habsburg armies. Memorable words, which he uttered during the battle, are engraved on the base of the monument.

Tiles on the Tomb of Gül Baba

❽ Tomb of Gül Baba

Gül Baba Türbéje

Mecset utca 14. **Map** 1 B1. 91. **Open** Mar–Oct: 10am–6pm daily; Nov–Feb: 10am–4pm daily.

Gül Baba was a Muslim dervish, who died in 1541, just after the capture of Buda. He was one of the few Turks who was respected and revered by the people of Hungary. His remains now lie in a tomb built between 1543 and 1598.

According to legend, it was Gül Baba who introduced roses to Budapest. From this came both the name of this area, Rózsadomb, meaning Rose Hill, and Gül Baba's own name, which means Father of Roses. Fittingly, his tomb is surrounded by a lovely rose garden.

A 400-year-old dome covers the octagonal tomb, which is adorned with religious items and rugs. It is a well-known place of pilgrimage for Muslims.

❾ Lukács Baths

Lukács Gyógyfürdő

Frankel Leo út 25–9. **Map** 1 C1. **Tel** (06 1) 326 16 95. **Open** 6am–8pm daily. 86. 19, 41, 61. **budapestspas.hu**
Veli Bej Baths: Árpád Fejedelem útja 7. **Tel** (06 1) 438 8641. **Open** 6am–noon, 3–9pm daily (admission to over 14s only; proof by ID or passport required).

This famous spa is named after St Luke. Although the Neo-Classical complex was established in 1894, the baths are one of a number still operating in the city *(see pp52–5)* that date back to the period of Turkish rule.

Set in peaceful surroundings, the complex comprises two outdoor swimming pools. Natural hot springs keep these pools heated all year round; bathing is comfortable even in winter.

It is also worth entering the overgrown courtyard to see a statue of St Luke, dating from 1760, and the plaques inscribed with thanks by bathers from around the world who benefited from the healing waters.

Nearby, the Veli Bej (Császár) thermal baths, built in 1574–5, are the oldest Turkish baths in Budapest and also some of the most beautiful. The baths have been fully renovated by the Ordo Hospitalarius (Brothers Hospitallers of St John of God) as part of their hospital, but are also open to the public. Visitors can enjoy bathing in four pools of different temperatures.

Lukács Baths, with beautiful old plane trees growing outside

❹ St Anne's Church

Szent Anna Templom

Budapest is home to many churches, but the twin-towered parish church of Víziváros is one of its most beautiful Baroque examples. Initially a Jesuit church, the architect who first designed it is unknown. Building was begun in 1740 by Kristóf Hámon and completed after his death by Mátyás Máté Nepauer. In 1763 an earthquake seriously damaged the building and the dissolution of the Jesuit order ten years later further delayed the completion of the church. Thus it remained unconsecrated until 1805.

The twin towers are crowned by magnificent Baroque spires.

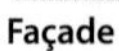

Façade
Buda's coat of arms appears in the centre of the tympanum. The symbol of the Trinity is above this, between two kneeling angels.

★ Pulpit
This magnificent, late Baroque pulpit was created by Károly Bebó in 1773. It features gilded details and angels that embody theological virtues. The reliefs were added at a later date.

Main entrance

Organ
The organ case from a former Carmelite church on Castle Hill was transferred to St Anne's Church in the late 18th century, after the dissolution of the order by Emperor Joseph II.

★ Painted Ceiling
The painted ceiling in the cupola of the chancel depicts the Holy Trinity. It was painted in 1771 by Gergely Vogl. There are also Neo-Baroque frescoes in the nave dating from 1938.

VISITORS' CHECKLIST

Practical Information
Batthyány tér 7. **Map** 1 C3 (9 B1). **Tel** (06 1) 201 63 64. **Open** Only for services. daily. Angelika café: **Tel** (06 1) 225 16 53. **Open** 9am–11pm daily.

Transport
H5. 11. 19, 41.
M Batthyány tér.

★ High Altar
The sculptures depict Mary, as a child, being brought into the Temple of Jerusalem by St Anne, her mother. Completed in 1773, it is regarded as one of the most beautiful works of Károly Bebó.

Church Pew
The choir pews are decorated with intricately carved wooden panels, which feature figurative scenes.

Baptismal Font
Concealed behind a pillar, this baptismal font has a carved pedestal and a simply, but beautifully, decorated cover.

Side Altar
This late Baroque altar of St Francis the Saviour, like the altar of St Cross on the opposite side of the church, is the work of Antal Eberhardt and dates from 1768. The picture in the centre was, however, executed by Franz Wagenschön.

Sights at a Glance

Historic Buildings and Palaces

1 *Parliament pp112–13*
3 Ministry of Agriculture
5 Post Office Savings Bank
6 Central European University
8 Gresham Palace
9 Hungarian Academy of Sciences
12 Drechsler Palace
13 Radisson Blu Béke Hotel, Budapest

Museums

2 Museum of Ethnography

Squares

4 Liberty Square
7 Széchenyi István Square

Theatres

11 *Hungarian State Opera pp122–3*
14 Budapest Operetta Theatre

Churches

10 *St Stephen's Basilica pp120–21*

Restaurants *pp198–200*

1 Alexandra Book Café
2 Belvárosi Lugas Vendéglő
3 Bombay Curry Bar
4 Borkonyha
5 Budapest Bisztró
6 Café Bouchon
7 Café Jubilee
8 Café Kör
9 Európa Kávéház
10 First Strudel House of Pest
11 Ganga Vega Café
12 Govinda Étterem
13 Gresham Restaurant
14 Hummus Bar
15 Hungarikum Bisztro
16 Iguana
17 Kispiac Bisztró
18 KNRDY Steakhouse
19 Krízia
20 Marquis de Salade
21 Momotaro Ramen
22 Okay Italia
23 La Pampa Steakhouse
24 La Plaza Étterem
25 Pomo D'oro
26 Rézkakas Bistro
27 Sir Lancelot Lovagi Étterem
28 Szeráj Török Étterem
29 Tigris
30 Via Luna

◀ The ornately decorated Chamber of Congress in Hungary's Parliament

AROUND PARLIAMENT

Towards the end of the 18th and throughout the 19th century Pest underwent a series of huge changes. In 1838 a flood destroyed most of the rural dwellings that had occupied the area until that time. The unification of Budapest in 1873 and the 1,000-year anniversary, in 1896, of the Magyar conquest also boosted the city's development. The medieval walls that originally marked Pest's limits were crossed as the area was gradually urbanized. This period produced a number of the most important buildings in Hungary, including St Stephen's Basilica, Parliament and the Hungarian Academy of Sciences, which were built in a variety of revivalist styles. Many Neo-Classical residences were also built, particularly on Nádor utca, Akadémia utca and Október 6 utca.

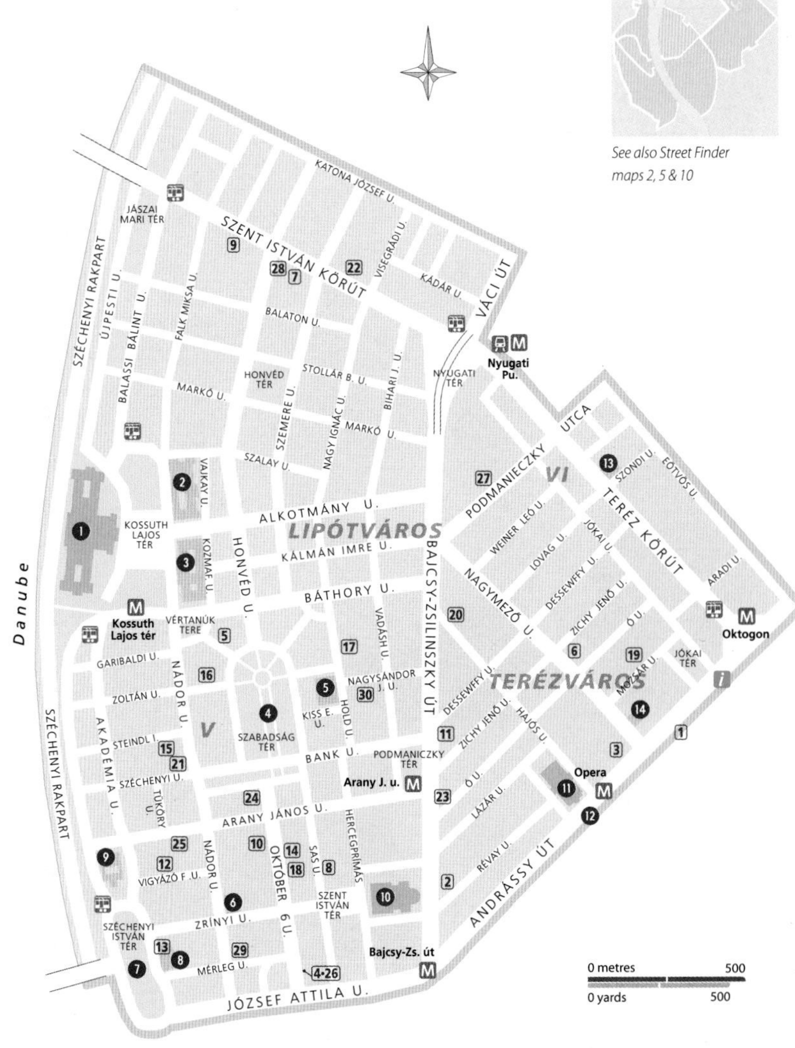

See also Street Finder maps 2, 5 & 10

For keys to symbols see back flap

Street-by-Street: Kossuth Square

This square expresses well the pomp and pride with which Pest was developed during the 19th and early 20th centuries. Parliament dominates the square on the Danube side, but equally imposing are the Ministry of Agriculture and the Museum of Ethnography on the opposite side. Several monuments commemorate nationalist leaders and provide a visual record of Hungary's political history.

2 ★ Museum of Ethnography
Among 250,000 exhibits amassed in the museum's collection is a captivating collection of folk costumes representing the various nationalities and ethnic groups in Hungary.

1 ★ Parliament
This building has become the recognized symbol of democracy in Hungary, despite the dome being crowned by a red star during the Communist period. Anchored in the Danube in front of the building is SMS *Leitha*, a warship originally launched in 1871, that has been restored and is now a floating museum.

Attila József was a radical poet whose work sensitively explored the human condition. In 1937 he committed suicide, aged 32. This statue by László Marton dates from 1980.

Lajos Kossuth (1802–94)

The popularity of Lajos Kossuth among the Hungarian people is immense. He led the 1848–9 uprising against Austrian rule *(see pp32–3)*, and was one of the most outstanding political figures in Hungary. He was a member of the first democratic government during the uprising, and briefly became its leader before being exiled after the revolt was quashed in 1849.

Stained-glass window depicting Lajos Kossuth

Shoes on the Danube Bank, a memorial honouring the Jews shot into the river during World War II

Ferenc II Rákóczi, the prince of Transylvania, led one of the earliest revolts for independence against the Habsburgs in 1703–11. This bronze equestrian monument can be seen in front of Parliament. It was completed by János Pásztor in 1937.

Locator Map
See Street Finder, maps 2 & 10

3 Ministry of Agriculture
A massive Corinthian colonnade, supporting an entablature, lends this Neo-Classical building a dignified character.

This monument to Imre Nagy symbolizes the insurgent prime minister's 1956 defection from the side of Communism to the side of the people – a protest that cost him his life.

The Exchange Palace is a historic landmark. This building, designed in the Late Eclectic style by Ignác Alpár, was constructed in 1905 and it originally housed the Stock Exchange.

Plaque commemorating Brigadier Woroniecki, hero of the uprising of 1948–9

❶ Parliament

Országház

Hungary's Parliament is the country's largest building and has become a symbol of Budapest. A competition was held to choose its design, the winner being Imre Steindl's rich Neo-Gothic masterpiece built between 1885–1902. Based on the Houses of Parliament in London, completed by Charles Barry in 1835–6, it is 268 m (880 ft) long and 96 m (315 ft) high, and comprises 691 rooms.

Exterior
The magnificent dome marks the central point of the Parliament building. Although the façade is elaborately Neo-Gothic, the ground plan follows Baroque conventions.

★ Domed Hall
Adorning the massive pillars that support Parliament's central dome are figures of some of the rulers of Hungary.

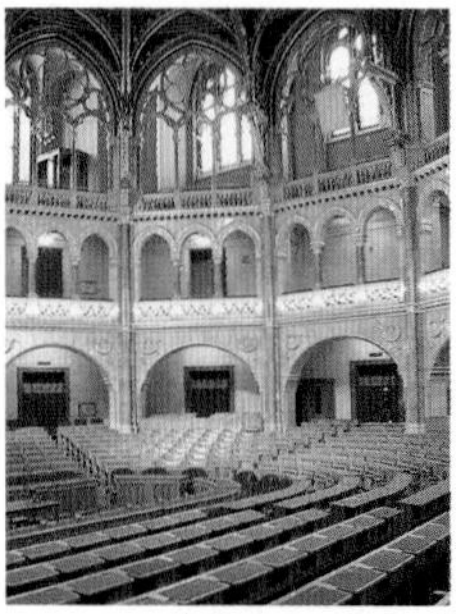

★ Deputy Council Chamber
Formerly the lower house, this hall is now where the National Assembly convenes. Two paintings by Zsigmond Vajda hang on either side of the Speaker's lectern. These were especially commissioned for the building.

①

②

Gables
Almost every corner of the Parliament building features gables with pinnacles based on Gothic sculptures.

Lobby
Lobbies, the venues for political discussions, are to be found along the corridors beneath stained-glass windows.

Dome
The ceiling of the 96-m (315-ft) high dome is covered in an intricate design of Neo-Gothic gilding combined with heraldic decoration.

VISITORS' CHECKLIST

Practical Information
Kossuth Lajos tér. **Map** 2 D3 (9 C1). **Tel** (06 1) 441 49 04. English 10am, noon, 1pm, 2pm, 3pm. Limited tickets available on door; book tickets in advance online. half-price adm with EU passport. **parlament.hu**

Transport
70, 78. 2. Kossuth tér.

Gobelin Hall
This hall is decorated with a Gobelin tapestry illustrating Prince Árpád, with seven Magyar leaders under his command, signing a peace treaty and blood oath.

Old Upper House Hall
International conferences are now held in the Old Upper House Hall. It is virtually a mirror image of the National Assembly Hall.

③

④

The main entrance on Kossuth Lajos tér

Main Staircase
The best contemporary artists were invited to decorate the interior. The sumptuous main staircase features ceiling frescoes by Károly Lotz and sculptures by György Kiss.

KEY

① **South wing**

② **Danube façade**

③ **North wing**

④ **The Royal Insignia**, excluding the Coronation Mantle *(see p136)*, are kept in the Domed Hall.

The magnificent façade of the Museum of Ethnography

❷ Museum of Ethnography

Néprajzi Múzeum

Kossuth Lajos tér 12. **Map** 2 D3 (9 C1). **Tel** (06 1) 473 24 00. 2. M Kossuth Lajos tér. **Open** 10am–6pm Tue–Sun. W **neprajz.hu**

This building, designed by Alajos Hauszmann and constructed between 1893–6, was built as the Palace of Justice and, until 1945, served as the Supreme Court.

The building's design links elements of Renaissance, Baroque and Classicism. The façade is dominated by a vast portico crowned by two towers. It also features a gable topped by the figure of the Roman goddess of justice in a chariot drawn by three horses, by Károly Senyei. The grand hall inside the main entrance features a marvellous staircase and frescoes by Károly Lotz.

The building was first used as a museum in 1957, housing the Hungarian National Gallery *(see pp78–81)*, which was later transferred to the Royal Palace. The Museum of Ethnography has been here since 1973.

The museum's collection was established in 1872 in the Department of Ethnography at the Hungarian National Museum *(see pp134–7)*. There are now around 240,000 exhibits, although most are not on display. The collection includes artifacts reflecting the rural folk culture of Hungary between the 18th and 20th centuries. A map from 1909 shows the settlement of the various communities who came to Hungary. Ethnic items relating to these communities, as well as aboriginal objects from North and South America, Africa, Asia and Australia, can also be seen through the programme of temporary exhibitions.

The museum's permanent exhibition presents the Traditional Culture of the Hungarian Nation.

❸ Ministry of Agriculture

Földművelésügyi Minisztérium

Kossuth Lajos tér 11. **Map** 2 D3 (9 C1). 2. M Kossuth Lajos tér.

On the southeast side of Kossuth Square is this huge building, bordered by streets on all its four sides. It was built for the Ministry of Agriculture by Gyula Bukovics at the end of the 19th century.

The façade is designed in a manner typical of late Historicism, drawing heavily on Neo-Classical motifs. The columns of the colonnade are echoed in the fenestration above the well-proportioned pedimented windows.

On the wall to the right of the building two commemorative plaques can be seen. The first is dedicated to the commanding officer of the Polish Legion, who was also a hero of the 1948–9 uprising *(see p32–3)*. Brigadier M Woroniecki, who was renowned for his bravery, was shot here by the Austrians in 1849. The second plaque honours Endre Ságvári, a Hungarian hero of the resistance, who died in 1944.

The two sculptures in front of the building are by Árpád Somogyi. The *Reaper Lad* dates from 1956 and the *Female Agronomist* from 1954.

The bullets on the wall of the Ministry of Agriculture building are a memorial to the civilian victims of the shooting at Kossuth tér on 25 October 1956, when a peaceful demonstration during the revolution turned violent.

❹ Liberty Square

Szabadság Tér

Map 2 E4 (10 D1). M Kossuth Lajos tér, Arany János utca.

After the enormous Neugebäude Barracks were demolished in 1886, Liberty Square was laid out in its place. The barracks, built for the Austrian troops, once dominated the southern part of Lipótváros (Leopold Town). It was here that Hungary's first independent prime minister, Count Lajos Batthyány was executed on 6 October 1849. Since 1926, an eternal flame *(see p33)* has been burning at the corner of Aulich utca, Hold utca and Báthory utca to honour all those executed during the uprising.

Two particularly impressive buildings by Ignác Alpár are on opposite sides of the square. The Exchange Palace, which was the former home of the Stock Exchange, dates from 1905 and shows the influence of the Secession style. The Hungarian National Bank (Magyar Nemzeti Bank) is decorated in a pastiche of Historicist styles and also dates from 1905. An obelisk by Károly Antal stands at the northern end

Bas-reliefs on the former Stock Exchange

Beautiful Secession interior of the Post Office Savings Bank

of the square commemorating the Red Army soldiers who died during the siege of Budapest in 1944–5. A second statue is to the US general Harry Hill Bandholtz. He led the allied forces that thwarted the Romanian troops looting the Hungarian National Museum. Also on the square is the Ronald Reagan Statue by István Máté, which was errected on the day of the former US president's 100th birthday to honour the important role the Reagan administration played in the collapse of Communism.

❺ Post Office Savings Bank

Postatakarék Pénztár

Hold utca 4. **Map** 2 E4 (10 D1). Ⓜ Kossuth Lajos tér.

A masterpiece by Ödön Lechner, the former Post Office Savings Bank was built between 1900–1901. Chiefly a Secession architect, Lechner *(see p58)* combined the curvilinear motifs of that style with motifs from Hungarian folk art to produce a unique visual style for his work.

Approaching the Post Office Savings Bank, one can see glimpses of the details that have made this building one of Pest's most unusual sights. The construction methods, interior design and exterior detailing of the building are remarkable. Lechner commissioned the tiles used in the design, including the vibrant roof tiles, from the Zsolnay factory *(see p58)*. The façades are decorated with floral tendrils and icons taken from nature. The bees climbing up the gable walls represent the bank's activity and the pinnacles, which look like hives, represent the accumulation of savings. These features were intended to help make the function of the building accessible to the people who banked here.

The building is not officially open to the public, but it is possible to see the Cashiers' Hall during office hours.

❻ Central European University

Közép-Európai Egyetem

Nádor utca 9. **Map** 2 E5 (10 D2). **Tel** (06 1) 327 30 00. Ⓜ Kossuth Lajos tér. Ⓦ **ceu.hu**

This Neo-Classical palace on Nádor utca, in the direction of Széchenyi Square, was built in 1826 by Mihály Pollack for Prince Antal Festetics. Since 1993 it has housed the Central European University (CEU).

Founded by financier and philanthropist George Soros, who was born in Budapest, CEU is a global institution of graduate education in the social sciences, the humanities, law, management, environmental studies, government and public policy, with students from over 100 countries, and a faculty drawn from major universities across the world.

The American Embassy

This beautiful house, at No. 12 Liberty Square, was designed by Aladár Kálmán and Gyula Ullmann and built between 1899–1901. The façade is decorated with bas-reliefs featuring motifs typical of the Secession style.

By the entrance to the embassy is a plaque with an image of the Catholic Primate, Cardinal Joseph Mindszenty, who was part of the movement seeking to liberate Hungary from the Communists after World War II. He was imprisoned by the regime in 1949 and was mistreated for many years. Released during the 1956 uprising, he asked for political asylum in the embassy. He lived here for 15 years in internal exile until, in 1971, the Vatican finally convinced him to leave Hungary.

Plaque commemorating Joseph Mindszenty

Street-by-Street: Széchenyi István Square

In 1867, a cermonial mound was made of earth from all over the country to celebrate the coronation of Franz Joseph as king of Hungary. At the head of the Chain Bridge on the eastern bank of the Danube, it features many of Pest's most beautiful buildings, such as the Hungarian Academy of Sciences and Gresham Palace. The square was named after American president Franklin D Roosevelt from 1947 until 2011, when it was renamed after the 19th-century political and social reformer István Széchenyi (1791–1860).

No. 1 Akadémia utca was built in the Neo-Classical style by Mátyás Zitterbarth the younger, in 1835. A plaque shows that in November 1848 General József Bem *(see p105)* stayed here when it was the Prince Stephen Hotel.

8 ★ Gresham Palace
One of the most expressive examples of Secession architecture in Budapest, now a Four Seasons hotel.

9 ★ Hungarian Academy of Sciences
The debating hall of the Hungarian Academy of Sciences is decorated with sculptures by Miklós Izsó and ceiling paintings by Károly Lotz.

House designed by József Hild in 1836

The Chain Bridge *(see p66)* was built between 1839–49 and was the city's first permanent river crossing. It was destroyed by the German forces in World War II and was reopened in 1949, 100 years after it was first finished.

The Pichler House is an unusual building. It was completed by Ferenc Wieser between 1853–7 in the style of a Venetian Gothic palace.

Locator Map

See Street Finder, maps 2 & 10

⑩ ★ St Stephen's Basilica
The interior of this church was decorated by leading Hungarian artists, such as Alajos Stróbl and Károly Lotz. It was seriously damaged in World War II, and renovation began in the 1980s.

No. 7 Nádor utca is a Neo-Classical building completed in 1830. It has a modest but well-balanced façade accented by pilasters with decorative capitals, and the large first-floor windows are crowned with elegant arches.

No. 8 József Attila utca, an impressive five-floor office building, was erected in 1898 by Artúr Meinig. It is an attractive example of the use of the Secession style *(see pp56–9)*.

Key

— Suggested route

Monument to Ferenc Deák in Széchenyi István Square

7 Széchenyi István Square

Széchenyi István tér

Map 2 D5 (9 C3). 105, 116. 2.

Previously, Széchenyi István Square was known by several different names – Franz Joseph Square, Unloading Square and Roosevelt Square among others – but it received its current title in 2010, named after the the leading social and political reformer. It is located at the head of the Pest side of the Chain Bridge, and is home to many important buildings.

At the beginning of the 20th century the square was lined with various hotels, the Diana Baths and the Lloyd Palace. The only building from the previous century still standing today is the Hungarian Academy of Sciences. The other buildings were demolished and replaced by the Gresham Palace and the Bank of Hungary, on the corner of Attila József utca. Two large modern hotels, the Sofitel Budapest Chain Bridge *(see p188)* and the Inter-Continental Budapest, stand on the southern side of the square.

There is a statue to Baron József Eötvös (1813–71) a reformer of public education, in front of the Inter-Continental. In the centre of the square there are monuments to Count István Széchenyi, and Ferenc Deák, who was instrumental in the Compromise of 1867, which resulted in the Dual Monachy *(see p34)*.

8 Gresham Palace

Gresham Palota

Széchenyi István tér 5–7. **Map** 2 D5 (9 C3). **Tel** (06 1) 268 60 00. 105, 116. 2. **W fourseasons.com/budapest**

This Secession palace aroused both controversy and praise from the moment it was built. One of Budapest's most distinctive pieces of architecture, it was commissioned by the London-based Gresham Life Assurance Company from Zsigmond Quittner and the brothers József and László Vágó, and completed in 1907.

This enormous edifice enjoys an imposing location directly opposite the Chain Bridge. The façade features characteristic Secession motifs *(see pp56–9)*, such as curvilinear forms and organic themes. The ornately carved window surrounds appear as though they are projecting from the walls, blending seamlessly with the architecture. The bust by Ede Telcs, at the top of the façade, is of Sir Thomas Gresham. He was the founder of the Royal Exchange in London and of Gresham's Law: "bad money drives out good".

On the ground floor of the palace there is a T-shaped arcade, covered by a multicoloured glazed roof. The entrance to the arcade is marked by a beautiful wrought-iron gate with peacock motifs. Still the original gate, it is widely regarded as one of the most splendid examples of design from the Secession era. Inside the building, the second floor of the Kossuth stairway has a stained-glass window by Miksa Róth, featuring a portrait of Lajos Kossuth *(see p110)*.

In 2004 the palace opened as a Four Seasons Hotel, the second in Central Europe, and the first in Hungary. Visitors can wander in and admire its many splendours.

Bust of Sir Thomas Gresham on the façade of the Gresham Palace

Miklós Izsó's sculptures inside the Hungarian Academy of Sciences

9 Hungarian Academy of Sciences

Magyar Tudományos Akadémia

Széchenyi István tér 9. **Map** 2 D4 (9 C2). **Tel** (06 1) 411 61 00. 16, 105, 116. 2. **Open** 11am–4pm Mon–Fri. by appointment. **W mta.hu**

Built between 1862–4, this Neo-Renaissance building was designed by the architect Friedrich August Stüler.

The statues adorning the façade represent six disciplines of knowledge – law, history, mathematics, sciences, philosophy and linguistics – and are the works of Emil Wolf and Miklós Izsó. On the Danube side are allegories of poetry, astronomy and archeology, and on the corners of the building are statues of renowned thinkers including Newton, Descartes and Révay. Inside are more statues and the library, which has a priceless collection of academic books.

The Neo-Renaissance façade of the Drechsler Palace

⑩ St Stephen's Basilica

See pp120–21.

⑪ Hungarian State Opera

See pp122–3.

⑫ Drechsler Palace

Drechsler Palota

Andrássy út 25. **Map** 2 F4 (10 E2).
M Opera.

Formerly the State Ballet Institute, the Drechsler Palace was originally built as Neo-Renaissance apartments for the Hungarian Railways Pension Fund in 1883. It was designed by Gyula Pártos and Ödön Lechner to harmonize with the façade of the Hungarian State Opera *(see pp122–3)*.

Its name derives from the Drechsler Café, which occupied the ground floor in the 1890s and early 1900s.

⑬ Radisson Blu Béke Hotel, Budapest

Radisson Blu Béke Hotel, Budapest

Teréz körút 43. **Map** 2 F3.
Tel (06 1) 889 39 00. 4, 6.
M Oktogon. W **radissonblu.com**

This elegant hotel was built in 1896 as an apartment building, and in 1912 was restyled by Béla Málnai as the Hotel Britannia. A mosaic of György Szondi, a Hungarian captain who fought against the Turks in the 16th century, was added to the façade at this time.

In 1978 the hotel was taken over by the Radisson group, which restored the rich interiors. Notable features are the stained-glass windows in the Szondi Restaurant, by Jenő Haranghy, illustrating the works of Richard Wagner. The Romeo and Juliet conference room and the Shakespeare Restaurant are named after the murals that decorate them. The café serves cake and coffee on porcelain from the Pécs factory *(see p58)*.

⑭ Budapest Operetta Theatre

Budapesti Operett Színház

Nagymező utca 17. **Map** 2 F4 (10 F1).
Tel (06 1) 472 20 30. 4, 6.
M Oktogon, Opera.
W **operettszinhaz.hu**

Budapest has a good reputation for musical entertainment, and its operetta scene *(see p216)* is over 100 years old. Operettas were first staged on this site in the Orfeum Theatre, designed in the Neo-Baroque style by the Viennese architects Fellner and Helmer, in 1898. The project was financed by the impressario Károly Singer-Somossy.

In 1922, the American entrepreneur Ben Blumenthal redeveloped the building and opened the Capital Operetta Theatre, which then specialized in the genre. After 1936, this theatre became the only venue for operetta in Budapest.

The repertoire of the theatre includes the works of both international and Hungarian composers of this genre, including Imre Kálmán, Ferenc Lehár and Pál Ábrahám.

Entrance to the Budapest Operetta Theatre on Nagymező utca

⑩ St Stephen's Basilica

Szent István Bazilika

Dedicated to St Stephen, or István, the first Hungarian Christian king *(see p24)*, this church was designed by József Hild in the Classical style, using a Greek cross floor plan. Construction began in 1851 and was taken over in 1867 by Miklós Ybl *(see p123)*, who added the Neo-Renaissance dome after the original one collapsed in 1868. József Kauser completed the church in 1905. It received the title of Basilica Minor in 1931, the 900th anniversary of St Emeric's death.

Dome
Reaching 96 m (315 ft), the dome is visible from all over Budapest.

St Matthew
St Matthew is one of the four Evangelists represented in the niches on the exterior of the dome. They are all the work of the sculptor Leó Feszler.

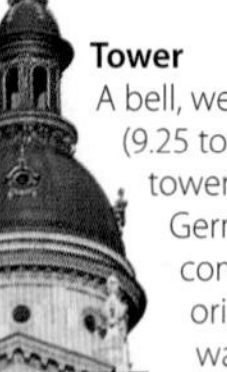

Tower
A bell, weighing 9,250 kg (9.25 tons) is housed in this tower. It was funded by German Catholics to compensate for the original bell, which was looted by the Nazis in 1944.

Main Portal
The oak wood door is decorated with carvings depicting the heads of the 12 Apostles.

Mosaics
The dome is decorated with mosaics designed by Károly Lotz. Other mosaics designed by Gyula Benczúr feature in the sanctuary.

VISITORS' CHECKLIST

Practical Information
Szent István tér. **Map** 2 E4 (10 D2). **Tel** (06 1) 338 21 51. Treasury: **Open** 9am–5pm Mon–Fri (to 1pm Sat), 1–5pm Sun. 10am–2pm.

Transport
M Deák Ferenc tér.

★ Main Altar
In the centre of the altar there is a marble statue of St István by Alajos Stróbl. Scenes from the king's life are depicted behind the altar.

★ Holy Right Hand
Hungary's most unusual relic is the mummified forearm of King István. It is kept in the Chapel of the Holy Right Hand.

St Gellért and St Emeric
This portrayal of St Gellért and his pupil, St Emeric, son of St István, is the work of Alajos Stróbl.

★ Painting by Gyula Benczúr
This image shows King István, left without an heir, dedicating Hungary to the Virgin Mary, who became *Patrona Hungariae*, the country's patron.

KEY

① **Observation point**

② **The basilica's lookout terrace** (accessed by 304 steps or an elevator) offers a beautiful panoramic view of the city.

③ **Figures of the 12 Apostles**, by Leó Feszler, crown the exterior colonnade at the back of the church.

⓫ Hungarian State Opera

Magyar Állami Operaház

Opened in September 1884, the Hungarian State Opera in Budapest was built to rival those of Paris, Vienna and Dresden. Its beautiful architecture and interiors were the life's work of the great Hungarian architect, Miklós Ybl. The interior also features ornamentation by Hungarian artists, including Alajos Stróbl and Károly Lotz. During its lifetime, the Hungarian State Opera has seen some influential music directors, including, Ferenc Erkel, composer of the Hungarian opera *Bánk Bán*, Gustav Mahler and Otto Klemperer.

Façade
The decoration of the symmetrical façade follows a musical theme. In niches on either side of the main entrance there are figures of two of Hungary's most prominent composers, Ferenc Erkel and Franz Liszt *(see p148)*. Both were sculpted by Alajos Stróbl.

Murals
The vaulted ceiling of the foyer is covered in magnificent murals by Bertalan Székely and Mór Than. They depict the nine Muses.

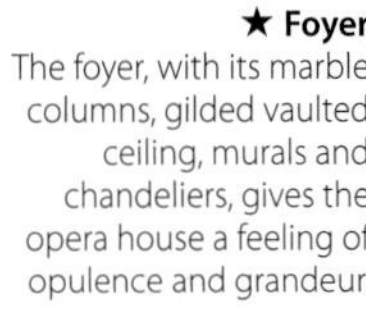

★ Foyer
The foyer, with its marble columns, gilded vaulted ceiling, murals and chandeliers, gives the opera house a feeling of opulence and grandeur.

Main entrance
Wrought-iron lamps illuminate the wide stone staircase and the main entrance.

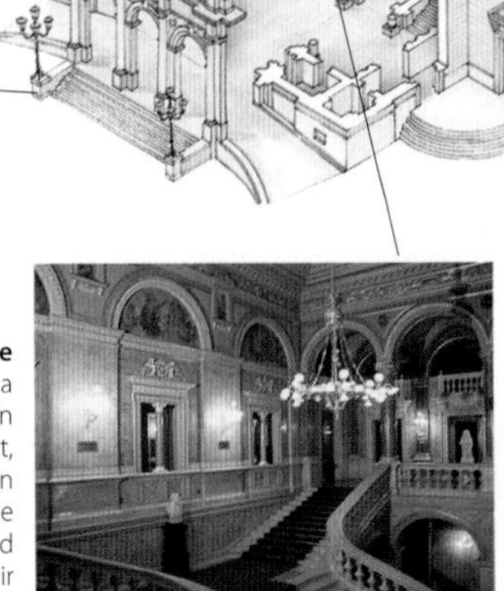

★ Main Staircase
Going to the opera was a great social occasion in the 19th century. A vast, sweeping staircase was an important element of the opera house as it allowed ladies to show off their new gowns.

Chandelier
The main hall is decorated with a bronze chandelier that weighs over 2,000 kg (2 tons). It illuminates a fresco, by Károly Lotz, of the Greek gods on Olympus.

VISITORS' CHECKLIST

Practical Information
Andrássy út 22. **Map** 2 F4 (10 E2). **Tel** (06 1) 332 81 97 or 353 01 70 (box office). during performances. 3pm & 4pm. **opera.hu**; **operavisit.hu**

Transport
Opera.

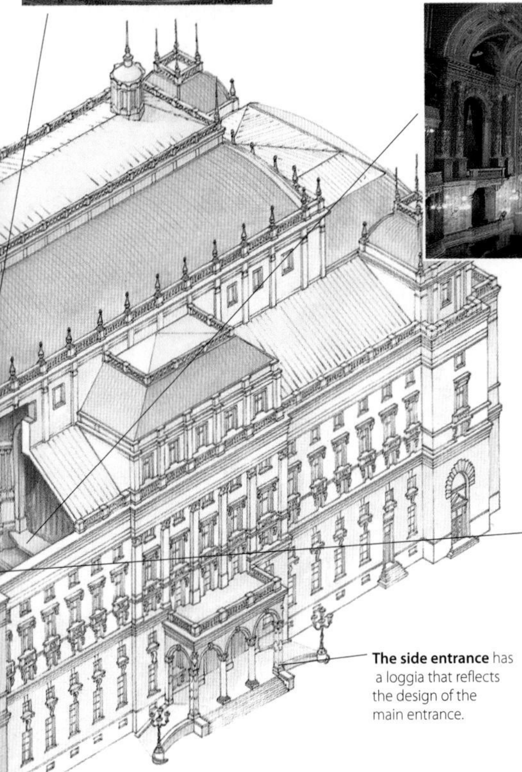

Central Stage
This proscenium arch stage employed the most modern technology of the time. It featured a revolving stage and metal hydraulic machinery.

The side entrance has a loggia that reflects the design of the main entrance.

★ Royal Box
The royal box is located centrally in the three-storey circle. It is decorated with sculptures symbolizing the four operatic voices – soprano, alto, tenor and bass.

Miklós Ybl (1814–91)

The most prominent Hungarian architect of the second half of the 19th century, Miklós Ybl had an enormous influence on the development of Budapest. He was a practitioner of Historicism, and tended to use Neo-Renaissance forms. The Hungarian State Opera and the dome of St Stephen's Basilica are examples of his work. Ybl also built apartment buildings and palaces for the aristocracy in this style. A statue of the architect stands on the western bank of the Danube, in Miklós Ybl Square *(see p99)*.

Bust of Miklós Ybl

The ornate façade of a building in Váci Street, a pedestrian shopping area in central Pest

Sights at a Glance

Churches

1 *Inner City Parish Church pp128–9*
10 Servite Church
11 Lutheran Church
17 Great Synagogue
18 Chapel of St Roch
22 Calvinist Church
26 Serbian Church
28 University Church
31 Franciscan Church

Museums

20 *Hungarian National Museum pp134–7*
23 *Museum of Applied Arts pp140–41*

Historic Buildings and Monuments

6 Klotild Palaces
7 Pest County Hall
8 Municipal Council Offices
9 Turkish Bank
12 Danube Fountain
13 New Theatre
14 Liszt Ferenc Academy of Music
15 New York Palace
21 Ervin Szabó Library
24 Central Market Hall
25 City Council Chamber
27 Loránd Eötvös University
29 Károlyi Palace
30 University Library

Streets and Squares

2 Vigadó Square
3 József Nádor Square
4 Vörösmarty Square
5 Váci Street
16 Jewish Quarter
19 Mihály Pollack Square

Restaurants *pp200–204*

1 Araz
2 Astoria Kávéház
3 Auguszt Cukrászda
4 Babel Étterem
5 BARbár Café
6 Bohémtanya
7 Borbiróság
8 Bors GasztroBár
9 Borssó Bistro
10 La Bourbon
11 Buena Vista Étterem
12 Café Alibi
13 Carmel Étterem
14 Central kávéház
15 Chess
16 Comme Chez Soi
17 Costes
18 Cucina
19 Cyrano
20 Dionysos Taverna
21 Drum Café
22 Fakanál
23 Falafel
24 Fausto's
25 Fresh Factory
26 Frici Papa
27 Frőhlich Kóser Cukrászda
28 Fruccola
29 Fülemüle Étterem
30 Gerbeaud Cukrászda
31 Gerlóczy Kávéház
32 Gotti Étterem
33 Il Terzo Cerchio
34 Kádár Étkezde
35 Kaltenberg Sörház és Étterem
36 Károlyi Étterem és Kávéház
37 Kárpátia Étterem
38 Két Szerecsen
39 Klassz
40 Király Cukrászda
41 Kőleves Vendéglő
42 Lou Lou
43 Macesz Huszár
44 Magdalena Merlo
45 Marie Kristensen Sandwich Bar
46 Menza
47 Művész Kávéház
48 Műzeum Kávéház es Étterem
49 Múzeum Cukrászda
50 New York Kávéház
51 Nobu
52 Onyx
53 Paris-Budapest Restaurant and Bar
54 Pata Negra
55 La Pizza di Mamma Sophia
56 Sahara
57 Shalimar
58 Soul Café
59 Spinoza
60 Sugar!
61 Trattoria Toscana
62 VakVarjú Étterem
63 Vapiano
64 Vörös Postakocsi Étterem
65 W35

CENTRAL PEST

At the end of the 17th century much of Pest was in ruins and few residents remained. Within the next few decades, however, new residential districts were established, which are today's mid-town suburbs. In the 19th century, redevelopment schemes introduced grand houses and apartment blocks, some with shops and cafés, as well as secular and municipal buildings. Perhaps the most prominent example of this work is the Hungarian National Museum. At this time Pest surpassed Buda as a centre for trade and industry. This was partly due to the area's Jewish community, who played an active role in its development.

See also Street Finder maps 4, 7 & 10

For keys to symbols see back flap

Street-by-Street: Around Váci Street

Váci Street has been Budapest's fashionable area for walking, meeting in cafés and shopping in elegant boutiques since the early 19th century. Its attractive promenade is an enjoyable place for an evening stroll, when it is stylishly illuminated.

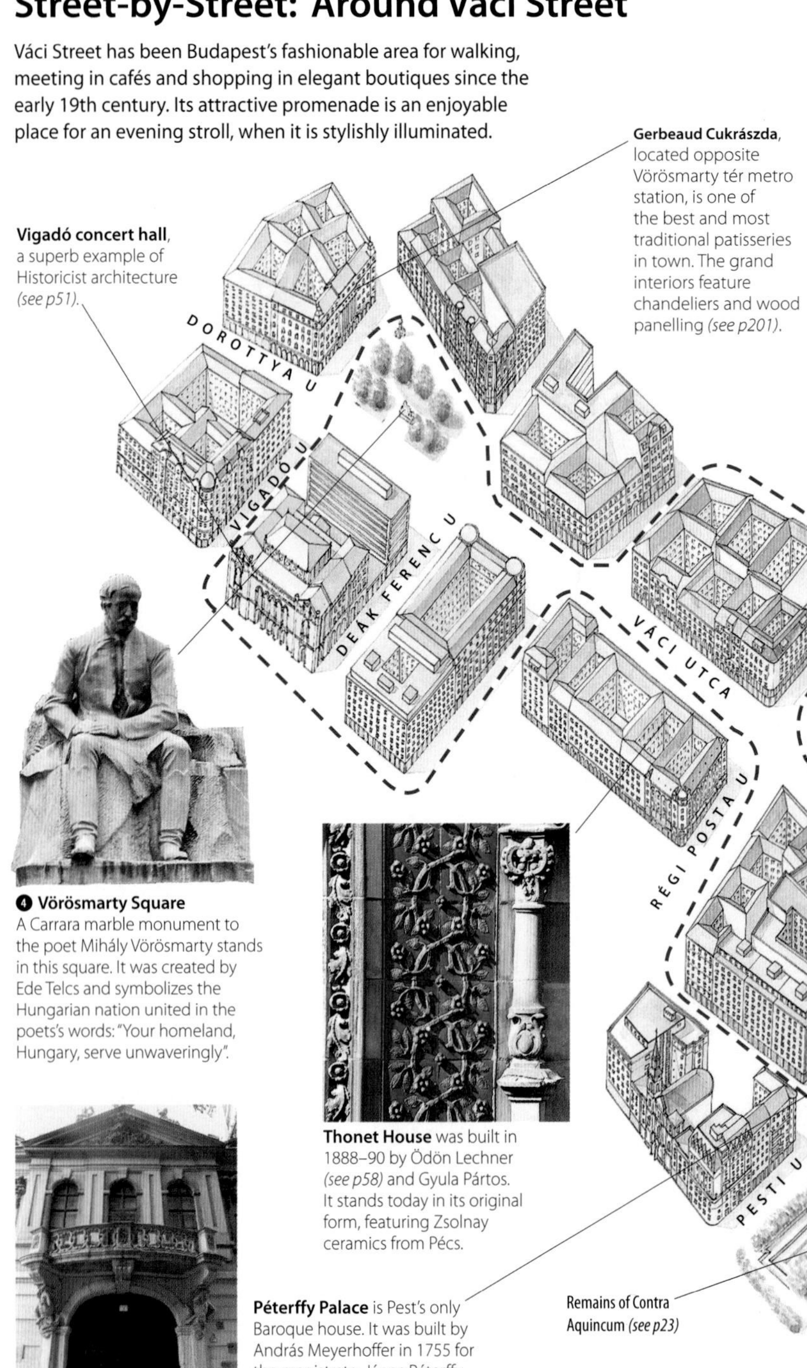

Gerbeaud Cukrászda, located opposite Vörösmarty tér metro station, is one of the best and most traditional patisseries in town. The grand interiors feature chandeliers and wood panelling *(see p201)*.

Vigadó concert hall, a superb example of Historicist architecture *(see p51)*.

❹ Vörösmarty Square
A Carrara marble monument to the poet Mihály Vörösmarty stands in this square. It was created by Ede Telcs and symbolizes the Hungarian nation united in the poets's words: "Your homeland, Hungary, serve unwaveringly".

Thonet House was built in 1888–90 by Ödön Lechner *(see p58)* and Gyula Pártos. It stands today in its original form, featuring Zsolnay ceramics from Pécs.

Péterffy Palace is Pest's only Baroque house. It was built by András Meyerhoffer in 1755 for the magistrate, János Péterffy. Above the gateway there is a beautiful balcony supported by atlantes.

Remains of Contra Aquincum *(see p23)*

Key

— Suggested route

⑩ Servite Church
Holy figures adorn the 19th-century façade of this Baroque church.

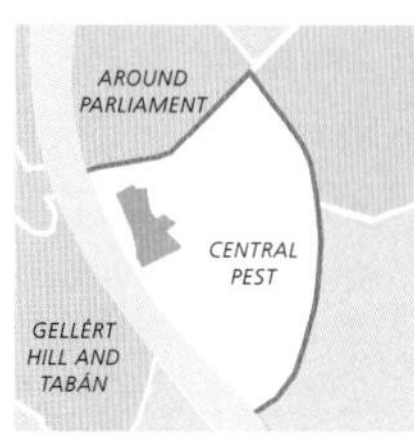

Locator Map
See Street Finder, maps 2, 4, 10

⑤ ★ Váci Street
Budapest's most elegant promenade and shopping area is lined with fashion boutiques, cafés, fountains and statues. Off the street there are old courtyards and shopping arcades.

⑥ ★ Klotild Palaces
This beautifully decorated block consists of two symmetrical buildings, which together form a magnificent gateway to the Elizabeth Bridge.

① ★ Inner City Parish Church
This white limestone and red marble tabernacle, in the church, dates from the early 16th century.

0 metres 50
0 yards 50

❶ Inner City Parish Church

Belvárosi Plébánia Templom

This church is the oldest building in Pest. It was first established during the reign of St István, the first king of Hungary *(see pp24–5)*, on the burial site of the martyred St Gellért. In the 14th century, a large Gothic church was built, which was used as a mosque under the Turks. Damaged by the Great Fire of 1723, the church was partly rebuilt in the Baroque style by György Pauer in 1725–39. The interior also features Neo-Classical elements by János Hild, as well as some 20th-century works. In May 2014, archeologists started excavation work on the site for an unforeseeable period. Some parts of the church may be closed to tourists.

★ Pulpit
This Neo-Gothic pulpit is beautifully carved from wood. It was produced in 1808 by Fülöp Ungradt.

Main Portal
The late Baroque portal is crowned by a sculpture of the Holy Trinity, inlaid with gold.

Nave
The interior of the church reflects the Gothic and Baroque periods in which it was built. The nave, in the western section of the church, is Baroque in design.

KEY

① **A fragment of a wall** from the Romanesque church is visible in the lower section of the façade.

② **The south tower** includes one of the surviving walls of the Romanesque church.

③ **Reconstructed Gothic tabernacle**

④ **The Turkish Prayer Niche**, or *mihrab*, which indicates the direction of Mecca, is one of the few remnants of the Turkish occupation *(see pp28–9)*.

★ Fresco
This fragment of a 15th-century Italianate fresco depicts the crucifixion of Christ. It was transferred from the cloister to its current location in the choir.

VISITORS' CHECKLIST

Practical Information
Március 15 tér 2. **Map** 4 E1 (10 D5). **Tel** (06 1) 318 31 08. **Open** 9am–7pm daily. ✝ daily.

Transport
🚌 2. Ⓜ Ferenciek tere.

Main Altar
The original altar was destroyed in World War II, and the current one, by Károly Antal and Pál C Molnár, dates from 1948.

★ Gothic Chapel
This vaulted chapel is entered through a painted archway. It features recreated tracery windows.

Crest of Pest
The crest of Pest adorns the pedestal of a Renaissance tabernacle, which was commissioned by Pest's city council in 1507. It is the work of a 16th-century Italian artist.

Historical Floorplan of the Church

Nothing remains of the first church: the oldest sections date from the 12th-century Romanesque church.

Key

- Romanesque church
- Gothic church
- Baroque church

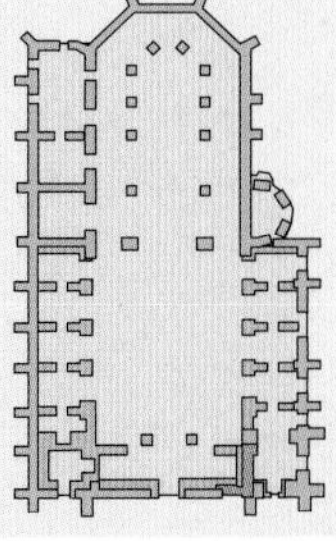

The opulent façade of the Vigadó concert hall, decorated with figures and busts of statesmen, leaders and other prominent Hungarians

❷ Vigadó Square

Vigadó Tér

Map 4 D1 (10 D4). 2. **Tel** (06 1) 235 4200. **Open** 10am–6pm Tue–Sun. **vigado.hu**

The Vigadó concert hall, incorporating a cultural centre and gallery, dominates the square with its mix of eclectic forms. It was built by Frigyes Feszl in 1859–64 to replace a predecessor destroyed by fire during the uprising of 1848–9 *(see pp32–3)*. The façade includes features such as folk motifs and busts of former monarchs, rulers and other Hungarian personalities. An old Hungarian coat of arms is also visible in the centre. The concert hall is run by the Hungarian Academy of Arts.

The Budapest Marriott Hotel *(see p188)*, located on one side of the square, was designed by József Finta in 1969. It was one of the first modern hotels to be built in Budapest.

On the Danube promenade is a statue of a childlike figure on the railings: *Little Princess (see p69)*, by László Marton. The square also has craft stalls, cafés and restaurants.

❸ József Nádor Square

József Nádor Tér

Map 2 E5 (10 D3). 105. Vörösmarty tér.

Archduke József, after whom this square is named, was appointed as the emperor's Palatine for Hungary in 1796 at the age of 20. He ruled the country for 51 years until his death in 1847. One of the few Habsburgs sympathetic to the Hungarian people, he was instrumental in the development of Buda and Pest and, in 1808, he initiated the Embellishment Commission *(see p32)*.

A statue of Archduke József, by Johann Halbig, stands in the middle of the square. It was erected in 1869.

Some of the houses on the square are worth individual mention. The Neo-Classical Gross Palace at No. 1 *(see p50)* was built in 1824 by József Hild. It now houses a bank. The building at Nos. 5–6, which overlooks the southern end of the square, dates from 1859 and was built by Hugó Máltás. At No. 11 is a shop run by the Herend company *(see p212)*. Its factory has produced world-renowned porcelain for almost 200 years.

Sculpture in Vigadó Square

❹ Vörösmarty Square

Vörösmarty Tér

Map 2 E5 (10 D3). Vörösmarty tér.

In the middle of the square stands a monument depicting the poet Mihály Vörösmarty (1800–55). Unveiled in 1908, it is the work of Ede Telcs. Behind the monument, on the eastern side of the square, is the former Luxus department store, which used to be one of the rare places in the Socialist era where you could buy fashionable clothes.

On the northern side of the square there is a renowned pâtisserie, opened by Henrik Kugler in 1858. It was taken over by the Swiss *patissière* Emil Gerbeaud, who was responsible for the richly decorated interior which survives to this day. A tempting selection of coffee, cakes, pastries and desserts are on offer. In summer, these can be taken on a terrace overlooking the square.

The elegant interior of the Gerbeaud pâtisserie, on Vörösmarty Square

Thonet House, decorated with Zsolnay tiles, at No. 11 Váci Street

❺ Váci Street

Váci Utca

Map 4 E1–F2 (10 E5).
Ⓜ Ferenciek tere.

Once two separate streets, which were joined at the beginning of the 18th century, Váci Street still has two distinct characters; the northern section is more of an elegant shopping street with luxury stores, the southern part has more restaurants and small shops. Most of the buildings lining the street date from the 19th and early 20th centuries. More recently, however, modern department stores, banks and shopping arcades have sprung up among the older original buildings.

Philantia, a Secession style florist's shop opened in 1905, now occupies part of the Neo-Classical block at No. 9, built in 1840 by József Hild. No. 9 also houses the Pesti Theatre, where classic plays by Anton Chekhov, among others, are staged. The building was once occupied by the Inn of the Seven Electors, which had a large ballroom-cum-concert hall. It was here that a 12-year-old Franz Liszt performed.

Thonet House, at No. 11, is most notable for the Zsolnay tiles *(see p58)* from Pécs, which decorate its façade. No. 13 is the oldest building on Váci Street and was built in 1805. In contrast, the postmodern Fontana department store at No. 16, was built in 1984. Outside the store there is a bronze fountain with a figure of Hermes, dating from the mid-19th century.

The Nádor Hotel once stood at No. 20 and featured a statue of Archduke Palatine József in front of the entrance. Today the Mercure Hotel *(see p188)*, designed by József Finta and opened in 1987, stands here.

In a side street off Váci Street, at No. 13 Régiposta utca, is a building from the Modernist period. An unusual sight in Pest, this Bauhaus-influenced building dates from 1937 and is by Lajos Kozma.

❻ Klotild Palaces

Klotild Paloták

Váci utca 34. **Map** 4 E1 (10 E5).
Ⓜ Ferenciek tere.

Flanking Szabadsajtó utca, on the approach to the Elizabeth Bridge, stand two massive apartment blocks built in 1902. The buildings were commissioned by the daughter-in-law of Palatine József, Archduchess Klotild, after whom they were named.

They were designed by Flóris Korb and Kálmán Giergl in the Historicist style, with elements of Rococo decoration. The Palace to the right houses apartments and the Buddha Bar Hotel *(see p187)*, while the left side houses a restaurant and a café.

One of the twin Klotild Palaces, from 1902, by the approach to the Elizabeth Bridge *(see p67)*

❼ Pest County Hall

Pest Megyei Önkormányzat

Városház utca 7. **Map** 4 F1 (10 E4).
Tel (06 1) 233 68 00. Ⓜ Ferenciek tere.
Open 8am–4:30pm Mon–Thu, 8am–2pm Fri.

Built in several stages, this is one of Pest's most beautiful, monumental Neo-Classical civic buildings. It was erected during the 19th century, as part of the plan for the city drawn up by the Embellishment Commission.

A seat of the Council of Pest has existed on this site since the end of the 17th century. By 1811, however, the building included two conference halls, a prison and a prison chapel. In 1829–32, a wing designed by József Hofrichter was added on Semmelweis utca, which was used to accommodate council employees.

In 1838 another redevelopment programme was begun, this time employing designs by Mátyás Zitterbarth Jr, a highly regarded exponent of Neo-Classical architecture. Completed in 1842, it included an impressive façade, which overlooks Városház utca. This features a portico with six Corinthian columns supporting a prominent tympanum.

Pest County Hall was destroyed in the course of World War II. During post-war rebuilding it was enlarged, with the addition of three internal courtyards, the first of which is surrounded by atmospheric cloisters. Due to the excellent acoustics, concerts are often held here during the summer.

Between Pest County Hall and the Municipal Council Offices building *(see p132)*, in the small Kamermayer Károly tér, there is a monument to the first mayor of Budapest. Károly Kamermayer (1829–97) took office in 1873 after the unification of Óbuda, Buda and Pest. The aluminium monument was designed in 1942 by Béla Szabados.

8 Municipal Council Offices

Fővárosi Önkormányzat

Városház utca 9–11. **Map** 4 E1 & F1 (10 E4). **Tel** (06 1) 327 10 00. Ⓜ Ferenciek tere. **Open** 8am–4:30pm Mon–Thu, 8am–12:30pm Fri. Ⓦ **budapest.hu**

The largest Baroque building in Budapest, this edifice was completed in 1735 to a design by the architect Anton Erhard Martinelli. It was originally a hospital for veterans of the war between the Christians and Turks at the end of the 17th century *(see pp28–9)*.

In 1894 the city authorities bought the building in order to convert it into council offices. Ármin Hegedűs was commissioned to refurbish the building.

Most notable are the bas-reliefs decorating the gates on the Városház utca side of the building. The scenes depicted in the bas-reliefs commemorate a victory of Charles III *(see p21)* and Prince Eugene of Savoy's role in the war against the Turks *(see p75)*. These are thought to be the work of the Viennese sculptor Johann Christoph Mader.

9 Turkish Bank

Török Bankház

Szervita tér 3. **Map** 4 E1 (10 D4). Ⓜ Deák Ferenc tér.

Dating from 1906 and designed by Henrik Böhm and Ármin Hegedűs, the building that formerly housed the Turkish Bank is a wonderful example of the Secession style.

The exterior used modern construction methods to create the glass façade, which is set in reinforced concrete. Above the fenestration, in the gable, is a magnificent colourful mosaic by Miksa Róth. Entitled *Glory to Hungary*, it depicts Hungary paying homage to the Virgin Mary, or *Patrona Hungariae (see p121)*. Angels and shepherds surround the Virgin, along with figures of Hungarian political heroes, such as Prince Ferenc Rákóczi *(see p30)*, István Széchenyi *(see pp32–3)* and Lajos Kossuth *(see p110)*.

Glory to Hungary, the mosaic on the façade of the Turkish Bank

10 Servite Church

Szervita Templom

Szervita tér 7. **Map** 4 E1 (10 D4). Ⓜ Deák Ferenc tér.

This Baroque church was built between 1725–32 to a design by János Hölbling and György Pauer. In 1871, the façade was rebuilt and the tower was covered with a new roof, designed by József Diescher.

Above the doorway there are figures of St Peregrin and St Anne, and above them sit St Philip and St Augustine. To the right of the entrance there is a bas-relief by János Istók, dating from 1930. It is dedicated to the heroes of the VIIth Wilhelm Hussar Regiment who gave their lives in World War I.

11 Lutheran Church

Evangélikus Templom

Deák tér 4. **Map** 2 E5 (10 E3). **Tel** (06 1) 317 34 13. Ⓜ Deák Ferenc tér. National Lutheran Museum: **Tel** (06 1) 483 21 50. **Open** reopens during 2015 following reconstruction; check website for times. by arrangement. Ⓦ **evangelikusmuzeum.hu**

Mihály Pollack designed this Neo-Classical church, built between 1799–1808. A portico, which features a tympanum supported by Doric columns, was added to the façade in 1856 by József Hild.

The church's simplicity is typical of early Neo-Classicism. It also reflects the notion of minimal church decoration, which was upheld by this branch of Protestantism. Above the modest main altar is a copy of Raphael's *Transfiguration* by Franz Sales Lochbihler, made in 1811. Organ recitals are held in the church.

Another Neo-Classical building by Mihály Pollack adjoins the church. Constructed as a Lutheran school, it is now the National Lutheran Museum. The museum illustrates the history of the Reformation in Hungary, and the most interesting exhibit is a copy of Martin Luther's last will and testament. The original document, dating from 1542, is held in the Lutheran Archives.

Neo-Classical main altar in the Lutheran Church

The Danube Fountain, built in 1880–83 by Miklós Ybl

⓬ Danube Fountain

Danubius Kút

Erzsébet tér. **Map** 2 E5 (10 D3). Ⓜ Deák Ferenc tér.

This fountain, which once stood in Kálvin tér, was designed and built by Miklós Ybl *(see p98)* in 1880–83. It is decorated with copies by Dezső Győri of original sculptures by Béla Brestyánszky and Leó Feszler, which were damaged in World War II.

The figure at the top of the fountain is Danubius, representing the Danube. The three female figures below symbolize Hungary's three principal rivers after the Danube: the Tisza, the Dráva and the Száva.

⓭ New Theatre

Új Színház

Paulay Ede utca 35. **Map** 2 F4 (10 E2). **Tel** (06 1) 269 60 21. Ⓜ Opera. **W ujszinhaz.hu**

Originally completed in 1909, this building has undergone many transformations. It was designed by Béla Lajta in the Secession style, and, as the home of the cabaret troupe Parisian Mulató, became a shrine to frivolity.

In 1921 it was completely restyled by László Vágó, who turned it into a theatre. After World War II, the theatre gained a glass-and-steel façade, and a children's theatre company was based here.

Between 1988–90 the building was returned to its original form using Lajta's plans. Now, gilding, stained glass and marble once more adorn this unusual building.

⓮ Liszt Ferenc Academy of Music

Zeneakadémia

Liszt Ferenc tér 8. **Map** 7 A1 (10 F2). **Tel** (06 1) 321 06 90. 4, 6 to Király utca. by arrangement. **W lisztacademy.hu**

The academy is housed in a late Historicist palace, built between 1904–7 by Kálmán Giergl and Flóris Korb. Above the main entrance there is a statue of Franz Liszt, by Alajos Stróbl. The six bas-reliefs above its base are by Ede Telcs, and depict the history of music.

Designed in a unique representation of Art Nouveau style, the building has regained its original splendour and has been outfitted with 21st-century technology. The jewel of the academy is the ornate 860-seat Grand Hall, which is a world-famous concert venue. The building also houses the 300-seat Sir George Solti Chamber Hall, where operas are staged.

⓯ New York Palace

New York Palota

Erzsébet körút 9–11. **Map** 7 B2. **Tel** (06 1) 886 61 11. 4, 6. Ⓜ Blaha Lujza tér. **W boscolohotels.com**

Built between 1891–5 to a design by the architect Alajos Hauszmann, the building was initially the offices of an American insurance firm.

This five-floor edifice displays an eclectic mix of Neo-Baroque and Secession motifs. The sculptures that animate the façade are the work of Károly Senyei.

On the ground floor is the renowned New York Café *(see p204)*. The beautiful, richly gilded Neo-Baroque interior, with its chandeliers and marble pillars, now attracts tourists, just as it once attracted the literary and artistic circles in its heyday. The Boscolo Budapest hotel *(see p187)*, occupies the rest of the building and a luxurious spa, and a restaurant serving international haute cuisine.

The magnificent Grand Hall at the Liszt Ferenc Academy of Music

20 Hungarian National Museum

Nemzeti Múzeum

The Hungarian National Museum is the country's richest source of art and artifacts relating to its own turbulent history. Founded in 1802, the museum owes its existence to Count Ferenc Széchényi, who offered his collection of coins, books and documents to the nation. The museum's constantly expanding collection of art and documents is exhibited in an impressive Neo-Classical edifice built by Mihály Pollack.

Placing the Cornerstone (1864)
This painting by Miklós Barabás shows the ceremony that marked the beginning of construction of the Chain Bridge *(see p66)* in 1842.

Campaign Chest
This carved Baroque campaign chest features the prince regent's decoration and the Hungarian crest. It dates from the insurrection led by Ferenc II Rákóczi *(see p30)*.

Armchair
Adorned with multi-coloured fruit and floral ornamentation, this armchair dates from the early 18th century. It is the work of Ferenc II Rákóczi, who learnt carpentry during his exile in Turkey.

★ Coronation Mantle
This textile masterpiece, made of Byzantine silk, was donated to the church in Székesfehérvár by St Stephen in 1031. It became the coronation mantle in the 12th century.

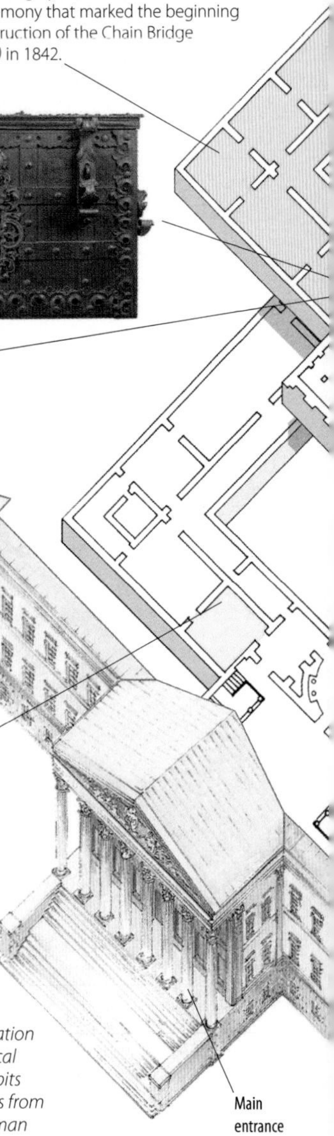

Key

- Coronation mantle
- Archaeological exhibition
- 11th–17th-Century exhibition
- 18th–19th-Century exhibition
- 20th-Century exhibition

Museum Guide

On the first floor is the coronation mantle and the archaeological exhibition. Second floor exhibits comprise Hungarian artifacts from 11th–20th centuries. The Roman Lapidarium is found in the basement.

Main entrance

VISITORS' CHECKLIST

Practical Information
Múzeum körút 14–16. **Map** 7 A4 (10 F5). **Tel** (06 1) 338 21 22 (327 77 73 for guided tours in English).
Open 10am–6pm Tue–Sun.
W **mnm.hu**

Transport
9, 15. 47, 49.
M Kálvin tér, Astória.

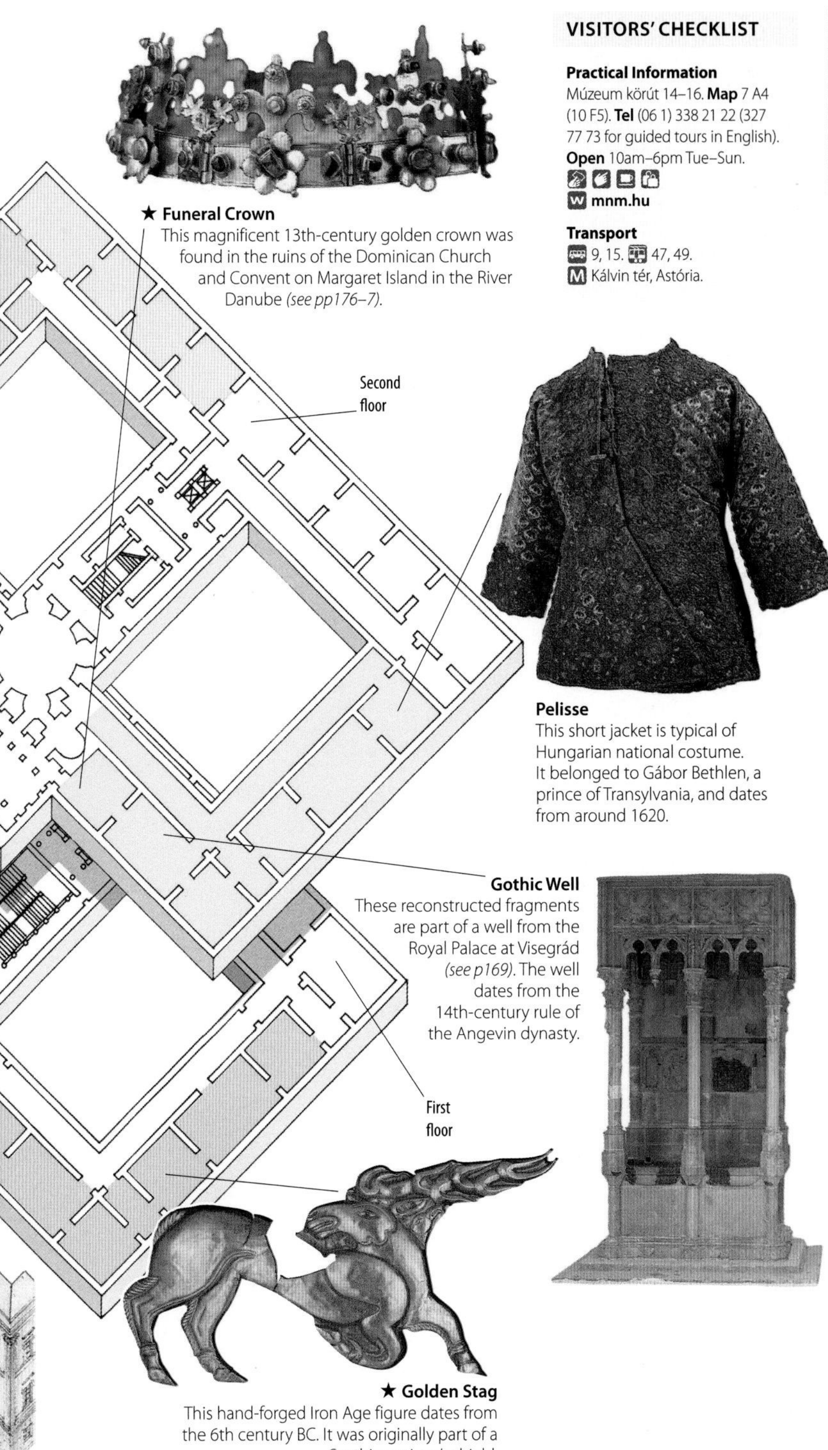

★ Funeral Crown
This magnificent 13th-century golden crown was found in the ruins of the Dominican Church and Convent on Margaret Island in the River Danube *(see pp176–7)*.

Pelisse
This short jacket is typical of Hungarian national costume. It belonged to Gábor Bethlen, a prince of Transylvania, and dates from around 1620.

Gothic Well
These reconstructed fragments are part of a well from the Royal Palace at Visegrád *(see p169)*. The well dates from the 14th-century rule of the Angevin dynasty.

★ Golden Stag
This hand-forged Iron Age figure dates from the 6th century BC. It was originally part of a Scythian prince's shield.

Exploring the Museum's Collection

The steps of the Hungarian National Museum were the scene of a major event in Hungary's history. According to tradition, it was from these steps that, in 1848, the poet Sándor Petőfi first read his *National Song*, which sparked the uprising against Habsburg rule *(see pp32–3)*. This day is commemorated each year on 15 March, when the museum is decorated in the national colours and a re-enactment is performed. Items from the museum's rich collection, including works of art, historical documents and photographs, vividly illustrate this and other events from Hungary's fascinating past.

Monument to poet János Arany in front of the Neo-Classical façade

Museum Building

Built between 1837–47, according to a design by Mihály Pollack, this imposing Neo-Classical building is one of the finest manifestations of that architectural epoch.

The façade is preceded by a monumental portico, which is crowned by a tympanum designed by Raffael Ponti. The composition depicts the figure of Pannonia *(see p22)* among personifications of the arts and sciences.

In the gardens surrounding the museum there are a number of statues of prominent figures from the spheres of literature, science and art. A monument to the poet János Arany, author of the *Toldi Trilogy*, stands in front of the main entrance. This bronze and limestone work dates from 1893 and is by Alajos Stróbl. The notable features of the interior include the magnificent paintings by Mór Than and Károly Lotz in the main staircase.

Coronation Mantle

One of the most important Hungarian treasures, the coronation mantle *(see pp24–5)*, is currently on display in a separate hall of its own in the museum. Made of Byzantine silk, it was originally donated to the church by St Stephen in 1031. The magnificent gown was then refashioned in the 13th century. The now much faded cloth features an intricate embroidered design of fine gold thread and pearls. Remarkably, the royal insignia, which includes a sceptre and golden crown, have survived Hungary's dramatic history. Discovered by the American forces during World War II, they were removed and stored in Fort Knox before being returned to Hungary in 1978.

In 2000, these other treasures of the royal insignia were transferred to the Domed Hall of Parliament *(see pp112–13)*, where they can also be visited.

Archaeological Exhibition

The archaeological display was opened in 2002 to celebrate the 200th anniversary of the museum's foundation. The visitor is taken through a display of Hungary's heritage, spanning the period between 400 BC and AD 804, from the first inhabitants of the country at Vértesszölős until the end of the Early Medieval period, immediately preceeding the Hungarian Conquest.

The exhibition presents some of the latest and important archaeological finds, and abounds in authentic reconstructions of the past.

11th–17th-Century Exhibition

The exhibition begins in the Árpád era and features one of the museum's most valuable exhibits, the crown of Constantine IX Monomachus, decorated with enamel work. Also on display in this section are the funeral decorations of Béla III, Romanesque sacred vessels, weapons and an interesting collection of coins and minting tools.

Carved base of a chalice dating from the 15th century

The period of Angevin rule *(see p20)* coincided with the birth of the Gothic style, which is represented here by some excellent examples of gold work. The next two halls explore the reign of Sigismund of Luxembourg *(see p26)* and the achievements of János Hunyadi *(see p26)*. On display here are copies of portraits of King Sigismund by Albrecht Dürer and a richly decorated ceremonial saddle. There are also several platinum and gold pieces, illuminated manuscripts and documents. The lifestyle of peasants from this era is illustrated, as well as the history of the royal court.

The reign of Mátyás Corvinus *(see pp26–7)* and the Jagiellonian dynasty *(see p20)* marks the decline of the Gothic period and the birth of the Renaissance. Exhibits from this era include a 15th-century glass goblet belonging to King Mátyás, late Gothic pews from a church in Bártfa, armour and weapons, as well as a 16th-century dress belonging to Maria Habsburg.

Magnificent examples of sculpture, art and artifacts from the 16th and 17th centuries follow. Of interest are items that survived the Turkish occupation *(see pp28–9)*, especially the everyday objects and weapons.

Brooch from the 18th-century

A separate hall is dedicated to the Transylvanian principality and the important historical role that it played. Exhibited here are vessels and jewellery elaborately crafted in gold, 17th-century costumes, and original ceramics produced by the people of Haban, who settled there in the early 17th century. This last section of the exhibition ends in 1686, at the time of the liberation of Buda by the Christian armies after the Turkish occupation. In this part of the museum there are also portraits of influential Hungarians from the period, and an interesting exhibition of jewellery dating from the 17th century.

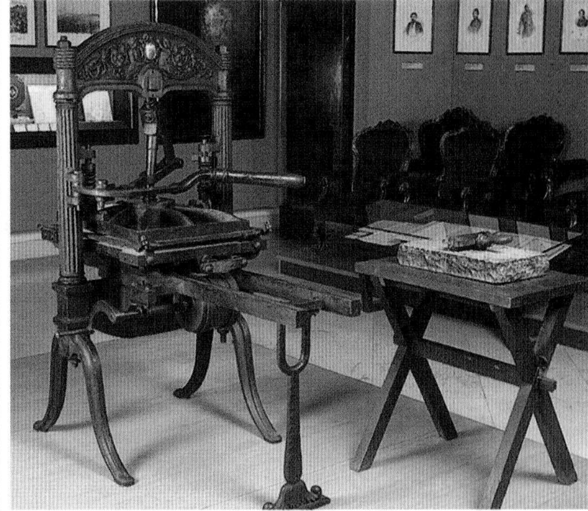

Printing press used in 1848 to print nationalist propaganda

18th–19th-Century Exhibition

This part of the museum covers Habsburg rule, a period of great civil unrest. The exhibition begins with artifacts connected to the Rákóczi insurrection of 1703–11 *(see pp30–31)*. Weapons, as well as furniture from Ferenc II Rákóczi's palace, are exhibited here. One item of particular interest is the armchair produced by Rákóczi himself.

The next hall is dedicated to 18th-century Hungarian art and culture.

The following rooms portray the Hungarian history of the first half of the 19th century. Artworks, including magnificent portraits and historic paintings, such as *Placing the Cornerstone of the Chain Bridge*, are

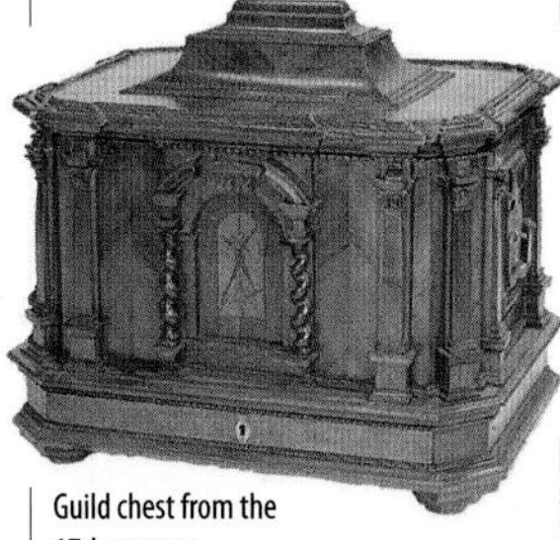

Guild chest from the 17th century

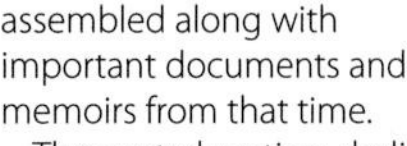

assembled along with important documents and memoirs from that time.

The central section, dedicated to the uprising of 1848–9 *(see pp32–3)*, features a printing press on which were printed leaflets outlining the 12 demands in Hungary's fight for independence from Austria.

The exhibits from the second half of the 19th century include collections of masonic items, official decorations, coins and historic manuscripts. Items relating to the coronation of Franz Joseph in 1867 and the Millennium Celebrations of 1896 are also displayed here.

20th-Century Exhibition

Reflecting the technical developments of this century, Hungary's recent history is presented in a documentary style. Photographs, and documents are widely used to illustrate this period. Artifacts relating to World War I and the era of revolution between the wars, and shocking documents from World War II can be found here. The post-war history of Hungary is depicted mainly from a political perspective. Emphasis is placed on significant episodes, such as the uprising of 1956 and the events of 1989, which signalled the end of Communism in Eastern Europe *(see p37)*.

⓰ Jewish Quarter

Zsidó Negyed

Király utca, Rumbach Sebestyén utca, Dohány utca & Akácfa utca. **Map** 2 F5 & 7 A2 (10 F3). 47, 49. M Deák Ferenc tér, Astoria.

Jews first came to Hungary in the 13th century and settled in Buda and Óbuda. In the 19th century, a larger Jewish community was established outside the Pest city boundary, in a small area of Erzsébetváros.

In 1251, King Béla IV gave the Jews of Buda certain priviliges, including freedom of religion.

Window of the Orthodox Synagogue

Holocaust Memorial

This sculpture of a weeping willow, designed by Imre Varga, was unveiled in 1991 in memory of the 600,000 Hungarian Jews killed by the Nazis in World War II. It was partly funded by the Hungarian-American actor Tony Curtis.

The Jewish community became well integrated into Hungarian society, until in 1941, a series of Nazi anti-Semitic laws were passed and the wearing of the Star of David was made compulsory. In 1944, a ghetto was created in Pest and the deportation of thousands of Jews to camps, including Auschwitz, was implemented. After heavy fighting between the Russian and German armies, the Soviet Red Army liberated the ghetto on 18 January 1945. In total, 600,000 Hungarian Jews were victims of the Holocaust. This persecution is commemorated by a plaque at the Orthodox Synagogue on Rumbach utca.

In the late 19th century, three synagogues were built and many Jewish shops and workshops were established. Kosher establishments, such as the butcher at No. 41 Kazinczy utca, were a common feature. Shops are now being reconstructed to recreate the pre-ghetto character of the Jewish Quarter.

⓱ Great Synagogue

Zsinagóga

Dohány utca 2. **Map** 4 F1 (10 F4). **Tel** (06 1) 462 04 77. M Astoria. Jewish Museum: **Open** Mar–Oct: 10am–6pm Sun–Thu, 10am–4pm Fri; Nov–Feb: 10am–4pm Sun–Thu, 10am–2pm Fri.

This synagogue is the largest in Europe. It was built in a Byzantine-Moorish style by the Viennese architect Ludwig Förster between 1854–9. It has three naves and, following orthodox tradition, separate galleries for women. Together the naves and galleries can accommodate up to 3,000 worshippers. Some features, such as the position of the reading platform, reflect elements of Judaic reform. The interior has valuable decorative fittings, particularly those on the Ark of the Law, by Frigyes Feszl. In 1931, a museum was established; a vast collection of historical relics, Judaic devotional items and everday objects, from ancient Rome to the present day, has been assembled. It includes the book of Chevra Kadisha from 1792. There is also a moving Holocaust Memorial Room.

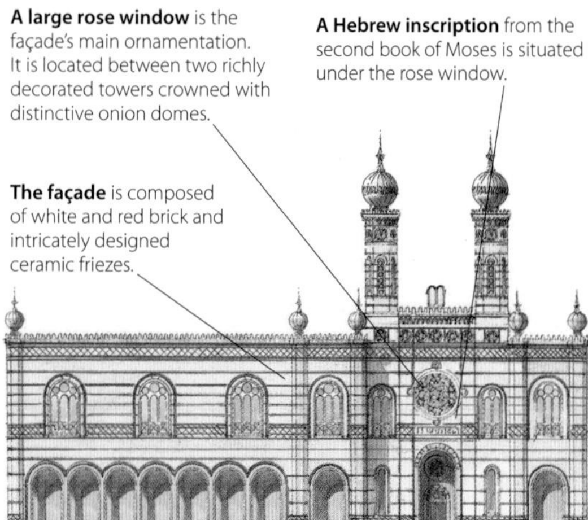

⑱ Chapel of St Roch

Szent Rókus Kápolna

Gyulai Pál u 2. **Map** 7 A3. **Tel** (06 1) 338 35 15. 7. 4, 6. Blaha Lujza tér.

Pest town council built this chapel in what was then an uninhabited area. It was dedicated to St Roch and St Rosalie, who were believed to provide protection against the plague, which afflicted Pest in 1711.

In 1740 the chapel was extended to its present size, and a tower was added in 1797. The façade is decorated with Baroque figures of saints, although the originals were replaced with copies in 1908.

Inside, on the right-hand wall of the chapel's nave, is a painting of the Virgin Mary from 1740. A painting by Jakab Warsch, depicting the Great Flood of 1838, is in the oratory.

⑲ Mihály Pollack Square

Pollack Mihály Tér

Map 7 A4 (10 F5). Kálvin tér. Festetics Palace: **Tel** (06 1) 266 31 01. by prior arrangement.

At the rear of the Hungarian National Museum *(see pp134–7)* is a square named after Mihály Pollack, the architect of several Neo-Classical buildings such as the museum and Sándor Palace *(see p77)*.

In the late 19th century, three palaces were built side by side on this square for the aristocratic elite of Hungary: Prince Festetics, Prince Eszterházy and Count Károlyi. The beautiful façades makes this one of the city's most captivating squares.

Miklós Ybl *(see p98)* built the French-Renaissance style palace at No. 6 for Lajos Károlyi, in 1863–5. The façade is decorated with sculptures by Károly Schaffer. There is also a covered driveway for carriages. Next door, at No. 8, is a small palace, which was built in 1865 for the Eszterházy family by Alajos Baumgarten. At No. 10 is the palace built for the Festetics family in 1862, again by Miklós Ybl. The interior, especially the Neo-Baroque staircase, is splendid.

Magnificent staircase inside the Festetics Palace on Mihály Pollack Square

⑳ Hungarian National Museum

See pp134–7.

㉑ Ervin Szabó Library

Szabó Ervin Könyvtàr

Szabó Ervin tér 1. **Map** 7 A4 (10 F5). **Tel** (06 1) 411 50 00. Kálvin tér. **Open** 10am–8pm Mon–Fri, 10am–4pm Sat. **fszek.hu**

In 1887, the wealthy industrialist Wenckheim family commissioned the architect Artur Meinig to build a Neo-Baroque and Rococo style palace. The result was the former Wenckheim Palace, regarded as one of the most beautiful palaces in Budapest. The magnificent wrought-iron gates, dating from 1897, are the work of Gyula Jungfer. Also worth particular attention are the richly gilded salons on the first floor, as well as the dome above an oval panel of reliefs.

Spiral staircase in one of the rooms of the Ervin Szabó Library

In 1926, the city council acquired the building and converted it into a public lending library, whose collection focuses on the city itself and the social sciences.

The Ervin Szabó Library was named after the politician and social reformer Ervin Szabó (1877–1918), who was the library's first director. It has over a hundred branches throughout Budapest and some three million books.

㉒ Calvinist Church

Református Templom

Kálvin tér 7. **Map** 4 F2. **Tel** (06 1) 217 67 69. Kálvin tér. **Open** 6pm Thu; 10am, 11:30am, 6pm Sun.

This single nave church was designed by József Hofrichter and built between 1816–30. In 1848 József Hild designed the four-pillared façade and tympanum, and a spire was added in 1859. Inside the church, the pulpit and choir gallery were designed by Hild in 1831 and 1854 respectively. The stained-glass windows are the work of Miksa Róth. Sacred artifacts from the 17th and 18th centuries are kept in the church treasury.

23 Museum of Applied Arts

Iparművészeti Múzeum

Opened in 1896 by Emperor Franz Joseph for the Millennium Celebrations, this collection is housed not within a Neo-Classical building, but in an outstanding Secession building designed by Gyula Pártos and Ödön Lechner *(see p58)*. The exterior incorporated elements inspired by the Orient as well as the Zsolnay ceramics characteristic of Lechner's work. Damaged in 1945 and again in 1956, the building has now regained its original magnificence. The collection, founded in 1872, includes many examples of arts and crafts workmanship.

18th-Century Perfumer
The base of this decorative perfumer comes from Paris, the porcelain figure from Meissen in Germany.

Inner Courtyard
This courtyard, covered by a glazed roof, is surrounded by cloisters with arcades designed in an Indian-Oriental style.

Main Entrance
The walls of the entrance are covered by Zsolnay ceramics.

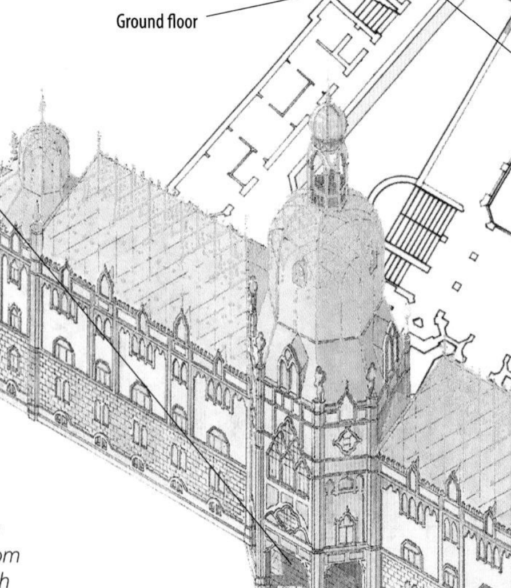

Museum Guide

The museum is home to various temporary exhibitions. Pieces from the permanent collections, which include furniture, textiles, precious metals, ceramics and glassware, are illustrated here. The major exhibitions change each year, while the smaller national and foreign displays change monthly. The library is located on the first floor and contains around 50,000 books. The second floor houses a permanent exhibition on Islamic art.

Key

- Library
- Temporary exhibitions
- Permanent collections

Renaissance Tile
This tile, which dates from around 1530, depicts Queen Anne, wife of Ferdinand I.

VISITORS' CHECKLIST

Practical Information
Űllői út 33–37. **Map** 7 B5.
Tel (06 1) 456 51 07. **Open** 10am–6pm Tue–Sun (closure for renovations is planned so phone ahead). **imm.hu**

Transport
4, 6. Corvin-Negyed.

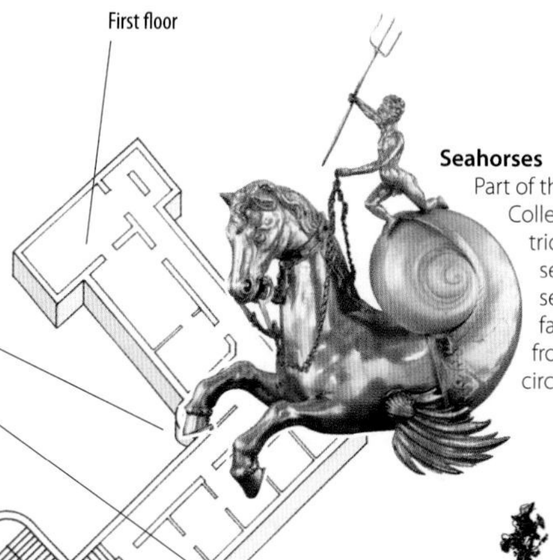

Seahorses
Part of the Goldsmiths' Collection, two trident-wielding sea satyrs ride seahorses in this fanciful piece from Germany, circa 1590.

Astronomical Clock
Medieval craftsmanship distinguishes this ornate astronomical clock from 1566, which displays the relative positions of the sun, moon and constellations.

Holics Dish
Animal and plant-shaped kitchen ceramics in the Holics style were manufactured in Hungary in the mid-18th century.

Devotional Tablet
This csóktábla or "kiss tablet" was crafted in Limoges, France, at the beginning of the 16th century.

㉔ Central Market Hall

Központi Vásárcsarnok

Vámház körút 1-3. **Map** 4 F3. **Tel** (06 1) 366 33 00. 🚋 2, 47, 49. Ⓜ Fővám tér. **Open** 6am–5pm Mon, 6am–6pm Tue–Fri, 6am–3pm Sat. **Closed** Sun.

Rebuilt in 1999, Budapest's main produce market is a great place to find local delicacies such as spicy *kolbász* salami and sheep's cheese. There are numerous farmers' stalls selling meat, sausage, fruit, vegetables and fish. The upper floor has a dozen or so food booths and souvenir stalls selling paprika, caviar, Hungarian dolls, T-shirts and chessboards. The basement level has a small grocery store selling imported delicacies.

Sausages for sale at the Central Market Hall

Decorative element on the façade of the City Council Chamber

㉕ City Council Chamber

Új Városháza

Váci utca 62–64. **Map** 4 F2 (10 E5). Ⓜ Deák tér. **Tel** (06 1) 235 17 00. **Open** 8am–noon Fri. compulsory

This three-floor edifice was built between 1870–75 as offices for the newly unified city of Budapest *(see p34)*. Its architect, Imre Steindl, was also responsible for designing Parliament *(see pp112–13)*.

The building is a mix of styles. The exterior is a Neo-Renaissance design in brick, with grotesques between the windows, while the interior features cast-iron Neo-Gothic motifs. The Great Debating Hall is decorated with mosaics designed by Károly Lotz.

Many antiquarian bookshops and galleries can be found around here. Fashionable bars, restaurants and cafés, and pedestrianization of the streets, make this a charming area.

㉖ Serbian Church

Szerb Templom

Szerb utca 2–4. **Map** 4 F2 (10 E5). Ⓜ Kálvin tér, Ferenciek tere. **Open** 10am–6pm Tue–Sun.

Serbs settled in the now largely residential area around the church as early as the 16th century. The end of the 17th century brought a new wave of Serb immigrants, and by the early 19th century Serbs comprised almost 25 per cent of Pest's home-owners.

In 1698, the Serb community replaced an earlier church on the site with this Baroque one. The church gained its final appearance after a rebuilding project that lasted until the mid-18th century, probably undertaken by András Meyerhoffer.

The interior of the church is arranged according to Greek Orthodox practice. A section of the nave, which is entered from the vestibule, is reserved for women. This area is divided from the men's section by a partition, and the division is further emphasized by the floor, which has been lowered by 30 cm (1 ft). The choir gallery is enclosed by an iconostasis that divides it from the sanctuary. This iconostasis dates from around 1850. The carving is by Serb sculptor Miahai Janic; Renaissance-influenced paintings are by Greek artist Károly Sterio.

Ceramic tile from the Serbian Church

㉗ Loránd Eötvös University

Eötvös Loránd Tudomány Egyetem Központja

Egyetem tér 1–3. **Map** 4 F2 (10 E5). Ⓜ Ferenciek tere, Kálvin tér. **Tel** (06 1) 411 65 00. **elte.hu**

In 1635, Cardinal Péter Pázmány, the leader of the Counter-Reformation, established a university in Nagyszombat (now Trnava in Slovakia). It moved to Buda in 1777, nearly a century after the end of the Turkish occupation *(see pp28–9)*, during the reign of Maria Theresa. Emperor Joseph II transferred the university to Pest, to the environs of the Pauline Church, now called the University Church.

It was not until 1889 that the university was endowed with a permanent home. This Neo-Baroque building, now the Law Faculty, was designed by architects including Sándor Baumgarten and Fülöp Herzog.

The university is named after the noted physicist Lóránd Eötvös (1848–1919).

㉘ University Church

Egyetemi Templom

Papnövelde utca 5–7. **Map** 4 F2 (10 E5). **Tel** (06 1) 318 05 55. Ⓜ Kálvin tér. **Open** 7am–6pm Mon–Sat, 8am–7:30pm Sun.

This single-nave church is considered one of the most impressive Baroque churches in the city. It was built for the Pauline Order in 1725–42, and was probably designed by András Meyerhoffer. The tower was added in 1771. The Pauline Order, founded in 1263 by Canon Euzsbius, was the only religious order to be founded in Hungary.

The magnificent exterior features a tympanum and a row of pilasters that divide the façade. Figures of St Paul and St Anthony flank the emblem of the Pauline Order, which crowns the exterior. The carved-wood interior of the main vestibule is also worth particular mention.

Inside the church a row of side chapels stand behind unusual marble pilasters. In 1776 Johann Bergl painted the vaulted ceiling with frescoes depicting scenes from the life of Mary. Sadly, these frescoes are now in poor condition.

The main altar dates from 1746, and the carved statues behind it are the work of József Hebenstreit. Above it, a copy of the painting *The Black Madonna of Czestochowa,* is thought to date from 1720. Much of the Baroque interior detail of the church is the work of the Pauline monks, such as the balustrade of the organ loft and the carved pulpit on the right.

Sculptures decorating the pulpit in the University Church

Tympanum adorning the façade of the University Library

㉙ Károlyi Palace

Károlyi Palota

Károlyi utca 16. **Map** 4 F2 (10 E5). **Tel** (06 1) 317 36 11. Ⓜ Ferenciek tere, Kálvin tér. Petőfi Exhibition: **Open** 10am–6pm Tue–Sun (until 4pm Nov–Feb). 317 36 11. **w** **pim.hu**

In 1696 there was a small Baroque palace on this site, which was extended by András Mayerhoffer between 1759–68. Subsequent rebuilding, which gave the palace a Neo-Classical appearance, was undertaken between 1832–41 by Anton Riegl. It is named after Mihály Károlyi, leader of the 1918–19 Hungarian Republic *(see p36),* who was born here in 1875.

The palace now houses the Hungarian Museum of Literature and the Petőfi Exhibition, dedicated to the poet Sándor Petőfi *(see p33).* Other poets remembered are Atilla József, Endre Ady and Mór Jókai.

㉚ University Library

Egyetemi Könyvtár

Ferenciek tere 6. **Map** 4 F1 (10 E5). **Tel** (06 1) 266 58 66. Ⓜ Ferenciek tere, Kálvin tér. **Open** 10am–8pm Mon–Fri.

This Neo-Renaissance Edifice, by Antal Szkalniczyky and Henrik Koch, was built from 1873–6. It is distinguished by the dome on the corner tower. The library's two million works include 11 *Corviniani (see p76)* and 160 medieval manuscripts and miniatures. The reading room has sgraffiti by Mór Than and frescoes by Károly Lotz.

㉛ Franciscan Church

Belvárosi Ferences Templom

Ferenciek tere 9. **Map** 4 F1 (10 E4). **Tel** (06 1) 317 33 22. Ⓜ Ferenciek tere. **Open** 7am–noon, 4–8pm daily.

A Franciscan church and monastery have stood on this site, beyond the old city walls, since the 13th century. In 1541 the Turks rebuilt the church as the Mosque of Sinan, but after the liberation *(see pp28–9)* the monks regained the building. Between 1727–43 they remodelled the church in the Baroque style, which it still retains today.

The façade features a magnificent portal incorporating sculptures of Franciscan saints, and the Franciscan emblem crowned by a figure of Mary being adored by angels.

The interior of the church is decorated with frescoes, dating from 1894–5, by Károly Lotz and paintings by Viktor Tardos Krenner, from 1925–6. The jewel of this church is the Baroque main altar with sculptures that date from 1741 and 1851. The side altars and the pulpit date from 1851–2.

AROUND VÁROSLIGET

Városliget, or City Park, was once an area of marshland, which served as a royal hunting ground. Leopold I gave the land to the town of Pest, but it was in the mid-18th century, under Maria Theresa, that the area was drained and planted. Today's park was designed towards the end of the 19th century in the English style, which was the fashion of the day. Városliget was chosen as the focus of the Millennium Celebrations in 1896 *(see p146)*, which marked the 1,000-year anniversary of the conquest of the Carpathian basin by the Magyars. A massive building programme was undertaken, which included the Museum of Fine Arts, Vajdahunyad Castle and the impressive monument in Heroes' Square.

Sights at a Glance

Museums

1 House of Terror Museum
2 Franz Liszt Museum
4 Kodály Memorial Museum
6 Postal Museum
7 Zelnik István Southeast Asian Gold Museum
9 Műcsarnok Art Gallery
10 *Museum of Fine Arts pp150–51*

Parks and Zoos

12 Zoo

Streets and Monuments

5 Városligeti Avenue
8 Millennium Monument
14 Hermina Street

Historic Buildings

3 University of Fine Art
11 Vajdahunyad Castle
13 Széchenyi Baths
15 Erkel Theatre

Restaurants *pp204–205*

1 Bagolyvár Étterem
2 Bock Bisztró
3 Ecocafe
4 Grundel Étterem
5 Haxen Király Étterem
6 Himalaya Nepáli Étterem
7 Kogart Étterem
8 Millennium da Pippo
9 Montenegrói Gurman
10 Napfényes Étterem
11 Olimpia Étterem
12 Paprika Vendéglő
13 La Perle Noire
14 Platán Étterem
15 Rákóczi Grillház
16 Regős Vendéglő
17 Robinson
18 Széchenyi Kertvendéglő
19 Zeller Bistro

See also Street Finder maps 5, 6, 7 & 8

◀ One of the outdoor pools at Széchenyi Baths

Street-by-Street: Around Heroes' Square

Heroes' Square is a relic of a proud era in Hungary's history. It was here that the Millennium Celebrations opened in 1896. A striking example of this national pride is the Millennium Monument. Its colonnades feature statues of renowned Hungarian leaders and politicians, and the grand central column is crowned by a figure of the Archangel Gabriel. Vajdahunyad Castle was built in Városliget, or City Park, adjacent to the square. Probably the most flamboyant expression of the celebrations, it is composed of elements of the finest architectural works found throughout Hungary.

⑩ ★ Museum of Fine Arts
This monumental museum building has an eight-pillared portico supporting a tympanum.

Entrance to the Zoo

Millennium Monument Dominating Heroes' Square, this monument includes a sculpted chariot representing war by György Zala.

⑨ Műcsarnok Art Gallery
The crest of Hungary decorates the façade of this building – the country's largest venue for artistic exhibitions.

City Park Boating Lake and Ice Rink

The Hungarian Millennium Celebrations

The Millennium Celebrations in 1896 marked a high point in the development of Budapest and in the history of the Austro-Hungarian monarchy. The city underwent modernization on a scale unknown in Europe at that time. Hundreds of houses, palaces and civic buildings were constructed, gas lighting was introduced and continental Europe's first underground transport system was opened.

Archangel Gabriel

Key

— Suggested route

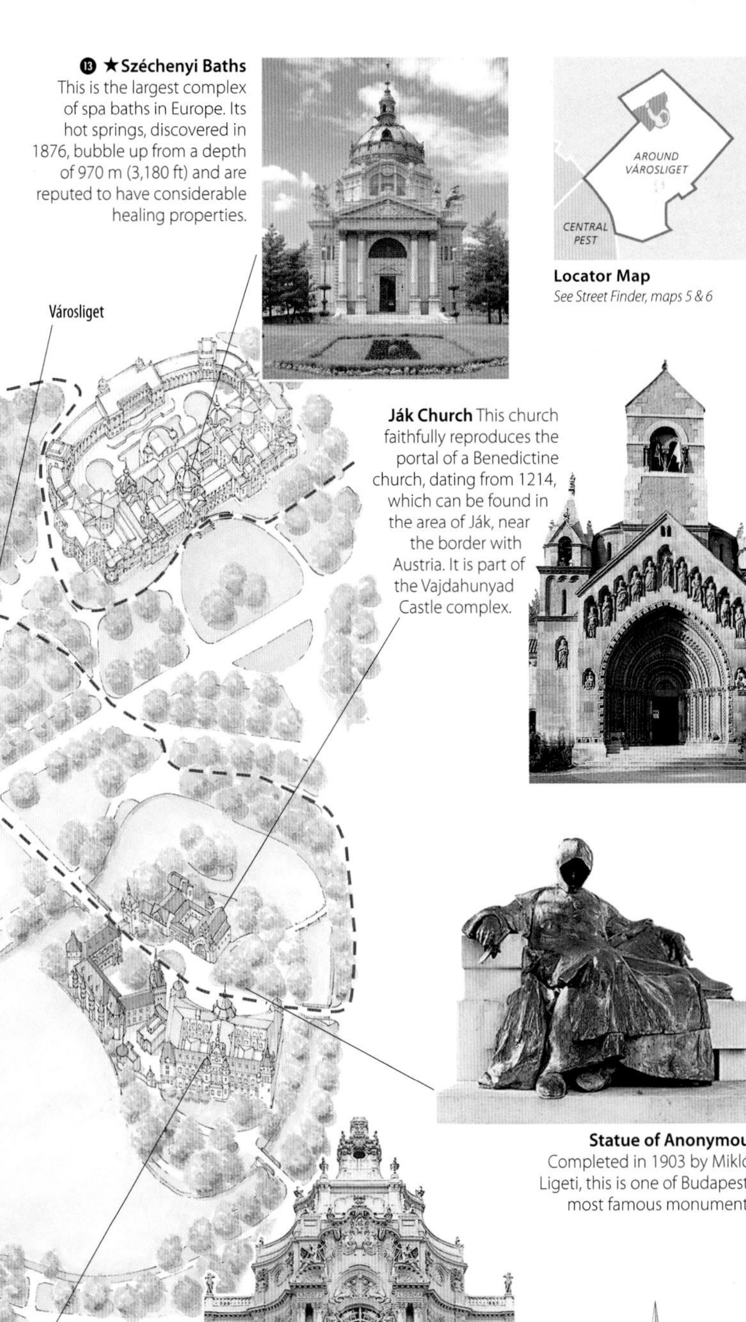

⓭ ★Széchenyi Baths
This is the largest complex of spa baths in Europe. Its hot springs, discovered in 1876, bubble up from a depth of 970 m (3,180 ft) and are reputed to have considerable healing properties.

Locator Map
See Street Finder, maps 5 & 6

Ják Church This church faithfully reproduces the portal of a Benedictine church, dating from 1214, which can be found in the area of Ják, near the border with Austria. It is part of the Vajdahunyad Castle complex.

Statue of Anonymous
Completed in 1903 by Miklós Ligeti, this is one of Budapest's most famous monuments.

⓫ ★ Vajdahunyad Castle
This Baroque section of the castle houses the Museum of Agriculture.

0 metres 200
0 yards 200

The former headquarters of the secret police on Andrássy Avenue

❶ House of Terror Museum

Teror Háza Múzeum

Andrássy út 60. **Map** 2 F5 (10 E2). **Tel** (06 1) 374 26 00. 4, 6 to Oktogon. Vörösmarty utca. **Open** 10am–6pm Tue–Sun. **terrorhaza.hu**

The museum is located in the former headquarters of the secret police of both the Nazi and Communist governments. It records the grim events and practices of the "double occupation" of Hungary at the end of World War II.

❷ Franz Liszt Museum

Liszt Ferenc Emlékmúzeum

Vörösmarty utca 35. **Map** 5 A5. **Tel** (06 1) 322 98 04. Vörösmarty utca. **Open** 10am–6pm Mon–Fri, 9am–5pm Sat. **lisztmuseum.hu**

This Neo-Renaissance corner house was designed in 1877 by Adolf Lang. Above the windows of the second floor are bas-reliefs depicting famous composers – J S Bach, Wolfgang Amadeus Mozart, Joseph Haydn, Ferenc Erkel, Ludwig van Beethoven, and Franz Liszt himself. Liszt not only lived in this house, but also established an Academy of Music in the city *(see p133)*.

In 1986, 100 years after Liszt's death, a museum was established in his house. Various items were assembled here, including documents, furniture and two pianos on which he composed and practised.

❸ University of Fine Art

Képzőművészeti Egyetem

Andrássy út 69–71. **Map** 5 A5. **Tel** (06 1) 342 17 38. Vörösmarty utca. Barcsay Gallery: **Open** 10am–6pm Mon–Fri, 10am–1pm Sat (seasonal). **mke.hu**

The university began as a drawing school, later becoming a Higher School of Art. Since 1876, it has occupied these adjacent buildings on Andrássy Street.

The two-floor Neo-Renaissance building at No. 71 was designed in 1875, by Lajos Rauscher. Its façade is decorated with sgrafitti by Robert Scholtz. The Italianate Renaissance exterior of No. 69, designed by Adolf Lang from 1875–7, is distinguished by Corinthian pilasters and a full-length balcony. The entrance hall and first-floor corridor feature frescoes by Károly Lotz. Only the Barcsay Gallery is open to visitors, but the interior can be glimpsed from here.

Sgrafitto by Robert Scholtz

Original furnishings in the salon at the Franz Liszt Museum

❹ Kodály Memorial Museum

Kodály Zoltán Emlékmúzeum

Andrássy út 89. **Map** 5 B5. **Tel** (06 1) 352 71 06. Kodály Körönd. **Open** 10am–noon & 2–4:30pm Wed–Fri (by appointment only). **Closed** Mon, Tue, Sat & Sun. **kodaly.hu**

Zoltán Kodály (1881–1967) was one of the greatest Hungarian composers of the 20th century. His profound knowledge of Hungarian folk music allowed him to use elements of it in his compositions, which reflected the fashion for Impressionism and Neo-Romanticism in music.

This museum was established in 1990 and occupies the house where he lived and worked from 1924 until his death in 1967. A plaque set into one of the walls of the house bears testimony to this fact. The museum consists of three rooms that have been preserved in their original style, and a fourth room that is used for exhibitions. An archive has also been created here, for the composer's valuable handwritten music scores and correspondence.

Worthy of attention are the composer's piano in the salon and a number of folklore ceramics which Kodály collected in the course of his ethnographical studies. Portraits and busts of Kodály by Lajos Petri can also be viewed.

❺ Városligeti Avenue

Városligeti Fasor

Map 5 C5. Hosök tere.

This beautiful street, lined with plane trees, leads from Lövölde tér to Városliget.

At the beginning of the avenue is Városliget Calvinist church built in 1912–13 by Aladár Árkay. This stark edifice is virtually bereft of any architectural features. However, stylized, geometric folk motifs have been used as ornamentation

Post delivery car and bike on display at the Postal Museum

and harmonize with the interior Secession decoration.

In front of the church is the Ráth György Museum, displaying artifacts from China, Korea and Japan collected in the 19th century.

Further along the avenue is a Lutheran church. It was constructed between 1903–5 to a Neo-Gothic design by Samu Pecz, who also designed the interior detail. Worthy of note is the painting on the high altar, by Gyula Benczúr, entitled *The Adoration of the Magi*.

❻ Postal Museum

Postamúzeum

Benczúr utca 27. **Map** 5 B5. **Tel** (06 1) 269 68 38. M Bajza utca. **Open** 10am–6pm Tue–Sun. W **postamuzeum.hu**

The Hungarian Postal Museum is located in the former mansion of the Egyedi Family. It was built in Neo-Renaissance style in 1897, with stained-glass windows crafted by Miksa Róth, a famous craftsman of the late 19th century. An exhibition on the history of the Royal Hungarian Post Office includes working telegraphs, telephone exchanges, the first post delivery car from 1905, and an electric car used in the 21st century.

❼ Zelnik István Southeast Asian Gold Museum

Zelnik István Délkelet-Ázsiai Aranymúzeum

Andrássy út 110. **Map** 5 B4. **Tel** (06 1) 482 31 90. M Bajza utca. **Open** 11am–5pm Mon–Thu, 11am–7pm Fri–Sat, 11am–5pm Sun. W **thegoldmuseum.eu**

Housed in a beautiful 19th-century villa, this private museum showcases a unique collection of Southeast-Asian art. The exhibits have been selected from the private collection of Dr. István Zelnik, a former diplomat from Southeast Asia.

The collection features Asian gold and silver objects from prehistoric times to the 20th century. The highlights of the collection include the artifacts from Khmer and tribal cultures. In the museum's teahouse rare Asian tea and coffee are served in porcelain cups.

❽ Millennium Monument

Millenniumi Emlékmű

Map 5 C4. M Hosök tere.

This monument was designed by György Zala and Albert Schikedanz to commemorate Hungary's Millennium Celebrations in 1896, but was not completed until 1929.

At the centre of the monument is a 36-m (120-ft) high Corinthian column, upon which stands the Archangel Gabriel holding St István's crown and the apostolic cross. These objects signify Hungary's conversion to Christianity under King István *(see p24)*. At the base of the column there are equestrian statues of Prince Árpád and six of the conquering Magyar warriors.

A stone tile set in front of the column marks the Tomb of the Unknown Soldier.

The column is embraced by two curved colonnades, featuring allegorical compositions at both ends. Personifications of War and Peace are nearest the column, while Knowledge and Glory crown the far end of the right-hand colonnade, and Labour and Prosperity crown the far end of the left. Statues of great Hungarians, including statesmen and monarchs, are arranged within the colonnades.

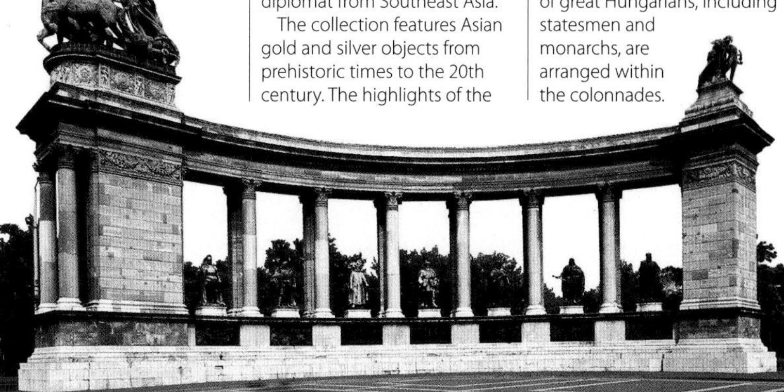

The right-hand colonnade of the Millennium Monument on Heroes' Square, completed in 1929

⑩ Museum of Fine Arts

Szépművészeti Múzeum

The origins of the Museum of Fine Arts' comprehensive collection date from 1870, when the state bought a magnificent collection of paintings from the artistocratic Esterházy family. The museum's collection was enriched by donations and acquisitions, and in 1906 it moved to its present location. The building, by Fülöp Herzog and Albert Schickedanz, is Neo-Classical with Italian-Renaissance influences. The tympanum crowning the portico is supported by eight Corinthian columns. It depicts the Battle of the Centaurs and Lapiths, and is copied from the Temple of Zeus at Olympia, Greece.

The Water Carrier
(c. 1810)
La Aquadora demonstrates the full range of Francisco de Goya's artistic talent.

First floor

The Fall of Man
(c. 1620)
The Flemish artist, Jacob Jordaens, worked alongside van Dyck and was Rubens' principal associate.

★ Esterházy Madonna
(c. 1508)
This unfinished picture by Raphael is so named because it became the property of the Esterházy family at the beginning of the 19th century.

Lower ground floor

St James Conquers the Moors
(1750)
Giambattista Tiepolo portrayed the miraculous appearance of the saint during a battle at Clavijo in 844.

Key

- Egyptian artifacts
- Classical artifacts
- German art
- Dutch and Flemish art
- European sculpture
- Italian art
- Spanish art
- French and British art
- Drawings and graphic art
- 19th- and 20th-century works
- Temporary exhibitions

View of Amsterdam (c. 1656)
Jacob van Ruisdael was a master of Dutch realist landscape painting. He greatly influenced the development of European landscape painting in the 19th century.

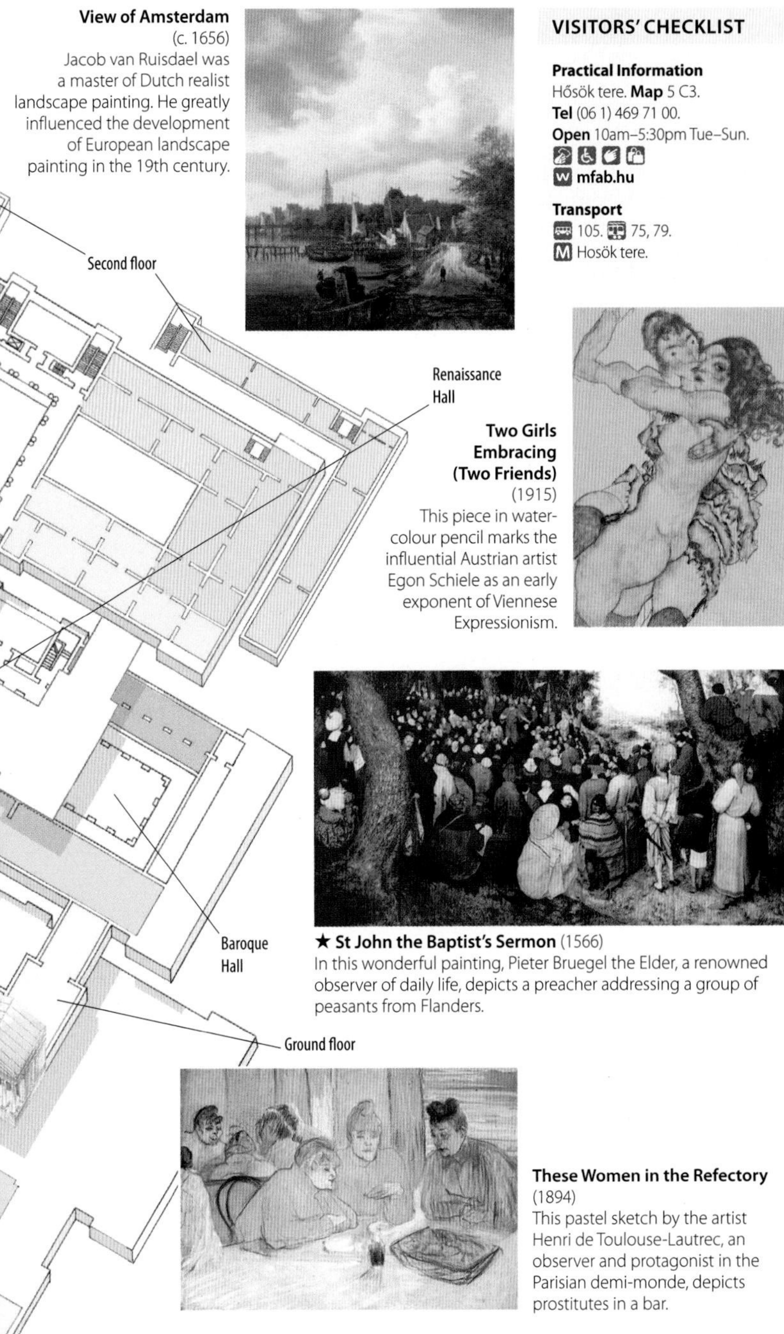

VISITORS' CHECKLIST

Practical Information
Hősök tere. **Map** 5 C3.
Tel (06 1) 469 71 00.
Open 10am–5:30pm Tue–Sun.
mfab.hu

Transport
105. 75, 79.
Hosök tere.

Two Girls Embracing (Two Friends) (1915)
This piece in watercolour pencil marks the influential Austrian artist Egon Schiele as an early exponent of Viennese Expressionism.

★ **St John the Baptist's Sermon** (1566)
In this wonderful painting, Pieter Bruegel the Elder, a renowned observer of daily life, depicts a preacher addressing a group of peasants from Flanders.

These Women in the Refectory (1894)
This pastel sketch by the artist Henri de Toulouse-Lautrec, an observer and protagonist in the Parisian demi-monde, depicts prostitutes in a bar.

Museum Guide

As a result of continuous renovation work on the building, not all the rooms are currently open to the public. Future reconstruction work will involve closure of the museum, so check the website before visiting.

Exploring the Museum of Fine Arts

The museum's collection encompasses international art dating from antiquity to the 20th century. As well as Egyptian, Greek and Roman artifacts, the museum houses galleries dedicated to a variety of modern art. Alongside its interesting collection of sculptures, there are priceless drawings and works of graphic art. Over the next few years the museum will be undergoing a process of redevelopment. In spite of this, exhibits will continue to be open to the public throughout the duration of the restoration work. Individual collections will simply be moved to different locations as building work progresses.

Egyptian Artifacts

Egyptian artifacts have been exhibited in the museum since 1939. Principally, they are the result of 19th-century excavations that involved Hungarian archaeologists.

The rich collection includes stone sculptures from each historic period, from the Old Kingdom to the Ptolemy dynasty. A nobleman's head of a votive statue dates from the New Kingdom and is a particularly beautiful example.

Also worthy of note is the collection of small bronze figures, which also date mainly from the New Kingdom, together with domestic objects that illustrate everyday life.

Classical Artifacts

The collection of Classical artifacts is rather varied. It encompasses works of Greek, Etruscan, and Roman works.

Detail of a hunting scene on a 3rd-century AD Greek sarcophagus

Albrecht Dürer's simple yet beautiful *Portrait of a Young Man*

The collection of Greek vases ranks as one of the best of its kind in Europe. A black-figure amphora by Exekias and a kylix from the studio of the painter Andokides are very fine examples of this work.

Bronze work, which dates from various epochs, including the famous Grimani jug from the 5th century BC, gold jewellery, and marble and terracotta sculptures are all exquisite artifacts from this era.

German Art

Among the most valuable works in the collection are the *Portrait of a Young Man*, by Albrecht Dürer, and the carefully composed painting of *The Dormition of Mary*, by Hans Holbein. The work of such masters as Hans Baldung Grien and Lucas Cranach are worth seeing, as is the collection of German and Austrian Baroque painting, which includes work by Franz Anton Maulbertsch.

Dutch and Flemish Art

The museum's Dutch and Flemish collection features works by the finest masters, including influential landscape artist, Jacob van Ruisdael, with *View of Amsterdam (see p151)*. The subtle *Nativity* by Gerard David and Pieter Bruegel's detailed masterpiece *St John the Baptist's Sermon (see p151)*, depicting Flemish peasants listening to the saint's words, are exemplary exhibits.

The museum also boasts canvases attributed to Rembrandt, including *St Joseph's Dream*, portraits by Frans Hals and Jan Vermeer's *Portrait of a Lady*. Not to be missed are the magnificent 17th-century Dutch paintings by artists including Adrian van Ostade, Jacob Ruisdael, Jan Steen and others.

The highlight of the Flemish collection is the 17th-century *Mucius Scaevola before Porsenna* by Peter Rubens and his then assistant, Anthony van Dyck. The latter was responsible for the picture of St John the Evangelist, also on display.

Also important is the painting of Adam and Eve in *The Fall of Man* by Jacob Jordaens *(see p150)*, who also worked as an assistant to Rubens.

Italian Art

This valuable collection of Italian art, which was the core of the Esterházy family's collection, is often considered the museum's biggest attraction. All the schools of Italian painting, from the 13th to the 18th centuries, are on display here. The Renaissance period is perhaps the best represented.

Of particular note is the captivating *Esterházy Madonna (see p150)*, an unfinished painting by Raphael. Another great work by this outstanding artist is the *Portrait of Pietro Bembo*.

There is no shortage of work by famous 16th-century Venetian artists among the paintings collected here. Important works by Titian, Bonifazio Veronese, Antonio Correggio, Jacopo Tintoretto,

Giorgione and Giovanni Boltraffio are all exhibited here. An excellent example of Baroque art is Giambattista Tiepolo's vast late 18th-century painting, *St James Conquers the Moors* *(see p150)*.

El Greco's *The Penance of St Mary Magdelene* (c. 1576)

Spanish Art

The most important features of this collection are seven paintings by El Greco, including *The Annunciation, Christ in the Garden of Gethsemane* and *The Penance of St Mary Magdalene*, a subtle though fully expressive work.

The dramatic *Martyrdom of St Andrew* by Jusepe de Ribera should not be missed, nor the work of artists such as Diego Velázquez, Bartolomé Murillo and Francisco de Zurbarán. Francisco de Goya's observations of daily life produced paintings such as *The Water Carrier* *(see p150)*, which also deserves special attention.

French and British Art

Works by French and British artists are not as numerous as Italian works, for example, but represent the various styles of the two countries.

French works include the well-composed *Resting on the Journey to Egypt* by Nicolas Poussin, the grandly majestic *Finding of Moses*, also by Poussin, and the bucolic landscape of *Villa in the Roman Countryside* by Claude Lorrain.

The collection of British paintings includes portraits by artists of the calibre of Joshua Reynolds, William Hogarth and Thomas Gainsborough.

European Sculpture

The collection encompasses the history of European sculpture up to the 19th century. Among its 600 items are such jewels as the *Man of Sorrows* by Verrocchio and a small bronze sculpture by Leonardo da Vinci (1452–1519). This is an unusually dynamic representation of King François I of France on his horse. Other superb examples of Italian sculpture, by masters such as Andrea Pisano of the Ronni family, can also be seen. The small bronzes from the Renaissance and Baroque periods are further highlights. The German, Dutch and French Middle Ages are well represented by various works, including the 14th-century *Beautiful Madonnas* and wooden sculptures from the Late Medieval Riemenschneider workshop. Donner and Messerschmidt represent Austrian Baroque art, the brightest period of sculpture in the region, with a number of fine works.

Drawings and Graphic Art

The collection of drawings and graphic art combines the work of old masters, including drawings by Leonard da Vinci, Raphael, Albrecht Dürer and Rembrandt, with pieces from artists of the 19th and 20th centuries. The collection is one of Europe's best.

19th- and 20th-Century Works

French painting makes up the largest constituent of the collection of 19th- and 20th-century art. The visitor can admire works by all the major painters of the time, including, Henri de Toulouse-Lautrec's *These Women in the Refectory* *(see p151)*, Gustave Courbet's *Wrestlers*, Edouard Manet's *Woman with a Fan* and Camille Pissarro's *Pont-Neuf*. Paul Gauguin's *Black Pigs*, one of his first Tahitian canvases, is also on display here. To complete the collection, the likes of Eugène Delacroix, Claude Monet, Pierre Bonnard, Pierre Renoir and Paul Cézanne are also represented.

Austrian and German 19th- and 20th-century art is represented with works by Waldmüller, Amerling, Lenbach, Leibl and Menzel.

Outstanding works from the collection of 20th-century and contemporary art are show-cased in the basement-level Majovszky Halls, which have been converted into a sterile white cube. Works from the museum's holdings are complemented by masterpieces of great value on loan from prominent private collectors, artists and foundations. Emphasis is given to the donations made by Victor Vasarely, and works by Marc Chagall, Corneille, Le Corbusier, Robert Rauschenberg and Timm Ulrichs are also included. There are also pieces such as Renato Guttuso's principle work titled *Occupation of Uncultivated Lands of Sicily*, Joseph Beuys' famous bag object exploring the opportunities inherent in direct democracy, and a lava stone sculpture by Antoni Tàpies.

Paul Cézanne's still life, *The Buffet*, dating from 1877

The façade of the Műcsarnok Art Gallery, featuring a six-columned portico

❾ Műcsarnok Art Gallery

Műcsarnok

Hősök tere. **Map** 5 C4. **Tel** (06 1) 460 70 00. Ⓜ Hosök tere. **Open** 10am–6pm Tue–Sun, noon–8pm Thu. **W** **mucsarnok.hu**

Situated on the southern side of Heroes' Square, opposite the Museum of Fine Arts *(see pp150–53)*, is Hungary's largest exhibition space. Temporary exhibitions of mainly contemporary painting and sculpture are held here.

The imposing Neo-Classical building, which was designed by Albert Schickedanz and Fülöp Herzog in 1895, is fronted by a vast six-columned portico. The colourful mosaic, depicting St István as the patron saint of fine art, was added to the tympanum between 1938–41. Behind the portico is a fresco in three parts by Lajos Deák Ébner: *The Beginning of Sculpture*, *The Source of Arts* and *The Origins of Painting*.

❿ Museum of Fine Arts

See pp150–53.

⓫ Vajdahunyad Castle

Vajdahunyad Vára

Városliget. **Map** 6 D4. **Tel** (06 1) 422 07 65. Ⓜ Széchenyi fürdő. Museum of Hungarian Agriculture: **Tel** (06 1) 422 07 65. **Open** Mar–Oct: 10am–5pm Tue–Sun; Nov–Feb: 10am–4pm Tue–Fri, 10am–5pm Sat & Sun. **W** **mmgm.hu**

This fairytale-like building is located among the trees at the edge of the lake in Városliget. Not a genuine castle but a complex of buildings reflecting various architectural styles, it was designed by Ignác Alpár for the 1896 Millennium Celebrations *(see p146)*.

Alpár's creation illustrated the history and evolution of architecture in Hungary. Originally intended as temporary exhibition pavilions, the castle proved so popular with the public that, between 1904–6, it was rebuilt using brick to create a permanent structure.

The pavilions are grouped in chronological order of style: Romanesque is followed by Gothic, Renaissance, Baroque and so on. The individual styles were linked together to give the impression of a single, cohesive design. Each of the pavilions either uses authentic details copied from Hungary's most important historic buildings or is a looser interpretation of a style inspired by a specific architect of that historic period.

The Romanesque complex features a copy of the portal from a church in Ják *(see p147)* as well as a monastic cloister and palace. The details on the Gothic pavilion have been taken from castles like those in Vajdahunyad and Segesvár (both now in Romania). The architect Fischer von Erlach was the inspiration for the Renaissance and Baroque complex. The façade copies part of the Bakócz chapel in the cathedral at Esztergom *(see p168)*.

The Museum of Hungarian Agriculture is housed in this wonderful building. It has exhibits on animals, forestry, wine-making, hunting, fishing and horse-racing.

The entire complex reflects more than 20 of Hungary's most renowned buildings. The medieval period, often considered to be the most glorious time in Hungary's history, is given greatest emphasis, while the controversial Habsburg era is pushed into the background.

⓬ Zoo

Fővárosi Állat- és Növénykert

Állatkerti körút 6–12. **Map** 5 C3. **Tel** (06 1) 273 49 00. Ⓜ Széchenyi fürdő. **Open** 9am–7pm daily. Holnemvolt Park **Open** May–Aug: 10am–5pm Mon–Thu, 10am–6pm Fri–Sun. **W** **zoobudapest.com**

Budapest's zoo is one of the city's great attractions. It was established in 1866 by the Hungarian Academy of Sciences *(see p118)*. In 1907 it was bought by

View across the lake of the Gothic (left) and Renaissance (right) sections of Vajdahunyad Castle

the State and totally redeveloped, between 1909–11, by Károly Kós and Dezső Zrumeczky. The animals are housed in enclosures, most of which strive to mimic their natural habitat. The elephant house, however, by Kornél Neuschloss-Knüsli, is a fine example of Secession style. Károly Kós, on the other hand, adopted a folk style for the aviary, in which a wide variety of birds fly freely. There is also a popular children's zoo.

Holnemvolt Park, which is adjacent to the zoo, was once a funfair, but now operates as a "Once Upon a Time Park" where children and families can meet about 30 different breeds of animals and let off steam in the playground. Historic features and games from the funfair have been retained, such as a carousel and a 1922 wooden roller coaster (one of the few remaining side-friction roller coasters in the world). Development of the park is on-going so planned features are still being added. Zoo tickets include entry to the park, but you can also buy tickets for the park only.

⓭ Széchenyi Baths

Széchenyi Strandfürdő

Állatkerti körút 11. **Map** 6 D3. **Tel** (06 1) 363 32 10. Ⓜ Széchenyi fürdő. **Open** Thermal Pool: 6am–7pm daily. Swimming pool and group thermal pool: 6am–10pm daily. **W szechenyibath.com**

A statue stands at the main entrance to the Széchenyi Baths depicting geologist Vilmos Zsigmond, who discovered a hot spring here while drilling a well in 1879.

The Széchenyi Baths are the deepest and one of the hottest baths in Budapest – the water reaches the surface at a temperature of 74–5° C (165° F). The springs, rich in minerals, are distinguished by their alleged healing properties. They are recommended for treating rheumatism and disorders of the nervous system, joints and muscles.

One of the outdoor pools at the beautiful Széchenyi Baths

The spa, housed in a Neo-Baroque building by Győző Cziegler and Ede Dvorzsák, was constructed in 1909–13. In 1926, three open-air swimming pools were added. The pools are popular all year due to the water's high temperature. Bathing caps are required.

⓮ Hermina Street

Hermina út

Map 6 E3, 6 E4 & 6 F4. 70. Transport Museum: **Tel** (06 1) 273 38 40. **Open** 10am–4pm Tue–Fri, 10am–5pm Sat & Sun. **Closed** Mon.

This beautiful street is worth walking along to experience the romantic atmosphere of the historic, elegant villas in this area. Particularly notable is the unusual Secession building at No. 47, Sipeky Balázs Villa *(see p57)*, built in 1905–6 by architects Ödön Lechner, Marcell Komor and Dezső Jakab. The asymmetric design of the villa's façade includes features such as a domed glass conservatory, an ironwork porch and a tall, narrow side tower. The villa's exterior decoration is inspired by national folk art.

A steam train exhibited at the Transport Museum, just off Hermina Street

Hermina Chapel at No. 23, by József Hild, was built in 1842–6 in memory of Palatine József's daughter, Hermina Amália, who died in 1842.

Backing onto Hermina Street, at No. 11 Városligeti körút, is the Transport Museum with exhibits on the evolution of air, sea, road and rail transport. Among the trains, helicopters and aeroplanes are some pre-World War II right-hand-drive cars and the first trams in Budapest.

Poster for a gala and ballet performance at the Erkel Theatre

⓯ Erkel Theatre

Erkel Színház

II. János Pál pápa tér 30. **Map** 7 C3. **Tel** (06 1) 332 61 50. Ⓜ II. János Pál pápa tér. **W opera.hu/en/erkel**

An alternative venue of the National Opera Company, the largest theatre in Hungary seats 2,500 people. Designed in 1911 by Marcell Komor, Dezső Jakab and Géza Márkus, its current form dates from the 1950s. It hosts concerts and operas.

FURTHER AFIELD

Budapest is a sprawling city and several sights on its periphery are well worth a visit. North from the centre of Buda are the fascinating ruins of Aquincum, a town founded by the Romans in approximately AD 100. To the west, the city is skirted by wooded hills, which offer walks around beautiful nature reserves and exciting cave visits. Out to the east of Pest is Kerepesi Cemetery, where a host of famous Hungarians are buried. To the south of the city is the Nagytétény Palace, one of the most beautiful Baroque palaces in all of Hungary. The setting for Socialist-era statues, Memento Park, is not far from the palace. All the sights can be reached easily using public transport.

Sights at a Glance

Museums and Theatres

- 10 Holocaust Memorial Center
- 11 Palace of Arts (MÜPA)
- 16 National Theatre
- 21 Gizi Bajor Theatre Museum
- 27 *Aquincum pp166–7*

Historic Buildings and Monuments

- 1 Raoul Wallenberg Monument
- 4 Geological and Geophysical Institute of Hungary
- 9 Ludovika Academy
- 17 Wekerle Estate
- 18 Technical University
- 23 Memento Park
- 24 Törley Mausoleum
- 25 Nagytétény Palace Museum

Parks and Recreation Areas

- 2 Szemlő-hegy and Pál-völgy Caves
- 5 Ferenc Puskás Stadium
- 8 ELTE Füvészkert Botanical Garden
- 12 Railway History Park
- 20 Budapest Congress Center
- 22 Eagle Hill Nature Reserve
- 26 Buda Hills

Cemeteries

- 6 Kerepesi Cemetery
- 14 *Municipal Cemetery pp162–3*
- 15 Jewish Cemetery

Churches

- 3 Újlak Parish Church
- 7 Józsefváros Parish Church
- 13 Kőbánya Parish Church
- 19 Cistercian Church of St Imre

Key

- City centre
- Motorway
- Main road
- Railway

0 kilometres 5

0 miles 3

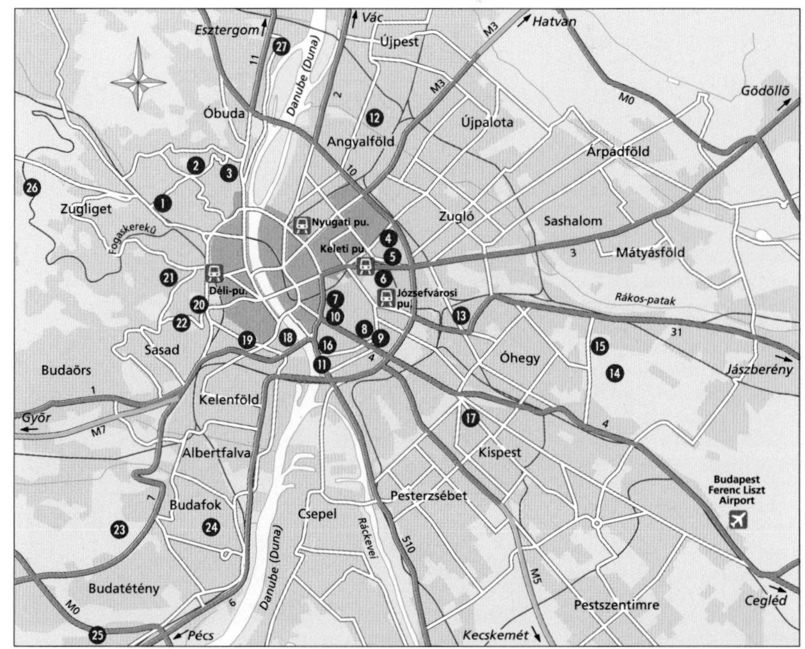

◀ A castle in the town of Esztergom, located on the Danube north of Budapest

For keys to symbols *see back flap*

❶ Raoul Wallenberg Monument

Raoul Wallenberg szobor

Szilágyi Erzsébet fasor. 56.

Tucked away at the junction of Szilágyi Erzsébet fasor and Nagyajtai utca, is this monument to an heroic but little known figure of World War II. Raoul Wallenberg was a Swedish diplomat who used his position to save over 20,000 Hungarian Jews from the extermination camps. He set up safe houses in the city and obtained fake Swedish documents for them.

Following the liberation of Budapest by the Soviet army, Wallenberg disappeared. It is thought he was arrested by the KGB and sent to a prison camp where he died. The memorial, by sculptor Imre Varga, was erected in 1987.

❷ Szemlő-hegy and Pál-völgy Caves

Szemlő-hegyi-barlang és Pál-völgyi-cseppköbarlang

Szemlő-hegy Cave: Pusztaszeri út 35. **Tel** 325 60 01. 29, 91, 291. **Open** 10am–4pm Wed–Mon. Pál-völgy Cave: Szépvölgyi út 162. **Tel** (06 1) 325 95 05. 65. **Open** 10am–4pm Tue–Sun. **caving.hu**

Thermal water springs have created a 120-km (75-mile) long system of caves in the Buda Hills, with picturesque formations. Two caves, less than a kilometre (half a mile) apart, are open to visitors.

Szemlő-hegy Cave features extraordinary formations called "cave pearls", produced when hot spring waters penetrate its limestone walls. There are guided tours every hour, as well as caving tours for the more adventurous; book in advance.

In Pál-völgy Cave, strange formations protruding from the rock face resemble animals.

Visitors are advised to wear warm clothes when entering the caves as they are cold and damp. Some claim, however, that the atmosphere in the caves has a relaxing and therapeutic effect on the respiratory system.

The Baroque interior of Újlak Parish Church, dating from 1756

❸ Újlak Parish Church

Újlaki pébániatemplom

Bécsi út 32. H5 Szépvölgyi út. 86, 160, 260. 19, 41, 61.

Bavarian settlers first built a small church here early in the 18th century. The present church, designed by Kristóf Hamon and Mátyás Nepauer, was finished in 1756. Its tower was added some years later.

In the Baroque interior there is a depiction of the Madonna, a gift from the inhabitants of Passau. The main altar, dating from 1798, also includes a painting entitled *The Visitation*, which was the work of Francis Falkoner.

Not far away, at Zsigmond tér, stands the Holy Trinity Column, built in 1691 as a memorial to the city's earliest plague epidemic. The Baroque monument was moved from central Buda to Újlak in 1712.

❹ Geological and Geophysical Institute of Hungary

Magyar Földtani és Geofizikai Intézet

Stefánia út 14. **Map** 8 F1. **Tel** (06 1) 251 09 99. 75. Museum: **Open** on week days by appointment only; email: muzeum@mfgi.hu at least one week ahead. **mfgi.hu**

This beautiful and unusual building, housing the Geological and Geophysical Institute of Hungary, dates from 1898–9 and was designed by Ödön Lechner *(see p58)*.

Lechner's very individual Secession style, also known as the Hungarian National Style, is on show here including motifs drawn from Hungarian Renaissance architecture.

Here and there Zsolnay blue-glazed ceramic ornaments adorn the walls and harmonize with the blue roof tiles. The central pitched roof is topped by four human figures bent under the weight of a large globe. Inside is a small museum with rock and mineral exhibits. Lechner's Secession

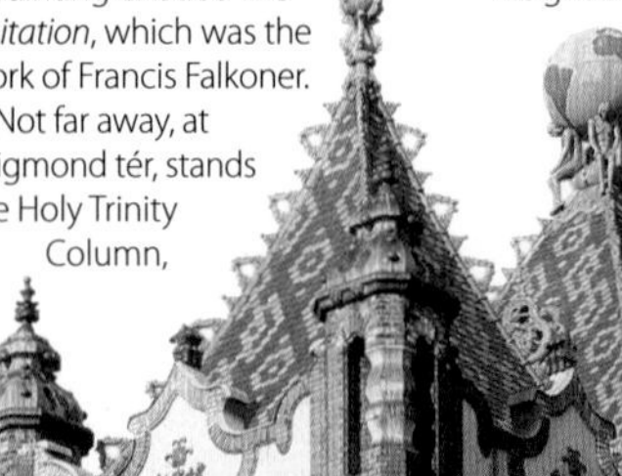

The Geological and Geophysical Institute of Hungary, with its stunning blue ceramic roof

interiors have been carefully preserved – the central hall is very grand, and can be seen when visiting the museum or with the caretaker's permission.

❺ Ferenc Puskás Stadium

Puskás Ferenc stadion

Istvánmezei u. 3-5. **Map** 8 F1. **Tel** (06 1) 473 42 21. 95, 95A, 130, 178. 1. Ⓜ Puskás Ferenc Stadion. **Open** 8am–2pm Mon–Thu, 8am–noon Fri. **magyarfutball.hu**

Hungary's biggest sports stadium, named after a national football hero, was built between 1948–53 to a design by Károly Dávid. The roofless structure seats 78,000, but generally only fills to capacity for major events. The entrance is at the end of the "Avenue of Youth", which is lined with Stalinist-era statues, depicting various sports, by well-known Hungarian sculptors.

❻ Kerepesi Cemetery

Kerepesi temető

Fiumei út 16–20. **Map** 8 E3. 24, 37. 24, 37.

Since 1847, the Kerepesi Cemetery has provided the resting place for many of Hungary's most prominent citizens. Fine tombstones mark the graves of some, while others were interred here inside large mausoleums.

The mausoleum of the leader of the 1948–9 uprising, Lajos Kossuth *(see p110)* and Lajos Batthyány, the first prime minister of Hungary *(see p33)* are found here. Ferenc Deák, who formulated the Compromise with Austria *(see p34)*, is buried here.

Also at the cemetery are the graves of poets Endre Ady and Attila József *(see p110)*, writers Kálmán Mikszáth Zsigmond Móricz and actors such as Lujza Blaha, whose tomb is particularly beautiful. Sculptors, painters and composers are buried close to great architects. Hungarian Communists who were sentenced to death in the show trials of 1949, were buried here. Their funerals inspired a revolutionary spirit which, a few years later, led to the 1956 Uprising *(see p36)*.

❼ Józsefváros Parish Church

Józsefváros plébániatemplom

Horváth Mihály tér 7. **Map** 7 C4. **Tel** (06 1) 313 63 13. Ⓜ Rákóczi tér.

Building work on this Baroque church began in 1797, but it was not completed until 1814. The main altar is by József Hild. A formidable architectural composition, it is based on a triumphal arch. This frames a magnificent painting, *The Apotheosis of St Joseph*, by Leopold Kupelwieser. The church also has two beautiful, late Baroque side altars.

❽ ELTE Füvészkert Botanical Garden

Füvészkert – ELTE Botanikus Kert

Illés utca 25. **Map** 8 D5. **Tel** (06 1) 314 05 35 or 210 10 74. Ⓜ Klinikák. **Open** Nov–Mar: 9am–4pm; Apr–Oct: 9am–5pm.

A garden was first established on this 3-ha (8-acre) site by the Festetics family. Their modest, early Neo-Classical villa is now the administration centre for the garden. It was built in 1802–3, probably to a design by Mihály Pollack. The palm house has a huge collection of tropical plants, while in the Victoria House the striking *Victoria cruziana* flowers once a year. The author Ferenc Molnár (1878–1952) used the garden as a setting in his novel, *The Paul Street Boys*, although the lake mentioned in the book no longer exists. Not far away are Pál utca (Paul Street) and Mária utca, the scene of a battle the boys fought.

The late Baroque façade of Józsefváros Parish Church

The tomb of actress Lujza Blaha at Kerepesi Cemetery

❾ Ludovika Academy

Ludovika Akadémia

Ludovika tér 2–6. Ⓜ Klinikák. **Tel** (06 1) 210 10 85. **Open** 10am–5pm Wed–Sun. Natural History Museum: **Open** 10am–5pm Wed–Sun. **mttm.hu**

The huge Ludovika Academy is in district IX, east of the city centre. It was designed in the 1830s by Mihály Pollack, the famous architect of the Hungarian National Museum *(see pp134–7)*. A military academy until 1945, it is an impressive example of Neo-Classical style, with many original features intact. It is now the city's Natural History Museum, with a rich paleontological collection.

⑩ Holocaust Memorial Center

Holokauszt Emlékközpont

Páva utca 39. 4, 6. M Corvin-Negyed. **Tel** (06 1) 455 33 33. **Open** 10am–6pm Tue–Sun. **W hdke.hu**

The Center was founded in order to collect and study material relating to the history of the Holocaust, and to honour its victims. The building complex is a mix of classical and modern architecture, and its asymmetrical outline and dislocated walls all symbolize the distorted and twisted time of the Holocaust.

A permanent exhibition examines the history of the suffering of Hungarian Jews and Roma during the Holocaust.

The impressive open-space interior of the Palace of Arts, a cultural hub

⑪ Palace of Arts (MÜPA)

Művészetek Palotája (MÜPA)

Komor Marcell utca 1. 1, 2, 2A, 24. **Tel** (06 1) 555 3000. **Open** 10am–10pm daily. Ticket Office: (all events) **Open** 10am–6pm. **W mupa.hu**

The Palace of Arts (MÜPA) in the Millennium City Centre, located on the Pest side of the Danube between the Lágymányos bridge and the National Theatre, brings together the different branches of the arts under one roof. Permanent residents include the Ludwig Museum of Contemporary Art, the National Philharmonic Orchestra, the Béla Bartók National Concert Hall and the National Dance Theatre.

⑫ Railway History Park

Vasúttörténeti Park

Tatai út 95. Vintage diesel shuttle from Nyugati station 10:20am, 11:20am, 1:20pm. 30A from Keleti station. **Tel** (06 1) 450 14 97. **Open** Apr–Oct: 10am–6pm Tue–Sun. **Closed** Nov–Mar. **W vasuttorteneti park.hu**

This open-air museum of railway history is one of Europe's largest. It boasts around 100 locomotives – most fully functioning – dating from the early days of steam to modern times. Visitors can drive a steam train, play with a model railway and ride in a line-inspection car. Every year, the legendary *Orient Express* makes several visits here. The park is popular with families as well as enthusiasts, and there is a full programme of events for children.

⑬ Kőbánya Parish Church

Kőbányai Plébániatemplom

Szent László tér. 9, 17, 32, 62, 185. 37.

An industrial suburb on the eastern side of Pest, Kőbánya is the unexpected home of the beautiful Kőbánya Parish Church. Designed by Ödön Lechner *(see p58)* in the 1890s, the church makes magnificent use of the architect's favourite materials, including vibrant roof tiles developed and produced at the now-famous Zsolnay factory in the town of Pécs. Like much of Lechner's work, including the Museum of Applied Arts *(see pp140–41)*, the church combines motifs and colours from Hungarian folk art with Neo-Gothic elements. Inside the church, both the altar and the pulpit are superb examples of early 20th-century wood carving. Somehow surviving heavy World War II bombing, a number of Miksa Roth's original stained-glass windows are still in place.

Gleaming ceramic tiles on the roof of Kőbánya Parish Church

⑭ Municipal Cemetery

See pp162–3.

⑮ Jewish Cemetery

Izraelita Temető

Kozma utca. 95, 202E.

Next door to the Municipal Cemetery is the Jewish Cemetery, opened in 1893. The many grand tombs here are a vivid reminder of the vigour and success of Budapest's pre-war Jewish community. At the end of the 19th century, nearly a quarter of the city's inhabitants were Jewish. Tombs to look out for as you stroll among the graves include that of the Wellisch family, designed in 1903 by Arthur Wellisch, and that of Konrád Polnay, which was designed five years later by Gyula Fodor.

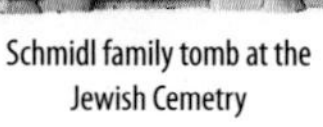

Schmidl family tomb at the Jewish Cemetry

Perhaps the most eye-catching of all belongs to the Schmidl family. The startlingly flamboyant tomb, designed in 1903 by Ödön Lechner and Béla Lajta, is covered in vivid turquoise ceramic tiles. The central mosaic in green and gold tiles represents the Tree of Life.

⑯ National Theatre

Nemzeti Színház

Bajor Gizi Park 1. **Tel** 476 68 68. 1, 2, 24. **nemzetiszinhaz.hu**

Situated at the foot of Rákóczi Bridge, the National Theatre showcases contemporary dance and drama. The architect, Mária Siklós, designed a Neo-Eclectic building surrounded by a park containing statues portraying Hungary's best actors.

⑰ Wekerle Estate

Wekerle Telep

Kós Károly tér. **Tel** (06 1) 280 01 14. Határ út, then 194.

Out in district XIX, the Wekerle Estate was built between 1909 and 1926, and represents a bold and successful experiment in 20th-century social planning. Named after Prime Minister Sándor Wekerle, the estate was originally known as the Kispest Workers and Clerks Settlement and was built to provide better housing for local workers.

Designed by a group of young architects, students of Ödön Lechner, the buildings have a uniquely Hungarian style. Other key influences were the English Arts and Crafts movement, and early English new towns such as Hampstead Garden Suburb in London.

Fanning out around Kós Károly tér, 16 types of family house and apartment block are separated by tree-lined streets. Wooden gables and balconies, and sharply pitched, brightly tiled roofs, contribute to the estate's lively and eclectic atmosphere.

Façade of the Technical University, as seen from the Danube

A police station on the early 20th-century Wekerle Estate

⑱ Technical University

Budapesti Műszaki Egyetem

Műegyetem rakpart 3. **Map** 4 F4. **Tel** (06 1) 463 11 11. 7, 86. 4, 6, 18, 19, 47, 49. Szent Gellért tér. **bme.hu**

Founded in 1857, the city's Technical University moved to its present site in 1904. Built on reclaimed marshland, the imposing building overlooks the Danube just south of Gellért Hill *(see pp92–3)*. Extended at the end of World War II, it is now the largest higher education establishment in Hungary. Former students include Imre Steindl, the architect of the Parliament building *(see pp112–13)*, and the richest and most widely known graduate to date, Ernő Rubik, inventor of the Rubik Cube.

⑲ Cistercian Church of St Imre

Cisztercita Szent Imre Plébániatemplom

Villányi út 25. **Map** 3 C4. 27, 40. 47, 49, 61.

Not far from the Technical University is the Cistercian Church of St Imre. The vast Neo-Baroque structure with its double tower was built in 1938 and is typical of the grand and rather sombre architecture in vogue in Budapest during the inter-war years.

Inside the church are relics of St Imre, canonized at the end of the 11th century. Other patron saints of the Cistercian order are depicted above the church's main entrance.

⓮ Municipal Cemetery

Rákoskeresztúr

A new, historic significance was gained by the Municipal Cemetery following the 1956 Uprising *(see p36)*. Here, at Budapest's southeastern limits, the leaders and victims of this bloody revolution against the oppressive Stalinist government were secretly buried in mass graves. During the 1970s, the country's democratic opposition began placing flowers on the site, at the far side of the cemetery. In 1990, after the fall of Communism, the revolutionary heroes were given a ceremonial funeral and reburied, and several memorials were set up to them.

View of Plot 300
Until 1989, the state militia guarded access to a thicket which covered the communal graves of the heroes of the 1956 Uprising.

Campanile
A wooden campanile is the type of decoration often found in old Hungarian cemeteries. It stands in front of panels listing the names of over 400 victims of the 1956 Uprising, giving the exact locations of their graves.

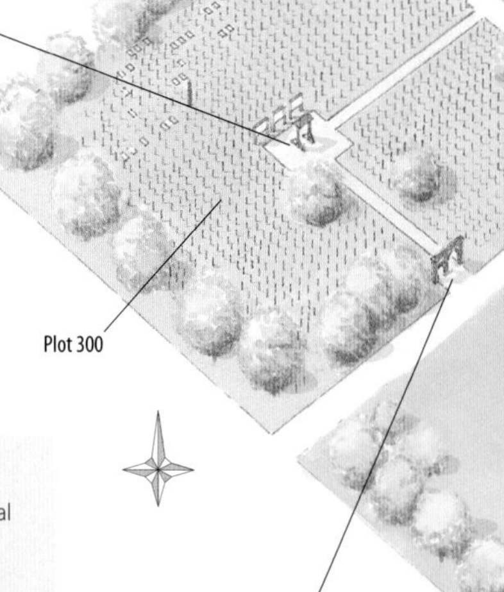

Plan of the Cemetery

In 1886, the city authorities opened a vast, new municipal cemetery in Rákoskeresztúr, on the outskirts of town. It became the largest cemetery in Budapest, occupying 30 sq km (12 sq miles).

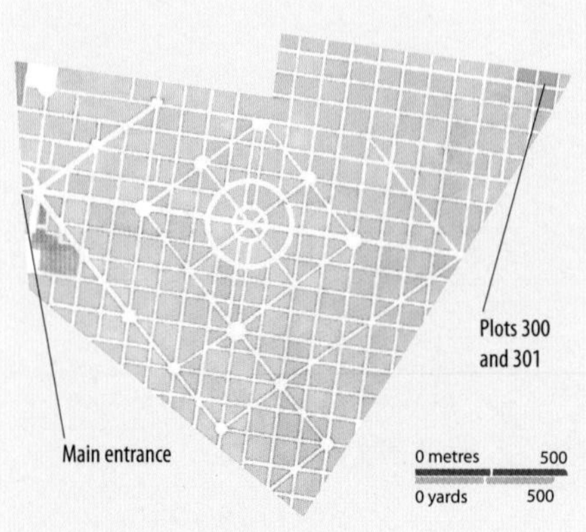

★ Transylvanian Gate
The 1956 Uprising Combatants' Association erected the carved Transylvanian Gate which stands at the beginning of one of the paths leading into plot 300. It is inscribed with the words: "Only a Hungarian soul may pass through this gate".

★ Imre Nagy's Grave
A marble slab bears the modest inscription: "Imre Nagy, Prime Minister of Hungary, 1956". Arrested after the uprising, Nagy was interned and shot dead on 16 June 1958 in Budapest, following a bogus political trial.

VISITORS' CHECKLIST

Practical Information
Kozma utca 8–10, Kőbánya.

Transport
95, 202E. M Puskás Ferenc Stadion. Plots 300 and 301: 30 mins walk from the main gate. Fee charged for cars.

Plot 301

Christ the Sorrowful
A figure of Christ the Sorrowful is traditionally placed in a plot containing Protestant graves.

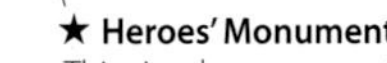

★ Heroes' Monument
This simple monument symbolizes the passage through purgatory. It was created by the leading modern Hungarian sculptor, György Jovánovics.

Protestant Graves
The tradition of Hungarian Protestants is to place a simple wooden post to mark each grave.

View from Eagle Hill Nature Reserve, down across the smart residential quarter below

⑳ Budapest Congress Center

Budapest Kongresszusi Központ

Jagelló út 1–3. **Tel** (06 1) 372 57 00. 8, 105, 112. 61. **Open** For events.
bcc.hu

Opened in 1975, this large arts complex houses a concert hall, conference rooms and a restaurant. It hosts international conferences and events such as dance performances and gala concerts. The building was designed, with the neighbouring Novotel Budapest City Hotel, by the architect József Finta. The *Tree of Life* decorating the main wall of the Congress Hall is by József Király.

㉑ Gizi Bajor Theatre Museum

Bajor Gizi Színészmúzeum

Stromfeld Aurél út 16. **Tel** (06 1) 375 11 84. 102, 105. **Open** 2–6pm Wed–Sun.

This museum was opened in 1952, in a garden villa which once belonged to Gizi Bajor, a leading Hungarian actress of her day. Its exhibits, which include furniture, portraits, theatrical props, fans, velvet gloves and personal letters, such as those exchanged between Gizi and her mother, transport visitors to the world of the theatre in the 19th century.

In 1990, the 200th anniversary of theatre in Hungary, the museum's collection was further extended, to include mementoes of well-known contemporary Hungarian actors. The garden features the busts of several writers, together with a number of other leading figures in Hungary's cultural history.

㉒ Eagle Hill Nature Reserve

Sashegy Természetvédelmi Terület

Tájék utca 26. **Tel** (06 1) 304 084 370. 8, 105. **Open** Mar–Oct: 10am–6pm Tue, Fri–Sun. available.

A nature reserve more or less in the centre of a city of nearly two million inhabitants is a remarkable phenomenon.

Access to the summit of this steep, 266-m (872-ft) high hill to the west of Gellért Hill *(see pp92–3)* is strictly regulated to protect the extremely rare animal and plant species found here. A smart residential quarter, which lies on the lower slope of Eagle Hill, extends almost to the fence of the reserve and the craggy 30-ha (74-acre) wilderness that it encloses.

It is well worth taking a guided walk, particularly in spring or early autumn. Only here is it possible to see *sesleria sadleriana*, also known as Pannonian Bluegrass, a cyan-coloured grass species. The reserve is also home to a type of spider not found anywhere else in the world, as well as to extraordinary, colourful butterflies and to *ablepharus kitaibelii*, a rare lizard.

㉓ Memento Park

Memento Park

Balatoni út & Szabadkai utca.
Tel (06 1) 424 75 00. 101, 150.
Open 10am–dusk daily.
mementopark.hu

In 1991, Budapest's City Council decided to gather in one place Communist monuments which had formerly occupied prestigious locations in the city.

The park, also known as Statue Park, has been enlarged and features gigantic monuments of the Communist regime. Statues of Karl Marx, Friedrich Engels, VI Lenin and Hungarian Communist heroes stand side by side, headed by the leader of the 1919 revolution in Hungary *(see p36)*, Béla Kun.

Stalin's Tribune is a replica of the original grandstand from which Communist leaders greeted the crowds. Above the tribune stood an 8m- (26 ft-) high bronze of Stalin, but it was pulled down during the national Uprising in 1956 and only the boots remain.

The Barakk Museum has exhibitions on everyday life under the Communist regime, and a cinema has a screening of the special methods used by the Communist secret services.

Cubist-style statues of Marx and Engels in the Statue Park

The marble Törley Mausoleum

㉔ Törley Mausoleum

Törley Mauzoleum

Sarló utca 6. 33. 47.

Until 1880 Budafok had a number of vineyards, but their cultivation was destroyed in that year by a plague of phylloxera (American aphid). It was then that József Törley, who had studied wine-making in Reims, started to produce sparkling wine in Budafok using the French model *(see p194)*. His wines sold well abroad and he quickly expanded his enterprise, storing the wines in the local cellars.

József Törley died in 1900 and was laid to rest in this monumental mausoleum, constructed in white marble and designed by Rezső Vilmos Ray. The Törley Mausoleum is not open to the public.

㉕ Nagytétényi Palace Museum

Nagytétényi Kastély Múzeum

Kastélypark utca 9–11. **Tel** (06 1) 207 00 05. from Déli to Kastélypark. 33. **Open** Mar–Dec: 10am–6pm Tue–Sun; Jan–Feb: 10am–6pm Sat & Sun; may close for renovations so phone or check website before visit. In period costume, by arrangement. **nagytetenyi.hu**

This is one of the best known Baroque palaces in Hungary. It was built in the mid-18th century, incorporating the remains of a 15th-century Gothic building. The work was started by György Száraz and completed by his son-in-law, József Rudnyánszky, acquiring its final shape in 1766. Based on the typical Baroque layout, it includes a main block and side wings. The coping features the Száraz and Rudnyánszky family crests.

The palace suffered severe damage during World War II, but the original wall paintings and furnishings survived. In 1949, the palace was rebuilt and turned into an interior design museum. Now it is a department of the Museum of Applied Arts *(see pp140–41)*. On display are fine pieces of Hungarian and European furniture from the 15th–18th centuries, early 19th-century paintings and more functional items, such as tiled stoves.

Standing close to the palace is an 18th-century Baroque church, built on the remains of a medieval church. Original Gothic features include the window openings in its tower and three supports on the outer wall of the presbytery. In 1760, the Austrian artist Johann Gfall created the painting in the dome which features illusory galleries. The altars, pulpit and baptistries also date back to the mid-18th century.

㉖ Buda Hills

Budai-hegység

M Széll Kálmán tér, then 18 or 56, then cog-wheel railway and chair lift.

To the west of the city centre are the wooded Buda Hills where Budapesters come to walk and relax.

The first station of a cog-wheel railway, built in 1874, is on Szilágyi Erszébet fasor. This runs up Sváb Hill – named after the Germanic Swabians, who settled here under the Habsburgs *(see p30)* – and then Széchenyi Hill.

From Széchenyi Hill a narrow-gauge railway covers a 12-km (7-mile) route to the Hűvös Valley. As in the days of the Soviet Young Pioneers movement, the railway is entirely staffed by children, apart from the adult train drivers. At the top of János Hill stands the Erzsébet Look-Out Tower, designed by Frigyes Schulek in 1910. A chair lift also connects the summit of János Hill with Zugligeti út and is a good way of making the descent.

The Erzsébet Look-Out Tower at the summit of János Hill

27 Aquincum

Aquincum

The remains of the Roman town of Aquincum *(see pp22–3)* were excavated at the end of the 19th century. Visitors are free to stroll along its streets, viewing the outlines of temples, shops, baths and houses, in what was once the centre of the town. This civilian town was founded at the beginning of the 2nd century AD, a couple of decades after a legionary fortress *(see pp174–5)* was established to its south. In the centre of the site there is a Neo-Classical museum building, which was built in 1894, and a mythological playground. On the other side of the road are the remains of an amphitheatre, where Aquincum's inhabitants once sought entertainment.

View Towards the Museum
The area opened to visitors is only a fragment of a much bigger town.

★ Public Baths
The walls of the thermal baths are immaculately preserved. Visiting the baths was a social event for the Romans.

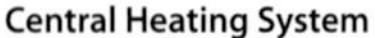

Central Heating System
Archaeologists have here unearthed the Roman version of central heating, an under-floor system in which hot air was circulated under mosaic floors.

★ Macellum
This was the covered market hall. Having stalls positioned around a cool inner courtyard kept the produce fresh and made shopping comfortable all year round *(see pp22–3)*.

★ Museum
This Neo-Classical Lapidarium is part of the museum, which houses an exhibition of objects found at Aquincum and at other Roman sites nearby. These include weapons and inscribed stone monuments.

VISITORS' CHECKLIST

Practical Information
Szentendrei út 135. **Tel** (06 1) 250 16 50. Park: **Open** Apr–Oct: 9am–6pm Tue–Sun. Museum: **Open** 10am–4pm Tue–Sun (Apr–Oct: to 6pm). **aquincum.hu**

Transport
Aquincum.

Thoroughfare
Paving stones can still be seen on the network of streets that run across the town at right angles.

Double Baths
Built mainly of stone, the baths were once richly decorated. Traces of wall paintings and mosaics can still be seen in some places.

Peristyle House
Surrounded by a colonnade, this courtyard once stood at the centre of a large town house.

The Painter's House
This elongated house is a reconstruction of the original house built in the 2nd century AD. Most rooms were decorated with wall paintings and one room was even heated.

Excursions from Budapest

Budapest is ten times bigger than any other Hungarian city. Sleepy and charming, the towns and villages on these pages are ideal for day or overnight trips. Coaches *(see p235)* and trains *(see p239)* are cheap and reliable. Esztergom, Visegrád and Szentendre to the north of the city can all be reached by boats *(see p234)*, which run throughout the summer along this beautiful stretch of the Danube. More off the beaten track, the towns and villages to the south offer a fascinating glimpse of traditional life.

Overlooking the Danube, the vast cathedral at Esztergom

❶ Esztergom

46 km (28 miles) NW of Budapest. 30,000. from Nyugati pu. from Árpád híd. from Vigadó tér (summer only), take local buses 1-6 and get off at Béke tér stop. Lőrinc utca Cathedral: Szent István tér 1. **Tel** (06 33) 41 18 95. **Open** Daily (times vary). Treasury: **Tel** (06 33) 40 23 54. **Open** Mar–Oct: 8am–5pm daily; Nov–Feb: 8am–4pm Tue–Sun. Castle: **Tel** (06 33) 41 59 86. **Open** Apr–Oct: 10am–6pm Tue–Sun (Nov–Apr: to 4pm). **esztergom.hu**

St István, Hungary's first Christian King, was baptized in Esztergom and crowned here on Christmas Day AD 1000. Almost completely destroyed by the Mongol invasion 250 years later, the city was gradually rebuilt in the 18th and 19th centuries.

Esztergom today is still the country's most sacred city, the seat of the archbishop of Hungary. Dominating the skyline is the huge Catholic **cathedral**, built in the early 19th century. By the southern entrance, built by 16th-century Florentine craftsmen, is the red marble Bakócz burial chapel. On the northern side is the **treasury** containing a collection of ecclesiastical treasures rescued from the ruins of the 12th-century church that existed on the cathedral site.

Below the cathedral are the remains of the 10th-century **castle**, rebuilt several times. It features a 12th-century chapel. The picturesque old town is also well worth exploring. At its heart is the town square, home to several cafés.

Sights at a Glance

❶ Esztergom
❷ Visegrád
❸ Szentendre
❹ Vác
❺ Fót
❻ Gödöllő
❼ Kecskemét
❽ Kiskunfélegyháza
❾ Ráckeve
❿ Martonvásár

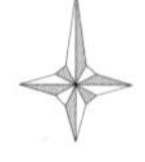

0 kilometres 20
0 miles 20

Key

Motorway
Main road
Minor road
Railway

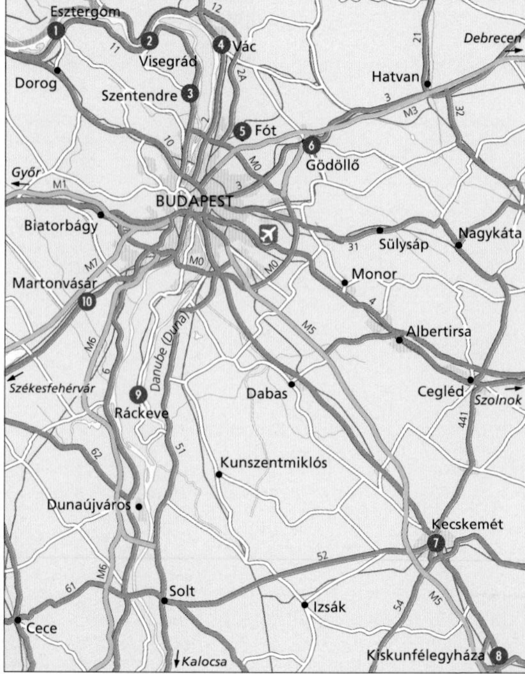

❷ Visegrád

40 km (25 miles) N of Budapest. 1,800. from Árpád híd. from Vigadó tér (summer only). Rév utca 15. **Tel** (06 26) 39 81 60. Castle: **Tel** (06 26) 39 81 01. **Open** Mar–Sep: 9:30am–6pm Mon–Sun; Oct–Nov: 9:30am–4pm Mon–Sun; Dec–Feb: 9:30am–4pm Sat & Sun. Mátyás Museum & Visegrád Palace: **Tel** (06 26) 39 80 26. **Open** 9am–5pm Tue–Sun. by arrangement. **visegrad.hu**

Set on the narrowest stretch of the Danube, the village of Visegrád is a popular tourist destination, thanks to its spectacular ruined **castle**.

A 25-minute walk, or a short bus or taxi ride will take you up to the castle from Visegrád. Built in the 13th century by King Béla IV, this was once one of the finest royal palaces ever built in Hungary. The massive outer walls are still intact, and offer stunning views over the surrounding countryside.

Halfway down the hill, in the Salamon Tower, is the **Mátyás Museum**, a collection of items excavated from the ruins of the **Visegrád Palace**. Built by King Béla IV at the same time as the castle, the palace was renovated two centuries later, in magnificent Renaissance style, by King Mátyás Corvinus *(see pp26–7)*. Destroyed in the 16th century after the Turkish invasion, then buried in a mud slide, the ruins were not rediscovered until 1934, when the excavations took place here.

❸ Szentendre

25 km (16 miles) N of Budapest. 20,000. from Batthyány tér. from Árpád híd. from Vigadó tér (summer only). Dumtsa Jenő utca 22. **Tel** (06 26) 31 79 66. Belgrade Cathedral: Pátriárka utca 5. **Tel** (06 26) 31 23 99. Museum of Serbian Ecclesiastical Art: Pátriárka utca 5. **Tel** (06 26) 31 23 99. **Open** May–Sep: 10am–6pm Tue–Sun; Oct–Apr: 10am–4pm Tue–Sun (Jan & Feb: Fri–Sun). Pajor Manor: Kossuth Lajos utca 5. **Tel** (06 26) 92 09 90. **Open** 10am–6pm Tue–Sun. **femuz.hu**. Hungarian Open Air Museum: Sztaravodai u. Pf 63. **Tel** (06 26) 50 25 11. **Open** Apr–Nov: 9am–5pm Tue–Sun. **skanzen.hu**

Only 25 km (16 miles) outside Budapest, Szentendre is a town built and inhabited by a succession of Serbian refugees. Most of Szentendre's older buildings date from the 18th-century.

Blagovestenska church in Fő tér, Szentendre's main square

Orthodox religious tradition lies at the heart of the town, which contains many Orthodox churches. The western European façades hide Slavic interiors filled with incense, icons and candlelight.

Blagovestenska Church on Fő tér, is just one example. Look out for the magnificent iconostasis that separates the sanctuary from the nave. Also of interest is Sunday mass at **Belgrade Cathedral**.

Next door is a **Museum of Serbian Ecclesiastical Art**, full of icons and other religious artifacts. Since the 1920s, Szentendre has been home to an ever-increasing number of artists and the town contains many galleries exhibiting the work of local artists.

The Ferenczy Museum has ten different exhibition locations, including **Pajor Manor** with its three permanent exhibitions on the art of Szentendre. Another notable part of the museum is the Margit Kovács Ceramics Museum located at Vastagh György út 1.

To the west of town is the **Hungarian Open Air Museum**, an ethnographical museum, illustrating the different Hungarian regions and their rural architecture and culture across the social groups, from the 18th to the 20th century.

❹ Vác

40 km (25 miles) N of Budapest. 36,000. from Nyugati pu. from Árpád híd. Március 15 tér 17. **Tel** (06 27) 31 61 60.

Vác has stood on the eastern bank of the Danube since AD 1000. Destroyed by war in the late 17th century, the town was rebuilt and today its centre, built around four squares, dates from the early 18th century. At its heart is Marcius 15 tér, where the **Town Hall** and **Fehérek Church** are located. At the northernmost end of the old town, on Köztársaság út, is Hungary's only **Arc de Triomph**. This was built in 1764, after a visit from the Habsburg Empress, Maria Theresa. The town's **cathedral**, built in Classicist late-Baroque style, is the third largest in Hungary

Arc de Triomph in Vác, built in honour of Empress Maria Theresa

For keys to symbols *see back flap*

Exterior of Fót's Church of the Immaculate Conception

5 Fót

25 km (15 miles) NE of Budapest. 16,000. Nyugati pu. Árpád híd. Vörösmarty tér 3. Károlyi Palace **Open** by appt. **Tel** (06 27) 36 13 39. ground floor only. obligatory. Park: **Open** Apr–Sep: 8am–8pm daily; Oct–Mar: 8am–6pm daily. Church of the Immaculate Conception: Vörösmarty út 2.

Just outside Budapest is the small town of Fót. Its main attraction is the **Károlyi Palace**, birthplace of the country's first president, Mihály Károlyi *(see p36)*. The palace was built in the 1830s, with a pavilion added on each side a decade later. Also worth a visit is the town's attractive 19th-century **Church of the Immaculate Conception**.

6 Gödöllő

30 km (18 miles) NE of Budapest. Hév from Örs vezér tere. Grassalkovich Mansion: **Tel** (06 28) 41 01 24. **Open** Apr–Oct: 10am–6pm daily; Nov–Mar: 10am–4pm Mon–Thu, 10am–5pm Fri–Sun. **Closed** Jan. **kiralyikastely.hu**

Gödöllő is most famous for its restored Baroque palace, the **Grassalkovich Mansion**. Built in 1741, it was the favourite residence of Queen Elizabeth, wife of Franz Joseph. The permanent exhibition in the Royal Museum incorporates the Ceremonial Hall and royal suites, and details the life of the Austro-Hungarian monarchy.

7 Kecskemét

86km (52 miles) SE of Budapest. 110,000. Nyugati pu. Népliget. Kossuth tér 1. **Tel** (06 76) 48 10 65. Town Hall: Kossuth tér 1. **Tel** (06 76) 51 35 13. **Open** 8am–4:30pm Mon–Thu, 8am– 2pm Fri. by appointment. Cifra Palace: Rákóczi utca 1. **Tel** (06 76) 48 07 76. **Open** 10am–5pm Tue–Sun. **kecskemet.hu**

Spreading out in a vast sweep around Budapest is the Great Hungarian Plain, or *Alföld*, which covers nearly half of modern Hungary. For hundreds of years, Kecskemét has been the major market town of the central-southern plain. Distributing and processing the products of the surrounding rich farmland, Kecskemét grew affluent, particularly towards the end of the 19th century. As a result, the town today boasts many gracious squares and splendid 19th and early 20th century buildings. The most famous is Ödön Lechner's massive **Town Hall**. Built between 1893–6, the building is a combination of both Renaissance and Middle-Eastern influences. The flamboyant **Cifra Palace** (Ornamental Palace), built as a casino in 1902, is a uniquely Hungarian variation of the Secession style *(see pp56–9)*.

Kecskemét Town Hall, designed by Ödön Lechner

8 Kiskunfélegyháza

110 km (66 miles) SE of Budapest. 40,000. Szent János tér 2. **Tel** (06 76) 56 14 20. Nyugati pu. Népliget. House of Nature Visitor Centre: Liszt Ferenc u. 19, Kecskemét (for information on Kiskunsági Park). **Tel** (06 76) 50 15 96. **Open** May–mid-Oct: 8am–4pm Tue–Fri, 10am–2pm Sat; mid-Oct–Apr: 8am–4pm Mon–Fri. **knp.hu** Kiskun Museum: Dr Holló Lajos utca 9. **Tel** (06 76) 46 14 68. **Open** Mar–Nov: 8am–4pm Mon, 9am–5pm Tue–Sat. **kiskunmuzeum.hu**

Much of the Great Hungarian Plain is used to grow maize and vines. Small areas, however, have been preserved as national parks. About 15 km (9 miles) to the west of Kiskunfélegyháza is the **Kiskunsági**

Detail of the ornate Town Hall façade at Kiskunfélegyháza

National Park. Many rare native animals and birds can be seen here, as well as the traditional way of life of the plains herdsman. Visitors can also explore nature trails; information is available from the Visitors' Centre in Kecskemét.

The poet Sándor Petőfi was born in Kiskunfélegyháza, and his childhood home is now part of the **Kiskun Museum**. The **Town Hall** combines influences of the Secession style *(see pp56–9)* with motifs from folk art.

❾ Ráckeve

43 km (26 miles) SW of Budapest. 8,500. Eötvös utca 11; H6 from Budapest, Közvágóhíd. Népliget. Kossuth Lajos út 51. **Tel** (06 24) 42 97 47. **tourinform.rackeve.hu**

The village of Ráckeve is built on Csepel Island, which extends 54 km (34 miles) south along the middle of the Danube from Budapest. Ráckeve (Rác means Serb in Hungarian) was founded in the 15th century by Serbs from Keve, who fled Serbia after the Turkish invasion *(see pp28–9)*.

The oldest building in the village is the **Orthodox church**, built by some of the first of the Serbian refugees. Dating back to 1487, this is the oldest Orthodox church in Hungary. Its walls are covered in well-preserved frescos, the first telling the story of the Nativity and the last showing the Resurrection. The church has a beautiful iconostasis separating the sanctuary from the nave.

Ráckeve's peaceful and convenient situation made it the country home of one of Europe's greatest military strategists, Prince Eugene of Savoy. Credited with the expulsion of the Turks from Hungary at the end of the 17th century, Prince Eugene built himself a country **mansion** on Kossuth Lajos utca. Now used as a hotel, the interior of the house has been modernized, but the façade has been preserved. The formal gardens can be seen from the river.

Well-preserved frescoes in the Orthodox church at Ráckeve

❿ Martonvásár

30 km (18 miles) SW of Budapest. 4,900. Buda út 13. **Tel** (06 22) 56 95 00. Déli pu. Brunswick Palace: Brunszvik utca 2. **Open** summer: 8am–5pm; winter: 8am–4pm *(park only)*. Beethoven Museum: **Open** 10am–noon, 2–4pm Tue–Fri, 10am–1pm, 2–5pm Sat & Sun (Nov–Mar: to 4pm Sat & Sun).

The village of Martonvásár has existed here since medieval times, but its principal tourist attraction is now the **Brunswick Palace**. Towards the end of the 18th century the whole village was bought by the German Brunswick family, and the original palace was built for Anton Brunswick in grand Baroque style. A century later, in 1875, the palace was totally rebuilt, this time in the Neo-Gothic style. Little evidence of the original palace remains today, among the flamboyant turrets and pinnacles. The magnificent parklands, however, are open to the public and are much as they always have been. The estate's church, built in 1775, also remains largely unaltered. The interior of the church is decorated with well-preserved frescoes.

Ludwig van Beethoven was a regular visitor to the original palace. He gave music lessons to the daughters of the house, Therèse and Josephine, with whom he is said to have fallen in love. Some of the palace rooms have been converted into a **Beethoven Museum**. The Beethoven festival is held in the gardens during the summer.

The Neo-Gothic Brunswick Palace at Martonvásár

THREE GUIDED WALKS

Budapest is a city made for exploring on foot. From Turkish bathhouses to Baroque palaces, evidence of the city's past is visible at every turn. These guided walks take you through three fascinating areas: Óbuda to the north of the city centre, once the site of a Roman garrison and now a residential district; Margaret Island, a park in the middle of the Danube; and the historic stretch that extends from Buda across Chain Bridge and into Pest. Óbuda has yielded some of the oldest archeological finds in Hungary. This walk takes in the ruins of a Roman amphitheatre, and more modern attractions. The walk around car-free Margaret Island includes an exotic landscaped garden. The third excursion encompasses the old buildings of Buda's Castle District and Pest's lively Central Market.

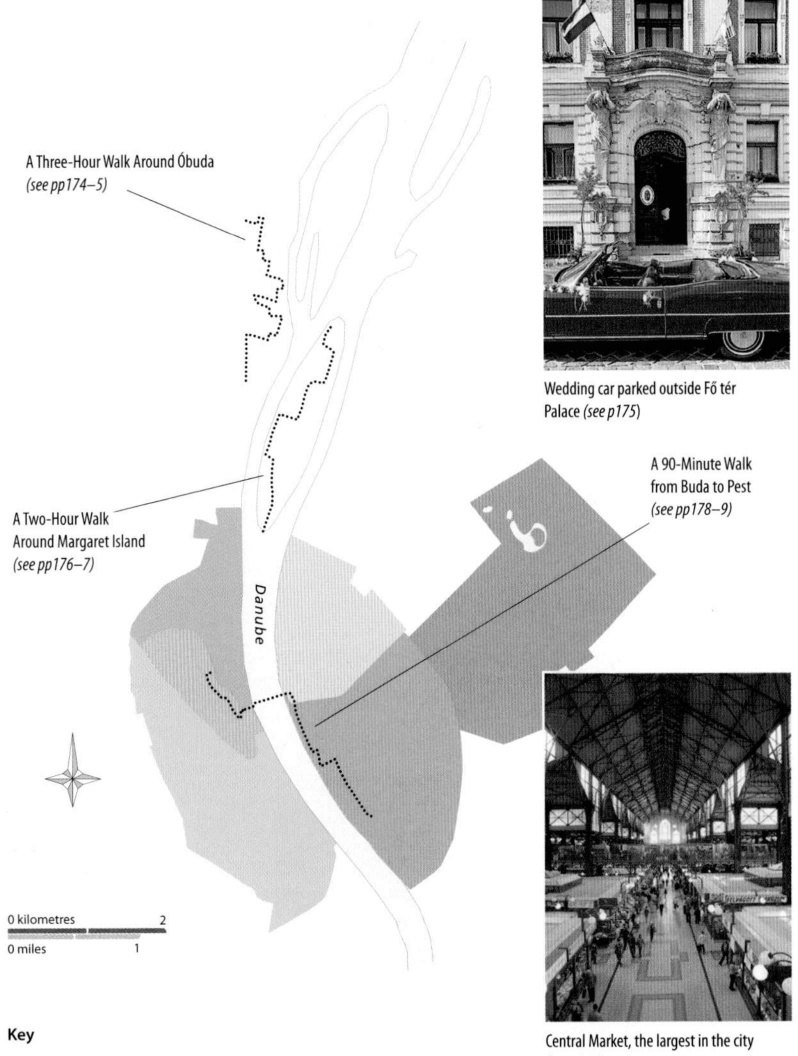

Wedding car parked outside Fő tér Palace *(see p175)*

Central Market, the largest in the city *(see p179)*

◀ Sculpture on Margaret Island, a haven of greenery in the middle of the Danube

A Three-Hour Walk around Óbuda

At first glance Óbuda today seems little more than a concrete jungle of tower blocks and flyovers. Behind the grey façade, however, there is a strong local identity and clues to the area's long and colourful past abound. Arriving here in AD 89, the Romans built a garrison in this district shortly before founding the civilian town of Aquincum *(see pp166–7)* to the north. After the departure of Romans in the 5th century AD, successive waves of invaders, including the Magyars *(see pp24–5)* all left their mark on Óbuda (literally "Old Buda"). By the end of the 16th century, Óbuda was a thriving market town, eventually forming part of the city of Budapest in 1873.

① A section of Óbuda's impressive Roman amphitheatre

⑩ The elegant, Neo-Baroque Fő tér Palace with its sentry box

The Roman Amphitheatre

Begin the walk at the corner of Bécsi út and Pacsirtamező út, which is dominated by the remains of a very fine Roman amphitheatre ①. The Romans arrived in the region soon after the time of Christ, building this impressive amphitheatre in the middle of the 2nd century AD, by which time Aquincum was the thriving capital of the province of Lower Pannonia *(see pp22–3)*. Originally used by the Roman soldiers from the nearby garrison, it became a fortress in the 9th century for the invading Magyar army. Not much remains of its once huge walls, but the scale of the theatre, which was designed to seat 14,000, is still awe inspiring.

Old Óbuda Synagogue to Flórián Tér

From the amphitheatre, continue along Pacsirtamező út and turn down Perc utca left up Mókus utca and Jós utca, turning left into Lajos utca. At No. 163 is the Óbuda Synagogue ②. Built in the early 1820s to serve the area's growing Jewish community, this is a Neo-Classical building with a six-columned portico. The synagogue once served as a television studio, but in 2010 Hungarian Television handed over the building to the Jewish community and it once again became a functioning synagogue. Some restoration work has already taken place, but the building requires further renovation. Also on Lajos utca, at No. 168, is Óbuda Parish Church ③. Constructed in 1744–9 on the site of the Roman military camp, the church has survived since then largely unchanged. The interior includes a magnificently carved pulpit showing the Good Shepherd and Mary Magdalene. Turning left up Óbudai utca, you will pass the house where the popular novelist, bon viveur and local character, Gyula Krúdy once lived ④. Writing in the early 20th century, much of Krúdy's work looks back at an idealized rural Hungary and is extremely popular in his country. This now houses the Hungarian Museum of Trade and Tourism. The museum's collection includes tools, scales

④ The former home of novelist and colourful local figure, Gyula Krúdy

and samples of the industry's products. From here, turn right along Tanuló utca and pass the ruins of the 14th-century St Clare's Nunnery ⑤. Then turn left towards Flórián tér. As you pass Kálvin köz, on the left at No. 2 is the 18th-century Óbuda Calvinist Church ⑥.

Key

••• Walk route

0 metres 400

0 yards 400

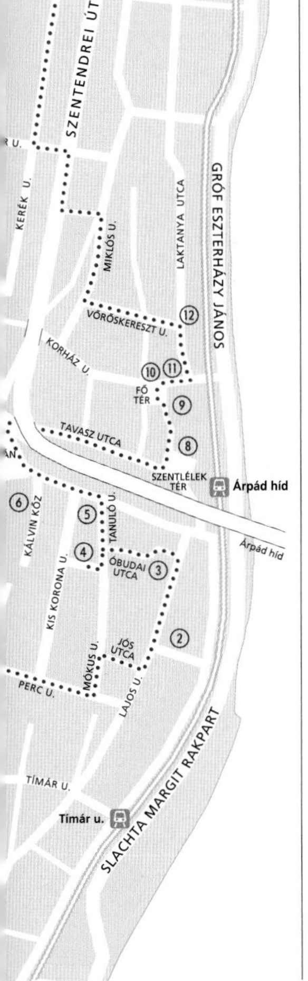

⑨ Zichy Palace, built in the 18th century for an aristocratic family

Next door is the presbytery, built in 1909 to a design by Károly Kós, better known for his work on the Wekerle Estate *(see p161)*. No. 4 is home to a collection of folk crafts. Walk back up to busy Flórián tér, where in 1778 Roman thermal baths were discovered. Hidden in the underpasses beneath the square are the Roman Baths Museum and the Roman Settlement Museum ⑦.

Szentlélek Tér and Fő Tér

Tavasz utca, off to the right from north of Flórián tér, leads to Szentlélek tér. In the south wing of the Zichy Palace, on Szentlélek tér, is the Vasarely Museum ⑧. The 20th-century artist Victor Vasarely is remembered as the founder of the Op-Art movement, producing work full of bright colours and optical illusions. The crumbling Zichy Palace ⑨ itself was built for the Zichy family in 1757.

⑪ One of several *Women with Umbrellas* by Imre Varga

Continue north up to Fő tér, one of the few areas of 18th- and 19th-century architecture remaining in Óbuda. On one side of the square stands the Neo-Baroque Fő tér Palace ⑩, its entrance still guarded by an 18th-century sentry box.

Imre Varga Gallery to the Hercules Villa

From Fő tér Palace walk up Laktanya utca, where there is a group of statues, *Women with Umbrellas*, by contemporary sculptor Imre Varga ⑪. At No. 7 Laktanya utca is the Imre Varga Gallery ⑫, where further examples of the sculptor's work can be seen. Finally, make your way up to Szentendrei út and cross it at an underpass. Turn right into Kerék utca (if you miss this, take the next right up Szél utca), then left into Herkules utca then onto Meggyfa utca to finish the walk at No. 21, the ruins of the Hercules Villa ⑬. Once a lavish Roman home, it takes its name from some stunning mosaics *(see p23)*. The villa is open only by arrangement (Tel (06 1) 430 1081). Near the villa are the remains of the *cella trichora*, an early Christian chapel dating from the 4th century AD.

Tips for Walkers

Starting point: Pacsirtamező utca.
Getting there: Bus 86 or tram 19, 41, 61.
Length: 3 km (1.8 miles).
Stops: Kéhli Vendéglö *(see p206)* on Mókus utca, or the Új Sipos Étterem on Fő tér for traditional Hungarian dishes.

A Two-Hour Walk around Margaret Island

Historically inaccessible in the middle of the Danube, Margaret Island was a retreat for religious contemplation from at least the 11th century onwards. Relics of the island's past include the remains of two monastic churches and also the ruins of the convent home of Princess Margit, daughter of King Béla IV, who gave the island its name. Opened to the public in 1869, Margaret Island is today Budapest's most beautiful park, a car-free haven of greenery in the middle of the city and the ideal location for a peaceful stroll. On the western shore, the Palatinus Strand bathing complex makes use of the mineral-rich hot springs rising on the island.

⑤ The Water Tower

⑧ A relief of Archangel Michael on St Michael's Church

Centenary Monument to Palatinus Strand

The walk begins amid the peace and greenery of the southern tip of Margaret Island. Proceeding to the north, the first landmark is the Centenary Monument ① *(see p66)*, which stands in front of a sizable fountain. Designed by István Kiss, the monument was made in 1973, to commemorate the centenary of the unification of the towns of Buda, Óbuda and Pest *(see p34)*. At night the fountain is dramatically illuminated. You can also rent four-wheel family bikes here called *Bringóhintó*. Taking a left turn ahead, the Hajós Olympic Pool Complex ② *(see p55)* is soon reached. Built in 1930, the complex was designed by the multi-talented Alfréd Hajós. He won gold medals in swimming events in the 1896 Olympic Games and was also a member of the Hungarian football team. Turn right and then left to continue northwards, there is a rose garden to the right before the ruins of the early 14th-century Franciscan Church ③ come into view. Constructed in the Gothic style of the time, the church was originally attached to a monastery. Visible in the west wall is the doorway which once led to the organ loft, as well as a spiral staircase and fine arched window. Further on is the busy Palatinus Strand ④ *(see p55)*. In front of the entrance to its pools stands a statue by French sculptor Emile Guilleaume.

③ Ruins of the 14th-century Franciscan Church

Water Tower to St Michael's Church

Clearly visible to the northeast of Palatinus Strand, is the 57-m (187-ft) high Water Tower ⑤. Built in 1911 and now protected by UNESCO, this graceful tower is currently used as an exhibition space for a variety of previously unexhibited modern crafts and artworks, ranging from puppets to paintings. At the foot of the Water Tower is the Summer Theatre, a large modern amphitheatre seating 3,500 people, which hosts a summer season of musical performances. To the

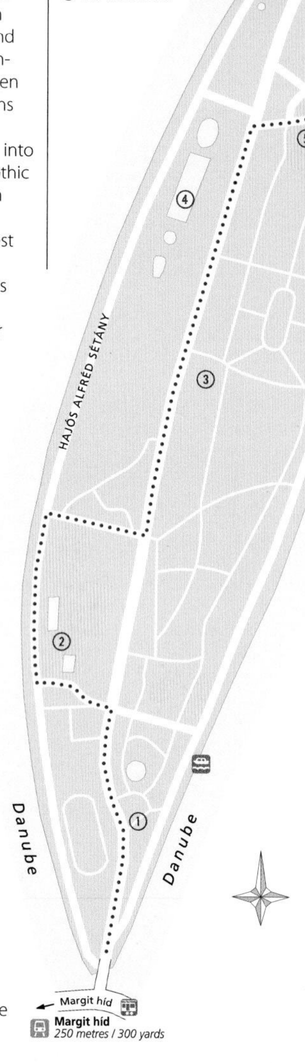

southeast of the Water Tower are the ruins of a 13th-century Dominican Church and Convent ⑥. The latter was once home to Princess Margit, after whom the island is named. King Béla IV *(see p25)* swore that if he succeeded in repelling the Mongol invasion of 1241 that he would offer his daughter to God. He kept his oath, building the church and convent, to which the 9-year-old Princess Margit was sent in 1251. She led a godly and ascetic life and died here at the age of 29. Nearly 300 years later, in 1541, the nuns of the convent fled to Pozsony (now Bratislava, capital of the Slovak Republic) in the face of the Turkish invasion, *(see pp28–9)*, leaving the church and the convent to be destroyed. Severe floods in 1838 led to the discovery of the ruined church and its underground vaults. The tomb of the now-canonized Margit was also excavated here 20 years later. Just to the north of the Dominican Church and Convent, near to the Water Tower, is the beginning of Artists' Avenue ⑦. A collection of contemporary busts of Hungarian writers, painters and musicians lines this promenade leading up to the Grand Hotel Margitsziget. A little way before the hotel is St Michael's Church ⑧. Originally built by members of the Premonstratensian Order, this is the oldest building on the island. In addition, the foundations of an 11th-century chapel have been excavated inside the 12th century church. Destroyed by the invading Turks in 1541, the church was eventually reconstructed in the 1930s, using materials from the original building. In the bell tower hangs a bell which, unusually, survived the Turkish invasion. Probably buried by the monks at the time of the invasion, the bell dates from the early 15th century. It was discovered in 1914 when its walnut-tree hiding place was uprooted during a violent storm.

⑦ Bust of Zsigmond Móricz on Artists' Avenue

⑪ Stepped pathway through the lush foliage of the Japanese Garden

Grand Hotel Margitsziget to Árpád Bridge

The Grand Hotel Margitsziget ⑨ was designed in 1872 by Miklós Ybl *(see p123)*. For many years it was the most fashionable hotel in Budapest, known simply as "The Grand". After World War II, the hotel was modernized and called the Danubius Grand, and in the 1970s the luxurious Danubius Health Spa Resort Margitsziget ⑩ was built nearby. The two hotels are joined by an underground walkway and offer thermal baths and a variety of spa treatments *(see p54)*. Heading west from the latter hotel, the final stretch of the walk passes beside the Japanese Garden ⑪. A variety of exotic plants, a rock garden, waterfalls and streams crossed by rustic bridges all add to the garden's atmosphere. The final stopping point on the walk is an unusual musical well, known as the Bodor Well ⑫. The original well was designed and constructed by Transylvanian Péter Bodor in 1820 and stood in the town of Marosvásárhely (modern-day Tirgu Mures, in Romania), which was then part of the Austro-Hungarian Empire. In 1936 this copy was built on Margaret Island. Continuing past the well, at the northern tip of Margaret Island the Árpád Bridge provides another link from the island back to the city.

⑫ The musical Bodor Well

Key

• • • Walk route

0 metres 500

0 yards 500

Tips for Walkers

Starting point: Southern end of Margaret Island, reached from Margaret Bridge (híd.

Getting there: Bus 26. Tram 4, 6.

Length: 3.3 km (2 miles).

Stops: There are numerous take-away kiosks and cafés on the island, selling drinks, snacks and ice creams. The Danubius Grand Hotel and Danubius Health Spa Resort Margitsziget ⑩ also have restaurants and cafés.

A 90-Minute Walk from Buda to Pest

Buda and Pest were unified in 1873, an act made possible by the construction of the monumental Chain Bridge some 20 years earlier. Before that, the two areas had shared a relatively common history, but they always retained separate identities. Even today, Buda remains more regal and relaxed than commercial, dynamic Pest. This walk reveals such differences, while highlighting the bond that makes Budapest's whole greater even than the sum of its sublime parts.

② The terrace and conical towers of Fishermen's Bastion

The Castle District

The walk begins at the 13th-century Mátyás Church ① *(see pp86–7)*, one of the oldest buildings in Buda, and coronation church of the Hungarian kings. Directly behind are the ramparts of Fishermen's Bastion ② *(see p84)*, from where there are famous views across the Danube to Pest. Return past the main portal of Mátyás Church and onto Tárnok utca, running the gauntlet of its myriad souvenir shops, before arriving at Dísz tér and the Honvéd Monument ③ *(see p77)*. The monument was raised in honour of those who died in the Hungarian revolution of 1848–9.

Head south out of the square, along stately Szinház utca to Sándor Palace ④ *(see p77)*, one of Buda's finest buildings and the residence of the Hungarian president. Past the terminus of the Sikló, the funicular that links the Royal Palace to the embankment below, an extravagantly ornamental gateway ⑤ *(see p74)* leads from the Habsurg Steps to the Royal Palace. A wide path meanders in front of the palace and offers more fine views of Pest.

Across the Danube into Pest

The path leads down through well-kept terraces to Clark Ádam tér, named after the Scottish engineer Adam Clark, who built the awe-inspiring Chain Bridge and the Neo-Classical Alagút tunnel ⑥ *(see p104)*, which channels traffic underneath the Royal Palace. In the centre of the square is the Zero Kilometre Stone ⑦, from which the official distance from Budapest to Vienna is measured. Walk to the centre of Chain Bridge ⑧ *(see pp66 and 116)* and look back towards the Castle District. On a clear day there are glorious views of the Royal Palace and the unmistakable Neo-Gothic silhouette of Mátyás Church.

View from Buda to the Parliament Building in Pest

Roosevelt tér to Váci utca

Facing the Pest side of the river there are rewarding vistas too: of Budapest's peerless Parliament building *(see pp112–13)*; and of the city's grandest hotel, the Four Seasons Gresham Palace ⑨ *(see p118)*, on the far side of Roosevelt tér. The hotel's astonishingly opulent foyer is well worth a visit.

From Széchenyi István tér, a walkway runs south next to the tram lines on Belgrád Rakpart.

Tips for Walkers

Starting point: Mátyás Church, Széll Kálmán tér.
Getting there: buses 16 and 16A from Széll Kálmán tér, or tram 2r.
Length: 3.8 km (2 miles).
Stops: Gresham Palace Kávéház on Széchenyi István tér, Corso Étterem at Vigadó tér 2, or 1000 Tea at Váci utca 65.

② The striking architecture of Vigadó Concert Hall on Vigadó tér

After a short walk, László Marton's charming sculpture of a little girl, entitled *Little Princess* ⑩ is perched on the railings on the right. Passing the small pier at Vigadó tér ⑪ *(see p130)*, you cannot miss the eclectic architecture of Vigadó Concert Hall ⑫ on the square's eastern side.

Nearby, the Budapest Marriott hotel ⑬, a modernist masterpiece, appears on the left.

Continuing along the embankment, take a left turn just before Petőfi tér onto Régiposta utca. Next, a sharp right turn onto Apáczai utca leads to the Roman remains of Contra Aquincum ⑭ *(see p126)*, and the Inner City Parish Church ⑮ *(see pp128–9)*, now sadly hemmed in by the approach to the Elizabeth Bridge. Turn right at the church, and, with the Danube at your back, head towards Váci utca to the point where it crosses the busy Szabadsajtó út. Here, the Klotild Palaces ⑯ *(see p131)*, massive twin apartment blocks built on either side of the road, provide a splendid gateway to the bridge.

Key

••• Walk route

0 metres 400

0 yards 400

Cafés and the Central Market Hall

The southern part of Váci utca ⑰ *(see p131)* is less charming and more commercial than its northern counterpart, but on summer afternoons it is thronged with people, many of whom stop to enjoy coffee or something stronger on its many terraces. Halfway along on the right is the hapless St Michael City Church ⑱, built around 1230, devastated by the Turks in 1541, rebuilt in 1701, and finally completely renovated from 1964-8. Its unimpressive exterior belies a rich interior.

From here, more cafés and bars lead along a widening street to Central Market Hall ⑲ *(see p211)*. The largest market in the city, its stalls sell fruit and vegetables, fish, meat and cheese, and Hungarian crafts.

⑰ The shops and busy terrace cafés of Váci utca

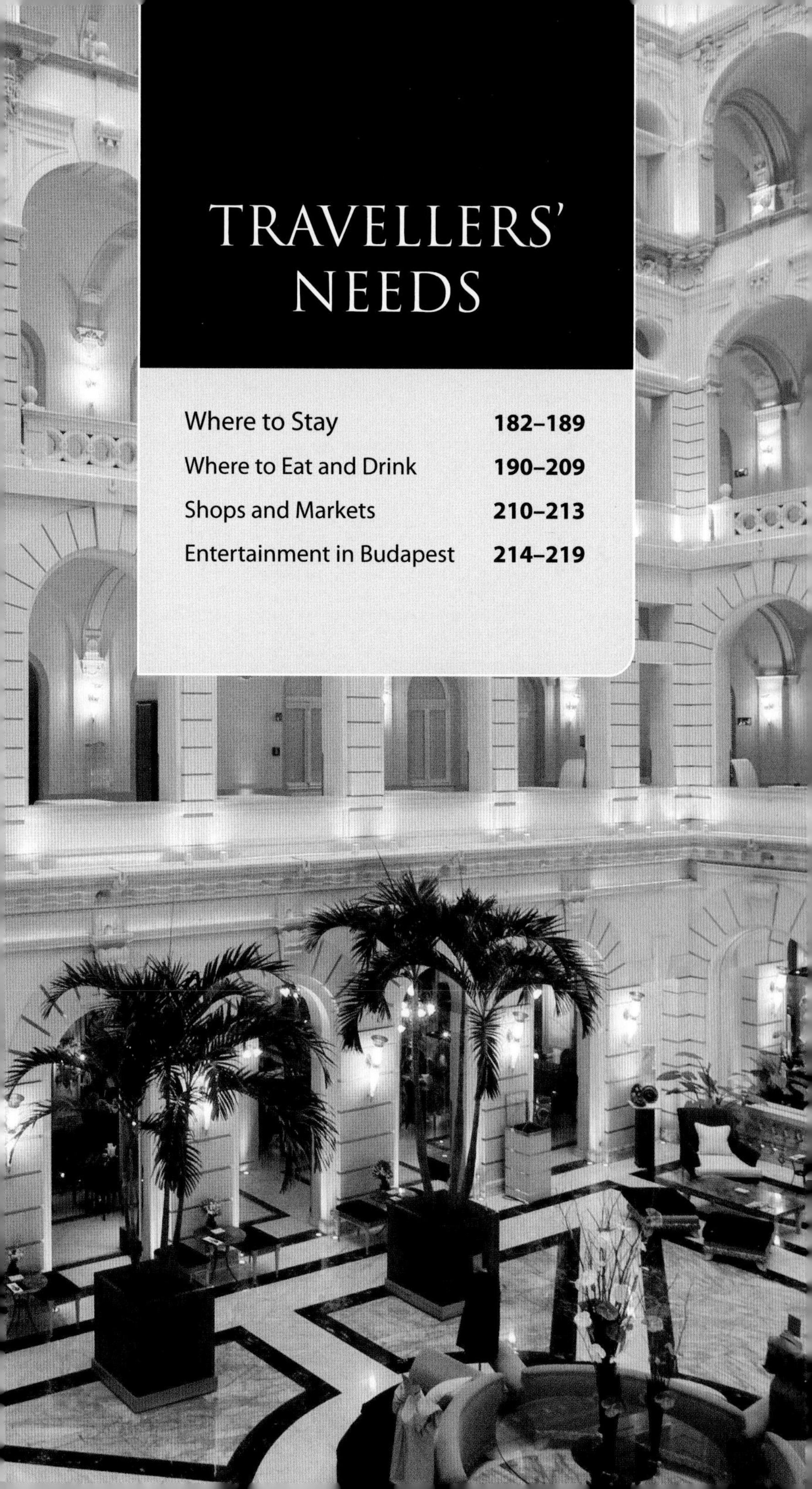

TRAVELLERS' NEEDS

WHERE TO STAY

Budapest's stock of accommodation is vast, and it's possible to find something to suit all tastes and budgets. Luxury and design hotels lead the way, though in this city of thermal springs, spa hotels are also plentiful. Cheaper accommodation can be found in hotels outside the city centre, as well as in the growing number of pensions and hostels. Travel agents and tourist information offices *(see p185)* can provide information on places to stay. The hotels on pages 186–9 include a selection of the best luxury, design, historic, spa, pension and business accommodation in Budapest, listed by area and in order of price category to help you choose the right hotel. Some entries are highlighted as DK Choice, which are establishments that offer a truly memorable stay.

Impressive façade of the Four Seasons Gresham Palace *(see p187)*

Where to Look

When deciding on accommodation, first choose the general location: Buda or Pest, or maybe even the picturesque suburbs further afield. The greatest concentration of accommodation is in low-lying Pest, where many hotels are literally only a few steps away from most of the major tourist attractions. Many luxury hotels are sited here, such as the Sofitel Budapest Chain Bridge *(see p188)*, set along the eastern bank of the Danube, while others, such as the Marriott *(see p188)* or the Kempinski Corvinus *(see p188)* are situated nearer to the centre of Pest, close to the theatres and shops. You'll also find most of the city's hostels in Pest.

There is a decent selection of hotels across the Danube on the Buda side, with many possessing spa facilities. Pensions abound here too, particularly up in the hills, where visitors can enjoy cool, fresh air and quiet surroundings.

Hotels located further out of town are usually an easy journey from the city centre, particularly since they are often situated close to metro stations.

Budapestinfo *(see p185)* is a chain of tourist offices that provide information (in several languages) on accommodation and places to eat, as well as on tourist and cultural events. Maps can be found on sale here, as well as free booklets and pamphlets.

Hotel and Pension Classification

Hotels are classified in five categories from one to five stars.

At the luxury end of the scale – the five-star and four-star hotels – all rooms have a bathroom, a telephone, a TV, a radio and a refrigerator, air conditioning and Wi-Fi. The majority of these hotels offer 24-hour service, including meals that can be brought to the room, as well as business and fitness facilities. Three-star hotels usually have at least one restaurant and one bar, and staff are expected to speak at least one foreign language, though both English and German are common. Two-thirds of the rooms in two-star hotels have their own shower or bath, while rooms in one-star hotels simply have wash-basins with hot and cold running water.

Accommodation in pensions is generally clean and simple, though usually very homely, with all the necessary services and amenities provided by friendly and helpful staff.

Spacious twin room at the Hilton Budapest Hotel *(see p188)*

◀ Atrium and lobby at the luxurious New York Palace, Budapest

Opulent guest room at the Buddha-Bar Hotel Budapest Klotild Palace *(see p187)*

Hotel Prices

Room tariffs reflect the hotel classification, though with online booking now prevalent, there are some great deals to be had if you book far enough in advance, even amongst the luxury hotels. Generally speaking, however, a centrally located, higher category hotel will be much more expensive than in an out-of-town, lower category hotel. Relatively cheap rooms can be found in pensions, and even cheaper ones in hostels, many of which now offer double rooms. Hotel prices usually include breakfast, which in hotels with three stars or more typically means a self-service buffet. Pensions also offer good value meals. Hostels may charge extra for breakfast.

Many luxury hotels offer substantial weekend reductions in the low season (mid-September to mid-March). During this period a three-night stay would cost the same as a two-night stay during the high season. Guests can also stay an extra night free of charge.

In spa hotels, such as the Danubius Hotel Gellért *(see p187)*, which offer hydrotherapy, the fee for using the pools and sauna is included in the room price. However, any treatments, such as massage, will incur an extra charge. Check these details with the hotel in advance.

Note that prices are often ramped up massively over the Christmas and New Year period, as well as around the time of the Formula 1 Hungarian Grand Prix and the Sziget Festival.

Prices in Budapest's hotels and pensions are usually quoted in euros, but you can pay in forints.

Hidden Extras

Both VAT and resort tax are included in the price of the room (resort tax is charged because Budapest is classed as a health resort), but there are often hidden surcharges that can greatly increase the overall cost of a stay. Avoid, for example, hotel currency exchange desks, which offer a poor rate of exchange, and making international telephone calls from your room.

Most hotels have their own car parks. Some, such as the Sofitel Budapest Chain Bridge *(see p188)* or the Victoria Hotel *(see p186)*, offer off-street or garage parking, for which a modest fee may be charged.

How to Book

The Budapest tourist season starts in the middle of June and lasts until the end of September. During this period, but particularly around New Year and the Formula 1 Hungarian Grand Prix weekend *(see p63)*, hotels can be booked months in advance. Otherwise, it is advisable to book at least two weeks ahead. Nearly all hotels accept bookings made via online booking systems.

It is possible to find accommodation without booking in advance, but rooms may be harder to come by, especially in high season. Bookings can be made in the tourist offices at the airport or at any of the Tourist Information offices located in the city centre.

Stained-glass window in the Danubius Hotel Gellért *(see p187)*

Stylish reception area at the La Prima Fashion Hotel *(see p186)*

Travelling with Children

Most hotels welcome children and offer free accommodation to those up to the age of four travelling with their parents. Additional beds can often be provided for older children in the parents' room for a small extra charge. Many higher-end hotels also offer a child-minding service.

Disabled Travellers

Budapest has been slow to acknowledge the needs of the disabled traveller, though specialist facilities are gradually being introduced throughout the city. Nearly all new hotels now have rooms for disabled guests, while some of the older ones continue to adapt their existing facilities. Further information is best obtained directly from the hotel before making your booking.

Self-Catering

A few hotels in Budapest, especially those in the embassy district, offer accommodation in suites with kitchenettes. This type of accommodation is particularly good for families as it gives them the option of eating "at home", rather than eating every meal at a restaurant. Another advantage is, of course, the extra space, which allows greater freedom of movement; often hotel suites in Budapest are equal in size to an apartment.

There are also some specially converted buildings that consist solely of self-catering apartments. The **Charles Apartment Hotel** is a good example of this type of accommodation; the apartments are spacious and well-equipped.

Hostels

Budapest possesses a huge number of hostels, and for visitors on a tight budget, these provide good, if basic, low-cost accommodation. As well as dormitories, many offer single, double and family rooms, often with en-suite facilities. **Marco Polo Hostel** and the **Citadella**, which is situated in the Citadel on Gellért Hill *(see pp96–7)*, are just two examples. Most hostels are open all year, though during the summer vacation in July and August, many students' halls of residence are turned into hostels, adding approximately 4,000 beds to Budapest's accommodation list and providing tourists with a convenient and inexpensive place to stay.

Given their popularity, it is advisable to book a hostel room in advance. This is best done online via the **Mellow Mood Travel Agency** or hostel booking companies such as www.hostels.com or www.hostelworld.com. International Youth Hostels Organisation members get a discount on rates with a membership card.

Staying in Private Rooms and Apartments

Accommodation in a private room usually consists of a separate bedroom and use of a kitchen and bathroom. The price depends on the facilities and the area, and varies from 6,000–12,000 Hungarian forints (€20-€40) per day for a double room and upwards of 6,000 forints (€20) for a single. **IBUSZ** is the most reputable agency through which this type of accommodation can be booked.

Renting an apartment is economical for longer stays. As well as using agencies to find private apartments, it is worth checking the *albérlet* (to rent) advertisements in newspapers such as *Expressz* and *Hirdetés* and on the Internet.

Camping

Camping is only permitted at designated campsites, of which there are several on the outskirts of Budapest. The biggest and most picturesque is **Római Camping**, which is located on the road leading from Óbuda to Szentendre. Campsites are open, in general, from May until the end of October. Some operations, such as **Haller Camping**, are open only from May to September, while others remain open throughout the year.

Stunning light installation in the lobby of the Hilton Budapest City *(see p188)*

Recommended Hotels

The accommodation on pages 186–9 is listed under six categories: Luxury, Design, Historic, Spa, Pension and Business/Chain. Budapest is home to an abundance of luxury hotels, all of which offer a supreme level of comfort as well as comprehensive facilities. Thanks to Budapest's wealth of grand architecture, historic accommodation is also plentiful, and there is a proliferation of brilliantly conceived design hotels throughout the city. Spa hotels are big business in Budapest, which is not surprising given that the city sits on more than a hundred springs. More affordable are the plethora of pensions located in the Buda Hills and around the city fringes, which is also where the majority of business and chain hotels are situated.

Any establishment highlighted as a DK Choice offers a singularly unique experience, be it distinguished rooms, cutting-edge amenities, fantastic views or first-class service, though it is typically a combination of some or all of these aspects.

Swimming pool and spa at the Boscolo Budapest *(see p187)*

DIRECTORY

Information

Hungarian National Tourist Office (UK)
Embassy of the Republic of Hungary, 46 Eaton Place, London SW1X 8AL.
Tel 020 7823 1055.
W gotohungary.co.uk

Hungarian National Tourist Office (US)
447 Broadway, Fifth Floor, Manhattan, New York, NY 10013.
Tel 212 695 1221.
W gotohungary.com

Budapestinfo Points
Airport Terminal 2A
Liszt Ferenc Budapest Airport Terminal 2A.
Open 8am–10pm.

Airport Terminal 2B
Liszt Ferenc Budapest Airport Terminal 2B.
Open 10am–10pm.

City Centre Liszt Ferenc tér
1061 Budapest, Liszt Ferenc tér 11.
Open noon–8pm.

City Centre Sütő u.
1052 Budapest, Sütő u. 2.
Open 8am–10pm.

Agencies

IBUSZ Travel Agency
1051 Budapest, József Attila utca 20.
Map 2 E5.
Tel (06 1) 501 49 10/11.
W ibusz.hu

Mellow Mood Travel Agency
1077 Budapest, Baross tér 15.
Map 7 C2.
Tel (06 1) 413 20 64.
W hostels.hu

Self-Catering

Charles Apartment Hotel
1016 Budapest, Hegyalja út 23.
Map 3 B2 (9 B5).
Tel (06 1) 212 91 69.
W charleshotel.hu

Hostels

Back Pack Guesthouse
XI, Takács Menyhért utca 33.
Map 3 B5.
Tel (06 1) 385 89 46.
W backpackbudapest.hu

Boat Hostel Fortuna
1137 Szent István Park, Alsó rakpart.
Map 2 D1.
Tel (06 1) 288 81 00.
W fortunahajo.hu

Citadella
1118 Budapest, Citadella sétány.
Map 4 D3.
Tel (06 1) 466 57 94.
W citadella.hu

Marco Polo Hostel
1072 Budapest, Nyár utca 6.
Map 7 A3.
Tel (06 1) 413 25 55.
W marcopolohostel.com

Red Bus Hostel
V. Semmelweis utca 14.
Map 4 F1.
Tel (06 1) 266 01 36.
W redbusbudapest.hu

Private Rooms and Apartments

IBUSZ Travel
1051 Budapest, József Attila utca 20.
Map 2 E5.
Tel (06 1) 501 49 10/11.
W ibusz.hu

Camping

Csillebérc Autós Camping
1121 Budapest, Konkoly Thege út 21.
Tel (06 1) 395 65 37/27.

Haller Camping
1096 Budapest, Haller utca 27.
Tel (06 1) 476 34 18.
W hallercamping.hu

Római Camping
1031 Budapest, Szentendrei út 189.
Tel (06 1) 388 71 67.
W romaicamping.hu

Where to Stay

Design

Castle District

Baltazár HUF HUF
Országház utca 31
Tel *(06 1) 300 7051* **Map** 1 A4
W baltazarbudapest.com
Artful rooms inspired by the likes of Warhol and Westwood, with clever extras like music systems that link into your smartphone.

DK Choice

Buda Castle Fashion Hotel HUF HUF HUF
Úri utca 39
Tel *(06 1) 224 7900* **Map** 1 B4
W budacastlehotelbudapest.com
This sublime 15th-century merchant's house has been converted into one of the city's leading hotels, presenting a mix of spacious rooms and luxurious mini-suites, all smartly furnished; the highlight, though, is taking breakfast in the impeccably manicured garden courtyard.

Lánchíd 19 
Lánchíd utca 19
Tel *(06 1) 419 1900* **Map** 1 C5
W lanchid19hotel.hu
A superb waterside location, with suspended glass walkways and colourful rooms.

North of the Castle District

art'otel 
Bem rakpart 16–19
Tel *(06 1) 487 9487* **Map** 1 C4
W artotels.com
From the artwork decorating the walls, to the carpets and chinaware, the individually designed rooms are extremely tasteful.

Victoria Hotel 
Bem rakpart 11
Tel *(06 1) 457 8080* **Map** 1 C4
W victoria.hu
Small hotel with big rooms, many with superlative river views from the floor-to-ceiling windows.

Around Parliament

Aventura Boutique Hostel HUF
Visegrádi utca 12
Tel *(06 1) 239 0782* **Map** 2 E2
W aventurahostelbudapest.com
There are four fantastic loft rooms at this agreeable, family-run hostel, each one reflecting a different country or culture.

Cotton House HUF
Jókai utca 26
Tel *(06 1) 354 2600* **Map** 2 F3
W cottonhouse.hu
With some of the best and most thoughtfully decorated rooms anywhere in the capital, all named after famous people, this hotel is full of character.

Home Made Hostel HUF
Teréz körút 22
Tel *(06 1) 302 2103* **Map** 2 F3
W homemadehostel.com
Superbly conceived, rustically styled hostel with bags of charm and first-rate facilities including a fabulous kitchen.

Central Pest

Bohem Art Hotel 
Molnár utca 35
Tel *(06 1) 327 9020* **Map** 4 E2
W bohemarthotel.hu
Former factory, now a high-class boutique hotel offering compact, creatively designed rooms. Great location and friendly staff.

Cosmo City Hotel 
Váci utca 77
Tel *(06 1) 799 0077* **Map** 4 F2
W cosmohotelbudapest.com
At this brilliantly central hotel the warm and amply sized rooms are a riot of bold colours.

Estilo Fashion Hotel 
Váci utca 83
Tel *(06 1) 799 7170* **Map** 4 F2
W estilohotelbudapest.com
Rooms at this enchanting hotel are lively, fresh and modern, if a little on the small side.

Stunning atrium at the Four Seasons Gresham Palace

Price Guide
Prices are based on one night's stay in high season for a standard double room, inclusive of service charges and taxes.

up to 25,000 forints
25,000–50,000 forints
over 50,000 forints

Gerlóczy 
Gerlóczy utca 1
Tel *(06 1) 501 4000* **Map** 4 F1
W gerloczy.hu
Spread over three floors, the variously coloured rooms (red, green and grey) feature beautifully designed fixtures and fittings.

La Prima Fashion Hotel HUF HUF
Piarista utca 6
Tel *(06 1) 799 0088* **Map** 4 E1
W laprimahotelbudapest.com
An effortlessly stylish hotel with plush rooms equipped with a host of mod cons.

Zara Boutique 
Só utca 6
Tel *(06 1) 577 0700* **Map** 4 F2
W boutiquehotelbudapest.com
Rooms are modestly sized but impressively turned out at this understatedly cool, and very central, hotel.

Continental Hotel Zara HUF HUF HUF
Dohány utca 42-44
Tel *(06 1) 815 1000* **Map** 7 A3
W continentalhotelbudapest.com
An Art Deco inspired hotel with a huge range of amenities, including a beautiful rooftop garden.

Soho HUF HUF HUF
Dohány utca 64
Tel *(06 1) 872 8292* **Map** 7 B2
W sohoboutiquehotel.com
A spectacular Pop Art lobby leads to funky rooms with bamboo covered walls and Swedish hardwood floors.

Around Városliget

Atrium Fashion Hotel HUF
Csokonai utca 14
Tel *(06 1) 299 0777* **Map** 7 B3
W atriumhotelbudapest.com
This cleverly conceived hotel offers bright rooms arrayed around a high glass atrium.

Royal Park Boutique Hotel HUF
Nefelejcs utca 6
Tel *(06 1) 872 8888* **Map** 7 C1
W royalparkboutiquehotel.hu
An imposing glass and brick building awash with style and colour, from the dazzling lobby to the accomplished rooms.

Mirage Fashion Hotel HUF HUF
Dózsa György út 88
Tel *(06 1) 462 7070* **Map** 5 C4
W miragehotelbudapest.com
This grand19th-century villa overlooking Heroes' Square offers sophisticated rooms.

Historic

Castle District

St George's Residence Hotel 
Fortuna utca 4
Tel *(06 1) 393 5700* **Map** 1 B4
W stgeorgehotel.hu
A medieval inn accommodating a stunning selection of suites furnished in Grand Empire style.

North of the Castle District

Antique Hostel 
Iskola utca 31
Tel *(06 1) 580 0056* **Map** 1 C3
W antiquehostel.eu
A splendid late 18th-century house that is now a lively hostel with doubles, multi and family rooms.

Around Parliament

DK Choice

Four Seasons Gresham Palace 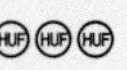
Széchenyi István tér 5-6
Tel *(06 1) 268 6000* **Map** 2 D5
W fourseasons.com
Following extensive restoration, this magnificent building is now one of the finest hotels in Central Europe. The rooms are complete, unbridled luxury, the staff are impeccable and the whole place is a real treat. Don't miss the Kavehaz Restaurant.

Central Pest

Danubius Astoria Hotel HUF
Kossuth Lajos utca 19
Tel *(06 1) 889 6000* **Map** 4 F1
W danubiushotels.com
A grand, Secessionist-style hotel with atmospheric rooms and a Neo-Baroque breakfast room.

Nemzeti HUF
József körút 4
Tel *(06 1) 477 2001* **Map** 7 B3
W accorhotels.com
Concealed behind the powder blue façade lies a grand staircase leading to sumptuous rooms. Friendly and helpful staff.

The piano room at the beautifully furnished Brody House

DK Choice

Brody House 
Bródy Sándor utca 10
Tel *(06 1) 266 1211* **Map** 7 A4
W brodyhouse.com
Named after the eponymous Hungarian writer, this unique residence has been fashioned into a super-cool retreat. It offers eight wonderfully idiosyncratic, artistically themed rooms, each one named after the artist whose studio it once was.

Casati Budapest Hotel HUF HUF
Paulay Ede utca 31
Tel *(06 1) 343 1198* **Map** 2 F4
W casatibudapesthotel.com
In this eighteenth-century apartment block with stripped-back walls, good-looking rooms overlook a pretty courtyard.

Hotel Palazzo Zichy HUF HUF
Lőrinc pap tér 2
Tel *(06 1) 235 4000* **Map** 7 B4
W hotel-palazzo-zichy.hu
A flamboyant hotel in the one-time residence of the eponymous Count. Stylish rooms.

Buddha-Bar Hotel Budapest Klotild Palace HUF HUF HUF
Váci utca 34
Tel *(06 1) 799 7300* **Map** 4 E1
W buddhabarhotelbudapest.com
Occupying the magnificent former palace, this place is almost overwhelming in its opulence.

Around Városliget

Three Corners Hotel Bristol HUF HUF
Kenyérmező utca 4
Tel *(06 1) 799 1100* **Map** 7 C2
W threecorners.com
While the rooms aren't quite as impressive as the façade, this is still a decent option with good transport links to the city centre.

Spa

Gellért Hill and Tabán

Danubius Hotel Flamenco 
Tas vezér utca 3-7
Tel *(06 1) 889 5600* **Map** 3 C5
W danubiushotels.com
This good value hotel offers smart rooms and a terrific breakfast served in the Bolero restaurant. Indoor swimming pool with sauna and solarium.

Danubius Hotel Gellért 
Szent Gellért tér 1
Tel *(06 1) 889 5500* **Map** 4 D2
W danubiushotels.com
Legendary spa hotel with indoor and outdoor pools, and an array of treatments. The rooms are a bit dated, but this adds to their charm.

Central Pest

DK Choice

Boscolo Budapest 
Erzsébet körút 9
Tel *(06 1) 886 6111* **Map** 7 B2
W budapest.boscolohotels.com
Built in 1894 and now magnificently restored, the rooms are the height of luxury, while the main hall is something to marvel at. Once a hub of literary life, the gilded domes of the Coffee House make for the perfect spot to while away an hour or so.

Further Afield

The Aquincum Hotel 
Árpád fejedelem útja 94
Tel *(06 1) 436 4100*
W aquincumhotel.com
A massive hotel with a host of great facilities, including pools, fitness and steam baths. Rooms are tastefully decorated.

For more information on types of hotels *see page 185*

Danubius Health Spa Resort Helia HUF HUF
Kárpát utca 62-64
Tel *(06 1) 889 5800*
W **danubiushotels.com**
Situated on the bank of the Danube, offering a full range of health and beauty facilities.

Danubius Health Spa Resort Margitsziget HUF HUF
Margitsziget
Tel *(06 1) 889 4700*
W **danubiushotels.com**
Hosting one of Europe's largest wellness centres, this island hotel sits atop a natural spring. All rooms have balconies.

Ramada Resort Aquaworld HUF HUF
Íves út 16
Tel *(06 1) 231 3600*
W **ramadaresortbudapest.hu**
Facilities here include a large indoor water park, an oriental-style fitness and wellness centre and a large playground for kids.

Luxury

Castle District

Hilton Budapest Hotel HUF HUF HUF
Hess András tér 1–3
Tel *(06 1) 889 6600* **Map** 1 B4
W **placeshilton.com**
This remarkable new-old building, perched high above the Danube, offers superb views from the rooms.

Around Parliament

Iberostar Grand Hotel HUF HUF
Október 6 utca 26
Tel *(06 1) 354 3050* **Map** 2 E4
W **iberostar.com**
The supremely luxurious rooms here feature huge bathrooms, high ceilings and large windows.

Striking modern exterior of the slick Expo Congress Hotel

Hotel Parlament HUF HUF HUF
Kálmán Imre utca 19
Tel *(06 1) 374 6000* **Map** 2 E3
W **parlament-hotel.hu**
Posh but not pompous, the first-rate facilities here include a wellness centre, library room and lounge bar. Chic, stylish rooms.

K&K Hotel Opera HUF HUF HUF
Révay utca 24
Tel *(06 1) 269 0222* **Map** 2F4
W **kkhotels.com**
Behind the splendid façade, the rooms are modern, immaculately turned out and spacious.

Sofitel Budapest Chain Bridge HUF HUF HUF
Széchenyi tér 2
Tel *(06 1) 266 1234* **Map** 2 D5
W **sofitel.com**
Most of the rooms here have outstanding views of Castle Hill. There are several elegant restaurants on site.

Central Pest

Queens Court Hotel HUF HUF
Dob utca 63
Tel *(06 1) 882 3000* **Map** 7 A2
W **queenscourthotelbudapest.com**
A range of high class suites and serviced apartments are available, all with attendant amenities.

Corinthia Grand Hotel HUF HUF HUF
Erzsébet körút 43
Tel *(06 1) 479 4000* **Map** 7 A2
W **corinthia.com**
From the distinguished façade and glittering lobby to the mahogany-furnished rooms, the Corinthia oozes class.

Kempinski Corvinus HUF HUF HUF
Erzsébet tér 7
Tel *(06 1) 429 3375* **Map** 2 E5
W **kempinski.com**
This grand, classy hotel is a favourite with the rich and famous, who are drawn to its large and expensively furnished rooms.

Marriott HUF HUF HUF
Apáczai Csere János utca 4
Tel *(06 1) 486 5000* **Map** 4 E1
W **marriottbudapest.com**
Banqueting rooms, three restaurants and a fitness centre are all features here. Rooms offer lovely river views.

Zenit Budapest Palace HUF HUF HUF
Apáczai Csere János utca 7
Tel *(06 1) 799 8400* **Map** 4 E1
W **budapest.zenithoteles.com**
This grandly titled hotel features immaculate rooms decked out in a beige and grey colour scheme.

Around Városliget

Mamaison Hotel Andrassy HUF HUF
Andrássy út 111
Tel *(06 1) 462 2100* **Map** 5 B4
W **mamaison.com**
Elegance and charm abound at this tasteful hotel. Spacious rooms.

Business/Chain

Gellért Hill and Tabán

Best Western Orion HUF
Döbrentei utca 13
Tel *(06 1) 356 8583* **Map** 4 D1
W **bestwestern.com**
This secluded hotel offers clean, plainly decorated rooms, as well as a good, small restaurant.

Mercure Budapest Buda HUF
Krisztina körút 41–43
Tel *(06 1) 488 8100* **Map** 1 A5
W **accorhotels.com**
Neat, clean rooms come with all the necessary amenities and the location is terrific. Friendly staff.

North of the Castle District

Hotel Regnum Residence HUF HUF
Ganz utca 8
Tel *(06 1) 265 5090* **Map** 1 C2
W **regnumresidence.hu**
A top-end hotel offering superior rooms and suites with sofas, desks and floor-to-ceiling windows.

Around Parliament

City Hotel HUF
Szent István körút 22
Tel *(06 1) 340 5450* **Map** 7 A1
W **cityhotel.hu**
Modern, well-appointed, comfortable rooms and cheerful, obliging staff.

Hilton Budapest City HUF HUF
Váci út 1–3
(inside WestEnd City Center)
Tel *(06 1) 288 5500* **Map** 2 F2
W **placeshilton.com**
Next to the hubbub of the shopping mall, this oasis of calm offers the usual Hilton mix of modernity and service.

Radisson Blu Béke HUF HUF
Teréz körút 43
Tel *(06 1) 889 3900* **Map** 2 F3
W **radissonblu.com**
A magnificently restored hotel with well-equipped rooms armed with all the latest facilities. Check out the exterior mosaic of St George and the Dragon.

Key to Price Guide *see page 186*

Central Pest

Budapest Museum Central HUF
1053 Budapest Muzeum korut 39
Tel *(06 1) 266 7868* **Map** 4 F2
W budapestmuseumcentral.com
This restored 19th-century building with well-equipped, pleasant rooms, all featuring high ceilings, is located in the historical heart of the city.

Mercure Museum HUF HUF
Trefort utca 2
Tel *(06 1) 485 1080* **Map** 7 A3
W accorhotels.com
The older, Italian-influenced half of this welcoming hotel is complemented by a sleeker modern part.

Around Városliget

Best Western Hotel Hungaria HUF
Rákóczi út 90
Tel *(06 1) 889 4400* **Map** 7 C2
W danubiushotels.com
Enormous, good-value place full of life and colour, with small but comfortable rooms and all the attendant facilities.

Hotel Ibis Heroes Square HUF
Dózsa György út 106
Tel *(06 1) 269 5300* **Map** 5 C3
W accorhotels.com
This bright, modern hotel offers pleasant rooms, a sauna, solarium and rent-a-bike. Buffet breakfast.

Further Afield

Expo Congress Hotel HUF HUF
Expo tér 2
Tel *(06 1) 263 6800*
W expohotelbudapest.com
Drab location but a thoroughly slick hotel complete with rooftop spa and Sky Bar. The rooms are decorated in warm colours.

Hotel Budapest HUF HUF
Szilágyi Erzsébet fasor 47
Tel *(06 1) 889 4200*
W danubiushotels.com
Distinguished by its cylindrical shape, this venerable hotel is a city landmark. The tasteful rooms have stunning views.

Pension

Castle District

Budavár Panzió HUF
Szabó Ilonka utca 15
Tel *(06 1) 201 5686* **Map** 1 B4
W budavar-pension.com
At this bright little pension in the heart of Buda the rooms all feature balconies that offer super river views.

One of the oppulent guest rooms at Boscolo Budapest

Gellért Hill and Tabán

Ábel Panzió HUF
Ábel Jenő utca 9
Tel *(06 1) 209 2537* **Map** 3 B4
W abelpanzio.hu
This early-1900s villa boasts ten rooms of considerable charm, as well as a drawing room and a garden terrace.

Central Pest

Leo Panzió HUF
Kossuth Lajos utca 2/a
Tel *(06 1) 266 9041* **Map** 4 F1
W leopanzio.hu
A charming little pension with private bathrooms, air-conditioning and TVs. A tasty buffet breakfast is included.

Around Városliget

Dominik Panzió HUF
Cházár András utca 3
Tel *(06 1) 460 9428* **Map** 8 E1
W centralhotel21.hu
Set over three floors, the private, dormitory-style rooms are clean and simple. Bathrooms and toilets are shared.

Further Afield

DK Choice

Beatrix Panzió HUF
Széher út 3
Tel *(06 1) 275 0550*
W beatrixhotel.hu
A warm welcome is assured at this homely pension in the peaceful and leafy villa district. The rooms are spacious and tastefully decorated. There are regular grill and goulash parties held in the pretty, landscaped garden. Breakfast can be enjoyed on the terrace in summer. Good transport links to the city centre.

Buda Villa Panzió HUF
Kiss Áron utca 6
Tel *(06 1) 275 0091*
W budapansio.hu
Ten tidy rooms complement the enjoyable lounge bar, but the best aspect here is the wonderful lush garden.

Hotel Manzard Panzió HUF
Bláthy Ottó utca 21
Tel *(06 1) 210 4141*
W manzardpanzio.com
Located in a pleasant neighbourhood, this laid back pension sports pine furnished rooms and a great outdoor pool.

Hotel Pension Helios HUF
Lidérc utca 5
Tel *(06 1) 246 4658*
W heliospanzio.hu
In a picturesque spot elevated above the city in a quiet area. Most of the rooms in this orderly pension have unbeatable views. Great breakfast, excellent staff.

Mohácsi Panzió HUF
Bimbó út 25a
Tel *(06 1) 326 7741*
W hotelmohacsipanzio.hu
This small, pleasant and inexpensive pension offers well-equipped rooms, the pick of which are on the upper floor.

Pál Panzió HUF
Pálvölgyi köz 15
Tel *(06 1) 388 7099*
There are just four rooms in this cosy guesthouse located up in the hills near the caves and close to local transport and restaurants.

Vadvirág Panzió HUF
Nagybányai út 18
Tel *(06 1) 275 0200*
W hotelvadviragpanzio.hu
At this neat, family-owned pension in a quiet, green district some rooms have balconies and there's a terrace and sauna.

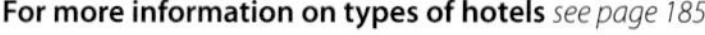

For more information on types of hotels *see page 185*

WHERE TO EAT AND DRINK

Following a visit to Budapest, the Nobel Prize-winning Latin American writer Miguel Ángel Asturias said that "the exquisite taste of Hungarian cuisine is a language understood by all". While classic traditional Hungarian cooking can still be found all over the city, it has been the evolution of contemporary Hungarian, as well as international, cooking that has really transformed Budapest's culinary landscape. A clutch of younger, more dynamic Hungarian chefs have brought age-old dishes and recipes into the present day, and allied to the fact that Hungary now produces some of central Europe's finest wines, it's not difficult to see why Budapest has become a serious foodie destination.

The most typical examples of traditional Hungarian cooking can be seen on pages 192–3, while information on what to drink is given on pages 194–5. A detailed guide to the city's best restaurants is provided on pages 196–207. Pubs, bars and nightlife can be found on pages 208–9.

Where to Look

There are large numbers of superb eating establishments all over the city and the surrounding suburbs. Central Pest has by far the greatest concentration of places to eat, though central Buda, and in particular the Castle District, has its fair share of decent restaurants. The city's main tourist areas, like Váci utca *(see p131)*, are well off for places to eat and drink, but often these do not equate to particularly good value for money. The rather annoying practice of touting for business is also very prominent here. Otherwise, it is often worth looking off the main roads or away from popular areas to find establishments frequented by local Budapest residents. For real high-end dining, you can't beat the top hotels, like the Gresham Palace or Le Meridien.

Luxurious banquette seating at La Pampa Steakhouse *(see p200)*

The best places for *al fresco* dining are Liszt Ferenc tér, which runs off Andrássy út, not far from Oktogon metro station; Ráday utca, which starts at Kálvin tér; and Gozsdu udvar (Gozsdu Court) which is in the heart of the Jewish disctrict. All these areas are full of cosy restaurants, bars and cafés, and attract a youthful clientele.

Types of Restaurants, Cafés and Bars

The differences between the types of establishments can be subtle, but they break down roughly into the following types: *Étterem* simply means restaurant, in which any type of cuisine may be served. A *csárda* comes in various forms, though most are folksy restaurants typically offering interesting local specialities – a *halászcsárda*, meanwhile, will offer mainly fish dishes and soups. There are two types of inn, a *vendéglő*, which has an informal, typically rustic ambience, and a *kisvendéglő*, (literally a "small inn"), which is similar to a cosy pub. Cafés range from a *kávéház* (coffee house), which include Budapest's great literary coffee houses of the early twentieth century, to a *cukrászda* (patisserie). Types of bars include a *borozó*, a *söröző* and an *eszpresszó* – though these often serve food too.

Lantern outside the Gerbeaud Cukrászda

What to Order

Ordering a Hungarian meal may not be as simple as it may first seem. There are many different varieties of Hungarian soups, some of which are a meal in themselves. *Bogrács*, which is often served in a kettle, and bean soups are the heartiest and would normally be followed by a light dish or pancakes. Hungarian fish soup is a particular speciality and owes its red colour to paprika. This should be followed by delicate homemade pasta served with crackling, cheese and cream. There are also many light soups, or small portions of the more substantial soups, which can be eaten as a starter, thus leaving room for the main course.

The archetypal Hungarian main dish is goulash soup *(gulyás leves)* and there are several versions of the basic thick meat stew. Another Hungarian speciality is *pörkölt* (a paprika stew very similar to goulash). This stew is made with all sorts of meat, typically veal, pork, poultry and game. Often, meals are eaten with bread; the white wheat variety is the most popular amongst Hungarians and it is particularly delicious.

Food served in bars or bought from butchers' shops typically involves spicy sausages, liberally seasoned with paprika and garlic, grilled chicken or various smoked meats. Another alternative is the delicious *lángos* (pronounced "langosh"), a flat, salty, fried yeast dough. It is traditionally eaten with garlic oil or sour cream and cheese.

For more detailed information on the types of food available in the city, including local dishes and specialities, see *The Flavours of Budapest* on pages 192–3.

Vegetarian Food

Although vegetarian cuisine *per se* is not found in abundance in Budapest, there are a growing number of vegetarian restaurants scattered around the city. Moreover, meat-free dishes can be found on most Hungarian menus. *Főzelék* is a vegetable dish that you can order on its own, or optionally with a slice of meat, a sausage or an egg. *Lecsó*, a type of ragout, is another popular vegetable side dish that makes a substantial meal by itself. There are also many sweet and savoury *palacsinta* (pancakes).

Reserving a Table

It is really only necessary to book in advance at Budapest's more exclusive restaurants. Interestingly, it is also still the custom in some cheaper establishments to be asked to join other diners at a table, especially during the busy lunchtime period.

Dining on the deck overlooking a lake at Hemingway *(see p196)*

Menus and Prices

Most Hungarian restaurants display a menu by the entrance, and it is usually translated into English or German. The name of the dish is generally followed by a brief description. The day's "specials" – a set meal consisting of a soup, a main course and a dessert – are listed at the head of the menu. Set menus are often very good value and provide an ideal opportunity for visitors to sample several Hungarian specialities.

The prices should also be displayed, but if they are not, go elsewhere or at least ask to see the prices, including any surcharges, before ordering the meal. In most Hungarian restaurants the waiters tend to round up the bill, particularly when serving foreign customers. Expect prices to be displayed in forints, as well as in euros in some places.

Al fresco dining at Café Pierrot *(see p196)*

Tipping

In some restaurants, a service charge is included in the final bill, in others it is customary to tip. If a service charge is added, this should be stated on either the menu or the bill; this could be up to 15 per cent. However, if there is any doubt, it is always courteous to leave a tip. In general, an acceptable tip is between 10–15 per cent of the cost of the meal.

Children

Children are welcomed in most restaurants without exception, though the higher-end establishments might be a little sniffy at their presence. If children's portions do not appear on the menu, the chef will prepare suitable dishes to order. These are usually charged at about 70 per cent of the price. The only exception is dessert, but this can often be shared. However, the desserts are so delicious that most children will happily eat a whole portion.

Recommended Restaurants

The restaurants in this guide are divided into seven geographical areas: Castle District, North of the Castle District, Gellért and Tabán, Around Parliament, Central Pest, Around Városliget, and Further Afield. Our listings include a selection of the best restaurants from across the city, and while traditional Hungarian cuisine is still heartily embraced amongst locals and visitors alike, we've also listed dozens more restaurants that reflect the changing, and more innovative, trends in Magyar cooking. The number, and quality, of ethnic eateries has also improved no end, with Italian, French, and Asian restaurants particularly to the fore, and this too is reflected in many of the establishments listed here. The highlighted restaurants, marked as DK Choice, have been chosen because they offer a unique experience – typically a combination of superb cuisine and a truly special atmosphere.

The Flavours of Budapest

The fusion of Magyar, Turkish, Austrian, Balkan and even French influences has made Hungarian cuisine one of the most interesting and flavourful in central Europe. Hungary is a country where cooking know-how has always been a key aspect of the national culture. The improvised stews of nomadic Asiatic settlers survive as a delicacy to this day. Noted for its game, *foie gras* and rich meaty preparations, such as goulash and the legendary Debrecziner sausages, it is also a good place to enjoy freshwater fish and an array of delicious cakes and pastries.

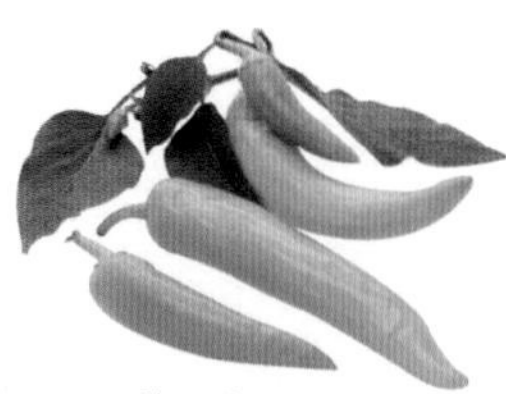
Hungarian peppers

Sausages and cured meats on sale in the Central Market

Meat

Pork is a popular meat in Hungary, while financial constraints mean that beef is more of an expensive delicacy. Pork is found in a wide range of stews and sausages, and is eaten as bacon. Cuts of beef do feature on tables and menus, especially in Budapest, and veal is becoming increasingly popular too. Steak is widely dished up, often with a rich sauce as in *Bélszín Budapest módra* (Budapest tenderloin medallions). Beef is also used to make the many different types of goulash, although this dish, as well as *gulyásleves* (goulash soup) can also be made from pork or venison.

Poultry & Game

Geese are an important farmyard animal in Hungary, which is the world's second biggest producer of *foie gras* (after France). *Foie gras* is almost the national dish, usually cooked in its own fat and served cold. It is also found in pâtés and *confits*. *Libatepertő* (goose skin) is widely enjoyed too, fried in its own fat

Selection of typical Hungarian cakes and pastries

Local Dishes and Specialities

White asparagus

Despite strong foreign influences, the classic dishes of Hungary dominate daily menus in the restaurants and cafés of Budapest. Many show their roots in one of the country's three historical regions. Goulash and its many variants, for example, is a dish of the Great Plain, the traditional method of cooking it in a kettle reflecting the nomadic past of the Plain's inhabitants. *Foie gras* may have been introduced into the country by the Austrian Habsburgs, but has become so popular that it is key to the cuisine of eastern Hungary, where most geese are now bred. The centre of the country, and the area around Budapest, has always had the sweetest tooth and nearly all the nation's favourite cakes and desserts originate from here.

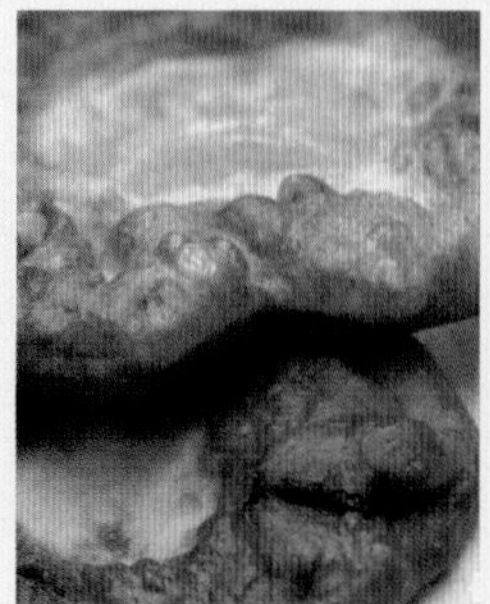
Lángos Crisp and golden, these deep-fried potato cakes make a popular, filling snack, served with soured cream.

Market stall, laden with root vegetables and strings of dried peppers

and served with pickles. Duck is another regular on Hungarian menus, often roasted with chestnuts or berries and served with red cabbage. Pheasant may also be on offer, normally in a rich soup. Venison is common, and usually served as a spicy *pörkölt* (goulash) or in a vegetable sauce with bread.

Fish

Traditional Hungarian dishes are made from freshwater fish, with carp the most widely eaten, although catfish, zander, bream and trout can also be found on most menus. A popular soup is *halászlé*, made with carp or catfish and seasoned with a generous dash of paprika. Another favourite is *harcsapaprikás*, a goulash-style fish stew with sour cream and served with *galuska*, a type of noodle.

Vegetables

Potatoes, tomatoes and cabbage are usually the main vegetables. But from May to July, fine white asparagus appears on market stalls, with many restaurants serving *spárgaleves*, a rich creamy soup made from asparagus and veal stock.

Roasting chestnuts, a common sight on Budapest's winter streets

Paprika peppers are a culinary staple and many types are grown. They are either cooked as part of a dish – *töltött paprika* (peppers stuffed with meat and rice) are served up everywhere – or dried and ground up to be used as a spice. There are hundreds of different types of ground paprika, which vary in flavour and strength. Although paprika is the emblematic spice of Hungary, it was not always so. During the 19th century national resistance movements, Hungarian cooks started the excessive use of paprika powder to differentiate Hungarian and Austrian gastronomy.

Best Local Snacks

Sausages Most buffets and butcher's shops offer the lightly smoked Debrecziner sausage, made from beef, pork, paprika and garlic. It is generally eaten with bread and mustard.

Chestnuts In winter, Budapest is crammed with stalls selling freshly roasted chestnuts.

Pancakes, fritters and doughnuts Snack bars all over the country serve tasty, fried, doughy snacks all day long. Try a salty *lángos* with garlic oil or sour cream and cheese.

Gingerbread Shops devoted to selling gingerbread are everywhere. At Christmas it is highly decorated and given as a gift.

Gulyásleves A type of goulash, this soup made of pork or beef with vegetables is flavoured with onion, caraway and paprika.

Csirkepaprikás Chicken ragout in a creamy sauce made from paprika and sour cream. Usually served with Hungarian noodles.

Dobos torta Fine slices of sponge cake are layered with chocolate cream and topped with glossy caramel.

What to Drink in Budapest

Hungary is famous for its excellent wines and, although it is not a big country, it has as many as 22 wine regions. These regions produce all the characteristic wine styles, from *pezsgő* (sparkling wine) and light whites that come from Mátra, near Lake Balaton, to dry reds from Villány or Eger, as well as Tokaji Aszú, a distinctive sweet dessert wine from the slopes of Tokaj. Many wines from different vineyards are matured in a maze of underground cellars in Budafok. They are all widely available in Budapest's many restaurants, wine bars and wine shops. As well as being a prominent wine producer, Hungary also makes beer, *pálinka* (a drink distilled from orchard fruits), several types of brandy and a bitter herb liqueur called Unicum.

Pálinka

Kecskemét is the largest region that produces the alcoholic drink *pálinka,* which is distilled from fruit grown in the orchards situated on the Great Hungarian Plain, some 100 km (60 miles) southeast of Budapest. *Pálinka* is a spirit native to Hungary and comes in a variety of flavours including *barack* (apricot) and *cseresznye* (cherry). The best of them, however, is *szilva* (plum) which comes from the Szatmár district and is much favoured by the Hungarians.

Barack pálinka

Pálinka is not the only spirit indigenous to Hungary. Other examples include Törköly, a spirit distilled from grape residues left over from winemaking, which possesses a very delicate flavour, and Vilmos, a brandy made from Williams pears.

Sparkling Wines

Sparkling wine, called *pezsgő* (the Hungarian word for "sparkling"), enjoys a good reputation in Hungary. The classic method of producing these wines was introduced to Hungary from France by József Törley, in 1881. It was Törley *(see p165)* who built the first production plant in Budafok in 1882, which continues to produce excellent sparkling wines and has an international reputation. Today, Hungary has several other factories producing *pezsgő*, mainly concentrated around Budapest, Pécs and Balatonboglár. As well as Törley, Hungaria is another good label to look out for.

Pezsgö by Törley and Hungaria

Light Hungarian beers

Hungarian Beers

Hungarians are turning increasingly to beer as their chosen drink, as its thirst-quenching quality goes well with many traditional, paprika-flavoured Hungarian dishes, goulash among them. There are some popular Hungarian beer brands worth trying, most notably Soproni, Borsodi and Dreher. The large Dreher factory in the Kőbánya district of Budapest was founded in 1854 and now offers pre-arranged beer-sampling events at their museum (www.dreherrt.hu). The number of small artisan breweries is also growing, with their beers on offer at festivals and some pubs and restaurants.

Hungarian Wines

The choice of good wine available in Hungary has increased dramatically over the past few years. This is thanks to the ever-improving wines being

One of Budafok's cellars, where wines are aged in barrels

Egri Bikavér, "Bulls' Blood", a full-bodied red wine

A dry white wine from the Badacsony vineyards

matured in private cellars. The styles currently favoured by the producers include dry white Chardonnay and Riesling, medium-dry Zöldszilváni, Hárslevelű and Szürkebarát, medium-sweet Tramini and the aromatic Muskotály, which is produced in Badacsony, Balatonboglár, Csopak and Somló.

Among red wines, the dry Kékfrankos, Burgundi, Oportó, Cabernet and Pinot Noir are popular, as is the medium-dry Merlot, which is produced in Siklós, Sopron, Szekszárd, Tihany and Villány.

Another vine-growing district is Eger, which is famous for its aromatic, robust red Egri Leányka and the dry red Egri Bikavér, or "Bulls' Blood", which is produced from a combination of three grape varieties. Other Hungarian wines take their names from their place of origin or the variety of grape from which they are produced.

Tokaji

The dessert wine Tokaji has a very different style. Its bouquet and flavour come from a mould that grows only in the fork of the Bodrog and Tisza rivers and the volcanic soil in which the vines grow.

Tokaji ranges from sweet to dry and is full-bodied and rich. Particularly worth sampling is Aszú, which is made with the addition of over-ripe grapes harvested after the first frost. The proportion of these grapes added to the must (grape ice) determines the wine's body and sweetness. The more of these grapes used, the sweeter and richer the Aszú.

Although cheap varieties of Tokaji do exist, they do not share the quality of the genuine article.

Spritzers

On hot days, Hungarians enjoy drinking refreshing spritzers. The various types are differentiated by the proportion of white wine to soda water:

	Quantity of wine	Quantity of water
Small spritzer *(Kisfröccs)*	10 cl	10 cl
Large spritzer *(Nagyfröccs)*	20 cl	10 cl
Long step *(Hosszúlépés)*	10 cl	20 cl
Janitor *(Házmester)*	30 cl	20 cl

Unicum

Originally, Unicum was prescribed in 1790 as a remedy for the king by the court physician, who was himself a member of the Zwack family. Since then, a blend of more than 40 Hungarian herbs has been used to create Unicum. The herbs, which are gathered in three separate areas, are combined to produce this bitter liqueur. Unicum can be drunk either as an apéritif before a meal or afterwards as a digestif with coffee.

Unicum herb liqueur

The recipe has been held by the Zwack family, and remained a secret, since the reign of Franz I *(see p21)*.

Sweet Tokaji Szamorodni

Dry Tokaji Szamorodni

Tokaji Aszú, a renowned golden dessert wine

Pear-flavoured Vilmos liqueur

Where to Eat and Drink

Castle District

Café Miró (HUF)
Café **Map** 1 B4
Úri utca 30
Tel *(06 1) 201 2375*
A popular, hip hangout with a Mediterranean vibe and a great summer terrace on which to enjoy an appealing range of salads and snacks.

Ruszwurm Cukrászda (HUF)
Patisserie **Map** 1 B4
Szentháromság utca 7
Tel *(06 1) 375 5284*
Budapest's oldest patisserie offers plenty of calorific strudels *(rétes)*, and some delicious coffees.

DK Choice

21 Magyar Vendéglő (HUF)(HUF)
Modern Hungarian **Map** 1 B4
Fortuna utca 21
Tel *(06 1) 202 2113*
A super stylish restaurant that strives to create traditional Magyar cuisine in a thoroughly contemporary setting. Brick walls, wooden floors and subdued lighting create the perfect atmosphere in which to enjoy the first-rate *foie gras* and other classic dishes like chicken paprika with buttered dumplings. The wine list is particularly inspired.

Café Pierrot (HUF)(HUF)
International **Map** 1 B4
Fortuna utca 14
Tel *(06 1) 375 6971*
This refined yet comfortable and relaxed, friendly restaurant is located in a 13th- century bakery house with a gorgeous secret garden.

Fekete Holló Vendéglő (HUF)(HUF)
Traditional Hungarian **Map** 1 B4
Országház utca 10
Tel *(06 1) 356 2367*
A little gem where the kitsch medieval decor does little to detract from the excellent food, though it is perhaps a little too touristy for some.

Pest-Buda Bistro (HUF)(HUF)
Traditional Hungarian **Map** 1 B4
Fortuna utca 3
Tel *(06 1) 225 0377*
A simple Hungarian bistro offering fresh, homestyle cooking made with love and the best ingredients. The atmosphere is traditional yet friendly and casual.

Rivalda Café & Restaurant (HUF)(HUF)
International **Map** 1 C5
Színház utca 5–9
Tel *(06 1) 489 0236*
Contemporary cuisine with a seasonal menu, using mostly local produce. Jazz evenings too.

Vár: a Speiz Étterem (HUF)(HUF)
International **Map** 1 B4
Hess András tér 6
Tel *(06 1) 488 7416*
This cultured restaurant offers the likes of *foie gras* with Tokaj. In the adjoining Ham and Wine Bar, you can sample a superb range of meats from all over Europe.

Alabárdos (HUF)(HUF)(HUF)
Modern Hungarian **Map** 1 B4
Országház utca 2
Tel *(06 1) 356 0851* **Closed** *Sun*
Exclusive place in an outstanding Gothic building, with Hungarian specialities of pre-paprika times made to please today's taste buds.

Halászbástya (HUF)(HUF)(HUF)
International **Map** 1 B4
Szentháromság tér 5
Tel *(06 1) 201 6935*
The Neo-Romanesque interior here is impressive, however it is the knockout views from the terrace that really make this place something special.

Zóna Budapest (HUF)(HUF)(HUF)
International **Map** 1 C5
Lánchíd utca 7–9
Tel *(06 1) 422 5981* **Closed** *Sun & Mon*
The breathtaking concept food here fuses modern Hungarian cuisine with a touch of the orient. Splendid views of the Danube. Fantastic Hungarian wines as well.

The stylish dining room opening onto the garden at Café Pierrot

Price Guide
Prices are based on a three-course meal per person, with a half-bottle of house wine, including tax and service.

(HUF) up to 6,000 forints
(HUF)(HUF) 6,000–12,000 forints
(HUF)(HUF)(HUF) over 12,000 forints

Gellért and Tabán

Gellért Espresso (HUF)
Café **Map** 4 E3
Szent Gellért tér 1
Tel *(06 1) 889 5500*
Situated on the ground floor of the Gellért Hotel, this sublime recreation of a Habsburg-era coffee house serves up good coffee and excellent cakes.

Hadik Kávéház Café (HUF)
Café **Map** 4 E5
Bartók Béla út 36
Tel *(06 1) 279 0290*
The classic interior here combines with a pleasant atmosphere, making for a good coffee stop. The lunch menu is worth trying too.

Marcello (HUF)
Italian **Map** 4 E4
Bartók Béla út 40
Tel *(06 1) 466 6231*
Housed in a cellar accessed by a low staircase, Marcello is famed for its pasta and salad bar, with a good choice for vegetarians.

Café Déryné (HUF)(HUF)
International **Map** 1 B5
Krisztina tér 3
Tel *(06 1) 225 1407*
In the atmosphere of a grand-scale dining room, the classic brasserie menu on offer here features simple local and French favourites.

Hemingway (HUF)(HUF)
Modern Hungarian **Map** 3 C5
Kosztolányi Dezső tér 2
Tel *(06 1) 381 0522*
The spread out, island resort feel of this lively, al fresco venue would have appealed to the famous writer. There's a weekly changing menu and a superb brunch buffet on Sundays.

János Étterem (HUF)(HUF)
Modern Hungarian **Map** 3 B2
Hegyalja út 23
Tel *(06 1) 202 3414*
The house restaurant of the Charles Hotel offers an interesting take on Hungarian classics, such as goose liver pie with Tokaj-wine mousse.

Márványmenyasszony Étterem
Traditional Hungarian **Map** 3 A1
Márvány utca 6
Tel *(06 1) 487 3090*
This old-style Hungarian outfit has long offered fine food, great prices and a relaxed atmosphere. Cracking gypsy music too. The menu changes weekly.

Szeged Vendéglő
Fish **Map** 4 E3
Bartók Béla út 1
Tel *(06 1) 209 1668*
River fish is the reason to come here, the *Szeged halászlé* (fish soup) being the one to go for. A lively gypsy band plays in the evenings.

Tabáni Gösser Restaurant
Traditional Hungarian **Map** 3 C1
Attila út 19
Tel *(06 1) 375 9482*
Authentic Hungarian restaurant whose vast menu includes a choice of juicy steaks prepared in various ways.

Vinopolis Naphegy
Traditional Hungarian **Map** 3 C2
Naphegy utca 67
Tel *(06 1) 799 0401*
Offering the widest variety of wines in Hungary, this restaurant also operates as a wine store. Choose from more than 600 Hungarian and imported wines. Of course, dishes served here all go well with wine.

DK Choice

Aranyszarvas Vendéglő 
International **Map** 3 C1
Szarvas tér 1
Tel *(06 1) 375 6451*
Despite the unalluring location, the handsome "Golden Deer" is a gem of a place, with a menu the envy of many restaurants in the capital; here you can sample wild boar tenderloin with white bean purée or duck breast with orange carrot and pak choi. The wine list is no less commendable, and there's an intriguing selection of palinkas to choose from.

Búsuló Juhász Étterem
Traditional Hungarian **Map** 3 C3
Kelenhegyi út 58
Tel *(06 1) 209 1649*
Sited on the slopes of Gellért Hill, Búsuló Juhász is well worth visiting as much for the views as the food, which is beautifully prepared. Seasonal menu.

Brick walls and wooden floors combine in the stylish dining room at 21 Magyar Vendéglő

North of the Castle District

Gusto Café
Café **Map** 1 C2
Frankel Leó út 12
Tel *(06 1) 316 3970*
A tiny cafe that's always rammed, and where the genial Gusto is ever-present behind the bar, offering drinks, light snacks, main meals and wonderful desserts. Great coffee.

Nagyi Palacsintázója
Light bites **Map** 1 C3
Batthyány tér 5
Drop in here for a prolific menu of sweet and sour pancakes, from sour cream and cheese to chocolate and whipped cream.

Roma Etelbar
Traditional Hungarian **Map** 1 B3
Fazekas utca 4
Tel *(06 1) 201 4545* **Closed** *Sun*
A fun 1970s style place that's a good bet for a cheap, homemade-style, no fuss lunchtime meal, be it goose or goulash.

Dining terrace at the handsome Aranyszarvas Vendéglő

Trófea Grill
International **Map** 1 C1
Margit körút 2
Tel *(06 1) 438 9090*
For a fixed price you can eat as much as you want from the self-service buffet, and that includes wine and champagne.

Arriba
Mexican **Map** 1 A3
Széna tér 1/a
Tel *(06 1) 201 3395*
Burritos, quesadillas and other delicious Mexican fast food at an excellent location.

Carne di Hall 
International **Map** 1 C4
Bem rakpart 20
Tel *(06 1) 201 8137*
This spot offers some of the more intriguing dishes this side of the Danube, such as catfish mousse with prawns.

Dunaparti Matróz Kocsma
International **Map** 1 C4
Halász utca 1
Tel *(06 1) 225 1673*
A fun bar/restaurant whose extensive, meat-heavy menu is complemented by a terrific selection of Belgian beers.

Horgásztanya Vendéglő
Fish **Map** 1 C4
Fő utca 27
Tel *(06 1) 212 3780*
This long-standing, enjoyable maritime-themed restaurant offers generous portions of fish soup, roasted trout and other fish treats.

Mandragóra
International **Map** 1 C2
Kacsa utca 22
Tel *(06 1) 202 2165* **Closed** *Sun*
A small restaurant close to the Buda banks of the Danube, with a particularly atmospheric shaded terrace.

For more information on types of restaurants *see page 191*

Traditionally-styled dining room at the First Strudel House of Pest

Pavillon de Paris HUF HUF
French **Map** 1 C4
Fő utca 20
Tel *(06 1) 509 3430* **Closed** *Sun*
Impressive in every aspect, from the sparsely decorated, tasteful dining room, to the cuisine and efficient service. There's also a lovely garden with a pavilion.

Vigadó Söröző HUF HUF
Traditional Hungarian **Map** 1 C3
Markovits Iván utca 4
Tel *(06 1) 214 9469*
The interior is a little staid, but the food is good, with steak and fish the mainstays of a long menu.

Arany Kaviár Étterem HUF HUF HUF
Fish **Map** 1 A3
Ostrom utca 19
Tel *(06 1) 201 6737*
At this fine Russian restaurant dishes are mostly based around fish, though there are some native specialities, such as *pelmenyi* (Russian ravioli).

DK Choice

Csalogány 26 HUF HUF HUF
Modern Hungarian **Map** 1 A3
Csalogány utca 26
Tel *(06 1) 201 7892* **Closed** *Sun & Mon*
The rather low-key location disguises a highly distinguished restaurant/café with a bright and breezy Mediterranean interior. Excellent poultry, fish and meat dishes are grilled on lava stones for a real burst of flavour. There are also some decent vegetarian options.

Kacsa Vendéglő HUF HUF HUF
International **Map** 1 C2
Fő utca 75
Tel *(06 1) 201 9992*
The service is as ostentatious as the food is splendid, with dishes presented under silver serving domes. Set lunch menu available.

Around Parliament

Alexandra Book Café HUF
Café **Map** 2 F4
Andrássy út 39
Tel *(06 1) 461 5835*
A beautiful café established in a historic, elegant bookstore where you can sit down with a book and enjoy it in the company of a fine coffee and cake.

Bombay Curry Bar HUF
Indian **Map** 2 F4
Andrássy út 28
Tel *(06 1) 332 8363*
A very basic, self-service, fast-food Indian sit-down and takeaway restaurant with a good lunchtime Express Menu. Favourite dishes, such as tandoori chiken, chicken korma and tikka masala, all feature.

Európa Kávéház HUF
Café **Map** 2 E2
Szent István krt 7–9
Tel *(06 1) 312 2362*
This large, bustling café is invariably packed to the gills with locals filling up on coffee and generously portioned slices of excellent cake.

One of several eclectic dining rooms at the Pomo D'Oro

First Strudel House of Pest HUF
Café **Map** 2 E4
Október 6 utca 22
Tel *(06 1) 428 0135*
Watch the many types of strudel – sweet and sour – being made before your eyes.

Ganga Vega Café HUF
Vegetarian **Map** 2 F4
Bajcsy-Zsilinszky út 25
Tel *06 70 633 8981*
This unfussy eatery has just a few tables, but the well thought out veggie food is undeniably tasty.

Govinda Étterem HUF
Vegetarian **Map** 2 D4
Vigyázó Ferenc utca 4
Tel *(06 1) 473 1310* **Closed** *Sun*
A fast-food style joint serving individual portions as well as set meals, in addition to an all-you-can-eat menu.

Hummus Bar HUF
Vegetarian **Map** 2 E4
Október 6 utca 19
Tel *(06 1) 354 0108*
This is one of a growing chain of veggie hangouts across the city, typically serving wrap sandwiches, salads and *falafel*.

Momotaro Ramen HUF
Asian **Map** 2 D4
Széchenyi utca 16
Tel *(06 1) 269 3802* **Closed** *Mon*
Cheep and cheerful, but still a cut above your average Chinese; try a bowl of dumplings followed by some steamed sea bass.

Szeráj Török Étterem HUF
Turkish **Map** 2 E2
Szent István körút 13
Tel *(06 1) 311 6690*
There's much more than kebabs available at this Turkish fast food restaurant where diners eat at simple wooden tables.

Belvárosi Lugas Vendéglő HUF HUF
Traditional Hungarian **Map** 2 E4
Bajcsy-Zsilinszky út 15/A
Tel *(06 1) 302 5393*
Well-made, hearty dishes served in a simple, appealing atmosphere, with daily specials chalked up on a blackboard.

Budapest Bisztró HUF HUF
Modern Hungarian **Map** 2 E3
Vécsey utca 3
Tel *(06 1) 783 0788*
This Hungarian bistro, with a view of the kitchen, and a state-of-the-art walk-in wine cellar, offers creative dishes ranging from classic to molecular gastronomy. One of the restaurant's favourite classics is their goulash soup.

DK Choice

Café Bouchon 
French **Map** 2 F3
Zichy Jenő utca 33
Tel *(06 1) 353 4094* **Closed** *Sun*
There's an outstanding combination of French and Hungarian flavours on offer at this welcoming little neighbourhood restaurant. It is also well-stocked with some of the country's finest wines. The lovely Art Deco furnishings and impeccable service round things off beautifully.

Café Jubilee
Italian **Map** 2 E2
Szent István körút 13
Tel *(06 1) 789 3357*
As well as being a buzzy place to drink, this is a good breakfast/ brunch and lunch option. Delicious home-made lemonade.

Café Kör
Modern Hungarian **Map** 2 E4
Sas utca 17
Tel *(06 1) 311 0053*
A popular bistro-style place serving enticing salad plates and grilled meat dishes. Fine wine too.

Hungarikum Bisztro
Traditional Hungarian **Map** 2 D4
Steindl Imre utca 13
Tel *06 20 352 3437*
Homestyle cuisine at its very best, from Grandma's noodles in onion stew to Hortobágyi crepes.

Iguana
Mexican **Map** 2 D4
Zoltán utca 16
Tel *(06 1) 331 4352*
The Tex-Mex fare is pretty much as you would expect in this expats' favourite, but it's a lot of fun. Good cocktails too.

Kispiac Bisztró
Modern Hungarian **Map** 2 E4
Hold utca 13
Tel *(06 1) 269 4321* **Closed** *Sun*
In the building of the Hold utca market hall, with a handful of tables, this place offers sumptuous dishes, all made by the staff themselves, including the bread and the marmalade. The roasted duck is the highlight.

Krízia
Italian **Map** 2 F4
Mozsár utca 12
Tel *(06 1) 331 8711* **Closed** *Sun*
This pretty restaurant showcases some fabulous Italian cuisine; the home-made pastas and noodles are superb, and there's a truffle menu too.

Gresham Restaurant at the magificent Four Seasons Gresham Palace Hotel

Marquis de Salade
International **Map** 2 F4
Hajós utca 43
Tel *(06 1) 302 4086*
Dishes from Azerbaijan and Georgia feature strongly in this beautifully decorated establishment – check out the Persian rugs downstairs.

Okay Italia 
Italian **Map** 2 E2
Szent István körút 20
Tel *(06 1) 349 2991*
Despite the noisy location and slightly overpriced menu, this lively joint is worth venturing to for its refreshingly creative Italian dishes.

Pomo D'oro
Italian **Map** 2 D4
Arany János utca 9
Tel *(06 1) 302 6473*
A labyrinthine trattoria with large wood-burning ovens firing up thin-crust pizzas; the charcoal grill is worth trying too.

Welcoming neighbourhood restaurant, Café Bouchon

Sir Lancelot Lovagi Étterem
International **Map** 2 F3
Podmaniczky utca 14
Tel *(06 1) 302 4456*
Hefty portions of Renaissance-inspired dishes are brought to the table by waiters in period costume, accompanied by Renaissance music.

Via Luna 
Italian **Map** 2 E4
Nagysándor József utca 1
Tel *(06 1) 312 8058*
Owned and operated by Italians, Via Luna offers an extensive menu of trattoria favourites, including pasta freshly made on the premises.

DK Choice

Borkonyha 
International **Map** 2 E5
Sas utca 3
Tel *(06 1) 266 0835* **Closed** *Sun*
From the moment you walk through the door of the "Wine Kitchen", you know you're in a for a treat at Budapest's third Michelin-starred restaurant. Beyond the gleaming bar, stacked high with beautiful bottles of wine, immaculately laid tables and a fabulous menu await. Expect dishes like rabbit *millefeuille* and suckling pig carpaccio.

Gresham Restaurant 
International **Map** 2 D5
Széchenyi István tér 5-6
Tel *(06 1) 268 6000*
Pick from an Italian or Hungarian menu for breakfast, lunch, or dinner at this excellent restaurant located in the magnificent Four Seasons Gresham Palace Hotel. A great selection of cakes, pastries and coffee is also available.

For more information on types of restaurants *see page 191*

KNRDY Steakhouse HUF HUF HUF
Steakhouse **Map** 2 E4
Október 6 utca 15
Tel *(06 1) 788 1685*
Enjoy some of the best steak meat from around the world cooked to perfection, along with a cocktail from the award-winning bartender. Excellent and attentive service.

La Pampa Steakhouse HUF HUF HUF
Steakhouse **Map** 2 F4
Bajcsy-Zsilinszky út 21
Tel *(06 1) 354 1444*
The decor is eye-catching, if not slightly over-the-top, while the steaks here are pretty much cooked to perfection.

La Plaza Étterem HUF HUF HUF
Spanish **Map** 2 E4
Október 6 utca 26
Tel *(06 1) 354 3050*
The dazzling restaurant of the Iberostar Hotel features gorgeous dishes like paella with rabbit and chicken, but it is expensive.

Rézkakas Bistro HUF HUF HUF
Traditional Hungarian **Map** 2 E5
Sas utca 3
Tel *(06 1) 318 0038*
The "Golden Cockerel" is a smart looking venture offering beautifully crafted classic Hungarian dishes. Good Hungarian wine list. Great live music.

Tigris HUF HUF HUF
Modern Hungarian **Map** 2 E5
Mérleg utca 10
Tel *(06 1) 317 3715* **Closed** *Sun*
Hungarian cuisine is cooked here with flare and ingenuity, from house-prepared smoked meats to a special *foie gras* menu. Excellent local wine list. Knowledgeable, helpful staff.

Central Pest

Astoria Kávéház HUF
Café **Map** 4 F1
Kossuth Lajos utca 19-21
Tel *(06 1) 889 6022*
Fill up on sandwiches, cakes and caffeine at the Astoria Hotel's elegant coffee house, which still retains an abundance of old-world charm.

Auguszt Cukrászda HUF
Patisserie **Map** 4 F1
Kossuth Lajos utca 14–16
Tel *(06 1) 337 6379* **Closed** *Sun*
One of a small chain of elegant patisseries offering delectable pastries, pies and ice creams, as well as more substantial lunch fare.

Auguszt cukrászda, one of a chain of elegant patisseries

BARbár Café HUF
Café **Map** 10 E5
Papnövelde utca 3
Tel *(06 1) 867 7987* **Closed** *Sun*
This enthusiastically-run café is renowned, above all, for its array of chocolate drinks, all made using imported Belgian chocolate.

Bors GasztroBár HUF
Light bites **Map** 10 F3
Kazinczy utca 10
Tel *06 70 953 3263*
At this above-average fast food joint the soups, in particular, are delicious, notably the wild mushroom and pumpkin.

Café Alibi HUF
Café **Map** 4 F2
Kecskeméti utca 1
Tel *(06 1) 317 4209*
A sunny little café where you can grab breakfast, something more substantial, or just pop by for a beer in the evening. There is plenty of outside seating in the lovely, covered patio area.

DK Choice

Central kávéház HUF
Café **Map** 4 F1
Károlyi utca 9
Tel *(06 1) 266 2110*
Budapest was littered with fabulous literary cafés in the early 20th century, but the Central remains the grandest, not only for its great-looking interior and laid-back atmosphere, but the service is exemplary and the coffee and pastries – if on the slightly expensive side – are truly spectacular.

Drum Café HUF
Café **Map** 2 F5
Dob utca 2
Tel *(06 1) 540 7422*
This quirky little cafe offers a large selection of Jewish and Hungarian dishes, like goulash soup and stuffed pancakes.

Fakanál HUF
Traditional Hungarian **Map** 4 F3
Vámház körút 1–3
Tel *(06 1) 217 7860* **Closed** *Sun*
Located upstairs inside the Great Market Hall, this unpretentious eatery is perfect for a quick, no-nonsense bite to eat.

Falafel HUF
Middle Eastern **Map** 7 A1
Paulay Ede utca 53
Tel *(06 1) 705 7142* **Closed** *Sun*
Still the city's most popular *falafel* joint, just pay your money and fill your pitta. Sit down or takeaway.

Fresh Factory HUF
Light bites **Map** 4 E1
Petőfi Sándor utca 7
Tel *06 30 443 6025*
A sit down and takeaway outlet where you can pick up omelettes, baguettes, juices and smoothies, and much more.

Ultra-modern decor at the KNRDY Steakhouse

Frici Papa (HUF)
Traditional Hungarian **Map** 7 A1
Király utca 55
Tel *(06 1) 351 0197* **Closed** *Sun*
There's not much that's classy here, but the food is hearty, cheap and served with efficiency. Popular with the locals.

Fröhlich Kóser Cukrászda (HUF)
Kosher Patisserie **Map** 2 F5
Dob utca 22
Tel *(06 1) 266 1733* **Closed** *Sat*
This warmly decorated kosher patisserie serves layered cakes, buns and sublime *flódni* (apple, walnut and poppy seed cake).

Fruccola (HUF)
Light bites **Map** 4 E1
Kristóf tér 3
Tel *(06 1) 430 6125* **Closed** *Sun*
A super little sandwich bar and coffee shop, with great breakfast and brunch options including plenty for vegetarians.

Gerbeaud Cukrászda (HUF)
Café **Map** 2 E5
Vörösmarty tér 7
Tel *(06 1) 429 9000*
An old gem that has been serving some of the best, and most expensive, coffees and cakes in the land since the mid-19th century.

Kádár Étkezde (HUF)
Hungarian/Jewish **Map** 7 A2
Klauzál tér 9
Tel *(06 1) 321 3622* **Closed** *Sun*
Delicious traditional home-cooking Jewish-Hungarian style in this retro-style eatery that has changed little over the years.

Király Cukrászda (HUF)
Patisserie **Map** 2 F5
Király utca 19
Tel *(06 1) 351 9532*
An age-old bakery that remains better than most, serving delicious cream cakes, pastries and ice-cream.

Marie Kristensen Sandwich Bar (HUF)
Light bites **Map** 7 A5
Ráday utca 7
Tel *(06 1) 218 1673* **Closed** *Sun*
There's a great choice of snacks here, with good vegetarian options, and a lovely terrace on which to enjoy them.

Művész Kávéház (HUF)
Café **Map** 2 F4
Andrássy út 29
Tel *(06 1) 343 3544*
This very popular coffee house is notable as much for its extravagant Baroque decor as for its coffee and cakes.

Traditional setting at the long-running Gerbeaud café

Múzeum Cukrászda (HUF)
Patisserie **Map** 4 F1
Múzeum körút 10
Tel *(06 1) 338 4415*
A friendly spot for a cup of coffee and a pastry, or even a full breakfast, this place is open round the clock.

La Pizza di Mamma Sophia (HUF)
Pizzeria **Map** 2 F5
Király utca 20
Tel *(06 1) 266 0444*
Head to this little outlet for cheap and tasty slices of pizza to eat on the go because there's no seating available.

Sahara (HUF)
Middle Eastern **Map** 7 B5
József Körút 82
Tel *(06 1) 313 0257*
Known to offer some of the best Turkish food in Budapest, this bright outlet, with shared tables, serves a range of kebabs and more substantial meals, as well as baklava and coffee.

Sugar! (HUF)
Café **Map** 7 A1
Paulay Ede utca 48
Tel *(06 1) 321 6672*
At this mesmerising confectioners-cum-café you can live out all your sweet-toothed fantasies at the same time as grabbing a coffee.

VakVarjú Étterem (HUF)
Traditional Hungarian **Map** 10 E3
Paulay Ede utca 7
Tel *(06 1) 268 0888*
Many patrons visit Vakvarjú for the *kenyérlángos* (a flat bread baked in the oven), which can only be sampled here. Service is friendly and efficient.

Vapiano (HUF)
Italian **Map** 4 E1
Bécsi utca 5
Tel *(06 1) 411 0864*
Collect a card, place your order (pizza or pasta) then watch it being prepared before your eyes. Great fun.

W35 (HUF)
Light bites **Map** 7 A2
Wesselényi utca 35
Tel *(06 1) 796 5370*
This tiny joint with just a handful of seats serves what are possibly the best burgers in town, as well as some Mexican dishes. Fans of very spicy food should try the 'Fire in the hole' burger.

Bohémtanya (HUF)(HUF)
Traditional Hungarian **Map** 2 F5
Paulay Ede utca 6
Tel *(06 1) 267 3504*
Customers at the "Bohemian Farm" are allocated places in wooden cubicles, which are typically shared with others.

DK Choice

Borbíróság (HUF)(HUF)
Modern Hungarian **Map** 4 F3
Csarnok tér 5
Tel *(06 1) 219 0902* **Closed** *Sun*
Across from the Great Market Hall, this fantastic looking restaurant possesses a split-level interior and small terrace. The highlights of a limited but exceptional menu are the duck carpaccio and duck steak, though there are many more appetising dishes, like tuna and veal with *foie gras*. The choice and quality of wine is second to none.

For more information on types of restaurants *see page 191*

Inviting terrace seating at Gerlóczy Kávéház

Buena Vista Étterem HUF HUF
International **Map** 7 A1
Liszt Ferenc tér 4-5
Tel *(06 1) 344 6303*
At this oasis of peace from the busy street, carefully prepared Hungarian and international dishes are offered alongside an extensive wine list.

Cucina HUF HUF
Italian **Map** 4 E1
Váci utca 20
Tel *(06 1) 266 4144*
This rustically styled trattoria is one of the more appealing places to eat along this popular tourist street.

Cyrano HUF HUF
International **Map** 4 E1
Kristóf tér 7
Tel *(06 1) 266 4747*
A wide variety of food and flavours are on offer here. Toasted goat's cheese with lavender and honey is the signature dish.

Dionysos Taverna HUF HUF
Greek **Map** 4 F3
Belgrád rakpart 16
Tel *(06 1) 318 1222*
At this fairly successful recreation of a traditional Greek taverna, you'll find an abundance of *meze* alongside authentic main dishes.

Fülemüle étterem HUF HUF
Jewish **Map** 7 A3
Kőfaragó utca 5
Tel *(06 1) 305 3000*
A homely, old-style family-run restaurant serving typical Jewish meals like *sólet*, *cholent* and goose soup with dumplings.

Gerlóczy Kávéház HUF HUF
Modern Hungarian **Map** 4 F1
Gerlóczy utca 1
Tel *(06 1) 501 4000*
Not only does this atmospheric street corner café offer delicious Hungarian fare, but it's also a great place for breakfast.

Gotti Étterem HUF HUF
International **Map** 7 A5
Ráday utca 29
Tel *(06 1) 783 4403*
This popular modern bar and restaurant in the buzzy café district serves everything from pasta and steak to stuffed pancakes. LIve music on Friday evenings.

Il Terzo Cerchio HUF HUF
Italian **Map** 7 A3
Dohány utca 40
Tel *(06 1) 354 0788*
The go-to Italian of choice for many in Budapest. It serves up enormous pizzas, though the seafood pasta dishes are also worth trying.

Kaltenberg Sörház és Étterem HUF HUF
Bavarian **Map** 7 A5
Kinizsi utca 30–36
Tel *(06 1) 215 9792*
An attractively furnished beer cellar where mammoth portions of sausage and cabbage are served. Superb list of locally brewed Hungarian beer. There's an on-site brewery too.

Károlyi Étterem és Kávéház HUF HUF
Traditional Hungarian **Map** 4 F2
Károlyi Mihály utca 16
Tel *(06 1) 328 0240*
At this elegant restaurant in the lovely courtyard of the Károlyi Palace, the veal paprika stew in a potato pancake is a speciality. Sit outside in the garden in summer.

Kárpátia Étterem HUF HUF
Traditional Hungarian **Map** 4 F1
Ferenciek tere 7–8
Tel *(06 1) 317 3596*
Open since 1877, standards in this beautifully ornamented establishment remain impeccably high, and the food is usually spot on. Classic dishes including goulash soup and strudel feature on the menu. Wonderful atmosphere.

Két Szerecsen HUF HUF
International **Map** 2 F4
Nagymező utca 14
Tel *(06 1) 343 1984*
At this bright, buzzy place, a varied tapas menu complements a strong selection of mains, such as salmon steamed in white wine. Try the meat tapas platter. Good vegetarian options as well.

Klassz HUF HUF
International **Map** 7 A1
Andrássy utca 41
As much a wine bar as a restaurant, this small but striking place offers a highly accomplished menu. Try the duck breast dish for a main course.

Kőleves Vendéglő HUF HUF
Traditional Hungarian **Map** 2 F5
Kazinczy utca 37–41
Tel *(06 1) 322 1011*
Jerusalem artichoke cream soup with roast walnuts is a typical dish in this quaint, rather idiosyncratic restaurant. The outside bar area has colourful tables, chairs and hammocks. Carefully selected wine list.

Macesz Huszár 
Jewish Bistro **Map** 7 A2
Dob utca 26
Tel *(06 1) 787 6164*
At this non-kosher Jewish bistro dishes are based on the traditional home cooking of Jewish families in Budapest. Seasonal menu.

Magdalena Merlo HUF HUF
Traditional Hungarian **Map** 7 A1
Király utca 59/b
Tel *(06 1) 322 3278*
Solid rather than spectacular, the food here is a mix of local specialities alongside a sprinkling of Italian dishes. Try the Hungarian steak or baked pork.

Elegantly simple dining room at the French Borssó Bistro

Key to Price Guide *see page 196*

Traditional dining booths at Kárpátia Étterem

DK Choice

Menza
Modern Hungarian **Map** 7 A1
Liszt Ferenc tér 2
Tel *(06 1) 413 1482*
If you only eat at one of the many places on this square, make it this one. Invariably packed to the gills, the retro 1970s decor is what makes this place such great fun, but the service is terrific and the food impeccably prepared and flavourful; sample the roasted duck liver with sour cherry sauce, or the house burger with smoked cheese. Decent sized portions and tasty desserts too. The drinks list is varied and includes green apple lemonade. Book in advance.

Múzeum Kávéház és Étterem
Traditional Hungarian **Map** 4 F1
Múzeum körút 12
Tel *(06 1) 267 0375* **Closed** *Sun*
This mid-19th century restaurant retains a vaguely distinguished air, and the food is excellent. Don't miss the veil paprikash served with sour cream.

Pata Negra
Spanish **Map** 7 A4
Kálvin tér 8
Tel *(06 1) 215 5616*
Traditionally prepared Serrano ham with Manchego cheese, and an all-Spanish wine list, are two very good reasons to visit here.

Shalimar
Indian **Map** 7 A2
Dob utca 53
Tel *(06 1) 352 0305*
The inviting menu here features all the Indian standards, including lots of mouthwatering tandoori dishes. Excellent starter platter.

Soul Café
International **Map** 7 A5
Ráday utca 11–13
Tel *(06 1) 217 6986*
The appeal of this vaguely North African themed establishment is the beautifully prepared French and Moroccan food. For dessert, try the *crêpe suzettes* (a sauce made with caramelized sugar, butter and zest).

Spinoza
Traditional Hungarian **Map** 2 F5
Dob utca 15
Tel *(06 1) 413 7489*
While the food is not particularly outstanding, many locals visit Spinoza to enjoy a meal while listening to the talanted pianist. Advisable to book ahead.

Trattoria Toscana
Italian **Map** 4 E2
Belgrád rakpart 13–15
Tel *(06 1) 327 0045*
Tuck into one of the terrific seafood pasta dishes on offer here while admiring the views across the Danube up to Castle Hill.

Vörös Postakocsi Étterem
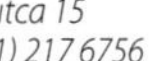
Modern Hungarian **Map** 7 A5
Ráday utca 15
Tel *(06 1) 217 6756*
The "Red Mail Coach" has been around for years, its reputation built on excellent goose liver dishes and Mangalica pork. Don't miss the baby pork ribs.

Araz
French **Map** 7 A3
Dohány utca 42-44
Tel *(06 1) 815 1100*
The mouthwatering French cuisine on offer here includes such dishes as chicken breast with creamy kale and spiced potatoes. The Sunday brunch is good too.

Babel Étterem
Traditional Hungarian **Map** 4 E2
Piarista köz 2
Tel *06 70 600 0800*
Babel is a Hungarian-regional restaurant. Although pricey, its creative cuisine will satisfy enthusiasts of fine dining. HIgh quality fish and meat dishes. Good wine list.

Borssó Bistro
International **Map** 4 F2
Királyi Pál utca 14
Tel *(06 1) 789 0975* **Closed** *Mon*
A charismatic split-level restaurant tucked away down a side street serving some intriguing French cuisine like duck liver terrine with pear salad. Four-course tasting menu available. Friendly service and live music.

Le Bourbon
French **Map** 2 E5
Erzsébet tér 9–10
Tel *(06 1) 429 57 70*
The principal restaurant inside Le Meridien Hotel serves exciting, seasonal menus, though at considerable cost. Fresh fish and seafood usually feature.

Carmel Étterem

Jewish **Map** 10 F3
Kazinczy utca 31
Tel *(06 1) 342 4585*
This legendary, kosher restaurant is invariably crowded with locals here to enjoy its famed *sólet (cholent)* with smoked goose. Book in advance for Friday and Saturday evenings.

Chess
French/Italian **Map** 7 A2
Dob utca 63
Tel *(06 1) 882 3080*
A small, upscale French, Italian and Hungarian bistro with touches of class and a seasonal menu. The decor is black and white throughout.

Dining room at modern Hungarian restaurant Vörös Postakocsi

For more information on types of restaurants *see page 191*

Comme Chez Soi (HUF)(HUF)(HUF)
Italian **Map** 4 E1
Aranykéz utca 2
Tel *(06 1) 318 3943* **Closed** *Sun*
Despite the name, this is essentially an Italian restaurant serving fine food that is elegantly presented. Save room for dessert. Also offered is homemade Hungarian *schnapps* and *limoncello*.

Costes (HUF)(HUF)(HUF)
International **Map** 7 A4
Ráday utca 4
Tel *(06 1) 219 0696* **Closed** *Mon & Tue*
One of only three Michelin-starred restaurants in Budapest; here you'll be treated to an unforgettable array of colour, flavour and texture combinations. Worth every penny.

Fausto's (HUF)(HUF)(HUF)
Italian **Map** 10 F4
Dohány utca 3
Tel *06 30 589 1813* **Closed** *Sun*
This gorgeously understated restaurant remains the best Italian in Budapest. Try the black ravioli filled with octopus served in broccoli cream.

Lou Lou (HUF)(HUF)(HUF)
French **Map** 10 E2
Székely Mihály utca 2
Tel *(06 1) 877 6202* **Closed** *Sun*
For superb fine dining, head to the classy Lou Lou, featuring exotic dishes such as halibut with lobster sauce and samphire.

New York Kávéház (HUF)(HUF)(HUF)
Café **Map** 7 B2
Erzsébet körút 9
Tel *(06 1) 886 6111*
This is another of Budapest's great literary cafés of yesteryear, though these days it is even more exclusive, and very pricey. The interior is simply stunning. Superb food.

Nobu (HUF)(HUF)(HUF)
Japanese **Map** 2 E5
Erzsébet tér 7–8
Tel *(06 1) 429 4242*
The global restaurant's first venue in Central Europe is expensive, but the food on offer is unquestionably stunning.

Onyx (HUF)(HUF)(HUF)
International **Map** 2 E5
Vörösmarty tér 7
Tel *06 30 508 0622* **Closed** *Sun & Mon*
Budapest's second Michelin-starred restaurant receives plaudits for its exquisite plates of food, like blanquette of veal with langoustine.

Paris-Budapest Restaurant and Bar (HUF)(HUF)(HUF)
French-Hungarian **Map** 2 D5
Széchenyi István tér 2
Tel *(06 1) 235 1230*
A fine establishment at the Sofitel, whose patrons know their food, which extends to French, Hungarian and international.

Around Városliget

Ecocafe (HUF)
Café **Map** 5 A5
Andrássy út 68
This cheery café and bakery uses organic and fair trade products and serves up a selection of fresh sandwiches, cakes and salads. Good coffee.

Montenegrói Gurman (HUF)
Light bites **Map** 7 B2
Rákóczi út 54
Tel *06 70 434 9898*
Fast food Balkan style, with loads of juicy grilled meats and oven baked breads, plus Slovenian beer to wash it all down.

Neo-Baroque interior at the Michelin-starred Onyx

Stylish bar seating at the Michelin-starred Costes restaurant

Bagolyvár Étterem (HUF)(HUF)
Traditional Hungarian **Map** 5 C3
Gundel Károly út 4
Tel *(06 1) 468 3110*
The little sister of Gundel, the "Owl Castle" is an enchanting restaurant offering homely cooking at reasonable prices.

Haxen Király Étterem (HUF)(HUF)
Bavarian **Map** 7 B1
Király utca 100
Tel *(06 1) 351 6793*
Leather-trouser-wearing gentlemen play accordion music as waitresses bring enormous plates of *bratwurst* and *sauerkraut*. There is also a huge selection of *pálinkas* (Hungarian fruit brandy).

Himalaya Nepáli Étterem (HUF)(HUF)
Asian **Map** 7 B1
Csengery utca 24
Tel *(06 1) 351 1289*
The chefs from Kathmandu rustle up a range of dishes to suit all palates and budgets, including some fairly spicy ones. Try the tandoori specialities. Tasty vegan options available.

Kogart Étterem (HUF)(HUF)
Modern Hungarian **Map** 5 B4
Andrássy út 112
Tel *(06 1) 354 3820*
Quite formal, this place only serves lunches, but the menu here is both interesting and reasonably priced.

Millennium da Pippo (HUF)(HUF)
Italian **Map** 5 A5
Andrássy út 76
Tel *(06 1) 374 0880*
A fun Italian place where the pasta and pizza dishes are only outdone by a great range of steaks in various sauces. There is a pleasant terrace.

Napfényes Étterem HUF HUF
Vegetarian **Map** 7 C1
Rózsa utca 39
Tel *(06 1) 313 5555*
An atmospheric, brick-vaulted cellar restaurant with a substantial vegan menu, including grilled platters and vegetarian pizzas.

Olimpia Étterem HUF HUF
International **Map** 8 E1
Alpár utca 5
Tel *(06 1) 321 0680* **Closed** *Sun & Mon*
A unique venture where the menu changes daily and can be anything from a three-to-six course meal. All dishes are full of flavour. Good value.

Paprika Vendéglő HUF HUF
Traditional Hungarian **Map** 6 D5
Dózsa György út 72
Tel *(06 1) 294 7944*
All the usual staples like goulash, Hortobágy pancakes (filled with meat) and leg of goose, but done with great style. Don't miss the duck with berry sauce.

Platán Étterem HUF HUF
Traditional Hungarian **Map** 5 C5
Városligeti fasor 46–48
Tel *(06 1) 322 6615*
At the base of a huge sycamore tree is this large dining hall serving à la carte dishes as well as fast-food options. Italian dishes, including pizza, also feature on the menu.

Rákóczi Grillház HUF HUF
Traditional Hungarian **Map** 7 C2
Rákóczi út 57/A
Tel *(06 1) 333 1342*
Enjoyable, all you can eat buffet-style menu. There's a selection of fish, meat and vegetables. Choose your ingredients and then watch them cooked in front of you. The price also includes drinks.

Regős Vendéglő HUF HUF
Traditional Hungarian **Map** 5 B5
Szófia utca 33
Tel *(06 1) 321 1921*
This cosy brick-cellar restaurant offers a lengthy menu of Hungarian standards but with a nod to French influences. Try the cold cherry soup or the veal paprikash and dumpling

Széchenyi Kertvendéglő 
Traditional Hungarian **Map** 6 D3
Állatkert körút 9–11
Tel (06 30) 906 1294
A smart restaurant in the building complex of the famous spa, offering delicious traditional Hungarian cuisine and an extensive wine list.

The magnificent New York Kávéház at the Boscolo Budapest Hotel

DK Choice

Bock Bisztró HUF HUF HUF
Modern Hungarian **Map** 7 A1
Erzsébet körút 43–49
Tel *(06 1) 321 0340*
Named after the eponymous Hungarian vintner, Bock is a classy establishment, from the elegant cork-filled glass tables to the beautifully crafted food. Well thought out tapas dishes complement exciting renditions of rich Hungarian offerings like veal paprika. The wine card is one of the finest in Budapest.

Gundel Étterem HUF HUF HUF
Traditional Hungarian **Map** 5 C3
Állatkerti körút 4
Tel *(06 1) 468 4040*
Budapest's most famous restaurant offers innovative Hungarian and international cuisine in posh surrounds. People flock here for their Sunday brunch.

Lively, modern dining room at the Bock Bisztró

DK Choice

La Perle Noire HUF HUF HUF
International **Map** 5 C4
Andrássy út 111
Tel *(06 1) 555 1545*
Inside the elegant MaMaison hotel, this restaurant offers an exclusive gourmet dining experience, with a fantastic fusion menu comprising the likes of sweet potato shiitake ravioli, and home-smoked salmon with wasabi yoghurt. The dining area is beautifully designed, and there's a pretty garden terrace for when the weather turns summery. It also has a fine selection of local and international wines, plus a good cocktail menu; try the RumBerry or Apricot Fizz. Excellent service and lovely atmosphere.

Robinson 
International **Map** 5 C3
Városligeti Tó
Tel (06 30) 663 6871
In an unbeatable location on the lake, the outdoor terrace is a wonderful spot to indulge in some exotic seafood dishes. HIghlights include grilled pikeperch on a bed of creamy spinach, duck leg served with cabbage and gnocchi and the risottos. Great cocktails as well.

Zeller Bistro 
Modern Hungarian **Map** 7 B1
Izabella utca 38
Tel (06 30) 651 0880 **Closed** *Sun & Mon*
This small but utterly charming restaurant serves outstanding nouvelle-cuisine. The flavourful dishes on the weekly changing menu are made using fresh local produce. You won't find better service anywhere in the city. Very popular, so book ahead.

For more information on types of restaurants *see page 191*

Cosy setting at traditional Hungarian restaurant Firkász Kávéház

Further Afield

DK Choice

Briós kávézó HUF
Café
Pozsonyi út 16
Tel *(06 1) 789 6110*
This delightful neighbourhood café serves super breakfasts, including American pancakes and filled croissants, French toast and fruit skewers. There's an appealing lunch menu too, including omelettes, sandwiches and salad. The family-friendly theme of this place extends to a dedicated kids' menu and a small play area upstairs, which is perfect as you indulge in coffee and cake downstairs.

Cziniel Cukrászda HUF
Patisserie
Nánási út 55
Tel *(06 1) 240 1188*
Fulfill all your sweet-toothed fantasies at this large and popular terrace patisserie-cum-café with ice-creams, sundaes and cakes galore.

Daubner Cukrászda HUF
Patisserie
Szépvölgyi út 50
Tel *(06 1) 335 2253*
Head here for some of the finest cakes and confectionery in Budapest, but there are no seats, and you will have to queue.

Kőbüfé Söröző HUF
Traditional Hungarian
Rege út 21
Tel (06 30) 212 6999
This small and welcoming family restaurant makes for a convenient pit-stop after an adventure on the nearby cogwheel railway. Sit outside on the terrace in summer.

Normafa Rétes HUF
Patisserie
Normafa Eötvös utca 50
At this hut on the top of the Buda Hills you can choose from a delectable selection of *rétes* to munch on alongside good coffee.

Árnyas Étterem HUF HUF
Traditional Hungarian
Diós árok 16
Tel *(06 1) 212 5681*
Despite the trek to get here, this early 20th-century restaurant is delightfully located and the food is generously portioned and tasty. Seasonally changing menu. Outside seating in summer.

Bajai Halászcsárda HUF HUF
Fish
Hollós út 2
Tel *(06 1) 275 5245*
Fresh river fish is the order of the day here, notably the Baja fish soup with a huge portion of carp fillet on the side. Live traditional Hungarian music most evenings. Helpful staff.

Bruno & Bruno Étterem HUF HUF
Modern Hungarian/International
Apor Vilmos tér 11–12
Tel (06 20) 243 1565
Head here for one of the best *schnietzel* in Budapest, prepared from the finest of Hungarian meat in a modern environment. Good service.

Dunapark Étterem és Kávéház HUF HUF
International
Pozsonyi út 38
Tel *(06 1) 786 1009*
The location is terrific and the food here is surprisingly varied. Good breakfasts, delicious cakes, superb ice cream and Italian coffee. Outside seating in summer and live piano music in the evenings.

Fenyőgyöngye Vendéglő HUF HUF
Traditional Hungarian
Szépvölgyi út 155
Tel *(06 1) 325 9783*
An incredibly popular, casual restaurant up in the Buda Hills, offering traditional Hungarian fare made in a lighter, healthier way. The long menu features tasty dishes, including soup, salad, fish meat and poultry.

Firkász Kávéház Étterem HUF HUF
Traditional Hungarian
Tátra utca 18
Tel *(06 1) 450 1118*
Appropriately meaning "Scribbler", this restaurant has a quiet, literary atmosphere, with old newspapers and posters covering the walls. Serves superb Hungarian food. Ideal for a sedate dinner.

Fuji Étterem HUF HUF
Japanese
Csatárka út 54
Tel *(06 1) 325 7111*
In a pagoda-style interior, you can watch the chef at work while enjoying dishes such as a beautifully presented selection of *sashimi*.

Kéhli Vendéglő HUF HUF
Traditional Hungarian
Mókus utca 22
Tel *(06 1) 368 0613*
Standards at this delightful inn have not dropped since Gyula Krúdy, the great Hungarian gourmet writer, ate here over a century ago. Don't miss the pikeperch, a speciality here.

Kerék Vendéglő HUF HUF
Traditional Hungarian
Bécsi út 103
Tel *(06 1) 250 4261*
Another landmark restaurant up in Óbuda, the pretty garden here is a lovely place to dine out on the likes of deer stew. Excellent soups.

Pretty outside dining area at Remiz

Pagoda-style interior at Fuji Étterem Japanese restaurant

Központ Bisztró
Modern Hungarian/International
Újpest, Szent István tér 1
Tel (06 20) 374 9785
A modern busy café and restaurant in the centre of the district of Újpest, next to the metro station. The appealing menu changes each season.

Larus Étterem
International
Csörsz utca 18/B
Tel *(06 1) 799 2480*
A large restaurant with a huge terrace in one of Buda's most pleasant parks. Quirky, creative menu. Try the asparagus and strawberry salad or the meat soup with marrow toast to start.

Náncsi Néni Vendéglője
Traditional Hungarian
Ördögárok utca 80
Tel *(06 1) 398 7127*
Offering a wide choice of home-style interpretations of traditional Hungarian meals. The giant *túrógombóc* (curd cheese dumplings) is a favourite dessert here.

Négy Muskétás Étterem
Traditional Hungarian
Tétényi út 18
Tel *(06 1) 203 1401*
This faintly kitsch restaurant with a leafy exterior and wooden interior offers an extensive menu of heart-warming Hungarian fare, including goose.

Öreghalász Étterem
Fish
Árpád út 20–22
Tel *(06 1) 231 0800*
The subtle nautical décor here gives away the fact that fresh river fish is the speciality. Don't miss the fish soups or the slightly spicey fish stew. Non-fish dishes are also available.

Porcellino Grasso
Italian
Ady Endre utca 19
Tel *(06 1) 886 7880*
Despite the dull location, this is a reasonably authentic Italian, with great pizzas and pasta, though duck also features prominently. Good for families, as there's a children's play area next to the terrace.

Premium Café & Restaurant
Traditional Hungarian
Országbíró utca 44–46
Tel *(06 1) 877 7600*
This elegant restaurant serves both well-prepared classic dishes, as well as international cuisine, alongside a stellar choice of beverages.

Remiz
Traditional Hungarian
Budakeszi út 5
Tel *(06 1) 384 1896*
An eclectic range of food, including Russian red caviar and Serbian carp is served up in a largely rustic-themed setting.

Rozmaring Kert Vendéglő
Traditional Hungarian
Árpád fejedelem útja 125
Tel *(06 1) 367 1301*
It is the pretty setting on the banks of the Danube, opposite Margit-Sziget, that makes this long-standing favourite really worth trekking to. Consistently good food.

Ypsilon Café
International
Stefánia út 1
Tel *(06 1) 468 3357*
Located in the Stadium district just by the Stadionok metro station, this establishment has a choice of local dishes alongside European dishes such as BBQ chicken.

Zöld Kapu Vendéglő
Traditional Hungarian
Szőlő utca 42
Tel *(06 1) 387 7028*
The "Green Door" restaurant is a long-standing favourite, serving huge portions of hearty food. There are some tasty vegetarian options too. The garden area is particularly lovely with its wooden green bench seating.

Chez Daniel
French
Szív utca 32
Tel *(06 1) 302 4039*
Choose from the daily specials chalked up on the blackboard, kick back and enjoy great food. There's a superb wine list too.

Kisbuda Gyöngye
Traditional Hungarian
Kenyeres utca 34
Tel *(06 1) 368 6402*
This gorgeous restaurant has a natural, old-time drawing room atmosphere, where guests can relax to the background of soft piano music. The fish soup and duck dishes are recommended.

DK Choice

Rosenstein
Traditional Hungarian
Mosonyi utca 3
Tel *(06 1) 333 3492*
In an area near Keleti station not known for fine dining, this is a true standout; an inviting, family-run establishment offering its guests a sophisticated menu, with plates such as wild boar ragout with forest mushrooms, as well as some Jewish favourites. The wine list is similarly of the highest order.

Terrace overlooking the Danube at Rozmaring Kert Vendéglő

For more information on types of restaurants *see page 191*

Pubs, Bars and Nightlife

To sample the true atmosphere of Budapest, it is essential to visit the smaller, often quirkier, drinking establishments that are scattered across the city and into the suburbs. Nowhere is this more evident than in the proliferation of uber-cool "ruin" pubs (also known as kerts – or garden bars), ramshackle bars set up in previously abandoned buildings and courtyards. There are also a number of superb wine bars, reflecting the country's strong, though still little known about, viticultural heritage. Elsewhere, bright neon and loud music reflect the contemporary cultural interests of Budapest's youth.

Drinking Customs

You will find Budapest a very friendly and informal place to drink; if you sit at an empty table, others will probably join you. Note that in traditional pubs a waiter will automatically bring more beer as soon as you appear to be close to finishing your glass, unless you indicate otherwise.

Toasting a fellow drinker in Hungarian is not the easiest task; *Egészségedre*! (literally "To Your Health") is the standard way to toast (and even trickier to say after a few drinks). Traditionally in Hungary it was not the done thing to clink beer glasses together with fellow drinkers. According to a legend, Austrians celebrated the execution of Hungarian generals after the uprising of 1848–9 with beer. The taboo has since passed, but don't be offended if some Hungarians may still politely refuse to clink beer glasses with you.

Wine Bars

Unlike in countries such as Britain or the United States where wine drinking is regarded as a somewhat middle-class pursuit, in Hungary it has traditionally been considered a workers' pastime. The old ways of drinking wine are still to be found underground, in the *borozók* of Budapest, like **Várfok Borozó**, in the Castle District, and **Grinzingi Borozó** and **Tokaji Borozó**, both in downtown Pest.

A traditional *borozó* is an unglamorous, cheap wine cellar with few tables and chairs, and where wine is served straight from the barrel and sold by the decilitre; here, too, you can normally grab a light snack, like *zsiros kenyér*, bread and pork dripping garnished with raw onion and sprinkled with paprika; or *pogácsa*, a yeast pan-bread, served with crackling, cheese, caraway seeds or paprika.

There are an increasing number of more modern and sophisticated equivalents, notably **Dobló** and **DiVino**. There is also **Drop Shop Wine Bar**, where you can taste wines from every region in Hungary. Then there are the hotel wine bars, the best of which is to be found in the Hilton Hotel *(see p188)*, which houses a stylish wine bar in a medieval cellar. Moreover, any good Budapest restaurant will have a decent selection of wines on offer.

Cocktail Bars

Budapest is alive with trendy cocktail bars that buzz from the early evening onwards with a young crowd, enjoying after-work drinks in the Italian fashion (*aperitivo*).

The trendiest establishments tend to be found on Liszt Ferenc tér, one of the city's main social hubs, particularly in spring and summer when the cafés and bars spill out onto the tree-lined pavements; here you'll find **Circus Bar** which has a repertoire of fancy cocktails and serves its own branded beer, while another nearby favourite is the casual **Boutiq'Bar**.

In Buda, within a stone's throw of the Castle District, a hip crowd meets every evening at the popular **Oscar's American Bar**, famous for its selection of more than 200 cocktails.

If money is no object, head for the **Bar and Lobby Lounge**, in the magnificent Gresham Palace hotel, or the super cool **Blue Fox Bar** in the Kempinski Corvinus Hotel. In fact, most of the top-end hotels have bars offering a superb, albeit expensive, selection of cocktails.

Pubs and Bars

The number, and variety, of places to drink in Budapest has improved beyond all recognition thanks in no small part to the evolution of the so-called "ruin" pub. Set up in dilapidated buildings or the courtyards of ruined blocks, these idiosyncratic dens are characterised by colourfully-decorated, graffiti-strewn rooms with furnishings seemingly plucked from the rubbish tip. Most ruin pubs are concentrated within the boundaries of the seventh (Erzsébetváros) and eighth (Józsefváros) districts, where you'll find big hitters such as **Szimplakert** and **Instant**, the latter with in excess of a dozen themed rooms. Others, like **Most Kortárs Bisztró** and **Szóda Cafe**, have a slightly more relaxed vibe.

Budapest is not short of conventional pubs and bars either; there are dozens of hip places to drink, particularly around Liszt Ferenc tér and Ráday utca, whose alfresco bars do a roaring trade as soon as the weather picks up. Pick of the bunch here include **Paris-Texas Kévéző**. On nearby Jókai tér, **Kiadó** is a more intimate venue, conducive to more contemplative drinking. In summer, you can find plenty of outdoor bars along the banks of the Danube, like **Spoon**, a large venue on the river itself with five bars.

One of the most lively and trendy areas for drinking, eating or just going out is in and around the Jewish Quarter. There are now more than 250 places for all tastes. Gozsdu Court is a good place to start. This renovated complex of eight buildings from 1901, with six inner yards connecting Király utca and Dob utca, is full of indoor and outdoor cafés, bars, pubs, buffets and restaurants.

Nightclubs and Discos

Nightlife in Budapest is now up there with other European capitals and there are stacks of clubs scattered throughout the city. One big party place is **Akvárium Klub** on central Erzsébet tér, with regular live music, and a terrific terrace to boot. Similarly, **Corvintető**, on the top floor of a department store on Blaha Lujza tér, has live music, DJs and the cities best drum'n'bass parties, while **Ötkert** has a regular roster of superstar DJs. **Kontra Club** is part of the Trafó House of Contemporary Arts, an innovative cultural space for alternative artists housed in a renovated power station; it's also the setting for numerous exhibitions and literary events, and music styles ranging from reggae beats to classical Indian music. Perhaps the most popular of the bohemian hangouts is **Piaf**, a decadent dive reminiscent of a speakeasy.

The outskirts of the city are home to some of the city's biggest and best clubs, not least **A38**, a concert boat moored just past Petőfi bridge on the Buda side of the river. It is a cultural centre with a restaurant, bars and a concert hall, and hosts numerous national and international cultural events, exhibitions and festivals.

Many clubs are often centered around student venues: **Liget** is a massive, sweaty joint that is popular with both locals and students alike.

Gay Venues

While not on the scale of most major European cities, there is an increasingly active gay scene in Budapest, with some terrific nightlife. The most well known of Budapest's gay bars are **Action Bar**, **AlterEgo Club** and **Coxx**, the latter a massive men-only complex with bar, disco, restaurant, Internet café and gallery – it's also famous for its theme nights, anything from fancy dress to no dress at all. For a more laid-back vibe, there's **Habroló**, a small, friendly place with a neighbourhood atmosphere, and **Mystery Bar**, the city's oldest gay bar and a good spot to start the evening.

DIRECTORY

Wine Bars

Drop Shop
Balassi Bálint 27.
Map2 D2. **Tel** (06 30) 345 37 39. **W dropshop.hu**

DiVino
Szent István tér 3
Map 2 E5.
Tel (06 70) 935 39 80.
W divinoborbar.hu

Dobló
Dob utca 20.
Map 2 F5.
Tel (06 20) 398 88 63.
W budapestwine.com

Grinzingi Borozó
Veres Pálné utca 10.
Map 4 F2 (10 E5).
Tel (06 1) 317 46 24.

Tokaji Borozó
Falk Miksa utca 32.
Map 2 D2.
Tel (06 1) 269 31 43.

Várfok Borozó
Várfok u.10. **Map** 1 A3.
Tel (06 1) 212 31 80.

Cocktail Bars

Blue Fox Bar
Kempinski Corvinus Hotel, Erzsébet tér 5–6. **Map** 2 E5.
Tel (06 1) 429 44 99.

Boutiq'Bar
1061 Budapest, Paulay Ede utca 5. **Map** 2 F5.
Tel (06 30) 229 18 21.
W boutiqbar.hu

Bar and Lobby Lounge
Four Seasons Gresham Palace Hotel. Széchenyi István tér 5–6.
Map 2 D5.
Tel (06 1) 268 51 20

Circus Bar
Liszt Ferenc tér 11.
Map 7 A1.
Tel (06 1) 413 67 64.

Oscar's American Bar
Ostrom utca 14.
Map 1 A3.
Tel (06 20) 214 25 25.

Pubs and Bars

Instant
Nagymező utca 38.
Map 2 F3. **Tel** (06 1) 311 07 04. **W instant.co.hu**

Kiadó Kocsma
Jókai tér 3
Map 7 A1.
Tel (06 1) 331 19 55.

Most Kortárs Bisztró
Zichy Jenő utca 17.
Map 2 F4.
Tel (06 70) 248 33 22.

Paris-Texas Kávézó
Ráday utca utca 22.
Map 7 A5.
Tel (06 1) 218 05 70.
W paristexaskavehaz.hu

Spoon
On river, moored next to the Pest side of the Chain Bridge.
Map 2 D4.
Tel (06 1) 411 09 33.
W spoon.hu

Szimplakert
Kazinczy utca 14.
Map 7 A3. **Tel** (06 20) 261 86 69. **W szimpla.hu**

Szóda Cafe
Wesselényiutca 18.
Map 7 A3. **Tel** (06 1) 461 00 07. **W szoda.com**

Nightclubs and Discos

A38 Ship
Pázmány Péter sétány, moored near the Buda end of Petőfi Bridge.
Tel (06 1) 464 39 40.
W a38.hu

Akvárium Klub
Erzsébet tér
Tel (06 30) 860 33 68.
W akvariumklub.hu

Corvintető
Blaha Lujza tér 1–2.
Map 7 B3. **Tel** (06 20) 378 29 88. **W corvinteto.hu**

Kontra Club
Trafó House of Contemporary Arts, Liliom utca 41
Tel (06 1) 456 20 40.
W trafo.hu

Liget
Népliget út 2.
Tel (06 70) 527 52 72.
W ligetclub.hu

Ötkert
Zrinyi utca 4.
Map 2 D5.
Tel (06 70) 330 86 52.
W otkert.hu

Piaf
Nagymező utca 25.
Map 2 F3.
Tel (06 1) 708 31 66.

Gay Venues

Action Bar
Magyar utca 42.
Map 4 F2.
Tel (06 1) 266 91 48.
W action.gay.hu

AlterEgo Club
Dessewffy utca 33.
Map 2 F4.
Tel (06 70) 345 43 02.
W alteregoclub.hu

Coxx
Dohány utca 38.
Map 7 A3.
Tel (06 1) 344 48 84.
W coxx.hu

Habroló
Szép utca 1.
Map 4 F1. **Tel** (06 1) 950 66 44. **W habrolo.hu**

Mystery Bar
Nagysándor József utca 3.
Map 2 E4. **Tel** (06 1) 312 14 36. **W mysterybar.hu**

SHOPS AND MARKETS

Shopping in Budapest has changed dramatically since the more spartan days of Communism. A huge variety of consumer goods, both foreign and home produced, are now available here. Major shopping streets include the pedestrianized and fashionable Váci utca (Váci Street, *see p131)* good for folk art and Zsolnay porcelain, and the less fashionable, but much cheaper Nagykörút, where locals come to do their shopping. For a more traditional shopping experience, don't miss a visit to some of Budapest's many markets. These range from stunning 19th-century food halls such as the Great Market Hall (Nagy Vásárcsarnok), to flea markets such as the huge and lively Ecseri Flea Market, for everything from bric-a-brac to furniture and antiques.

Opening Hours

Most shops in Budapest open from 9am to 5:30 or 6pm Monday to Friday, and from 9am to 1pm on Saturday. Greengrocers, bakeries and supermarkets open from 7am until 8pm. Shopping centres, department stores and plazas are open from 10am to 9pm except Sundays, when they close at 6pm. Indoor markets open on Sunday, and most cafés sell milk and bread on Sunday morning. A large number of shops stay open 24 hours a day.

Westend City Center shopping mall

How to Pay

Credit and debit cards can be used to pay for goods and services in many shops (check for signs at the entrance), but it is advisable to carry some cash in Hungarian forints as smaller vendors may not accept cards.

Traditional folk crafts, on sale around Váci utca

VAT Exemption

The price of all goods in Hungary includes a value-added tax of 27% (ÁFA). With the exception of works of art and antiques, it is possible for non-EU residents to claim back the value-added tax on anything costing more than 50,000 forints. However, before buying expensive goods with the intention of reclaiming the VAT, it is advisable to consult the vendor about whether they have the necessary VAT-reclaim form. Then, present your goods at customs within 90 days of purchase, along with the VAT-reclaim form, to receive your customs certification. You will need your sales receipt and currency exchange or credit card receipt, plus the customs certification, to apply for your refund within 183 days of your return home.

Department Stores and Malls

Budapest's most luxurious department store is **Il Bacio di Stile** on Andrássy út. More of a mall than a department store, the **Duna Plaza** on Váci út is smart but not centrally located.

Many large stores are clustered in the old buildings of Váci utca, such as C&A and Zara, though most of these brands can also be found in one place in the modern shopping centres.

There are than 20 major shopping malls in the city, which have proved popular with both locals and visitors. The most centrally-located mall is **Westend City Center**. One of Central Europe's largest, it has over 350 stores, including Massimo Dutti, Gap, Nike and Marks & Spencer, in addition to a 14-screen cinema and a food court with Hungarian and international fast food options.

The huge and stylish **Mammut** on Széna tér (next to Széll Kálmán tér) is frequented by the better off inhabitants of Buda, and is easily accessible for those who do not have the good fortune to live nearby.

More than 200 shops, including Mango, Benetton, and Gant are housed in the modern **Arena Plaza** shopping mall.

Delicate lace, an example of traditional Hungarian folk art

Markets

Markets of all sorts are an essential part of life in Budapest, and offer a delightfully traditional shopping experience to visitors. Perhaps the most spectacular are the five cavernous market halls found around the city. All were built in the late 19th century and several are still used as markets.

Fruit and vegetable stalls at Central Market Hall

The three-level Great Market Hall (Nagy Vásárcsarnok) known officially as the **Central Market Hall** (Központi Vásárcsarnok) on Fővám tér is the largest of all. More than 180 stalls display a huge variety of vegetables, fruit, meat and cheese, under a roof of brightly-coloured Zsolnay tiles. The market opens from 6am–5pm Mon–Fri and 6am–2pm Sat *(see p142)*.

In many markets you will see independent farmers selling fruit and vegetables, as well as local cheeses, honey and sausages. Some of the best markets are at Lehel tér (district XIII), Bosnyák tér (XIV), Fehérvári út (IX) and Fény utca (II). Delicious hot sausages with mustard and fresh bread, or *lángos,* a flat salty dough fried in oil served with or without cream or grated cheese, are traditional and popular market snacks.

Beginning at 156 Nagykőrösi út in district XIX, is the **Ecseri Flea Market**, open on weekends. Outside, a maze of wooden tables is covered in Communist artifacts, second-hand clothes and all sorts of bric-a-brac, while from tiny cubicles inside the market, serious antique dealers sell porcelain, icons, silverware, jewellery and much more. It is necessary to obtain permission from Gyula Forster National Centre for Cultural Heritage Management, located at Táncsics Mihály utca 1 (Tel (06 1) 225 4800 or email: info@forsterkozpont.hu), before you can take antiques out of the country.

Another market well worth a visit is the **Inner City Market Hall** (Belvárosi Vásárcsarnok). Located in the middle of the city, it was built in 1897 and fully renovated in 2014. The market specializes in fruit, vegetables and food products that come directly from small country farms.

Held every second weekend in two locations depending on the season, the **WAMP Design Fair** gives young Hungarian designers an opportunity to sell their handmade items, including textiles, jewellery and kitchenware. There are also stalls selling homemade delicacies like artisan sweets.

Marks & Spencer, a branch of the British department store

What to Buy in Budapest

Despite price rises since the return to a free-market economy, many Hungarian goods are still great bargains. Embroidered peasant blouses and wooden carvings make unique souvenirs, as does the distinctive porcelain produced at the world-famous Zsolnay and Herend factories. Cheap, good quality CDs and records are widely available, and Hungarian wines, salamis and other foodstuffs can be bought in the city's many lively markets. Clothes and shoes made to your specifications represent one of the city's most luxurious bargains.

Folk Art

Hungarian folk culture is still alive and well in many parts of rural Hungary. You can buy textiles, ceramics and woodwork from flea markets *(see p211)* and from folk art and souvenir shops around Váci utca and in the Castle District *(see pp73–89)*. Folk art shops such as **Tekla Folklór**, sell machine-made products, and, for genuine Transylvanian textiles there is the **Korona Folklór** hand-made shop. For the cheapest authentic folk costumes, head for the **Central Market Hall** (Nagy Vásárcsarnok). To buy folk, modern art, souvenirs and Hungarian delicacies, or just look at the unique whale-shaped building on the bank of the Danube, visit **Bálna**, which has several such shops and a market.

Antiques

Dominated by 18th- and 19th-century pieces in the Habsburg style, the Budapest antiques scene is concentrated in the Castle District, around Falk Miksa utca and on Váci utca (Váci Street, *see p131*). **Moró Antik** is a tiny shop specializing in 18th-century weapons, while the huge **Nagyházi Gallery** sells everything from jewellery to furniture. The **Ecseri Flea Market** *(see p211)* is also a good place for antiques.

Porcelain

There are two major porcelain manufacturers in Hungary, **Herend** and **Zsolnay**. Herend enjoys a reputation as the producer of the country's finest porcelain, while Zsolnay's brightly glazed tiles can be seen on many of the city's notable buildings. Second-hand porcelain can be bought in antiques shops and markets. Both companies have shops selling new pieces.

Clothes and Shoes

Made-to-measure clothes and shoes, and ready-made designer clothes offer some of the best deals to be had by visitors to Budapest. Many people have clothes made up in their choice of fabric by a local tailor – who is likely to be happy to oblige for a fairly modest fee. At the smart end of the market, there is **Náray Tamás Atelier**, the showcase for one of the most famous fashion designers in Hungary. **Orex** is one of the country's most exclusive jewellers. Shoemakers in Budapest tend to make only men's shoes. **Vass** will make a one-off pair of dress shoes in about a month for around 200,000 Hungarian forints.

Food and Wine

Food and wine in Hungary are great value and make excellent souvenirs. Sausage is a national passion and can be bought in shops and markets all over the city. Some of the most popular types include spicy sausages from Debrecen, smoked sausages from Gyulai and a whole range of world-famous salamis. Also worth bringing home are dried mushrooms, *paté de foie gras*, a string of paprika or some fresh sheep's cheese. All these can be bought in Budapest's markets and in delicatessens like **Memories of Hungary**. Hungary's national beverage is wine *(see pp194–5)* and there are various top-quality bottles to look out for. These include fine dessert wines from the Tokaji region, Muscats from Kiskunhalas on the central plain, and Chardonnays from Mátraalja. Also popular are the herbal liqueur Unicum, and the strong, fiery pálinka, which is made from plums, cherries or apricots. Wines and spirits are available in supermarkets and in specialist shops such as **Borház** and **House of Hungarian Pálinka**.

Music

Hungary's rich folk and classical music traditions make low-priced CDs, tapes and vinyl a tempting purchase in Budapest. For Hungarian folk music, from traditional Roma (Gypsy) music to recordings of village folk music, the old-style **Rózsavölgyi Zeneműbolt** is a good choice. Many record shops now operate online only, but most book shops and secondhand book shops still sell CDs and music DVDs.

Books

For illustrated books and English-language guide-books, try the **Litea Bookstore and Café**, where you can browse while enjoying coffee and cakes at tables set among the shelves. **Bookstation** stocks new and secondhand books, as well as many books in English. A range of English-language newspapers, magazines and novels are available at **Bestsellers**. **Írók Boltja** sells art books and some English-language books, while **Pendragon** stocks a varied assortment of fiction in English. **Librotrade-Kodex** stocks books in English, French and German. For antique books, etchings and maps a good place to try is **Központi Antikvárium**. **Famulus Foreign Language Bookshop** has English literature and books about Hungary, as well as dictionaries and books for language learners.

DIRECTORY

Department Stores

Arena Plaza
Kerepesi út. **Map** 8 E2.
Tel (06 1) 880 70 10.
Open 10am–9pm Mon–Sat, 10am–7pm Sun.
W arenaplaza.hu

Duna Plaza
Váci út 178.
Tel (06 1) 465 16 66.
W dunaplaza.hu

Il Bacio di Stile
Andrássy út 19.
Map 2 F4.
Tel (06 1) 211 10 00.
W ilbaciodistile.com

Mammut I–II Mall
Lövőház út 3. **Map** 1 A2.
Tel (06 1) 345 80 20.
Open 10am–9pm Mon–Sat, 10am–6pm Sun.
W mammut.hu

Westend City Center
Váci út 1–3. **Map** 2 F2.
Tel (06 1) 238 77 77.
W westend.hu

Markets

Central Market Hall (Központi Vásárcsarnok)
Vámház Körút 1–3 (Fővám tér). **Map** 4 F3.
Tel (06 1) 217 60 67.
Open 6am–5pm Mon, 6am–6pm Tue–Fri, 6am–3pm Sat.

Ecseri Flea Market
Nagykőrösi út 156.
Tel (06 1) 348 32 00.
Open 8am–4pm Mon–Fri, 5am–3pm Sat, 8am–1pm Sun.

Fehérvári út Market
Fehérvári út 20.
Map 4 D5.

Fény utca Market
Near Széll Kálmán tér.
Map 1 A3.

Inner City Market Hall (Belvárosi Vásárcsarnok)
Hold utca 13.
Tel (06 1) 353 11 10.
Open Mon–Sat.

Lehel tér Market
Lehel tér.
Map 2 F1.

WAMP Design Fair
Late May–early Sep: Erzsébet tér. **Map** 2 E5.
Late Sep–early May: Millenáris, Kisrókus utca 16–20. **Map** 1 A2.
W wamp.hu

Folk Art

Bálna
Fővám tér 11–12.
Map 4 F3.
W balnabudapest.hu

Korona Folklór
Szentháromság utca 5.
Map 1 B4.
Tel (06 1) 212 76 40.

Tekla Folklór
Váci utca 58.
Map 4 E1 (10 D3).
Tel (06 1) 486 00 58.
Open 9am–9pm daily.

Antiques

Moró Antik
Falk Miksa utca 13.
Map 2 D2.
Tel (06 1) 311 08 14.

Nagyházi Gallery
Balaton utca 8. **Map** 2 D2.
Tel (06 1) 475 60 00.

Porcelain

Herend Shops
József Nádor tér 11.
Map 2 E5 (10 D3).
Tel (06 1) 317 26 22.
Szentháromság utca 5.
Tel (06 1) 225 10 50.
Andrássy út 16.
Map 2 F4.
Tel (06 1) 374 00 06.

Zsolnay Shops
József krt. 59–61.
Map 7 B4.
Tel (06 1) 318 70 93.
Kecskeméti u.14.
Map 4 F2.
Tel (06 1) 318 26 43.
Bajcsy Zs.u.23.
Map 2 F3.
Tel (06 1) 311 40 94.
W porcelan.hu

Clothes and Accessories

Náray Tamás Atelier
Hajós utca 17.
Map 10 E5.
Tel (06 1) 266 24 73.

Orex
Petőfi Sándor utca 6.
Map 4 E1.
Tel (06 1) 266 63 04.

Vass Cipőbolt
Haris köz 2. **Map** 4 E1.
Tel (06 1) 318 23 75.
W vass-cipo.hu

Food and Drink

Borház
Jókai tér 7.
Map 2 F3 (10 F1).
Tel (06 1) 353 48 49.

House of Hungarian Pálinka
Rákóczi út 17.
Map 7 A3.
Open 9am–7pm Mon–Sat. **W magyar palinkaha za.hu**

Malatinszky Wine Store
József Attila utca 12.
Map 2 E5 (10 D3).
Tel (06 1) 317 59 19.
W malatinszky.hu

Memories of Hungary
Hercegprimas utca 8.
Map 2 E5.
Tel (06 1) 80 52 47.
W memoriesof hungary.hu

Music

Liszt Ferenc Book and Music Store
Andrássy út 45.
Map 2 F5 (10 E2).
Tel (06 1) 322 40 91.

Rózsavölgyi Zeneműbolt
Szervita tér 5.
Map 4 E1 (10 D4).
Tel (06 1) 318 35 00.
Open 10am–10pm Mon–Sat.

Books

Bestsellers
Október 6 utca 11.
Map 2 E4 (10 D2).
Tel (06 1) 312 12 95.
W bestsellers.hu

Bookstation
Katona József utca 13.
Map 2 E1
Tel (06 1) 413 11 58.
W bookstation.hu

Famulus Foreign Language Bookshop
Ujpesti rakpart 6.
Tel (06 1) 288 07 71.
W famuluskonyv.hu

Írók Boltja
Andrássy út 45.
Map 2 F4 (10 E2).
Tel (06 1) 322 16 45.

Központi Antikvárium
Múzeum Körút 13–15.
Map 4 F1 (10 E4).
Tel (06 1) 317 35 14.

Librotrade-Kodex
Honvéd utca 5.
Map 7 C3.
Tel (06 1) 428 10 10.

Litea Bookstore and Café
Hess András tér 4.
Map 1 B4 (9 A2).
Tel (06 1) 375 69 87.
Open 10am–6pm.

Pendragon
Pozsonyi út 21–23.
Map 2 F1.
Tel (06 1) 340 44 26.
Open 10am–6pm Mon–Fri, 10am–2pm Sat.

Pendragon at CEU
Zrínyi utca 12.
Map 2 D4.
Tel (06 1) 327 30 96.
Open 10am–7pm Mon–Fri, 10am–3pm Sat.

ENTERTAINMENT IN BUDAPEST

Budapest has been known as a city of entertainment since the late 19th century, when people would travel here from Vienna in search of a good time. Its nightclubs were frequented for their exciting atmosphere and the beautiful girls that danced the spirited *csárdás* and the cancan. It was said that there was nowhere else where fiddlers played such heartrending music or casinos witnessed such staggering losses as in Budapest. Between the wars the city was as famous for its glittering society balls as for its libertine delights. The half-century of Communist rule dampened the revelry, but since 1990 the music scene flourished and theatres, cabarets, festivals, cinemas and discotheques are all buzzing again. Budapest continues to offer something for every interest, whether you prefer opera to jazz or horse racing to a football match.

Entertainment Highlights

Budapest has two opera houses, an orchestral concert hall at the **Liszt Ferenc Academy of Music** *(see p216)*, several other concert halls including the city's largest venue, the **Béla Bartók National Concert Hall** with Europe's largest concert hall organ at the Palace of Arts *(see p160)*. Also located at the Palace of Arts, is the **Festival Theatre**, which serves as an outstanding venue for dance, chamber operas, musical and theatrical performances, and concerts. Plus, there is an operetta theatre, numerous cabarets and more than 50 theatres, including the fringe.

The greatest concentration of theatres is in district V, in Nagymezö utca, which has been nicknamed "Budapest's Broadway". Along this 100-m (328-ft) stretch there are theatres such as the **Operetta Theatre** *(see p216)* and **Új Színház (New Theatre)** *(see p217)*, which puts on performances in English. Film-lovers are spoilt for choice, as Budapest boasts many **cinemas** *(see p217)*.

Actors in satirical cabaret performed in many theatres

Városliget *(see pp146–7)* offers a permanent circus and a zoo, with bars and beer tents in the summer.

A38 Ship is a music club in a converted ship and **Millenáris** is a concert venue and cultural centre with a varied programme, including festivals and exhibitions. The **Budapest Arena** holds 12,000 spectators, and stages a range of cultural events. There are also a few casinos and striptease shows to enjoy as part of Budapest's nightlife.

Free Entertainment

It is not difficult to find excellent, free entertainment in Budapest. During the summer, there always seem to be street entertainers and musicians wandering around the **Castle District**, often in elaborate period costume, playing instruments or acting out scenes from Hungarian history. During the **Budapesti Búcsú** in June *(see p63)*, all entertainments, from singing and dancing to theatre, are staged by the city council for free. In July, the **Danube Water Carnival** offers most of its thrills without charge, and the **Budapest Summer Festival**, Budapest's largest summer festival, offers a series of events every weekend, from mid-July to September. Hungarian culture, handicrafts, music and folklore are celebrated.

Unfortunately, entry to Budapest's museums is not free, although permanent exhibitions are usually cheaper than temporary ones.

Lavishly staged opera at the Hungarian State Opera *(see p216)*

Buying Tickets

Tickets for all plays and concerts can be purchased in advance, either at a booking office or by telephoning the venue direct. Addresses and telephone numbers are listed in the directory on pages 216–17. The most difficult tickets to obtain are those for the **Liszt Ferenc Academy of Music** concerts, as these tend to be sold many days in advance; try the website or ticket office. Similarly, seats at opera and operetta performances sell out quickly. The best way of securing a seat, particularly for summer performances, is via **Rózsavölgyi Jegyiroda** or **Ticket Express**, which are located right in the centre of town, close to Vörösmarty tér.

In Budapest, like anywhere else, you can risk it and try buying returned tickets at the last minute. A cheap option, but not for the weary, is to buy a standing-room pass.

Late Night Transport

Budapest's metro *(see p238)* runs until just after 11pm. Night services (buses plus tram 6 on the Grand Boulevard) run from around 11:50pm through the night until the regular service resumes at around 4:30am. Night services are numbered 900–999. Separate schedules for night and day buses are posted at the relevant stops. A major hub for night bus lines is Astoria. The solo night buses are front-door boarding only; on articulated vehicles ticket inspection is carried out at every door. The stop-request button is situated above the exit door.

Poster pillar

Disabled Access

Much work has been done since Hungary joined the European Union to make the country's venues accessible to as wide a range of people as possible. However, a lot of Budapest's older venues are far from wheelchair-friendly. Places which are equipped for disabled visitors include the **Mátyás Church** *(see pp86–7)*, the **Hungarian State Opera** *(see pp122–3)* and the **Liszt Ferenc Academy of Music** *(see p133)*. The pedestrianized **Liszt Ferenc tér**, with its preponderance of outdoor cafés and terraces is also perfect for disabled travellers. The bars and pubs of Central Pest, many of which are located in basements, are not.

Note that many venues (including the State Opera House) offer small reductions for disabled visitors.

The Hungarian Disabled Association
San Marco utca 76.
Tel 250 90 13. **W** meosz.hu

Listings Magazines

The best Budapest listings publication is the bi-weekly *Funzine*, which is published in Hungarian as well as in English. It is available in bars, restaurants, hotels and shops. Visitors should also try the *Budapest Times*, an English-language weekly newspaper that lists the best current events. *Pesti Est*, although in Hungarian only, is also available online. A useful listings website is welovebudapest.com, which has pages in English and an extensive list of programmes.

The elegant interior of the Liszt Ferenc Academy of Music *(see p216)*

Dancers of the Hungarian National Ballet Company perform at the State Opera House

Both port.hu and est.hu list the most popular film, music, television and theatre programme guides, but are only available in Hungarian.

Late-Night Scams

Budapest is generally a very safe city, but it is not without its dangers, especially late at night. Tourists are seen as easy prey by fraudsters, and it is important to stay alert at all times. Attractive peroxide-blondes promenading Váci utca and introducing themselves to single men may appear friendly and genuine at first sight, but, alas, they are not. If they insist you join them for a drink in a bar of their choice, you should refrain from doing so. They are not prostitutes, but "consumption girls", employed by bars to bring in foreign men to buy them drinks – which, as will become apparent only after the bill arrives, cost tens of thousands of Hungarian forints.

Although a number of bars that carry out this practice have been closed by the authorities, it still goes on. Always check how much you are paying for a drink and be wary of instant female friends.

Late nights are also the delight of unscrupulous taxi drivers, eager to make a killing from tipsy tourists. Never get into a taxi that does not clearly state it belongs to a reputable taxi company, or which does not display its tariffs on the side of the driver's door. Licensed taxis are painted yellow and must use the same fixed prices. Always ask for a rough estimate of the cost before getting in.

Music

Thanks to great composers such as Liszt, Bartók and Kodály *(see p148)*, and the wealth of its folk tradition, Hungary is famous for its music. Hungarians have always been a nation of music lovers; in addition to performances by national artists, Budapest is frequently visited by revered musicians from around the world.

Opera and Operetta

The standard of opera in Budapest is high. Performances are at the **Hungarian State Opera** *(see pp122–3)* or the **Erkel Theatre** *(see p155)*. At both there is a mainly classical repertoire, sung in Italian. The secondary focus is on Hungarian works. The **Operetta Theatre** *(see p119)* stages Hungarian operettas.

Classical Music

The **Liszt Ferenc Academy of Music** *(see p133)* is the leading venue for classical music. The city's largest venue is the **Béla Bartók National Concert Hall** *(see p160)*. Concerts are sometimes held in the domed hall of **Parliament** *(see pp112–13)*, which has great acoustics, and at the **Budapest Congress Center** *(see p164)*. Budapest also has a strong tradition of music festivals, *(see pp62–5)*.

Sacred Music

Concerts of organ music are held between March and December in the magnificent setting of the **Mátyás Church** *(see pp86–7)*. Among the composers whose works are featured, Bach is the most popular. **St Stephen's Basilica** *(see pp120–21)* serves sporadically as the venue for concerts of choral music. Between March and October the Musica Sacra Agency organizes concerts in the **Great Synagogue** *(see p138)*.

Folk and Gypsy Music

Performances of folk and gypsy music are held at the **Duna Palota** and **Hungarian Heritage House**. Watch out for shows by the Hungarian State Song and Dance Ensemble and a gypsy band that is part of the ensemble but also stages independent concerts. During July and August the city is visited by folk troupes from all over the country.

From October to May, the city's dance houses rock to the sounds of fiddles and flutes. One of the most renowned is **Fonó Budai Zeneház**, which stages peasant and gypsy bands from Transylvania. The popular **Marczibányi téri** cultural centre stages folk and gypsy music events, and house music, as well as playing host to various other arts events and shows.

Jazz

Jazz was very late in reaching Hungary. The best known and revered Hungarian jazz band is the Benkó Dixieland Band, which during Spring Festivals *(see p62)* plays in various theatres and large halls. The best place for jazz-lovers to congregate is **Columbus Jazz Club**, where Hungary's best players perform from 8:30pm every evening. The club boasts views of the Danube and it is a good idea to reserve a table. The **Cotton Club** at the Cotton House hotel *(see p186)* is also very popular.

DIRECTORY

Tickets

Rózsavölgyi Jegyiroda
Szervita tér 5. **Map** 4 E1.
Tel (06 1) 266 83 37.

Ticket Express
Váci út 1 (Westend City Center mall). **Map** 10 E2.
Tel 0630 303 09 99.
Dalszinház utca 10.
Map 2 F4. **W tex.hu**

Opera and Operetta

Erkel Theatre
II. János Pál pápa tér 30.
Map 7 C3.
Tel (06 1) 332 61 50.

Hungarian State Opera
Andrássy út 22. **Map** 2 F4.
Tel (06 1) 353 01 70.

Operetta Theatre
Nagymező utca 17. **Map** 2 F3. **Tel** (06 1) 312 48 86.

Classical Music

Béla Bartók National Concert Hall
Palace of Arts
Komor Marcell utca 1.
Tel (06 1) 555 30 00.

Budapest Congress Center
Jagelló út 1–3.
Tel (06 1) 372 54 00.

Liszt Ferenc Academy of Music
Liszt Ferenc tér 8. **Map** 7 A1. **Tel** (06 1) 321 06 90.

Parliament
Kossuth Lajos tér.
Map 2 D3 (9 C1).
Tel (06 1) 441 49 04.

Sacred Music

Great Synagogue
Dohány utca 2–8.
Map 7 A3.
Tel (06 1) 462 04 77.

Mátyás Church
Szentháromság tér 2.
Map 1 B4 (9 A2).
Tel (06 1) 355 56 57.

St Stephen's Basilica
Szent István tér.
Map 2 E4 (10 D2).
Tel (06 70) 407 85 94 (concert ticket bookings).

Folk and Gypsy Music

Duna Palota
Zrínyi utca 5.
Map 2 E5 (10 D2).
Tel (06 1) 235 55 00.

Fonó Budai Zeneház
Sztregova utca 3.
Map 2 E5 (10 D3).
Tel (06 1) 206 53 00.

Hungarian Heritage House
Corvin tér 8.
Map 1 C4 (9 A2). **Tel** (06 1) 225 60 56.

Marczibányi téri
Müvelödesi Központ
Marczibányi tér 5/A.
Tel (06 1) 212 28 20.

Jazz

Columbus Jazz Club
Vigadó tér, Dock 4.
Map 4 D1.
Tel (06 1) 266 90 13.

Cotton Club
Jókai utca 26. **Map** 2 F3.
Tel (06 1) 354 08 86.

Theatre, Cinema and Casinos

Budapest has many theatres, which are worth visiting not only for their impressive repertoires, but also because they are invariably located in beautiful, historic buildings. Cinemas show the latest films, although few retain the original soundtrack. For late-night dancing, the city has a wealth of popular clubs to choose from.

Theatre

The first theatre to stage plays in Hungary was the **National Dance Theatre** *(see p77)*. Other established theatres include the **Madách Theatre**, **Festival Theatre**, **Nemzeti Theatre** and **Pesti Theatre**. The **Új Színház (New Theatre)** also performs in English. **Trafó** is an exciting showcase for all the contemporary arts.

The **Budapest Secret Theatre** produces and shares English language theatre performances in Budapest and Central Europe. They have no permanent venue or repertoire, but create opportunites for the English-speaking community in Hungary to experience English theatre in the original language, and for actors working in Hungary to perform in English. Visit their website for the latest information on performances.

Budapest has over 30 drama and cabaret theatres, which host satirical cabaret shows. The most prestigious is the **József Katona Theatre**, which became famous following performances in Paris and London. The **Vígszínház**, meaning "comedy theatre", specializes in musicals (as does the Madách Theatre). In summer rock-operas are staged on Margaret Island. These shows are remarkable both for the quality of the production and the magnificent island setting.

Cinema

Many of Budapest's cinemas were built during the 1920s and 1930s and, despite renovations, have been superceded by modern multiplexes such as those in the shopping malls **Duna Plaza, Westend City Center**, and **Corvin Filmpalota**.

Most foreign films in Hungary are now both dubbed and subtitled into Hungarian, leaving cinema-goers free to choose which version they prefer. Those who do not understand Hungarian should choose the *angol nyelvű* (English soundtrack) version of the film. For films in English with no subtitles at all, look out for the words, *angol nyelvű, felirat nélkül.*

Apart from foreign films, the cinemas also show native Hungarian films. The range covers both the latest releases and vintage films from a time of Hungarian cinematic glory, notably when Miklós Jancsó and István Szabó received international awards for directing. The Moorish style **Uránia Nemzeti Filmszínház** film palace has operated as a cinema since 1899.

All cinema tickets can be bought a few hours in advance. Some cinemas will sell tickets for showings the next day.

Casinos

Budapest has two casinos, although more are planned. To enter a regular casino you must show a passport or official ID.

At the casinos listed below, players can try roulette, Black Jack, poker and the wheel of fortune. Both are open 24 hours a day. ,**Casino Tropicana**, requires evening dress.

DIRECTORY

Theatre

Budapest Secret Theatre
W budapestsecret theatre.com

Festival Theatre
Palace of the Arts,
Komor Marcell utca 1.
Tel (06 1) 555 30 00.

József Katona Theatre
Petőfi Sándor utca 6.
Map 4 E1 (10 D4).
Tel (06 1) 317 40 61.

Madách Theatre
Erzsébet körút 29–33.
Map 7 A2.
Tel (06 1) 478 20 41.

National Dance Theatre
Színház 1-3.
Map 9 A3.
Tel (06 1) 201 44 07.

Nemzeti Theatre
Bajor Gizi Park 1.
Map 7 B1.
Tel (06 1) 476 68 68.

Pesti Theatre
Váci utca 9.
Map 4 E1 (10 D4).
Tel (06 1) 266 55 57.

Trafó
Liliom utca 41.
Map 7 B5.
Tel (06 1) 215 16 00.

Új Színház (New Theatre)
Paulay Ede utca 35.
Map 2 F5.
Tel (06 1) 269 60 21.

Vígszínház
Szent István körút 14.
Map 2 E1.
Tel (06 1) 329 23 40.

Cinema

Corvin Filmpalota
Corvin köz 1.
Tel (06 1) 459 50 50.

Palace Duna Plaza
Váci út 178.
Tel (06 1) 999 61 61.

Palace West End
Váci út 1–3.
Map 2 F2.
Tel (06 1) 999 61 61.

Uránia Nemzeti Filmszínház
Rákóczi út 21
Map 7 A3.
Tel (06 1) 486 34 13.

Casinos

Casino Tropicana
Vigadó utca 2.
Map 4 D1.
Tel (06 1) 266 30 62.

Las Vegas Casino
Széchenyi István tér 2 (Sofitel Budapest Chain Bridge).
Map 2 D5.
Tel (06 1) 266 20 82.

Sports

Hungarians are fine athletes, as is testified by their consistently outstanding performances at competitive events, such as the Olympic Games. Budapest's world-class sports facilities serve as venues for many of these international events, including European and World championships. Sporting opportunities for visitors to the city are both varied and accessible.

Spectator Sports

Most competitive sporting events are held either in the **Ferenc Puskás Stadium** *(see p159)*, which currently seats 78,000 spectators and is planned to be fully reconstructed by 2017, or in the modern, indoor **Papp László Budapest Sportaréna**.

Football remains the most popular spectator sport, although it's been some time since the national side was highly successful. In the 1950s, for instance, Hungary beat England 6:3 at Wembley. League matches in Budapest attract big crowds. The atmosphere is particularly electric when local favourites Ferencváros, FTC, take to the pitch.

Two of the three great events regularly held in Budapest are the Vivicitta Half Marathon and the Budapest Marathon. These are run mid-April and mid-October, respectively. The third big sporting event is the Formula 1 Hungarian Grand Prix *(see p63)*, which takes place in August at the Mogyoród racing circuit.

Hungarians achieve impressive results in boxing, canoeing, swimming, water polo and fencing, which are all widely supported.

Horse Racing and Riding

As a nation of former nomads, the Hungarians have retained a great love of horses. In Budapest this passion finds its expression in horse racing, which is enormously popular. A few hours spent at a racetrack can be a cheap and fun way of soaking up the local atmosphere. Near the Albertirsai út is the Trotters' Racecourse, at the **Kincsem Park**.

Those wishing to be rather more energetic and ride instead of watch horses, should contact the **National Riding School**, the **Petneházy School**, the **Aranypatkó Riding Club** or the **Budapest Riding Club**.

Sporting Activities

Practising sport for fitness and pleasure is both cheap and popular in Budapest.

Strolling through the city's parks, particularly on Margaret Island, you will encounter scores of eager joggers, both young and not so young. The indoor and outdoor swimming pools are also full of regular visitors, who come here for an hour or so of healthy exercise. Particularly popular is the **Hajós Olympic Pool** on Margaret Island, which is named after Hungary's first Olympic gold winner for swimming, who was also the pool's architect. Busy open-air swimming options include **Császár Komjádi Uszoda** and the neighbouring **Lukács Baths** *(see p105)*, both of which can be enjoyed even in winter as the hot spring water creates a steamy atmosphere over the water's surface. For the deepest spa water in the city, head to the Széchenyi Baths *(see p155)*, which is the largest bathing complex in Europe. However, the most atmospheric and beautiful baths, and also the hottest, are undoubtedly the 16th-century Turkish **Rudas Baths** *(see p97)*.

Cycling is also gaining in popularity, particularly since the introduction of cycling lanes to the city's roads *(see p237)*. If you want to play tennis, there are numerous courts available, but these tend to be monopolized by local Hungarians. Your best bet for a game is to befriend a local tennis player, or find a hotel that has its own court.

Despite the moderate climate, it is also possible to undertake winter sports in Budapest. From December until March the **Városliget Lake** *(see pp146–7)* is turned into a skating ring and many people take to the ice. **Sváb Hill** *(see p165)* is generally snow-covered from December to March and has several ski runs and ski lifts.

DIRECTORY

Spectator Sports

Ferenc Puskás Stadium
Istvánmezei út 3–5.
Map 8 F1.
Tel (06 1) 471 41 00.
W **magyarfutball.hu**

Papp László Budapest Sportaréna
Stefánia út 2.
Map 8 F1.
Tel (06 1) 422 26 00.
W **budapestarena.hu**

Horse Racing and Riding

Aranypatkó Riding Club
Aranyhegyi út 18.
Tel (06 70) 363 15 53.

Budapest Riding Club
Albertirsai út 4.
Tel 0630 92 12 36.

Kincsem Park
Albertirsai út 2–4.
Tel (06 1) 433 05 20.

National Riding School
Kerepesi út 7.
Tel (06 1) 210 26 63.

Petneházy School
Feketefej utca 2–4.
Tel (06 1) 397 50 48.

Swimming Pools

Császár Komjádi Uszoda
Frankel Leó út 55.
Map 1 B1.
Tel (06 1) 212 27 50.

Hajós Olympic Pool
Margitsziget.
Tel (06 1) 450 42 20.

Lukács Baths
Frankel Leó utca 25–29.
Map 1 C1. **Tel** (06 1) 326 16 95. **W** **budapestspas.hu**

Rudas Baths
Döbrentei tér 9. **Map** 4 D2. **Tel** (06 1) 356 13 22.

Széchenyi Baths
Allatkerti körút 11. **Map** 6 D3. **Tel** (06 1) 363 32 10.

Children's Budapest

Visiting Budapest can be made great fun for children. There are several choices of energetic outdoor pursuits, including a funfair, a terrific zoo and, of course, a range of glorious of swimming venues. If the weather is poor, the city's historic buildings, museums and art galleries will entertain and inform. In addition, a handful of puppet theatres cater specifically for younger audiences, although the shows are in Hungarian.

Sightseeing for Kids

Busy Pest is a difficult area in which to entertain kids, but the **Postal Museum***(see p149)*, set in an opulent 19th-century mansion, is well worth a visit.

In Buda's **Royal Palace** *(see pp74–5)* and **Castle District** *(see pp72–89)*, the city's long history can be appreciated just by wandering round the ancient and lovely buildings. The **Hungarian National Gallery** *(see pp78–81)* feeds young imaginations, as does the fabulous *turul*, the statue of a mythical giant bird that stands in the Palace Courtyard. The magnificently carved **Mátyás Fountain** *(see pp76–7)* is also worth a look.

In the Old Town, the **Labyrinth in the Buda Castle** *(see p85)* on Lords' Street is a bizarre underground exhibition that fascinates kids, and there are displays of armour and weapons in the **Museum of Military History** *(see p89)*. A final "must" is a ride on the **Budavári Sikló** funicular railway *(see p239)*.

Swimming

The most suitable complex for young families is the seasonal **Palatinus Strand** *(see p55)* on Margaret Island, where there are pools of varying temperatures, water slides and artificial waves.

During the winter season, the **Gellért Hotel and Baths Complex** *(see pp94–5)* is a better alternative. Here, the large swimming pool has artificial waves, and the paddling pool's warm water is wonderful for toddlers.

Aquaworld Budapest, a vast indoor water theme park, is a great place for a family day out.

Circus and Zoo

People of all ages love the Budapest **Zoo** *(see pp154–5)*, which is one of the best in Europe. Attractions include a large sea-water aquarium, a terrarium and an aviary.

A visit to the **Great Capital Circus** is an easy way to keep kids occupied. The daily shows often star international artists.

Indoor Attractions

Budapest Bábszínház and **Kolibri Színház** are two of several puppet theatres that stage international favourites, such as *The Jungle Book*, *Cinderella* and *Snow White*, as well as Hungarian classics. The shows are all performed in Hungarian.

Tropicarium Budapest is the largest sea aquarium in Central Europe. As well as the thousands of colourful fish in the aquariums, there are exotic birds, squirrel monkeys, alligators and tortoises.

Next to the Tropicarium is the **Center of Scientific Wonders**, a "physics playhouse" where more than 100 interactive games and installations help children to learn about the laws of physics in a fun and exciting way.

Scenic Railways

Children love the trip up into the **Buda Hills** *(see p165)*. The first stage is a ride on the cogwheel railway that runs up Széchényi Hill. At the top, there is a playground and the start of the Children's Railway, which follows the ridge of the hills to the Hűvös Valley. The way back down is on the Libegő chair-lift that runs from the top of János Hill to Zugliget (linked by bus 291 to Nyugati Railway Station). Young railway enthusiasts also enjoy the **Railway History Park** *(see p160)*.

DIRECTORY

Sightseeing

Budavári Sikló
Clark Ádám tér, Szent György tér.
Map 1 C5 (9 B3).

Hungarian National Gallery
Szent György tér 2.
Map 3 C5.
Tel (06 1) 375 55 67.

Labyrinth in the Buda Castle
Úri utca 9.
Map 1 A4 (9 A2).

Mátyás Fountain
Royal Palace.
Map 1 C5 (9 B3).

Museum of Military History
Tóth Árpád Sétany 40.
Map 1 A4.
Tel (06 1) 356 95 22.

Postal Museum
Benczúr utca 27. **Map** 5 B5. **Tel** (06 1) 322 42 40.

Royal Palce
Map 1 5C (9 B4).

Swimming

Aquaworld Budapest
Íves út 16.
Tel (06 1) 231 37 60.
W aqua-world.hu

Gellért Hotel and Baths Complex
Kelenhegyi út 4. **Map** 3 C3. **Tel** (06 1) 466 61 66.

Palatinus Strand
Margitsziget.
Tel (06 1) 340 45 05.

Circus and Zoo

Great Capital Circus
Állatkerti körút 7.
Map 5 C3.
Tel (06 1) 343 83 00.

Zoo
Állatkerti körút 6–12.
Tel (06 1) 273 49 00.
Map 5 C3.

Indoor Attractions

Budapest Bábszínház
Andrássy út 69. **Map** 5 A5 (10 E2). **Tel** (06 1) 321 52 00.

Center of Scientific Wonders (Csodák Palotája)
Nagytétényi út 37–43.
Tel (06 30) 210 55 69.
W csopa.hu

Kolibri Színház
Jókai tér 10. **Map** 2 F3 (10 F1). **Tel** (06 1) 311 08 70.

Tropicarium Budapest
Nagytétényi út 37–43.
Tel (06 1) 424 30 53.
W tropicarium.hu

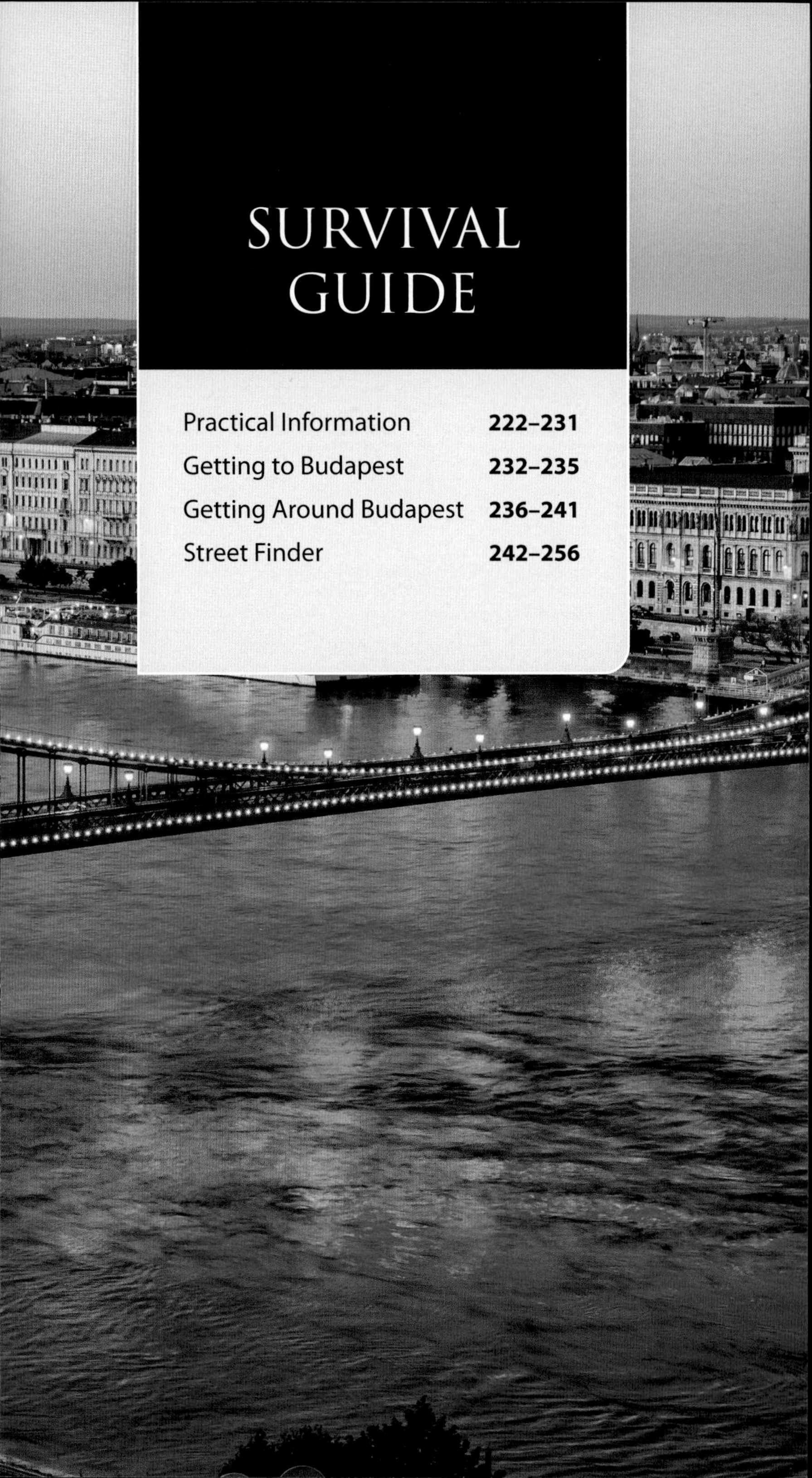

SURVIVAL GUIDE

PRACTICAL INFORMATION

Budapest was always famous for its hospitality, and the Hungarians have been increasingly emphasizing tourism as an important part of the national economy. The biggest problem in its development has been the formidable barrier posed by the Hungarian language, which hinders access to information. Familiarizing yourself with a few Hungarian words and phrases is a good idea *(see pp271–2)*. However, English and German are spoken in all tourist offices and bigger hotels, and tourist brochures and pamphlets are now published in several languages. Budapest is generally safe, but it still has its share of pickpockets. It is therefore wise to take care in the busy shopping centres and on public transport.

When to Go

The best time to visit Budapest is between March and the end of June, and from the middle of August until October. July and early August are generally hot, while the winter months can be very cold.

Various festivals and cultural programmes take place throughout the year, the biggest events being the Spring and Autumn Festivals and the Sziget Festival (August). The end of the year is an enjoyable time, when visitors can experience the Christmas Fair and the New Year's Eve street party *(see pp62–5)*.

Visas and Passports

Citizens of the UK, Ireland, the US, Canada, Australia and New Zealand need only a valid passport to visit Hungary for up to 90 days. Visitors from any country in the European Economic Area (EEA) and Switzerland can enter with just an ID card for a stay of up to 90 days. Some EEA countries do not issue ID cards; citizens of these countries require a passport.

All other visitors should check their visa requirements – and, if necessary, apply for a visa at their local Hungarian embassy before travelling. Note that visas for other Schengen countries are also valid for Hungary. For more information, see the **Hungarian Ministry of Foreign Affairs** website.

One of several tourist information offices in Budapest

Tourist Information

Prior to your arrival in Budapest it is worth getting in touch with your nearest **Hungarian National Tourist Office**, which can supply useful information and put you in touch with reputable tour operators.

Many agencies specialize in organizing individual trips and tours to Hungary, including **Great Escapes**, **Kirker Holidays** and **Page & Moy**. They can all provide you with detailed information on itineraries and accommodation and help you to make reservations. Official tourist information centres in Budapest, **Budapestinfo**, can be found at a number of locations in the city, including at Liszt Ferenc tér, Sütő utca at Deák tér, Buda Castle and at the airport terminals. General tourist information in a variety of languages is provided by these centres. They also sell the Budapest Card *(see below)* as well as souvenirs, guide books and maps.

Brown tourist signs can be found at all the important sights of the city to help visitors find their way around.

Budapest Card

Budapest Card

The Budapest Card is designed for tourists visiting the city for two or three days. It entitles a visitor to use most city transport – metro, bus, tram, trolley bus, Danube public transport boats and hév – free of charge, as well as providing discounted or free entry to some museums. In addition, you can also enjoy two walking tours and visit the zoo. It also entitles you to a significant discount on tickets to selected spas and restaurants as well as many cultural events.

The card costs 7,500 forints for 48 hours and 8,900 forints for 72 hours. Cards can be purchased at tourist offices, hotels, museums and most large metro stations. Enclosed with the card is information, in four languages, which lists where to use the card.

◀ Széchenyi Chain Bridge illuminated at night, with Orszaghaz Parliament behind

Ludwig Museum of Contemporary Art, Palace of Arts *(see p160)*

Opening Hours

Museums and galleries are generally open year round. Most museums are closed on Monday; one exception is the Jewish Museum (*see p138*), which is closed on Saturday. Opening times for specific venues are given under their individual entries.

During winter (November to March) most museums have shorter opening hours. In summer, from April until October, they tend to stay open a couple of hours longer, typically from 10am until 6pm. Most museums charge an entrance fee, though it is worth checking to see if there are any discounts.

Shopping centres in Budapest are open daily until 8 or 9pm; grocery stores are open from 7am to 6pm and other shops from 10am until 6pm Monday to Friday. On Saturdays many shops, except shopping centres, close at 1pm. Further information on the opening hours of shops and markets in Budapest can be found on pages 210–13.

Admission Prices

Tickets to museums and historical monuments can be purchased at the sight. Some may also be bought in advance on museum websites. Average prices are around 2,500 forints per person, but some can be as much as 4,000 forints. Students, schoolchildren and seniors are often entitled to reductions. Opera, concert and other tickets can be bought at ticket agencies *(see pp214–17)*. Theatre and opera tickets are also sold at individual box offices, either for shows on the same day or in advance. Ticket prices can vary from 1,500 to 20,000 forints, depending on the type of show.

Social Customs and Etiquette

Traditionally, Hungarians attach great importance to being properly dressed when going to an opera or concert hall so theatre performances, classical music concerts and operas are smart affairs. Hungarians usually wear evening dress or at least a suit when going to any theatre or concert hall. Tourists will therefore feel more comfortable wearing evening dress too.

In Hungary, when introduced to someone it is customary to shake hands and say your name. Hungarians also shake hands when meeting people with whom they are already acquainted, though between friends kissing on both cheeks is the norm, for men as well as women. Some older men still bow to kiss a woman's hand *(see also Senior Travellers, p224)*.

Tipping

It is standard practice to tip when paying for taxis, meals and drinks (though not for drinks at a bar counter); 10 per cent of the total or thereabouts is acceptable. In restaurants, check to see whether between 10 and 12 per cent has been added to the bill – in which case you don't have to leave more. Rather than leaving the tip on the table, the usual practice is to include the tip when you pay – just indicate the amount you want to pay and you will be given change accordingly. If you expect change back, don't say *köszönöm* (thank you) when handing over payment, as it will be assumed that you want the change to be kept.

Note that when visiting baths and pools in Hungary it is customary to tip the attendant who unlocks your cubicle (100–200 forints is usual).

Travellers with Special Needs

Budapest is gradually becoming more accessible for disabled visitors. However, it is best to call ahead to the sights or obtain specialist information prior to your visit to ensure it is as hassle-free as possible. Newer buses are now equipped for easier boarding and some metro stations have special lifts.

For advice and help, contact the **Hungarian Disabled Association**. Many museums and monuments present difficulties for the disabled, although increasingly they are being renovated to be wheelchair-friendly.

Hungarian State Opera *(see pp122–3)*, a venue with disabled access

A Europride parade on the streets of Budapest

Gay and Lesbian Travellers

While Hungarian society is largely conservative, Budapest is a cosmopolitan city and its gay scene is thriving, with overtly gay clubs now replacing the old covert meeting places.

This greater prominence is also reflected in Hungarian law – the age of consent is 14 for homosexuals and heterosexuals alike. The Budapest gay scene is male-dominated, however. The **Gay Guide Network** has information on gay-friendly accommodation, bars, clubs, restaurants and baths. **Magnum Sauna** (for men only) at Csepreghy utca 2 is the largest and one of the most popular gay saunas in Budapest. It also has a gym and a lounge.

It is worth noting that in the past, extreme right-wing groups, such as Magyar Gárda, have attacked Gay Pride marches (Europride) – so caution is always advised at this annual summer event.

Senior Travellers

The older generation in Hungary is accorded great respect. You shouldn't be surprised if people allow older ladies to cut ahead in shop and post office queues, for instance. Senior travellers to Hungary are also afforded some special courtesies. Many museums offer discounts of up to 50 per cent for EU citizens between the ages of 62 and 70, and free admission for those aged 70 and over. On the public transport system, seniors are also entitled to reductions on ticket prices of 50 per cent, and more for monthly and quarterly passes. For EU residents over the age of 65, travel on the metro, buses and trolley buses is free.

Travelling on a Budget

The days when you could live like a prince on a pauper's budget in Hungary are long gone – today the top hotels and restaurants charge international rates. However, there are still plenty of places in the city where you can sleep and eat well for a modest cost.

For cheap accommodation try the **Top Hostels** chain of student hostels, which has an office by the platforms in Keleti station. For cheap places to eat, look for an *önkiszolgáló étterem* (a self-service restaurant), *étkezde* (lunchtime diner), or a *főzelék bár* (*főzelék* is dish of creamed vegetables). More restaurants are now offering a lunchtime menu – an inexpensive two-course lunch. There are also many Turkish kebab restaurants in the city centre, as well as a number of cheap Chinese restaurants.

International Student Identity Card

Student cards (ISICs) are widely accepted in Budapest. They are useful for obtaining discounts at many museums and monuments throughout the city. If you don't already have an ISIC card, go to the Vista Travel Office at Andrássy út 1 – they should be able to issue you with one. If you are travelling as a family, renting an apartment can help keep costs down – try the Internet-based **Budapest Lets** *(see also pp182–5)*.

Budapest Time

Budapest uses Central European time, in keeping with the rest of mainland Europe, which means it is 2 hours ahead of Greenwich Mean Time (GMT) in the summer and 1 hour ahead in the winter.

Examples of the summer time differences between Budapest and other major cities are as follows: London: -1 hour; New York: -6 hours; Dallas: -7 hours; Los Angeles: -9 hours; Perth: +6 hours; Sydney: +8 hours; Auckland: +10 hours; Tokyo: +7 hours.

Electrical Appliances

Hungarian electricity supply is 230 V and the plugs needed are the standard Continental 2 pin type. Adapters can be purchased in most countries. Since sockets are generally earthed, the most commonly used plugs are the flat type.

Public Toilets

There are few public toilets in Budapest, and most require a small fee for their use. It is worth carrying some small change for this eventuality.

Cubicles can be found in some squares and parks and these are usually free. In cafés and restaurants there are toilet attendants and the price for using the facility is usually clearly displayed.

There are no public toilets in metro stations, except for Batthyány tér. Apart from the generally understood picture symbols, the toilets are signed in Hungarian: *Hölgyek* (ladies) and *Urak* (gentlemen), or *Nők* (women) and *Férfiak* (men).

Sign for a ladies' toilet

Sign for a men's toilet

Responsible Tourism

Environmental awareness has been slowly gathering strength in Hungary. As far back as the 1980s there were protests against the hydroelectric scheme on the Slovakian border which diverted the Danube. Today, however, environmental issues are a low priority for most households struggling to meet daily costs. Nevertheless, some attention is paid to green matters.

There are recycling centres in every district of the city for paper, glass and cardboard, and many bottles can be returned to shops on a deposit basis.

There are several organic food outlets in the city. The largest organic market is the Bio-piac, which takes place on Saturday mornings from 6:30am to noon on Csörsz utca, not far from Déli station. Another option is the Bioritmus Csarnok, located inside Cédrus Piac market Hall on Fehér út.

To ease the city's air pollution, Budapest has become more pedestrian-friendly, with greater areas of downtown Pest, in particular, blocked to traffic. Parks are being established in place of former industrial buildings, and cycling is also increasing in popularity as the network of cycle lanes continues to expand.

A useful organization which has a website packed with green facilities in Budapest is **Green Map**.

DIRECTORY

Tourist Offices Abroad

Hungarian National Tourist Office (UK)
46 Eaton Place,
London SW1X 8AL,
United Kingdom.
Tel 0207 823 1055.
W gotohungary.co.uk

Hungarian National Tourist Office (US)
447 Broadway,
Fifth Floor, Manhattan,
New York, NY 10013.
Tel 212 695 12 21.
W gotohungary.com

Tourist Offices in Budapest

Budapestinfo Points

Airport Terminal 2A
Liszt Ferenc Budapest Airport Terminal 2A.
Open 8am–11pm.

Airport Terminal 2B
Liszt Ferenc Budapest Airport Terminal 2B.
Open 10am–10pm.

City Centre Liszt Ferenc tér
1061 Budapest, Liszt Ferenc tér 11.
Open 10am–8pm.

City Centre Sütő u.
1052 Budapest,
Sütő u. 2.
Open 8am–10pm.

Travel Agents Abroad

Great Escapes
Cutter House 1560
Parkway, Solent Business Park, Fareham,
Hampshire,
PO15 7AG,
United Kingdom.
Tel 0845 330 2084.
W greatescapes.co.uk

Kirker Holidays
4 Waterloo Court,
10 Theed St, London
SE1 8ST,
United Kingdom.
Tel 020 7593 1899.
W kirkerholidays.com

Page & Moy
Compass House,
Rockingham Road,
Market Harborough,
Leicestershire
LE16 7QD,
United Kingdom.
Tel 0116 217 8005.
W pageandmoy.com

Hungarian Embassies

United Kingdom
35 Eaton Place,
London SW1X 8BY.
Tel 020 7201 3440.
W hungary.embassyhomepage.com

United States
3910 Shoemakers Street
NW, Washington D.C.
20008.
Tel 202 362 6730.
W huembwas.org

Foreign Embassies and Consulates in Budapest

Canada
Ganz utca. 12–14.
Map 1 B2.
Tel (06 1) 392 33 60.
W canadainternational.gc.ca

South Africa
Gárdonyi Géza utca 17.
Tel (06 1) 392 09 99.
Tel 200 72 77.

United Kingdom
Harmincad utca 6.
Map 2 E5.
Tel (06 1) 266 28 88.
W gov.uk/government/world/organisations/british-embassy-budapest

United States
Szabadság tér 12.
Map 2 E4.
Tel (06 1) 475 44 00.
W hungary.usembassy.gov

Travellers with Special needs

Hungarian Disabled Association
San Marco utca 76.
Tel (06 1) 250 9013.
W meosz.hu

Gay and Lesbian Travellers

Gay Guide Network
W gayguide.net

Travelling on a Budget

Budapest Lets
W budapestlets.com

Top Hostels
W mellowmood.hu

Responsible Tourism

Green Map
W zoldterkep.hu

Useful Websites

Budapest Tourism Office/Tourinform
W budapestinfo.hu

Hungarian Ministry of Foreign Affairs
W mfa.gov.hu

Personal Security and Health

Budapest is safe for visitors as long as common-sense precautions are taken to guard your personal safety and possessions. Emergency services are reliable, and hospitals and medical clinics are clean and efficient. Nevertheless, as in any large city, social problems can have an impact. Petty crime rates are on the rise, with an increase of pickpocketing in particular. Sadly, any visitors to Budapest will also be aware of the growing numbers of homeless people living on the city's streets.

Police

Budapest is a pleasant city, with most neighbourhoods still safe to walk around at night. However, as with any large city, it has its share of crime so sensible precautions should be taken.

The Hungarian police *(rendőrség)* are frequently seen patrolling the streets on motorbikes, on foot or in cars. Every district has its own police station, some of which offer 24-hour tourist assistance. In the event of loss or theft, a report should be made immediately to the police. For lost passports, *see Lost and Stolen Property.*

Police car

Ambulance

Road policeman on a motorbike

In an Emergency

The number to call in an emergency is the **Central Emergency Number** – 112. If you are involved in a police case as a witness or injured party, you should ask for consular assistance. For other emergency numbers see the Directory *(opposite)*.

What to be Aware of

Documents and money should be carried in a secure inside pocket or in a money belt. Money should be exchanged at a bank, your hotel or an exchange bureau, never on the black market. There is generally no need to carry your passport with you, although it is advisable to have some form of ID – such as a driving licence.

Do not leave valuables in your car. If taking a taxi, use registered vehicles, which offer more security and are less likely to overcharge than unmarked ones *(see p239)*. Pickpockets operate during rush hours, targeting people in crowded metro stations, buses and shopping centres. They also operate at all the main tourist sights, and on nearby public transport. When working as a group, they may surround unsuspecting tourists and jostle or distract them. For this reason, it is a good idea to have a photocopy of your passport and your travel insurance documents.

It is also worth noting that the rise of extreme nationalist and right-wing groups has created pockets of violence, which it is wise to avoid. In the past, violent clashes have taken place on major national holidays such as 15 March (Spring Uprising) and 23 October (Remembrance Day), and at Gay Pride marches, so it is wise to keep an eye out for trouble.

Women should not walk unaccompanied late at night in poorly lit areas and should avoid deserted streets. Rákóczi tér and Mátyás tér, in district VIII, have been infamous for their brothels since the 19th century and have a long-standing tradition as hangouts for prostitutes, although legislation has now made prostitution much less visible on the streets.

When eating in restaurants make sure that your menu includes prices, as some restaurants may try to take advantage of tourists. Single men should also beware of predatory females inviting them to a bar for a drink or meal, which then results in a disproportionately huge bill. Such scams are most often found in the less appealing places in the centre of Pest.

Lost and Stolen Property

The loss or theft of a passport should be reported to the local police station and then the appropriate embassy immediately *(see p225)*.

Any items left on public transport may be traced at the Lost Property Office, at No. 18 Akácfa utca, or by calling **BKK Lost Property**.

Hospitals and Pharmacies

First aid and ambulance services in Hungary are free for citizens of the UK and most other European countries. Before travelling to Hungary you should obtain a European Health Insurance Card (EHIC), which allows you to access state-provided healthcare at a significantly reduced cost. In the case of an accident or emergency, the largest state hospital in central Budapest is the **Szent János Kórház** in the XII district (or call an ambulance).

There are also a number of international clinics, such as the **First Med Centre** and **Főnix-Med Medical Service**, with English-speaking staff and a high standard of care, although these are expensive. Hungary has a well-deserved reputation for good dentistry at very reasonable prices. One popular, centrally located dental care specialist is **Dental Care Budapest**.

The shop front of a pharmacy in Budapest

Budapest's pharmacies *(gyógyszertár or patika)* are well stocked and, in the case of a minor ailment, the chemist will be able to recommend a suitable treatment. Some drugs require a prescription, while others can be sold over the counter in pharmacies such as **Déli Gyógyszertár**. If your nearest pharmacy is closed, there should be a list displayed, on the door or in the window, of all the local chemists – it will indicate which ones are on 24-hour emergency duty, one of which is **Teréz Patika**.

Pharmacy sign

Travel Insurance and Medical Matters

When travelling to Hungary it is highly recommended that visitors take out travel insurance before leaving home. Foreign nationals are only entitled to free medical help in emergencies, such as accidents or a sudden illness requiring immediate medical intervention. Any other medical care, including hospitalization, must be paid for. The cost depends on the type of insurance policy held and the relevant agreement between Hungary and the visitor's home country. Most insurance companies expect policy holders to pay for their treatment as they receive it and then apply for a refund on their return home. All the relevant bills and police reports must be submitted with any insurance claim. Remember that a report must be made to the police within seven days of any incident.

No special vaccinations are required for Hungary and the general standard of hygiene in the country is reasonably good. That said, allergy sufferers and people with breathing difficulties should take account of the air pollution during the summer months, which is particularly acute in the crowded streets of Pest. Those susceptible should consider staying in the Castle District, from which cars are banned, or retreating to the wooded Buda Hills or the greenery of Margaret Island *(see p189)*.

The water in Budapest is of good quality. It is generally considered safe to drink water straight from the tap. The city's numerous thermal baths *(see pp52–5)* have richly mineralized water.

DIRECTORY

In an Emergency

Ambulance
Tel 104.

Fire
Tel 105.

Central Emergency Number
Tel 112.

Police
Tel 107.

Police Stations with 24-hour Assistance
I district: Pauler utca 13.
V district: Szalay utca 11–13.
XI district: Bocskai út 90.
XIII district: Szabolcs utca 36.

Lost Property

BKK Lost Property
Akácfa utca 18.
Tel (06 1) 258 46 36 (Mon–Fri).

Hospitals and pharmacies

Szent János Kórház
Diósárok utca 1-3.
Tel (06 1) 458 4500.

Déli Gyógyszertár
Alkotás utca1/b.
Tel (06 1) 355 46 91.
Open 8am–8pm Mon–Fri, 8am–2pm Sat.

Teréz Patika
Teréz krt. 41. **Map** 10 F1.
Tel (06 1) 311 44 39.
Open 24 hours daily.

International Clinics

Avicenna Medical and Dental
Podmaniczky utca 33, 3rd floor, 8. **Map** 2 F3.
Tel (06 1) 302 5005.

Dental Care Budapest
SOS Dent Nonstop Clinic, Király utca 14. **Map** 2 F5.
Tel (06 1) 269 60 10 (24 hours).
W **dentalcarebudapest.com**

First Med Center
Hattyúház 14, 5th floor Hattyú utca.
Map 1 A5.
Tel (06 1) 224 9090.
W **firstmedcenters.com**

Főnix-Med Medical Service
Diósárok utca 1–3.
Tel (06 1) 2000 100.
W **fonixmed.com**

Local Currency and Banking

The Hungarian banking system is on a par with European standards. Budapest boasts many modern banks, both Hungarian and foreign, which are located in smart buildings. The service is efficient and courteous. There are numerous automatic cash dispensers and bureaux de change in the town centre and around the railway stations. An increasing number of shops and restaurants now accept credit cards, but it is still more common in Budapest to pay for goods and services in cash. The official currency of Hungary is the forint (HUF or Ft). Most banks also advance money on a credit card.

An ATM (cash machine) outside a Budapest bank

Banks and Bureaux de Change

For the best rate of exchange, take foreign currency to a bureau de change such as **Northline** or **Exclusive Change**; these generally give better rates than Hungarian banks. Before changing money, check the rates of exchange, as they tend to vary quite widely. The rates quoted by some exchange offices can be misleading as they could apply only to sums in excess of 200,000 forints, which may be stated only in very small print.

The least favourable rates are in hotels and at the airport, while the best are offered by the smaller bureaux de change a little way off the usual tourist tracks. A reasonable, average rate can usually be found at Hungarian banks.

Branches of the **Budapest Bank** are open Monday to Friday, from 9am until 5pm. **K & H Bank** are open Monday to Thursday, between 8am and 4pm, and on Friday between 8am and 3pm. Most banks are closed on Saturdays and Sundays, but the bureaux de change and ATMs remain open. Exchanging money is only permitted in licensed, designated places. Transactions on the street are illegal, and often involve counterfeit money.

Entrance to a branch of the Budapest Bank, on Váci utca

ATMS

The easiest way of getting money is from cash machines (ATMs), which have instructions in various languages (including English). These can be found all over the city. Don't be put off if a bank machine rejects your card; try at another bank and it is likely to work. There are also exchange machines, which change foreign notes.

Credit Cards and Traveller's Cheques

Most hotels, shops and restaurants accept credit cards, but older establishments and some of the more inexpensive restaurants do not. It is therefore wise to carry some cash with you.

The most widely accepted cards are Visa and MasterCard. American Express and Diners Club have very limited acceptance. The logos of accepted credit cards are usually on display – it is always worth checking before you order, however. Traveller's cheques can be changed at most banks, as well as at some hotels. In Hungary, shops never accept traveller's cheques as payment.

Wiring Money

Wiring is an effective way to receive and transfer money abroad. Western Union has branches all over Budapest. Look for their logo at foreign exchange bureaux, or the Intercash symbol (www.intercash.hu), the Western Union agent in Hungary. Some Western Union offices also exchange foreign currency, though they generally offer poor rates. Since Hungary joined the EU, many shops and restaurants accept euros. Always check the exchange rate and the money returned.

DIRECTORY

Banks

Budapest Bank
Bajcsy-Zsilinszky út 5.
Map 2 E4 (10 E1).
Tel (06 1) 477 77 77.

K & H Bank
Apáczai Csere János utca 4.
Map 4 E1.
Tel (06 1) 327 80 80.

Magyar Külkereskedelmi Bank Rt
Váci utca 38.
Map 4 E1.
Tel 0640 333 666.

Bureaux de Change

Exclusive Change
Váci utca 12.
Map 4 E1.
Tel (06 70) 383 06 54.

Northline
Central Market Hall, Vámház Körút 1.
Map 4 F3.
W northline.hu

Hungarian currency

The Hungarian currency unit is the forint (HUF or Ft). Banknotes are issued in denominations of 500, 1,000, 2,000, 5,000, 10,000 and 20,000 forints. Both an old and a new style of some notes are currently legal tender, but an older version of the 5,000 forint note than the one shown here is no longer accepted.

500 HUF

1,000 HUF

2,000 HUF

5,000 HUF

10,000 HUF

20,000 HUF

Coins

The forint has coin denominations of 5, 10, 20, 50, 100 and 200 forints currently in circulation. As with Hungarian banknotes, new coins are gradually being phased in – the 200 forint coin with a nickel disc inside a brass ring is now the only legal version.

10 HUF

5 HUF

20 HUF

50 HUF

100 HUF

200 HUF

Media and Communications

The prevalence of mobile phones has transformed communications in Hungary, giving reliable access to the phone network for many who had struggled with the relatively inefficient landline telephone operating system. There remain many telephone boxes throughout the city, although card-operated telephones are much more widespread than coin-operated ones. Wi-Fi access is also available at many places around the city.

International and Local Phone Calls

Calling cards (such as Telecard, Neophone or Barangoló) are the best option for making landline calls, and are widely available from post offices, street vendors, fuel stations and some newspaper kiosks in a variety of denominations. These cards usually offer better international rates than when using coins. Alternatively, coin phone boxes accept 10, 20, 50 and 100 forint coins and also €1 and €2 coins; some also accept credit or debit cards.

The minimum rate for a local call is 20 forints, and 100 forints for an international call. To make an international call dial 00, wait for the dialling signal and then dial the country code, followed by the rest of the number. You can also phone abroad using a pre-paid international phonecard such as the Barangoló, available at post offices, which offers good rates to countries around the world.

Budapest telephone numbers consist of seven digits (when combined with the city dialling code 06-1 there are 10 digits). Hungarian mobile phone numbers consist of 11 digits: they start with 06-20, 06-30, 06-31 or 06-70, followed by seven digits. If you are calling any of these numbers from abroad the initial 06 is replaced by the country code, 36. To call the operator dial 11818, or 11824 for the international operator, but be aware that calls to these numbers are usually billed at high rates. There is little advantage in using the services of a hotel operator, and this only makes the call more expensive.

Mobile Phones

If you plan to bring your mobile phone when travelling, check with your provider about whether you have a roaming facility, and bring an adaptor and transformer with you to recharge your phone. US cell phones need to be tri-band to work in Hungary.

Alternatively, you can buy a Hungarian SIM card to use in your phone. You'll find providers such as **Telekom**, **Telenor**, **Vodafone** and others in all big shopping malls.

Visitor using a mobile phone

Internet

Cafés and bars offering a wireless connection are now common in Budapest. It is easy to find Wi-Fi hotspots, too: go to www.hotspotter.hu. Plus, more and more cafés and restaurants are providing free Wi-Fi. Budapest also has several Internet cafés offering coffee and snacks while you check your emails, search the Internet or play online games. It is worth noting that connection speeds can vary.

In some cafés the keyboards are laid out according to the Hungarian template, with extra letters.

Addresses

Budapest is divided into 23 districts, identified by Roman numerals. A Budapest address is usually written with the district number placed first; in addition, the street number comes after the street name – for example, V Kossuth Lajos utca 4. However, in correspondence a four-digit postal code is used in place of the district number, the middle two digits indicating the district (so that 1054 refers to an address in the fifth district).

Internet café in Vaci utca, a pedestrianized street in Pest

After the street number, an additional combination of numerals denotes the floor, and the number of individual apartments (eg Kossuth utca 14.III.24). Confusingly, some old buildings in Pest are designated as having a half-floor *(félemelet)* or upper ground floor *(magas földszint)* between the ground *(földszint)* and first floor *(első emelet)* proper. So what the British would call the second floor, and Americans the third, Hungarians might describe as the first floor.

Postal Services

Postage stamps cost between 70 and 190 Hungarian forints for sending a postcard. Always ask the clerk at the post office as rates depend on the weight and even the format of the envelope. Apart from ordinary stamps, all post offices sell various special issues. Care should be taken when sending valuable items, as packages often go missing.

Red post box for national and international mail

On weekdays, most post offices are open from 8am until 5pm. They are closed on Saturday and Sunday. The branch at Keleti station is open till 9pm on weekdays and until 2pm on Saturdays.

International couriers such as **DHL** operate in Budapest, but if you need to courier something within the city, local couriers such as **Hajtás Pajtás Bicycle Messengers** are faster and cheaper.

Newspapers, Magazines and Listings

In Budapest all the world's top newspapers and magazines are easily accessible at hotels. A number of the larger newsstands maintain a constant stock of international newspapers and magazines. The largest number of these can be found at the underpasses near Nyugati and Keleti stations. There are also various shops around town which specialize in English-language newspapers, books and maps *(see pp212–13)*.

Bear in mind that the foreign daily newspapers on sale tend to be yesterday's editions, but even so they often sell out by lunchtime. For English-speaking visitors there are also a few magazines, including *The Budapest Times*, *Budapest Funzine* and *Where Budapest* (the last two are free). These provide the most comprehensive information on local events and full entertainment guides.

A kiosk selling newspapers on a Budapest street

Two useful websites for news and events in the city are www.xpatloop.com and www.caboodle.hu.

TV and Radio

The city's larger hotels are geared up for the needs of the international traveller and, in addition to the state and independent Hungarian television channels, most offer tens of satellite TV and radio channels in English and other European languages.

DIRECTORY

Mobile Phones

Telekom
Petőfi Sándor utca 12.
Map 4 E1.
Tel (06 1) 266 57 23.

Telenor
Károly korút 3/A.
Map 10 E3.
Tel (06 20) 960 07 54.

Vodafone
Váci út 1.
Map 2 F1.
Tel 0670 288 32 88.

Internet

Király Internet Kávézó
Király utca 54.
Map 7 A1.
Tel (06 1) 321 0106.

Törpe Kávézó
XIII Béke út 69.
Map 2 E1.
Tel (06 1) 239 45 73.
Open 11am–1am Mon–Fri, noon–1am Sat & Sun.

Vist@Net Café
XIII Váci út 6.
Map 2 F2.
Tel (06 1) 320 43 32.
Open 24 hours.

Postal Services

Bajcsy-Zsilinszky út 16
Map 10 E1.
Open 8am–8pm Mon–Fri.

Fővám tér 5
Map 4 F3
Open 10am–6pm Mon–Fri.

Pauler utca 3
Map 1 B5.
Open 8am–6pm Mon–Fri.

Teréz körút 51
Map 10 F1.
Open 7am–8pm Mon–Fri, 8am–6pm Sat.

Couriers

DHL
Szabadság tér 7.
Map 2 E4.
Tel (06 40) 45 45 45.

Hajtás Pajtás Bicycle Messengers
Vörösmarty utca 20.
Map 5 A5.
Tel (06 1) 327 90 00.

GETTING TO BUDAPEST

Hungarians like to boast that Budapest is the heart of central Europe – a claim with some justification, as the city acts as a major crossroads linking north to south and west to east. It has excellent rail links with the whole of Europe and its two largest railway stations, Keleti and Nyugati *(see pp234–5)*, are conveniently situated in the centre of town. Another main railway station is Déli pályaudvar, which serves the western part of the city. The country's motorway network has undergone improvements, making up for decades of neglect. Budapest can now be reached by motorway, with the fastest route, via France, Brussels, Germany and Austria, taking 17 hours if driving non-stop but for convenience, it is better to make use of the air links Budapest has with major cities throughout Europe. A flight from London to Budapest, for example, takes just 2 ½ hours. Transfers from the airport by taxi or on public transport are quick and efficient.

Arriving by Air

Airlines from around 90 towns and cities, in 40 different countries, now fly to Budapest. The city's airport receives flights from major international airlines that include **Air France**, **British Airways** and the larger low cost airlines such as **Jet2.com** and **Wizz Air**. Between them, British Airways and the low-cost airlines operate over a dozen flights daily between Budapest and London's international airports.

In the UK, it is also possible to fly to Budapest from Edinburgh and Manchester, and there are indirect connections from a large number of other British cities. Seasonally there are direct flights from New York, and several airlines fly from the US and Canada via other European cities. Direct flights from New York take around 8 ½ hours. A direct service operates between Beijing and Budapest.

Budapest Airport

Budapest's international airport has three terminals, 1, 2A and 2B are 16–20 km (10–12 miles) from the city centre. Terminal 1, the oldest terminal, is currently closed although it may reopen in the future. When Malév Hungarian Airlines went bankrupt, the low-cost airlines moved to the better equipped terminal 2A which had been used solely by Malév. Terminals 2A and 2B currently serve all departures and arrivals – flights to and from Schengen and non-Schengen zone countries alike.

All terminals offer good amenities and services. Catering facilities include bars, cafés and restaurants. There are numerous boutiques and shops, as well as tourist offices, currency exchange facilities and desks of major car rental firms.

In 2011, Terminal 2 benefitted from the opening of Bud:SkyCourt, a centrally located building, which links Terminals 2A and 2B. Bud:SkyCourt has significantly increased the commercial area of the terminals and provides a wide range of retail outlets, international brands and dining options for travellers. Passengers can move through the terminal building much faster and the installation of six security lanes on each side of the building has made security screening speedier and more comfortable.

Passengers inside the Bud:SkyCourt terminal

Package Deals and Bargains

Low-cost airlines, such as **Easyjet**, make getting to Budapest much more affordable than in the past. Good deals are available year round, and the further in advance you book, the better the chance of a bargain.

Promotional offers from British Airways frequently stipulate that journeys include a Saturday night, and will often include stays at top hotels in the city centre. These kinds of deals are more plentiful during the low season, between September and March.

There are also specialist tour operators, such as Leisure To Taste, which offer reasonably priced, all-inclusive itineraries and special-interest holidays.

If you are booking accommodation separately from your flights, look at travel websites such as Hotel Room Finder (hotelroomfinder.co.uk), which searches more than 15 databases for the best hotel, deals. It also has special deals in Budapest and all over Hungary.

Airport shuttle company logo

Airport taxi company logo

Getting to the Centre

Bus No. 200E runs from Budapest Airport Terminals 2A and 2B to Kőbánya-Kispest metro station. Tickets cost 350 forints if bought at BKK Customer Service Points in the terminals or 450 forints on the bus. From Kőbánya-Kispest station, take the blue M3 metro line into the centre (350 forints).

The airport taxi, **FőTaxi**, charges 6,000–8,000 forints, depending on which zone in Budapest you are travelling to.

Shuttle buses waiting outside Budapest Airport

The drive into the centre is usually fairly brisk and a pleasant introduction to the city.

A cheaper option is the Airport Minibus Shuttle. For around 3,200 forints (5,500 forints return) the shuttle takes passengers from both terminals to any address in the city centre (prices are lower if booked on the Internet). Minibuses have wheelchair access and can pick up returning passengers – they advise calling 24 hours before departure to book.

Terminal 1 is currently closed, but may reopen in 2017. The cheapest and quickest way to get into the city centre from Terminal 1 is to catch the mainline train to Nyugati railway station. You will need to walk 300 m with your luggage from Terminal 1 to Ferihegy station, but the fare is reasonable at 300 forints. The trains run as often as three times an hour, but only once an hour between midnight and 6am.

Aircraft at Budapest Airport

DIRECTORY

Airport and Airlines

Air France
Tel (06 1) 483 88 00.
W airfrance.com

British Airways
Tel (06 1) 777 47 47.
W **britishairways.com**

Budapest Airport
Tel (06 1) 296 96 96 (general information).
Tel (06 1) 296 70 00 (flight information).

Easyjet
W **easyjet.com**

Jet2.com
Tel 44 203 059 8336.
W **jet2.com**

Wizz Air
Tel 06 90 181 181.
W **wizzair.com**

Tour Operator

Leisure To Taste
Ribáry utca 1, 1022 Budapest.
Tel 0800 686 0619 (UK); +36 1 336 1917 (Hungary).
W **leisuretotaste.com**

Airport Minibus

Airport Minibus Shuttle
Tel (06 1) 296 85 55.
W **airportshuttle.hu**
(Phone booking 6am–10pm daily.)

Airport Taxi

FőTaxi
Tel (06 1) 222 22 22.

Ticket offices at Nyugati Railway Station in Budapest

Travelling by Rail

Budapest has direct rail links with 25 other capital cities. Every day, more than 50 international trains, many of them express services, arrive and depart from the city's three railway stations. The modern Hungarian trains used on the mainline services are generally considered to be an efficient means of transport, although some international services suffer occasional delays.

Trains from Budapest to Vienna, the main communication hub for western Europe, depart approximately every hour or two from Keleti station. The fastest trains run at top speeds of 140–160 km/h (85–100 mph). The travelling time is an efficient 2 hours 50 minutes.

Detailed information on all domestic and international rail services running to and from Budapest can be obtained from either Keleti station or on the **MÁV-START** (Hungarian Railways) website.

It is worth knowing that there are several concessionary fares available. Foreign visitors to Hungary can buy a season ticket that is valid for between seven and ten days and offers unlimited travel throughout the country. There are also a number of Europe-wide passes that allow you to travel cheaply on trains in Hungary.

Local trains *(személyvonat)* are slow and make frequent stops. The best option if time is tight is to take modern Intercity trains, which go to Pécs, Miskolc, Debrecen, Szeged and all the larger cities in Hungary in around 1–3 hours. Seat reservations are required on these trains. Reserve in advance and expect to pay a small fee.

Railway Stations

There are three main railway stations in Budapest – Keleti (East), Nyugati (West) and Déli (South) *(see opposite)*.

The Hungarian for station is *pályaudvar*, often shortened in writing to *pu*. Most international trains run from Keleti station. Some trains to Vienna and one of the express trains to Croatia ("Maestral") leave from Déli station, as do trains to the Lake Balaton resorts, which go almost hourly in high season. Déli pu is on the red M2 metro. Keleti pu can be reached using the red M2, as well as the green M4 metro lines. For Nyugati pu take the blue M3 metro line, or trams 4 or 6.

Travelling by Boat

Between April and October hydrofoils cruise the Danube from Vienna to Budapest, via Bratislava. It is also possible to take a hydrofoil or pleasure boat along to the Danube bend, to towns such as Esztergom and Visegrád *(see pp168–9)*. See the timetable at the departure point at Vigadó tér for details, or contact cruise companies such as **AMA Waterways**, **Legenda** or **Mahart Passnave**.

Travelling by Car

Eight main roads lead out of Budapest, four of them motorways, which are marked "M". The M1 stretches from Budapest to the Hegyeshalom border crossing, where it joins the Austrian motorway network. The M3 links Budapest with Miskolc and Nyíregyháza to the northeast, the M5 leads south to Kecskemét *(see p170)* and Szeged, M6 takes you to Pécs, and the M7 links to the Balaton resorts. The M0 is being built as a ring motorway around Budapest, with only the west section still to be completed. Drivers must purchase an electronic motorway sticker for all motorways except the M0; these can be bought at petrol stations near or on the motorway or online.

Traffic regulations include driving with the headlights on, day and night. All car occupants, in the front and back seats, are required by law to wear seat belts. Motorcycle drivers and passengers must wear helmets at all times.

The speed limits are 50 km/h (30 mph) in built-up areas, 90 km/h (60 mph) outside built-up areas, 110 km/h (68 mph) on main roads and 130 km/h (80 mph) on motorways.

In Hungary it is strictly forbidden to drive following any alcohol consumption. If any trace of alcohol is found in the bloodstream, the fine for drink-driving can be as high as 50,000 Hungarian forints (approximately US $220) and is only payable in forints.

Visitors coming to Budapest by car are obliged to have the green insurance card, while

The imposing exterior of the Nyugati Railway Station

A luxury air-conditioned tourist coach

those hiring a car need only present their driving licences. Hitchhiking, while not against the law, is not recommended.

Regulations permit the use of mobile phones by drivers only when the car is fitted with a hands-free system. Otherwise, it is advisable to pull over and stop when using your phone.

Travelling by Coach

Budapest's international coach station, Népliget (Üllői út 131) lies 5 km (3 miles) southeast of the centre, and is on the blue M3 metro line.

There are three national coach stations: Népliget (with buses to western Hungary), Stadionok (to eastern Hungary) and Árpád Bridge (to northern Hungary and the Danube bend). Stadionok station can be reached by the M2 metro line, while Árpád Bridge is served by the M3 line. International routes are served by luxury coaches, which have all the usual facilities such as air-conditioning and toilets. The domestic and main international traffic is served by Volánbusz coaches (Eurolines), which operate on routes to the major towns in Hungary.

DIRECTORY

Travelling by Rail

MÁV-START
Tel (06 40) 49 49 49 (domestic); + 36 (1) 444 44 99 (international).
W **mav-start.hu**

Travelling by Boat

AMA Waterways
Tel +44 (0) 808 223 5009 (UK).
W **amawaterways.co.uk**
800 626 0126 (US toll free).
W **amawaterways.com**

Legenda
Tel (06 1) 317 22 03.
W **legenda.hu**

Mahart Passnave
Tel (06 1) 484 40 13.
W **mahartpassnave.hu**

Travelling by Car

Road and Motorway Information
Tel (06 1) 336 24 00.
W **internet.kozut.hu**

Vehicle Assistance
Tel (06 1) 266 63 83 or 188 (for breakdowns).

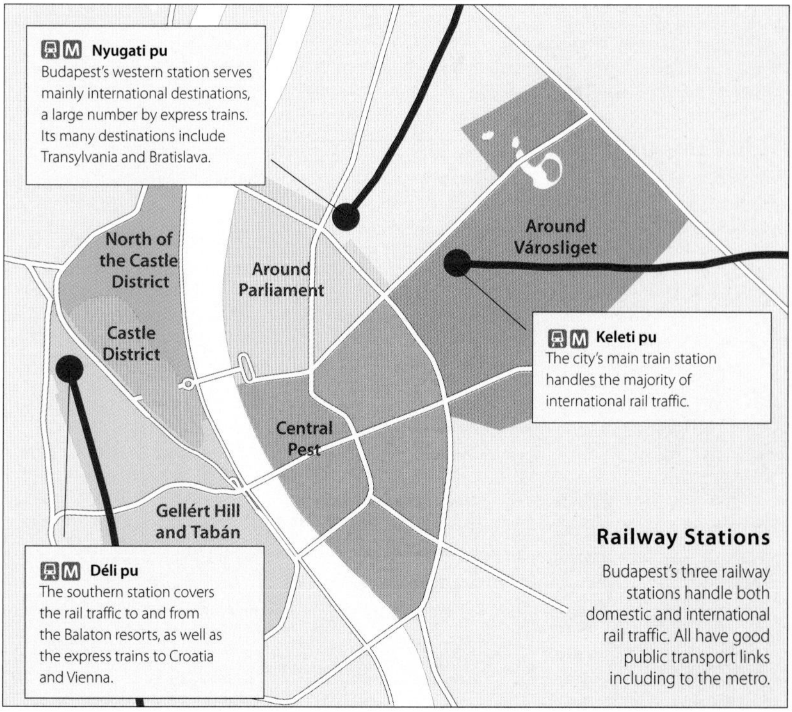

Nyugati pu
Budapest's western station serves mainly international destinations, a large number by express trains. Its many destinations include Transylvania and Bratislava.

North of the Castle District

Around Parliament

Around Városliget

Castle District

Central Pest

Gellért Hill and Tabán

Keleti pu
The city's main train station handles the majority of international rail traffic.

Déli pu
The southern station covers the rail traffic to and from the Balaton resorts, as well as the express trains to Croatia and Vienna.

Railway Stations

Budapest's three railway stations handle both domestic and international rail traffic. All have good public transport links including to the metro.

GETTING AROUND BUDAPEST

Budapest is a sprawling city with many suburban districts. However, most of its main tourist attractions are centrally located and can be easily reached by the city's public transport system, or on foot. The many choices of transport by rail, road and even water provide visitors to Budapest with ample opportunity to travel through and around the city to reach their chosen destinations. The infrastructure of Budapest is chiefly determined by the *körúts* (ring roads) and the boulevards that radiate out from the city centre and into the city's suburbs. The metro system mainly operates in Pest with some stations in Buda, while efficient tram and bus networks are easy to use and extend to all parts of the city. The overland hév trains provide a service from the city centre to the suburbs.

Green Travel

Budapest has long suffered from air pollution, and the proliferation of cars has made the problem worse. Moreover, the difficulties of parking in the city make it highly advisable to leave your car outside the centre.

A much better option is to use the excellent public transport system, which covers the whole city very well. The preservation of trolley buses and the extension of the tram network *(see pp240–41)* is good news for environmentalists. An increase in the number of cycle routes and the public bike-sharing system MOL Bubi have also resulted in the growing use of bicycles in Budapest.

Public Transport in Budapest

Budapest has an excellent public transport system, which makes it easy to get around the city. Organised by the **BKK** (Centre for Budapest Transport), it covers the metro, trams, buses, trolley buses, cogwheel railway, Danube boat and suburban hév lines up to the city boundaries *(see pp238–41)*. Daytime services run from about 4:30am to 11pm, with a good range of night buses operating across the city every 15–60 minutes. Timetables for buses, trams and trolley buses are displayed at each stop.

Budapest on Foot

Budapest is a city in which every pedestrian will find something of interest. Those who like to stroll through picturesque alleyways should make a point of visiting the cobbled streets of Buda's Castle District. Another option might be to wander around the backstreets of central Pest. Here, there are plenty of opportunities to peer into historic courtyards and admire the wrought-iron balconies and exterior decorative details of Secession apartment blocks *(see pp56–9)*. Váci utca *(see p131)* is fully pedestrianized and has seats where weary walkers can rest and watch the bustle. The promenade along the Danube is also a pleasant place to walk in Budapest. Visitors who enjoy rambling along leafy trails should take the railway or bus Nos 20 or 21A from Széll Kálmán tér to the Buda Hills *(see p165)*.

Pedestrians beside the Danube

When walking in the city it is worth remembering that you need to keep an eye on the traffic. Drivers in Budapest expect pedestrians to get out of their way – they will often swerve around you rather than stop if you use a zebra crossing.

Driving in Budapest

The large number of one-way streets in Budapest makes it a very difficult city for visitors to navigate by car. The many changes of direction often result in drivers unfamiliar with the city becoming lost. Any confusion brought about by the complex system of roads is further aggravated by the heavy rush-hour traffic. There are also few places to park in the city, so it is much better to sightsee on foot or by public transport. Most road signs follow the European pattern, and people drive on the right-hand side of the road. In towns the use of the horn is legally restricted to cases of imminent danger.

Pedestrian zone

Pedestrian crossing

Walk signal at a pedestrian crossing

New street name plate

OKTOBER 6. UTCA

Old street name plate

Hiring a Car

Cars can be hired from the airport on arrival in Budapest, or from one of several car hire offices in the city, such as **Avis**, **Budget Hungary**, **Europcar** or **Hertz**. Be prepared to leave a credit card deposit ranging between 100,000 forints and 800,000 forints, and to pay US$100–240 per day for unlimited mileage.

Stopping and parking prohibited

Parking of cars allowed in this zone for a maximum of 2 hours

Parking

There are several multi-storey car parks in the city centre, including at Nos. 4–6 Aranykéz utca, No. 20 Nyár utca, and Szervita tér. There are underground car parks at Szabadság tér and Sas utca. A lot of the larger hotels also have an underground garage. There are attended and unattended car parks situated in other busy parts of the city as well. In addition, hotels with car parks may offer spare parking spaces to non-guests, all of which helps to ease the problem of on-street parking.

Budapest is split into several parking zones that all have different hourly rates. When parking on the street, you must get a ticket from the nearest ticket machine to display in the car, specifying how long you will stay. Parking charges vary from 175 to 600 Hungarian forints per hour. Parking without a valid ticket or overstaying the allocated time can lead to either a parking fine or wheel-clamping.

Cars parked improperly may be clamped or towed away to a car park outside the centre. Fines of up to 30,000 forints can also be imposed for parking offences.

Clamping and Towing

Wheel-clamping is growing in Budapest; all illegally parked vehicles are subject to clamping.

As well as paying a fine, it costs around 16,000 forints (US $70) to release a car from a clamp, and around 20,000 forints (US $90) if a car has been towed away – usually to a car park outside the city. Parking meters often display the telephone number to contact in the event of wheel-clamping. It is also worth asking a car park attendant for advice. If the car has been towed away, call the Removed Cars Information line (Tel (06 1) 301 75 00) to find out where it has been taken.

Cycling

Cycling in Budapest is often difficult and fairly dangerous. Cyclists have to be careful of the tram rails and the uneven, cobblestoned surfaces of some roads. The poor air quality is an additional disadvantage. However, Budapest's main roads are usually open to cyclists, and designated cycle lanes are available on a growing number of roads. The provision of cycle routes in Budapest and the opening of one-way streets to contraflow cycling (indicated by signs allowing this) have made cycling an increasingly popular pastime. Bike-hire shops such as **Bikebase**, **Budapest Bike** and **BudaBike Tours** are also a good source of information about bicycle routes in the city.

The **MOL Bubi** public bike-sharing scheme is another way of cycling around Budapest. It consists of 76 docking stations and 1,100 bicycles found at several locations in the city. After buying an initial ticket, you can use the bikes free for 30 minutes or for longer periods with modest charges. A deposit is blocked on your credit card and released a few days after your ticket has expired.

An enjoyable way to spend time in Budapest is to take a cycling trip around Margaret Island *(see pp176–7)*. There are several bike-hire stalls on the island, and they also rent out children's bikes, thus enabling family groups to explore. The Danube riverbank also has dedicated cycle lanes.

Using one of Budapest's cycle routes

DIRECTORY

Public Transport

BKK (Centre for Budapest Transport)
Rumbach S. utca 19–21.
Map 2 F5 (10 E3).
Tel (06 1) 325 52 55.

Car Hire

Avis
Arany János utca 26–28.
Tel (06 1) 296 64 21. **W** **avis.com**

Budget Hungary
Hotel Mercure Buda, Krisztina körút 41–43. **Map** 3 C1.
Tel (06 1) 214 04 20.
W **budget.hu**

Europcar
Erzsébet tér 7–8. **Tel** (06 1) 505 44 00. **W** **europcar.hu**

Hertz
Apáczai Csere János utca 4.
Tel (06 1) 266 43 61. **W** **hertz.hu**

Bike Hire

Bikebase
Podmaniczky utca 19 (closed in winter). **Tel** (06 1) 269 59 83.
W **bikebase.hu**

BudaBike Tours
Szent István tér 6 (in front of Basilica). **Tel** (06 70) 242 5736.
W **budabike.com**

Budapest Bike
Wesselényi utca 13. **Tel** (06 30) 944 55 33. **W** **budapestbike.hu**

MOL Bubi
W **molbubi.bkk.hu**

Getting Around by Metro

Budapest has four metro lines *(see inside back cover)*, most easily distinguished by their colours: yellow, red, blue and green. Three lines (M1, M2 and M3) intersect at Deák Ferenc tér station, while the M4 line intersects with M2 at Keleti pályaudvar, and M3 at Kálvin tér. The oldest line, the yellow M1 line, runs just beneath the surface of the city. Built in 1894, it is known as the Millennium Line after the celebrations that took place two years later *(see p146)*, but its more common name is the *Földalatti* (Underground). Two more lines – the red M2 and blue M3 lines – were added after 1970. The M4 line opened in 2014 and has some architecturally remarkable stations. The modern trains on this line are driverless.

Signs for the M2 metro

The Metro System

A journey on the World Heritage Millennium Line (M1) is an event in itself, with some beautifully tiled late-19th century stations.

Three words to remember when using the metro system are: *bejárat*, meaning entrance; *kijárat*, meaning exit (both are always clearly marked); and *felé*, meaning towards (the direction of trains is indicated by the name of the station at the end of the line). Remember to validate your ticket. Validation machines are located at the station entrances.

To plan a journey, consult the map at the back of this guide. A recorded voice message announces when the door is closing and gives the name of the next station and transfer possibilities. The M4 stations are accessible by lift, but the other lines are only accessible by escalators or stairs. Smoking and eating are not permitted on the trains, and you must use headphones to listen to music. Dogs can travel on the metro, but only when muzzled and require an extra ticket or a dog pass.

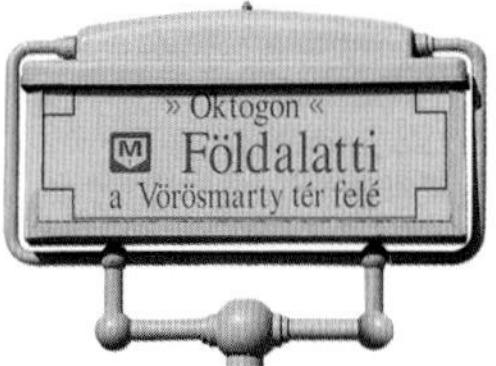

Sign over the entrance to the M1 metro line at Oktogon tér station

Tickets

The same types of ticket and pass cover all forms of BKK transport. Single tickets must be validated in a machine at the start of your journey: on the metro they must be validated at the station before boarding; on buses, trams, trolley buses and the cog-wheel railway they must be validated on board.

Tickets are checked frequently, and there is a fine of 8,000 forints to be paid in cash on the spot for travelling without a valid ticket. Each time you board a bus or tram, you must validate a new ticket, but on the metro system you can change lines within one hour, provided you do not leave the stations.

A typical station on the M4 metro line

One-day travel card valid for all forms of public transport

A 72-hour travel card valid for all forms of public transport

Tickets *(jegy)* can be purchased separately or, more economically, in booklets of 10 for 3,000 forints. Individual tickets cost 350 forints if you buy them in advance at metro stations and newspaper kiosks. You can buy tickets on board buses and some trams for 450 forints *(see p241)*. You can also buy transfer tickets *(Átszállójegy)* costing 530 forints, which are valid for two immediately consecutive journeys on any form of public transport. On the metro you can also get cheaper tickets for journeys of three stops *(Metrószakaszjegy)*, with no transfers. Automated fare collection and electronic tickets are being introduced in 2015 so schedules and prices may change.

Travelcards and Passes

Travelcards are available for 24 hours, 72 hours or one week. Passes for 14 or 30 days, or an entire year, are also available. There are discounts for students, seniors, the disabled and parents with small children, but these only apply for periods of at least two weeks. Make sure you bring photographic ID with you when buying your pass, which can be purchased on the spot. The Budapest Card *(see p222)* entitles the holder to free city transport, free guided tours, as well as a range of discounts at some museums and restaurants, for periods of two or three days.

Travelling on the hév

The overland hév railway is an essential means of transport connecting Budapest with its suburban districts. It carries residents to and from work and tourists to attractions located 20–30 km (12–20 miles) away from the city centre. The standard tickets used on other forms of transport *(see p238)* can be used to travel to central destinations and other places within the city limits, such as the Roman town of Aquincum, but passengers leaving the city boundaries by suburban railway have to purchase an extension ticket at the ticket office, ticket vending machines or from the conductor on board.

Suburban Rail Lines

The hév line H5 is most commonly used by tourists and runs north from Batthyány tér *(see p104)* towards Szentendre *(see p169)*, taking in such sights as Aquincum *(see pp166–7)* along the way. Many of the trains on this line terminate at Békásmegyer rather than running on to Szentendre. You should check the destination on the front of the train before boarding.

Another line (H8) runs from Örs vezér tere (at the eastern terminus of the M2 metro line) to Gödöllő, passing the Hungaroring Grand Prix race track *(see p63)* near Mogyoród en route.

The hév line (H9) runs from Örs vezér tere and terminates in the village of Csömör just off the northeast boundary of Budapest.

A fourth hév line (H6) begins at Közvágóhíd and terminates approximately 40 km (25 miles) away at Ráckeve on Csepel Island *(see p171)*. Tourists who make this long journey can enjoy a visit to the palace of Prince Eugene of Savoy.

The fifth hév service (H7) between Boráros tér and Csepel Island is the shortest, extending only 7 km (4 miles).

Hév trains run regularly between 4am and 11.30pm. BKK tickets are valid up to the city boundary; a supplementary ticket is required to go further.

A standard hév train carriage

Other Town Transport

Several modes of transport operate in the Buda Hills west of the city *(see p165)*. A cog-wheel railway connects Szilágyi Erzsébet fasor with Széchenyi Hill, with its picturesque walking trails – BKK tickets and passes are valid right along the line.

The Children's Railway runs from Széchenyi Hill to Hűvössvölgy *(see p11)*. A chair lift, or *libegő*, descends from the top of János Hill down on to Zugligeti út.

In the centre of the city the Budavári Sikló is an old funicular railway which runs between the Buda end of the Chain Bridge and the top of Castle Hill.

Buy tickets for all three modes of transport at the ticket offices before boarding.

Getting Around by Taxi

It has always been easy to find a taxi in Budapest. The competition was so fierce that some companies used unfair methods to attract passengers or exploited foreign visitors, especially those unfamiliar with Budapest. To reduce this risk, the municipality of Budapest devised taxi regulations. All licensed taxis have to be yellow, apply the same fares and conform to strict standards, such as having air conditioning and accepting payment by credit card.

Using Taxis

Taxi ranks can be found throughout Budapest and are seldom empty. Taxis can also be hailed on the street but to avoid problems it is often better to book from your hotel or by phone. All of the companies listed in the Directory are likely to have English-speaking operators on duty. The total fare you will be asked to pay is made up of three parts; a basic charge, a per-kilometre charge, and a waiting charge. On getting into the taxi, ensure that the meter is set at the beginning of the journey and ask for an estimate of what the fare will be.

A licensed Budapest taxi

DIRECTORY

Taxi Companies

Budapest Taxi
Tel (06 1) 777 77 77.
W budapesttaxi.hu

City Taxi Tel (06 1) 211 11 11.
W citytaxi.hu

Főtaxi Tel (06 1) 222 22 22.
W fotaxi.hu

Taxi 2000 Tel (06 1) 200 00 00.
W taxi2000.hu

Getting Around by Tram

There are more than 30 tram lines in Budapest, which extend to practically every part of the city except the hilly parts of Buda. Trams are yellow in colour and are a good way of travelling for sightseeing in the centre. They are easy to use and an efficient and speedy means of getting around Budapest, as they avoid traffic and run very frequently. Services start early in the morning, from about 4:30am, and run regularly throughout the day until 11pm or midnight, depending on the route. Night trams operate only on line 4, every 10 to 15 minutes. More information on late-night transport is given on page 215.

One of the city's yellow trams, on route No. 2

The Tram System

Tickets *(see p238)* for trams can be bought at metro stations and some newspaper kiosks. You can also get them from vending machines on some tram platforms. Validate your ticket in the machine inside the tram. All tram stops display the relevant tram numbers and the timetable. Some have electronic displays.

When a tram line is closed for maintenance, replacement buses *(potlóbusz)* are provided.

Travelling with Luggage

Every passenger on all forms of public transport is entitled to carry two small pieces of luggage. You can also carry one pair of ice skates and one pair of skis, providing they are clean, as well as a child's buggy. For transporting a bicycle or a larger item of luggage, the rack railway or the designated carriages of the hév trains should be used and an extra ticket is needed.

Sightseeing by Tram

Trams provide a cheap, pleasant way to explore the city. Tram 2, runs along the river Danube in Pest between Kozvágóhíd and Jászai Mari tér. It passes in front of the Parliament building and is one of the most beautiful and famous tramlines in the world, offering passengers an unforgettable vista of Buda Castle across the river. For the best views, sit on the river side of the tram. Trams 4 and 6 are also useful routes for travelling though the Central Pest area of the city.

For a nostalgic trip, look out for the wonderfully restored vintage trams that are frequently operated by BKK along the tramline 2 line at weekends.

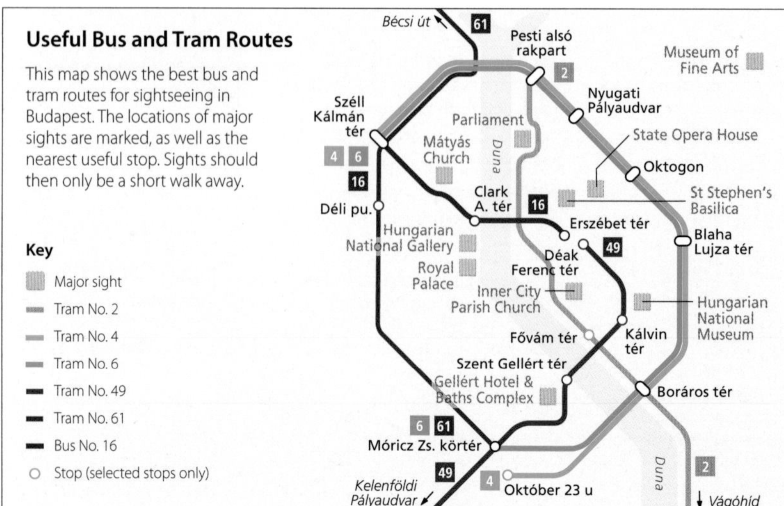

Getting Around by Bus

Budapest has about 200 different bus routes, covering the whole city. They are a recommended mode of transport for visitors, except during rush hour. Daytime services run from about 4:30am to 11pm, with departures on most routes every 10–20 minutes. There is a good range of night buses operating across the city every 15–60 minutes. Departure times and a list of destinations are on display at each stop. All buses are blue – ordinary buses are indicated by black numbers and halt at every stop. Buses with the letter "E" follow express routes and omit a number of stops.

It is worth noting that buses sometimes get caught in heavy traffic congestion in the centre of the city during rush hours, and their progress at these times can be slow. If you are in a hurry it might be better to take a tram or the metro, or even to walk.

The Bus System

Budapest's bus system is extremely efficient and makes exploring the city easy, even for first-time visitors. Many bus stops now have electronic displays showing real-time transport information. Tickets must be punched upon entering the bus. The next stop is always announced, often informing passengers about any interchanges. To ensure that the bus stops, you should press the button located by the door before your required stop. Remember that Budapest's bus drivers tend to drive fast and that the streets, particularly in Buda, can be steep. This combination makes it advisable to hang on tightly to the hand grips when standing on a bus.

Some of Budapest's modern buses

Bus stop with a real-time display board

Sightseeing by Bus

Buses are especially helpful for exploring the hilly area of Buda. Bus 16 will take you close to Buda Castle.

Various hop-on/hop-off bus tour companies operate in the city. These cover the major sights and allow you to explore the city at your own pace.

Getting Around by Trolley Bus

Trolley buses, which are red, operate only in Pest. It is advisable to hold on tight if you are standing, as they can accelerate very suddenly. Timetables are displayed at each stop.

The Trolley Bus System

The same rules apply for travelling on a trolley bus as when travelling on a bus. Remember to signal to the driver by pressing the button located above the door when approaching your stop. Otherwise, if there are no passengers waiting at the stop, the driver will not automatically come to a halt.

Trolley buses are numbered from 70 upwards and there are about 15 different routes in Budapest. Tickets must be punched upon boarding. A particularly pleasant and useful route is taken by trolley bus No. 70, which runs from Parliament on Kossuth Lajos tér, past the City Park to Erzsébet királyné útja.

A red trolley bus in Budapest

Ticket Vending Machine

Tickets are sold at metro stations and the vending machines at major transport junctions. Besides cash (forints), the new machines also accept credit and debit cards, even contactless (PayPass) ones.

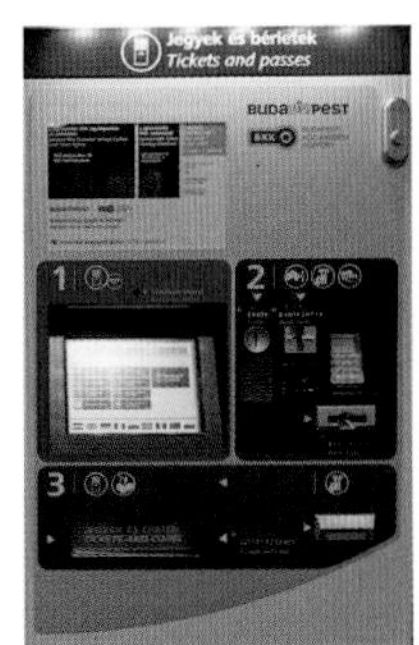

Ticket vending machine

STREET FINDER

The map references for all the sights, hotels, bars, restaurants, shops and entertainment venues described in this book refer to the maps in this section. A complete index of street names marked on the maps appears on *pages 254–6*. The map below shows the area of Budapest covered by the *Street Finder* and is colour-coded by area. The *Street Finder* also includes bus and tram routes, major sights and places of interest together with other useful information listed in the key below. As an aid to navigation, all street names, both on the *Street Finder* and in the index, are in Hungarian. Slightly confusing are the terms *utca* (often abbreviated to *u*), which means street, and út meaning avenue, a term mainly applied to wide, busy roads. Other commonly used terms are *körút* (ring road), *tér* (square), *köz* (lane), *körtér* (circus) and *hid* (bridge).

Key to Street Finder

- Major sight
- Place of interest
- Other building
- Metro station
- Hév station
- Train station
- River boat boarding point
- Main bus stop
- Tram stop
- Funicular station
- Tourist information point
- Hospital with casualty unit
- Police station
- Church
- Synagogue
- Railway line
- Pedestrianized street

Scale of Maps 1–8: 1:12,000

0 metres 200

0 yards 200

Scale of Maps 9–10: 1:10,500

0 metres 200

0 yards 200

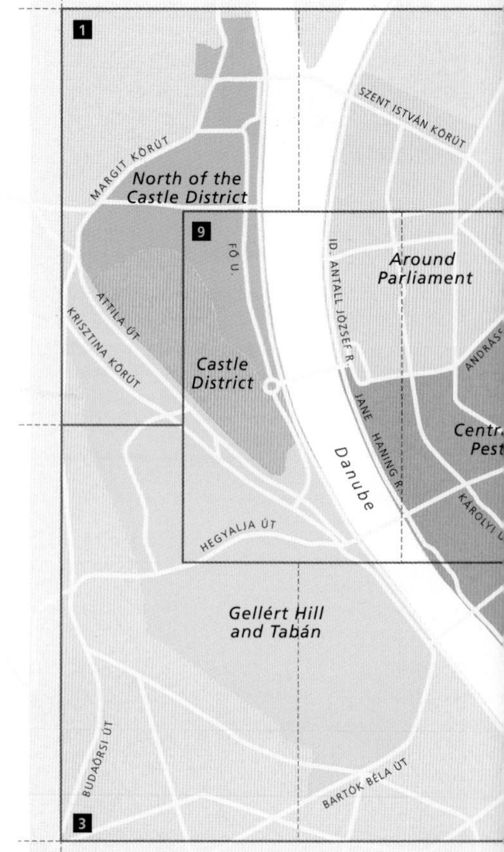

House in the leafy Tabán district *(see p98)*

Deák Ferenc tér *(see p125)*, named after politician Ferenc Deák and home to the city's first ever public toilet

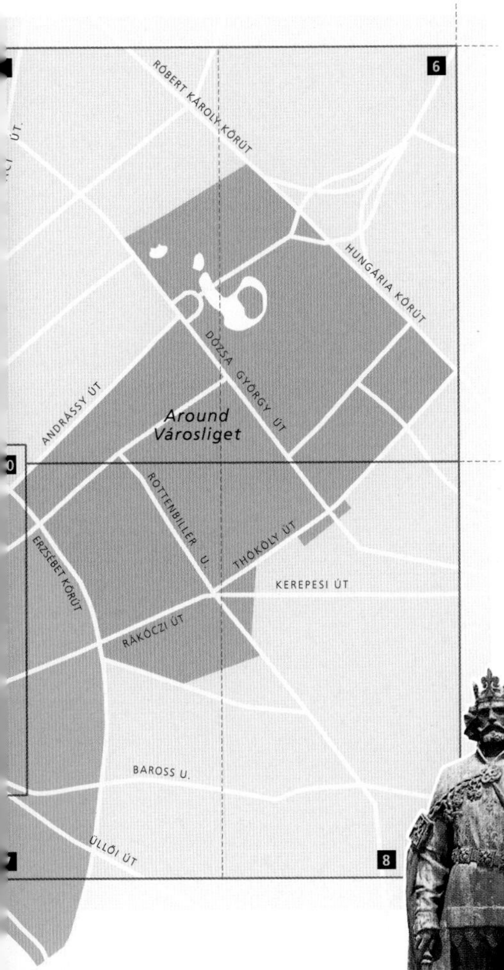

6

RÓBERT KÁROLY KÖRÚT

HUNGÁRIA KÖRÚT

DÓZSA GYÖRGY ÚT

ANDRÁSSY ÚT

Around Városliget

ROTTENBILLER U.

THÖKÖLY ÚT

ERZSÉBET KÖRÚT

KEREPESI ÚT

RÁKÓCZI ÚT

BAROSS U.

ÜLLŐI ÚT

8

Flag-lined avenue in the Castle District *(see pp82–3)*

0 kilometres 2

0 miles 1

Statue of King Ludwig I, part of the colossal Millennium Monument on Heroes' Square *(see p149)*, which was completed in 1929

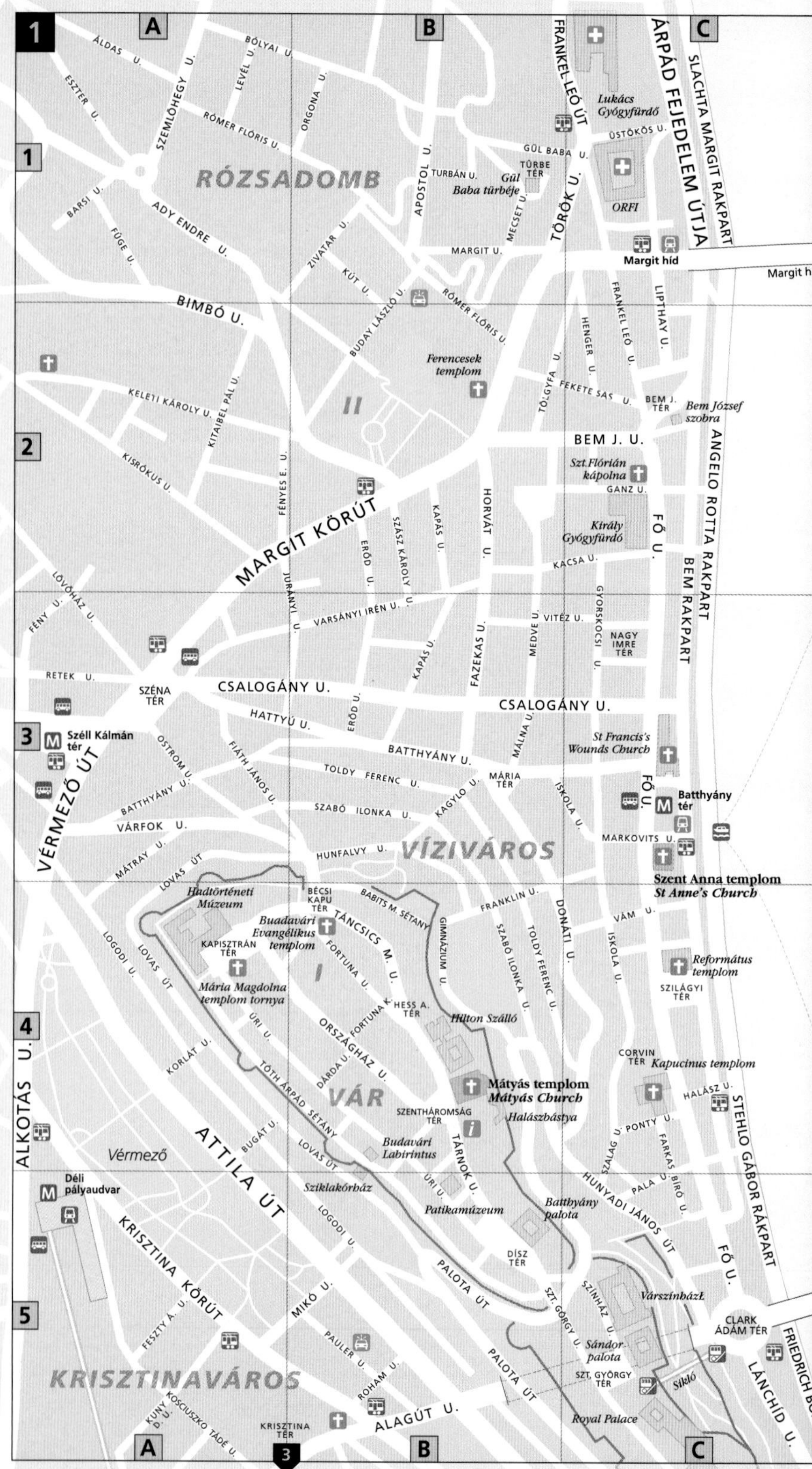

1
A
B
C
RÓZSADOMB
II
VÍZIVÁROS
I
VÁR
KRISZTINAVÁROS
Lukács Gyógyfürdő
ORFI
Gül Baba türbéje
Margit híd
Ferencesek templom
Bem József szobra
Szt.Flórián kápolna
Király Gyógyfürdő
St Francis's Wounds Church
Széll Kálmán tér
Batthyány tér
Szent Anna templom
St Anne's Church
Hadtörténeti Múzeum
Buadavári Evangélikus templom
Mária Magdolna templom tornya
Református templom
Hilton Szálló
Kapucinus templom
Mátyás templom
Mátyás Church
Halászbástya
Budavári Labirintus
Vérmező
Déli pályaudvar
Sziklakórház
Patikamúzeum
Batthyány palota
Várszínház
Sándor palota
Sikló
Royal Palace
MARGIT KÖRÚT
CSALOGÁNY U.
VÉRMEZŐ ÚT
ATTILA ÚT
KRISZTINA KÖRÚT
ÁRPÁD FEJEDELEM ÚTJA
ANGELO ROTTA RAKPART
BEM RAKPART
STEHLO GÁBOR RAKPART
ALKOTÁS U.
ALAGÚT U.
CLARK ÁDÁM TÉR
LÁNCHÍD U.
3

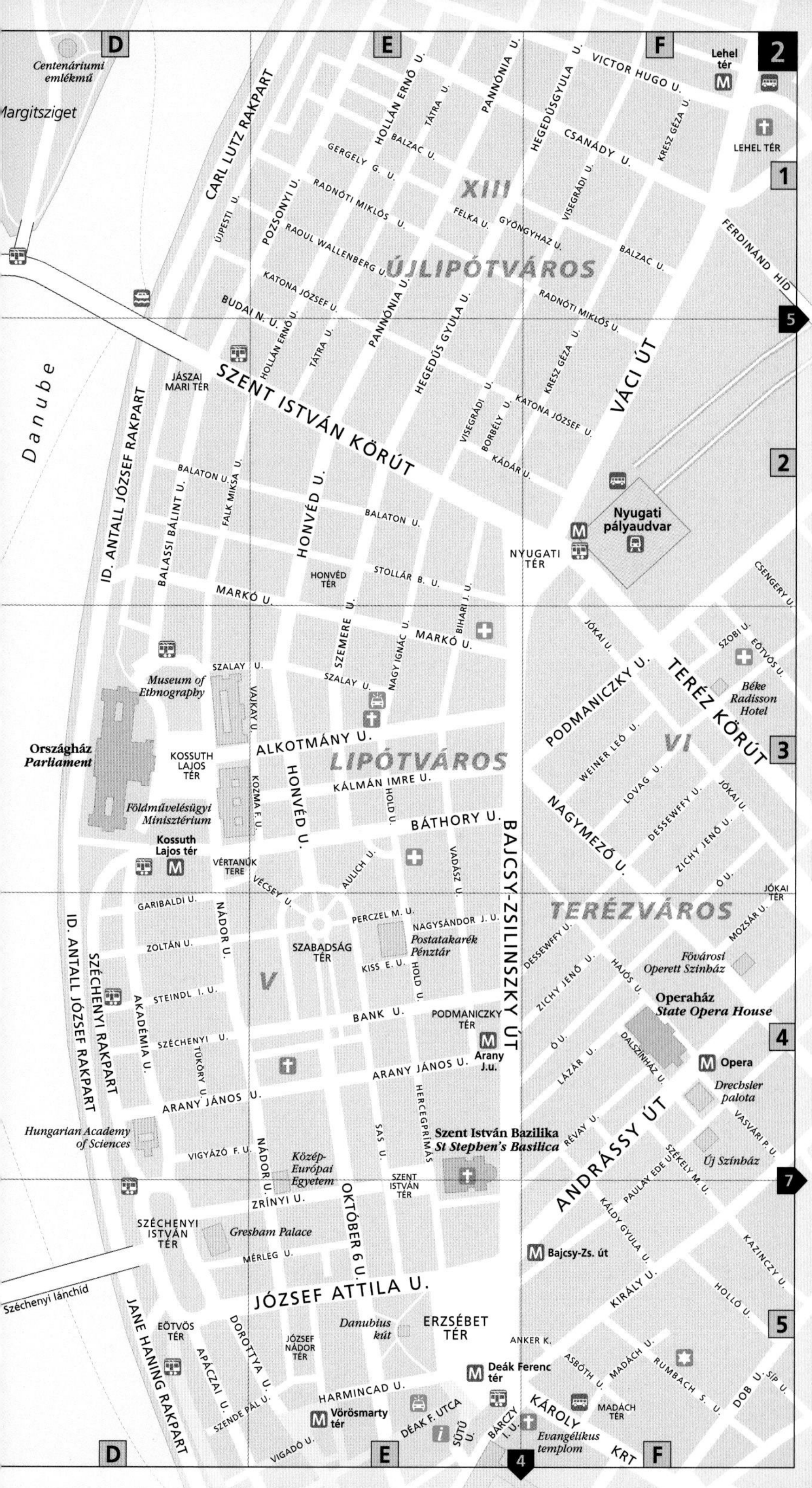

D
E
F
2
Centenáriumi emlékmű
Margitsziget
Lehel tér
LEHEL TÉR
CARL LUTZ RAKPART
HOLLÁN ERNŐ U.
TÁTRA U.
PANNÓNIA U.
HEGEDŰSGYULA U.
VICTOR HUGO U.
BALZAC U.
GERGELY G. U.
CSANÁDY U.
KRESZ GÉZA U.
XIII
ÚJPESTI U.
POZSONYI U.
RADNÓTI MIKLÓS U.
FELKA U.
GYÖNGYHÁZ U.
VISEGRÁDI U.
RAOUL WALLENBERG U.
ÚJLIPÓTVÁROS
BALZAC U.
FERDINÁND HÍD
KATONA JÓZSEF U.
RADNÓTI MIKLÓS U.
BUDAI N. U.
HOLLÁN ERNŐ U.
TÁTRA U.
PANNÓNIA U.
HEGEDŰS GYULA U.
KRESZ GÉZA U.
VÁCI ÚT
5
Danube
JÁSZAI MARI TÉR
SZENT ISTVÁN KÖRÚT
VISEGRÁDI U.
BORBÉLY U.
KATONA JÓZSEF U.
KÁDÁR U.
ID. ANTALL JÓZSEF RAKPART
BALATON U.
FALK MIKSA U.
BALASSI BÁLINT U.
HONVÉD U.
BALATON U.
Nyugati pályaudvar
NYUGATI TÉR
HONVÉD TÉR
STOLLÁR B. U.
CSENGERY U.
MARKÓ U.
BIHARI J. U.
SZEMERE U.
NAGY IGNÁC U.
MARKÓ U.
JÓKAI U.
SZOBI U.
EÖTVÖS U.
SZALAY U.
SZALAY U.
Museum of Ethnography
VAJKAY U.
PODMANICZKY U.
TERÉZ KÖRÚT
Béke Radisson Hotel
Országház Parliament
KOSSUTH LAJOS TÉR
ALKOTMÁNY U.
LIPÓTVÁROS
VI
3
KÁLMÁN IMRE U.
KOZMA F. U.
HONVÉD U.
HOLD U.
WEINER LEÓ U.
LOVAG U.
Földművelésügyi Minisztérium
BÁTHORY U.
NAGYMEZŐ U.
DESSEWFFY U.
JÓKAI U.
Kossuth Lajos tér
VÉRTANÚK TERE
AULICH U.
VADÁSZ U.
BAJCSY-ZSILINSZKY ÚT
ZICHY JENŐ U.
Ó U.
JÓKAI TÉR
VÉCSEY U.
GARIBALDI U.
PERCZEL M. U.
NAGYSÁNDOR J. U.
TERÉZVÁROS
MOZSÁR U.
ZOLTÁN U.
NÁDOR U.
SZABADSÁG TÉR
Postatakarék Pénztár
DESSEWFFY U.
ZICHY JENŐ U.
HAJÓS U.
Fővárosi Operett Színház
V
KISS E. U.
HOLD U.
ID. ANTALL JÓZSEF RAKPART
SZÉCHENYI RAKPART
AKADÉMIA U.
STEINDL I. U.
Operaház State Opera House
BANK U.
PODMANICZKY TÉR
SZÉCHENYI U.
TÜKÖRY U.
Arany J.u.
Ó U.
LÁZÁR U.
DALSZÍNHÁZ U.
4
Opera
ARANY JÁNOS U.
Drechsler palota
ARANY JÁNOS U.
HERCEGPRÍMÁS
Hungarian Academy of Sciences
SAS U.
Szent István Bazilika St Stephen's Basilica
RÉVAY U.
ANDRÁSSY ÚT
VASVÁRI P. U.
VIGYÁZÓ F. U.
NÁDOR U.
Közép-Európai Egyetem
SZÉKELY M. U.
Új Színház
SZENT ISTVÁN TÉR
PAULAY EDE U.
7
ZRÍNYI U.
OKTÓBER 6 U.
KÁLDY GYULA U.
SZÉCHENYI ISTVÁN TÉR
Gresham Palace
KAZINCZY U.
Bajcsy-Zs. út
MÉRLEG U.
Széchenyi lánchíd
JÓZSEF ATTILA U.
KIRÁLY U.
HOLLÓ U.
JANE HANING RAKPART
EÖTVÖS TÉR
DOROTTYA U.
Danubius kút
ERZSÉBET TÉR
JÓZSEF NÁDOR TÉR
ANKER K.
ASBÓTH U.
MADÁCH U.
RUMBACH S. U.
DOB U.
SÍP U.
APÁCZAI U.
Deák Ferenc tér
HARMINCAD U.
SZENDE PÁL U.
Vörösmarty tér
DEÁK F. UTCA
SÜTŐ U.
BARCZY I. U.
KÁROLY KRT
Evangélikus templom
MADÁCH TÉR
VIGADÓ U.
4

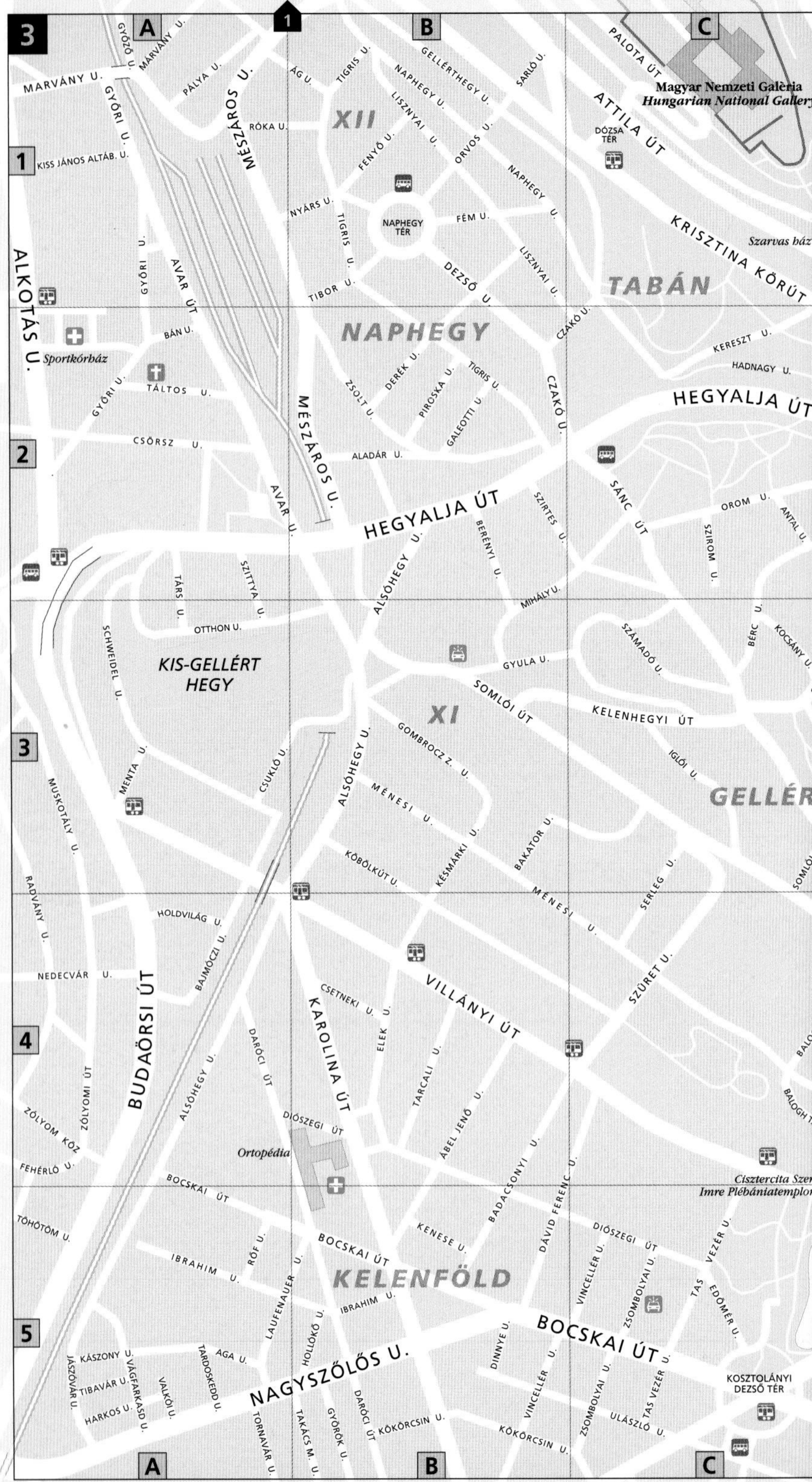

3
A
B
C
1
2
3
4
5
Magyar Nemzeti Galéria
Hungarian National Gallery
Szarvas ház
XII
NAPHEGY
TABÁN
XI
GELLÉR
KIS-GELLÉRT HEGY
KELENFÖLD
Sportkórház
Ortopédia
Cisztercita Szent Imre Plébániatemplom
NAPHEGY TÉR
DÓZSA TÉR
KOSZTOLÁNYI DEZSŐ TÉR
PALOTA ÚT
ATTILA ÚT
KRISZTINA KÖRÚT
HEGYALJA ÚT
ALKOTÁS U.
BUDAÖRSI ÚT
VILLÁNYI ÚT
KAROLINA ÚT
BOCSKAI ÚT
NAGYSZŐLŐS U.
MÉSZÁROS U.
AVAR ÚT
MARVÁNY U.
GYŐRI U.
GYŐZŐ U.
PÁLYA U.
RÓKA U.
ÁG U.
TIGRIS U.
NAPHEGY U.
GELLÉRTHEGY U.
SARLÓ U.
LISZNYAI U.
ORVOS U.
FENYŐ U.
NYÁRS U.
FÉM U.
DEZSŐ U.
TIBOR U.
KISS JÁNOS ALTÁB. U.
BÁN U.
TÁLTOS U.
CSÖRSZ U.
CZAKÓ U.
KERESZT U.
HADNAGY U.
ZSOLT U.
DERÉK U.
PIROSKA U.
GALEOTTI U.
ALADÁR U.
SÁNC ÚT
OROM U.
ANTAL U.
SZIROM U.
SZIRTES U.
BERÉNYI U.
ALSÓHEGY U.
MIHÁLY U.
TÁRS U.
SZITTYA U.
OTTHON U.
SCHWEIDEL U.
SZÁMADÓ U.
BÉRC U.
KOCSÁNY U.
GYULA U.
SOMLÓI ÚT
KELENHEGYI ÚT
GOMBROCZ Z. U.
IGLÓI U.
MENTA U.
CSUKLÓ U.
MÉNESI U.
KÉSMÁRKI U.
BAKATOR U.
MUSKOTÁLY U.
KÖBÖLKÚT U.
SERLEG U.
RADVÁNY U.
HOLDVILÁG U.
BAJMÓCZI U.
NEDECVÁR U.
SZÜRET U.
CSETNEKI U.
ELEK U.
DARÓCI ÚT
TARCALI U.
BALOGH T.
ZÓLYOMI ÚT
ZÓLYOM KÖZ
ÁBEL JENŐ U.
DIÓSZEGI ÚT
FEHÉRLÓ U.
BADACSONYI U.
DÁVID FERENC U.
TÖHÖTÖM U.
RŐF U.
KENESE U.
VINCELLÉR U.
TAS VEZÉR U.
EDÖMÉR U.
IBRAHIM U.
LAUFENAUER U.
ZSOMBOLYAI U.
KÁSZONY U.
AGA U.
HOLLÓKŐ U.
DINNYE U.
JÁSZÓVÁR U.
TIBAVÁR U.
VÁGFARKASD U.
TARDOSKEDD U.
VALKÓI U.
HARKOS U.
TORNAVÁR U.
TAKÁCS M. U.
GYÖRÖK U.
KÖKÖRCSIN U.
ULÁSZLÓ U.

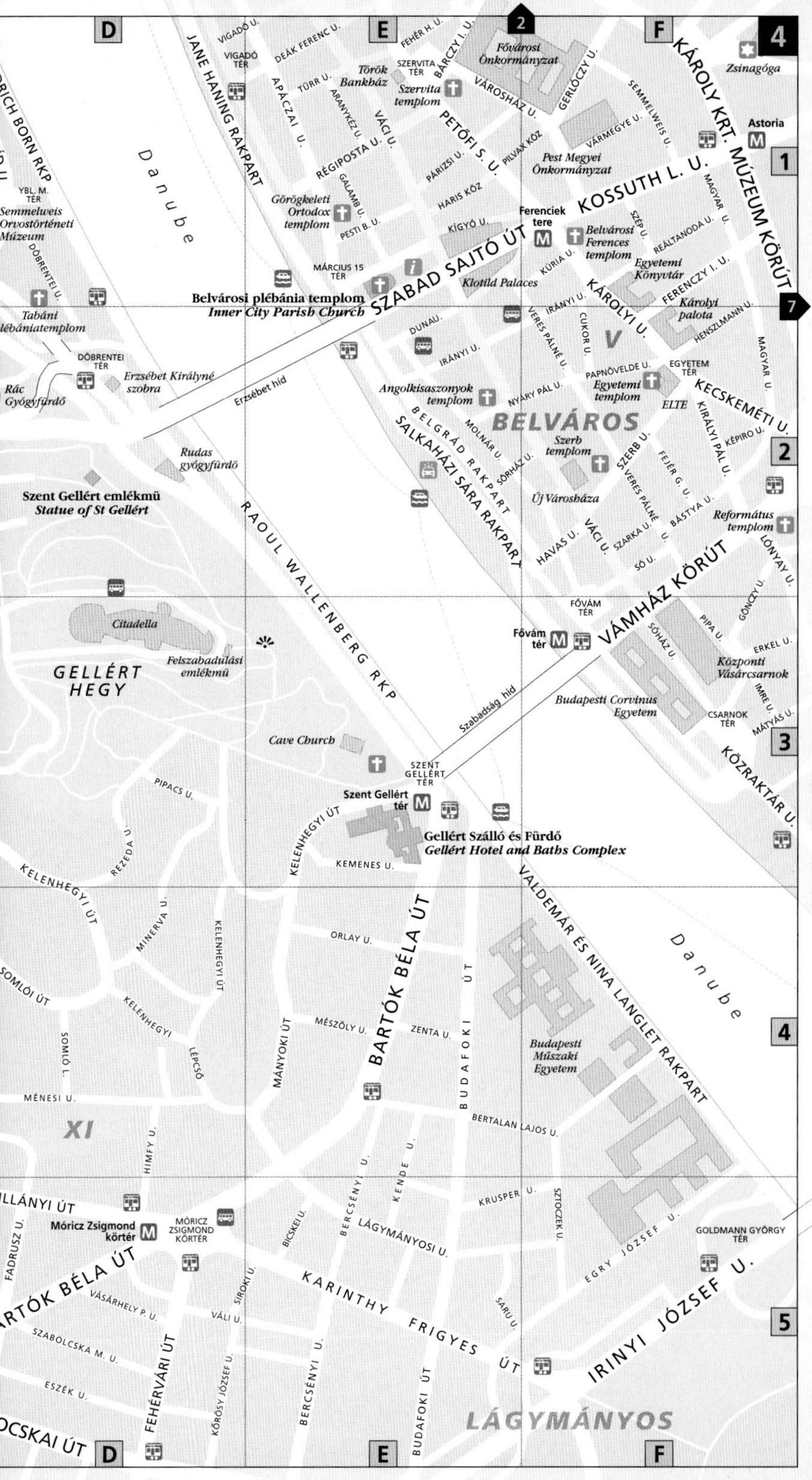

D
E
F
4
2
7
1
2
3
4
5
Danube
Fővárosi Önkormányzat
Zsinagóga
Astoria
Török Bankház
Szervita templom
Pest Megyei Önkormányzat
Görögkeleti Ortodox templom
Semmelweis Orvostörténeti Múzeum
Ferenciek tere
Belvárosi Ferences templom
Egyetemi Könyvtár
Klotild Palaces
Belvárosi plébánia templom
Inner City Parish Church
Károlyi palota
Tabáni plébániatemplom
Erzsébet Királyné szobra
Rác Gyógyfürdő
Erzsébet híd
Angolkisaszonyok templom
Egyetemi templom
ELTE
BELVÁROS
V
Rudas gyógyfürdő
Szerb templom
Új Városháza
Szent Gellért emlékmű
Statue of St Gellért
Református templom
Citadella
Felszabadulási emlékmű
GELLÉRT HEGY
Fővám tér
Központi Vásárcsarnok
Budapesti Corvinus Egyetem
Szabadság híd
Cave Church
Szent Gellért tér
Gellért Szálló és Fürdő
Gellért Hotel and Baths Complex
Budapesti Műszaki Egyetem
XI
Móricz Zsigmond körtér
LÁGYMÁNYOS
KÁROLY KRT.
MÚZEUM KÖRÚT
KOSSUTH L. U.
SZABAD SAJTÓ ÚT
JANE HANING RAKPART
PETŐFI S. U.
VÁROSHÁZ U.
KÁROLYI U.
KECSKEMÉTI U.
BELGRÁD RAKPART
SALKAHÁZI SÁRA RAKPART
RAOUL WALLENBERG RKP
VÁMHÁZ KÖRÚT
KÖZRAKTÁR U.
VALDEMÁR ÉS NINA LANGLET RAKPART
BARTÓK BÉLA ÚT
KELENHEGYI ÚT
BUDAFOKI ÚT
KARINTHY FRIGYES ÚT
IRINYI JÓZSEF U.
VILLÁNYI ÚT
FEHÉRVÁRI ÚT
BOCSKAI ÚT

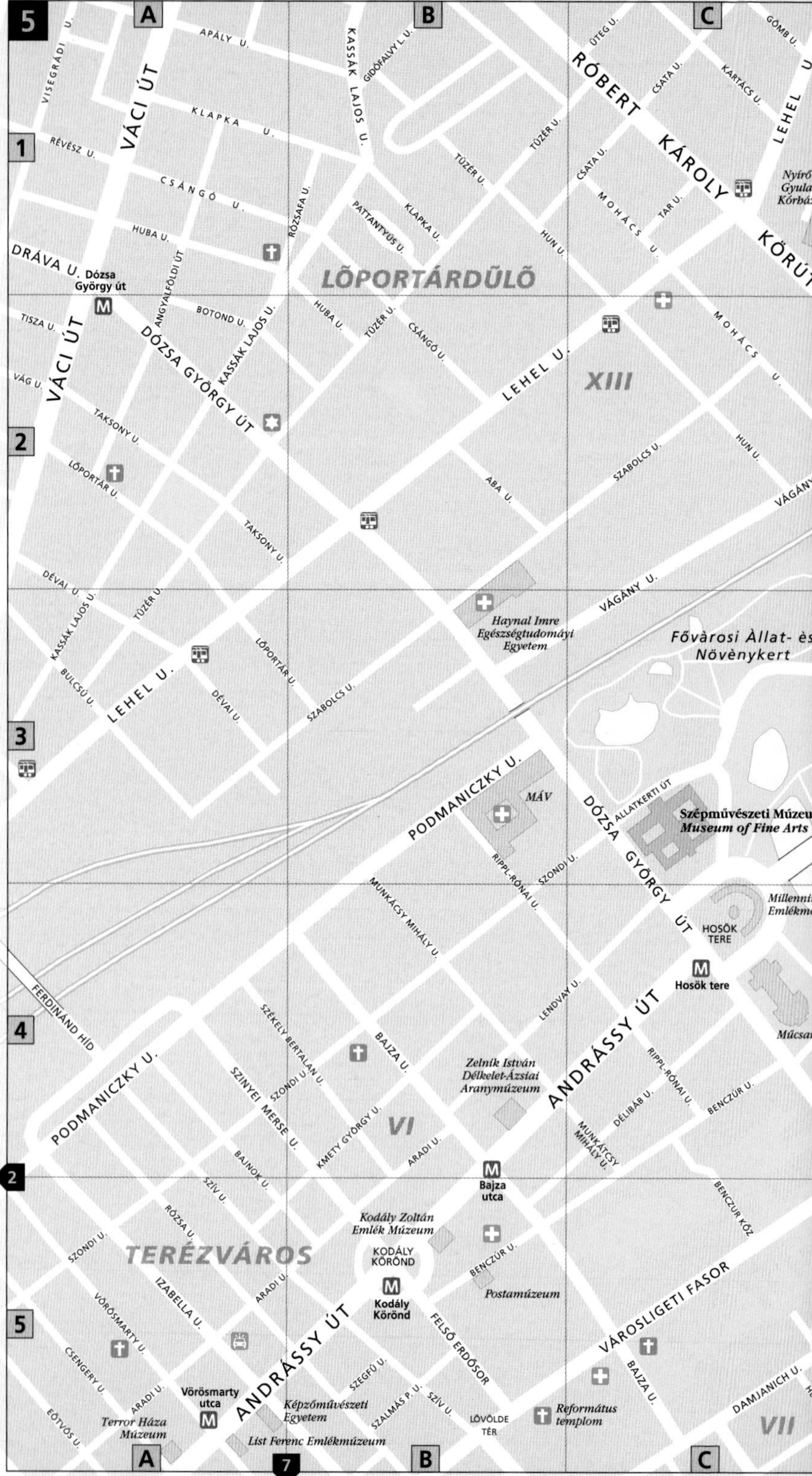

5
A
B
C
1
2
3
4
5
APÁLY U.
VISEGRÁDI U.
VÁCI ÚT
KLAPKA U.
RÉVÉSZ U.
CSÁNGÓ U.
HUBA U.
DRÁVA U.
Dózsa György út
ANGYALFÖLDI ÚT
RÓZSAFA U.
KASSÁK LAJOS U.
GIDÓFALVY L. U.
PATTANTYÚS U.
KLAPKA U.
TÜZÉR U.
ÜTEG U.
RÓBERT KÁROLY KÖRÚT
CSATA U.
KARTÁCS U.
GÖMB U.
LEHEL U.
MOHÁCS U.
TAR U.
HUN U.
Nyírő Gyula Kórház
LÕPORTÁRDÛLÕ
TISZA U.
BOTOND U.
HUBA U.
TÜZÉR U.
CSÁNGÓ U.
DÓZSA GYÖRGY ÚT
VÁG U.
TAKSONY U.
LŐPORTÁR U.
XIII
ABA U.
SZABOLCS U.
VÁGÁNY U.
DÉVAI U.
KASSÁK LAJOS U.
TÜZÉR U.
Haynal Imre Egészségtudományi Egyetem
Fővárosi Állat- és Növénykert
BULCSÚ U.
LEHEL U.
DÉVAI U.
LŐPORTÁR U.
SZABOLCS U.
PODMANICZKY U.
MÁV
ÁLLATKERTI ÚT
Szépművészeti Múzeu
Museum of Fine Arts
RIPPL-RÓNAI U.
SZONDI U.
MUNKÁCSY MIHÁLY U.
DÓZSA GYÖRGY ÚT
HŐSÖK TERE
Millenniu
Emlékmű
Hősök tere
FERDINÁND HÍD
LENDVAY U.
Műcsar
SZÉKELY BERTALAN U.
BAJZA U.
SZONDI U.
Zelnik István Délkelet-Ázsiai Aranymúzeum
ANDRÁSSY ÚT
RIPPL-RÓNAI U.
PODMANICZKY U.
SZINYEI MERSE U.
VI
KMETY GYÖRGY U.
ARADI U.
DÉLIBÁB U.
MUNKÁCSY MIHÁLY U.
BENCZÚR U.
BAJNOK U.
2
SZÍV U.
Bajza utca
BENCZÚR KÖZ
RÓZSA U.
Kodály Zoltán Emlék Múzeum
SZONDI U.
TERÉZVÁROS
KODÁLY KÖRÖND
BENCZÚR U.
IZABELLA U.
ARADI U.
Kodály Körönd
Postamúzeum
VÁROSLIGETI FASOR
VÖRÖSMARTY U.
ANDRÁSSY ÚT
FELSŐ ERDŐSOR
CSENGERY U.
SZEGFŰ U.
BAJZA U.
DAMJANICH U.
Vörösmarty utca
Képzőművészeti Egyetem
SZALMÁS P. U.
SZÍV U.
Református templom
ARADI U.
EÖTVÖS U.
Terror Háza Múzeum
LÖVÖLDE TÉR
VII
List Ferenc Emlékmúzeum
7

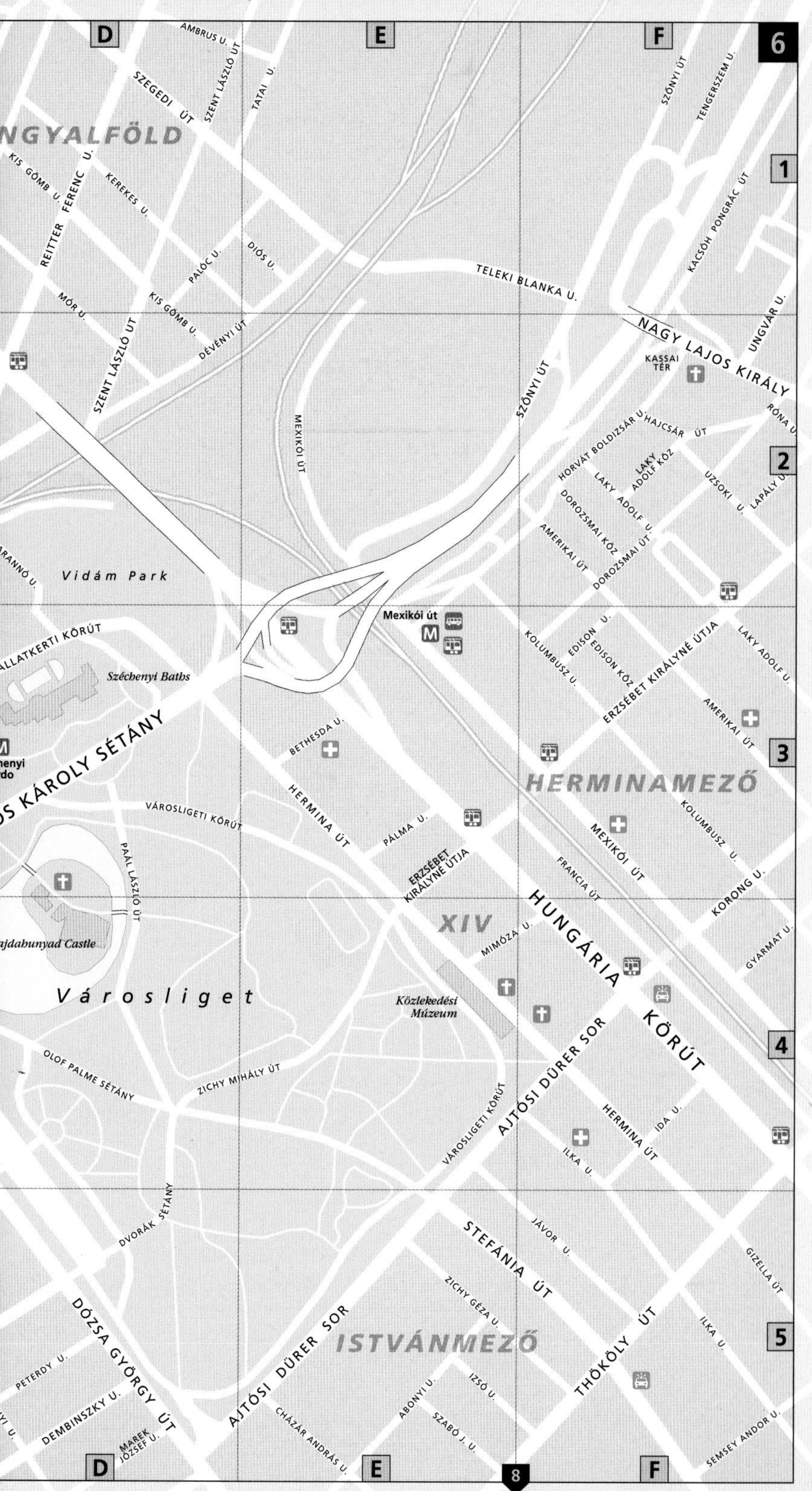
D
E
F
1
2
3
4
5
NGYALFÖLD
Vidám Park
Széchenyi Baths
HERMINAMEZŐ
XIV
Vajdahunyad Castle
Városliget
Közlekedési Múzeum
ISTVÁNMEZŐ
Mexikói út
AMBRUS U.
SZENT LÁSZLÓ ÚT
TATAI U.
SZEGEDI ÚT
KIS GÖMB U.
REITTER FERENC U.
KEREKES U.
DIÓS U.
PALÓC U.
MÓR U.
KIS GÖMB U.
DÉVÉNYI ÚT
SZENT LÁSZLÓ ÚT
MEXIKÓI ÚT
TELEKI BLANKA U.
SZŐNYI ÚT
TENGERSZEM U.
KACSÓH PONGRÁC ÚT
UNGVÁR U.
NAGY LAJOS KIRÁLY
KASSAI TÉR
SZŐNYI ÚT
RÓNA U.
HAJCSÁR ÚT
HORVÁT BOLDIZSÁR U.
LAKY ADOLF KÖZ
LAKY ADOLF U.
UZSOKI U.
LAPÁLY U.
DOROZSMAI KÖZ
DOROZSMAI ÚT
AMERIKAI ÚT
VARANNÓ U.
ÁLLATKERTI KÖRÚT
KOLUMBUSZ U.
EDISON U.
EDISON KÖZ
ERZSÉBET KIRÁLYNÉ ÚTJA
LAKY ADOLF U.
AMERIKAI ÚT
OS KÁROLY SÉTÁNY
BETHESDA U.
HERMINA ÚT
PÁLMA U.
VÁROSLIGETI KÖRÚT
PAÁL LÁSZLÓ ÚT
ERZSÉBET KIRÁLYNÉ ÚTJA
MEXIKÓI ÚT
KOLUMBUSZ U.
FRANCIA ÚT
HUNGÁRIA KÖRÚT
KORONG U.
MIMÓZA U.
GYARMAT U.
OLOF PALME SÉTÁNY
ZICHY MIHÁLY ÚT
VÁROSLIGETI KÖRÚT
AJTÓSI DÜRER SOR
HERMINA ÚT
IDA U.
ILKA U.
DVORÁK SÉTÁNY
JÁVOR U.
STEFÁNIA ÚT
GIZELLA ÚT
ZICHY GÉZA U.
DÓZSA GYÖRGY ÚT
ILKA U.
THÖKÖLY ÚT
PETERDY U.
AJTÓSI DÜRER SOR
IZSÓ U.
ABONYI U.
DEMBINSZKY U.
MAREK JÓZSEF U.
CHÁZÁR ANDRÁS U.
SZABÓ J. U.
SEMSEY ANDOR U.

8

7
A
B
C
5
Oktogon
ANDRÁSSY ÚT
JÓKAI TÉR
HUNYADI TÉR
KIRÁLY U.
ERZSÉBET KÖRÚT
Liszt Ferenc Zeneakadémia
LISZT F. TÉR
DOB U.
ROTTENBILLER U.
DAMJANICH U.
DEMBINSZKY U.
ISTVÁN ÚT
HEVESI S. TÉR
BETHLEN GÁBOR TÉR
VII
Terézvárosi Plébániatemplom
ALMÁSSY TÉR
RÓZSÁK TERE
Szent Erzsébet
Erzsébet Kórház
ERZSÉBETVÁROS
KLAUZÁL TÉR
New York palota
RÁKÓCZI ÚT
Erkel Színház
II. JÁNOS PÁL PÁPA TÉR
Blaha Lujza tér
Szent Rókus Kápolna
JÓZSEF KÖRÚT
NÉPSZÍNHÁZ U.
II. János Pál pápa tér
GUTENBERG TÉR
RÁKÓCZI TÉR
Rákóczi tér
BRÓDY SÁNDOR U.
POLLACK M. TÉR
Magyar Nemzeti Múzeum
Hungarian National Museum
JÓZSEFVÁROS
Kálvin tér
KÁLVIN TÉR
SZABÓ E. TÉR
Szabó Ervin Könyvtár
HORVÁTH MIHÁLY TÉR
Józsefvárosi plébániatemplom
BAROSS U.
ÜLLŐI ÚT
IX
FERENCVÁROS
MARKUSOVSZKY TÉR
Iparművészeti Múzeum
Museum of Applied Arts
Corvin Negyed
PRÁTER U.
1
2
3
4

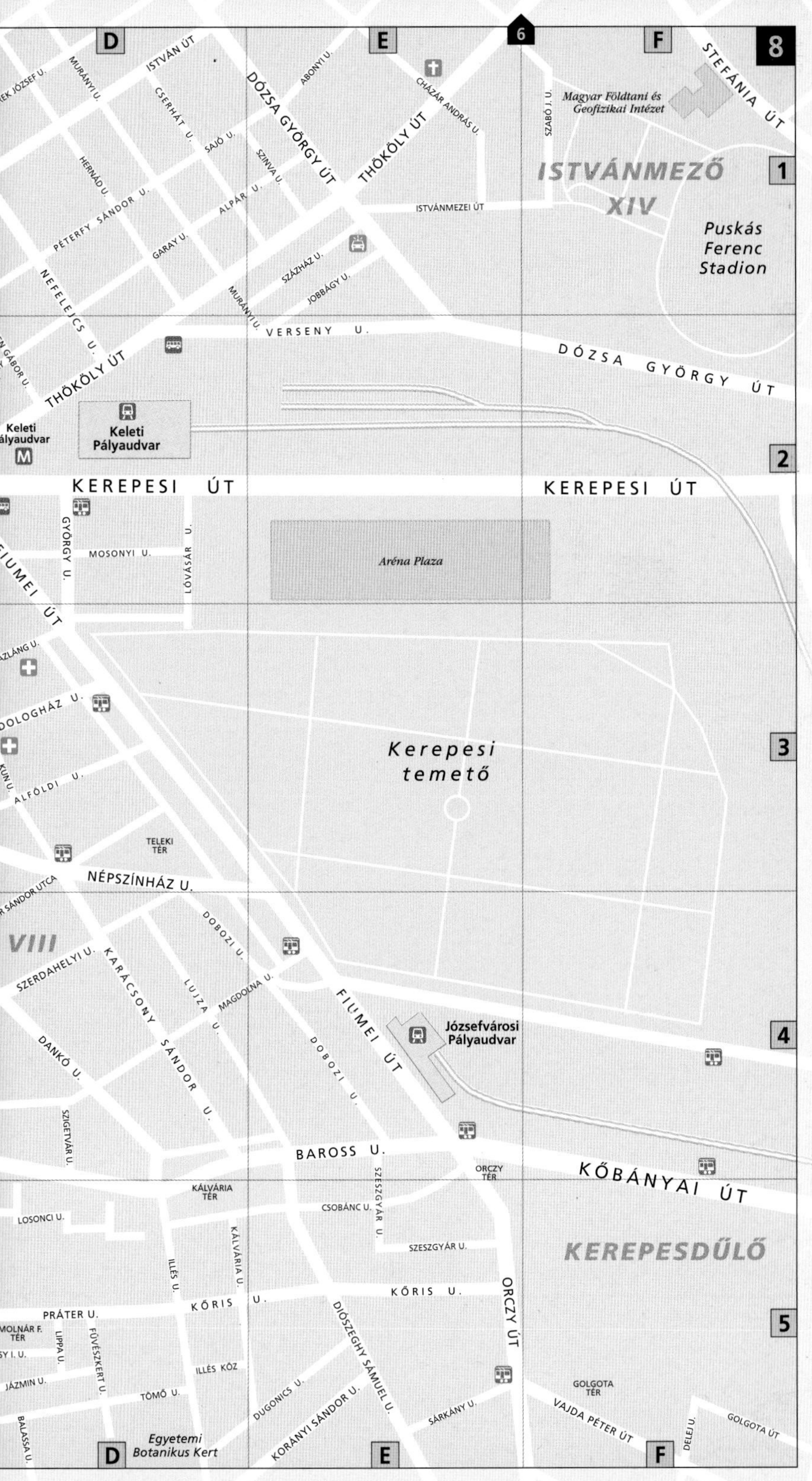
D
E
6
F
8
ISTVÁN ÚT
MURÁNYI U.
CSERHÁT U.
DÓZSA GYÖRGY ÚT
ABONYI U.
CHÁZÁR ANDRÁS U.
THÖKÖLY ÚT
SZABÓ J. U.
Magyar Földtani és Geofizikai Intézet
STEFÁNIA ÚT
SAJÓ U.
SZINVA U.
HERNÁD U.
ISTVÁNMEZŐ
XIV
1
PÉTERFY SÁNDOR U.
ALPÁR U.
ISTVÁNMEZEI ÚT
Puskás Ferenc Stadion
GARAY U.
SZÁZHÁZ U.
JOBBÁGY U.
NEFELEJCS U.
MURÁNYI U.
VERSENY U.
DÓZSA GYÖRGY ÚT
THÖKÖLY ÚT
Keleti Pályaudvar
2
KEREPESI ÚT
KEREPESI ÚT
GYÖRGY U.
MOSONYI U.
LÓVÁSÁR U.
Aréna Plaza
FIUMEI ÚT
DOLOGHÁZ U.
Kerepesi temető
3
KUN U.
ALFÖLDI U.
TELEKI TÉR
NÉPSZÍNHÁZ U.
DOBOZI U.
VIII
SZERDAHELYI U.
KARÁCSONY SÁNDOR U.
LUJZA U.
MAGDOLNA U.
FIUMEI ÚT
Józsefvárosi Pályaudvar
4
DANKÓ U.
DOBOZI U.
SZIGETVÁR U.
BAROSS U.
ORCZY TÉR
KŐBÁNYAI ÚT
KÁLVÁRIA TÉR
SZESZGYÁR U.
LOSONCI U.
CSOBÁNC U.
SZESZGYÁR U.
KEREPESDŰLŐ
KÁLVÁRIA U.
ILLÉS U.
KŐRIS U.
KŐRIS U.
ORCZY ÚT
PRÁTER U.
DIÓSZEGHY SÁMUEL U.
5
MOLNÁR F. TÉR
LIPPA U.
FÜVÉSZKERT U.
ILLÉS KÖZ
JÁZMIN U.
TÖMŐ U.
DUGONICS U.
GOLGOTA TÉR
KORÁNYI SÁNDOR U.
SÁRKÁNY U.
VAJDA PÉTER ÚT
GOLGOTA ÚT
DELEJ U.
BALASSA U.
Egyetemi Botanikus Kert
D
E
F

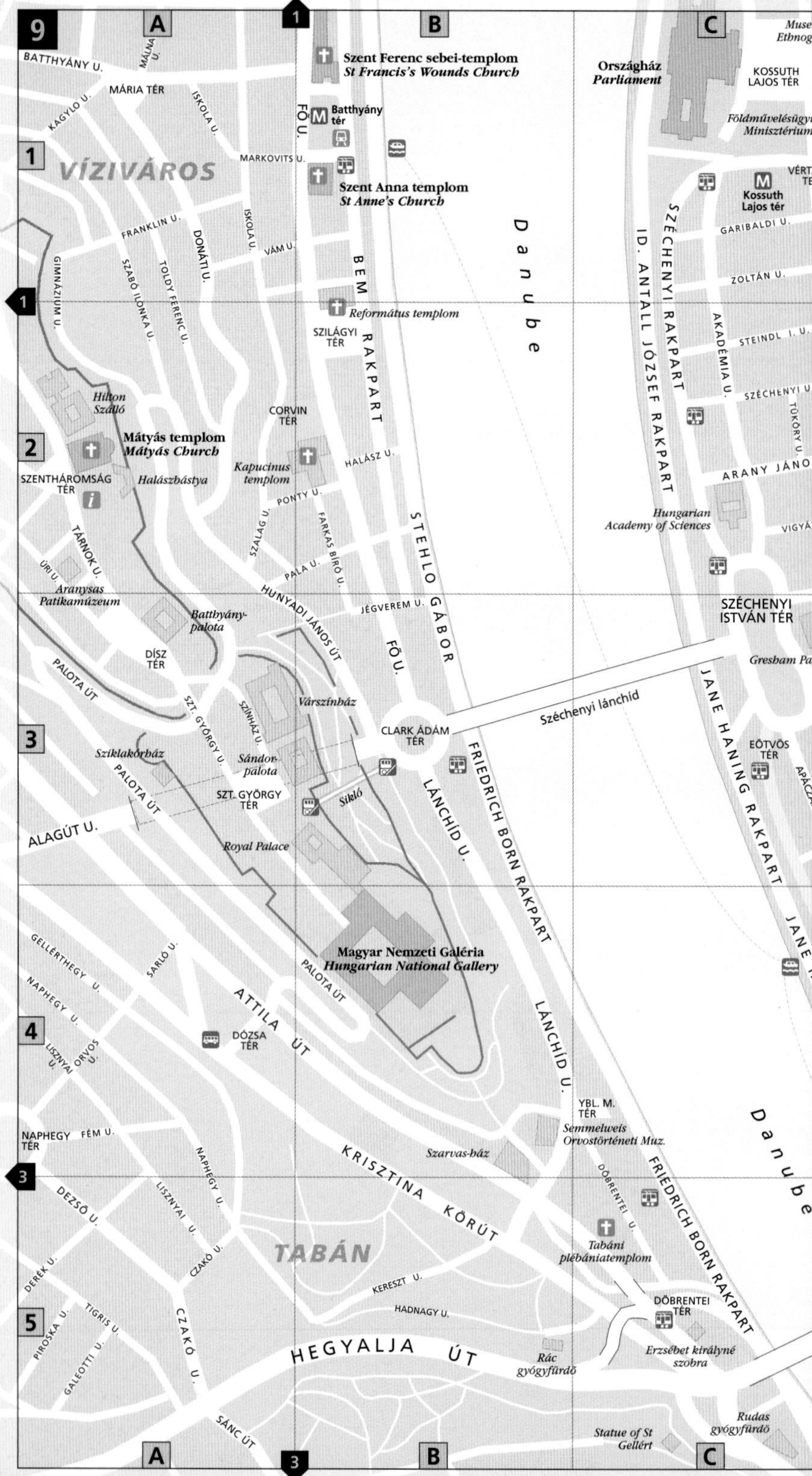
9
Szent Ferenc sebei-templom
St Francis's Wounds Church
Országház
Parliament
Batthyány tér
Szent Anna templom
St Anne's Church
VÍZIVÁROS
Danube
Református templom
Hilton Szálló
Mátyás templom
Mátyás Church
Halászbástya
Kapucinus templom
Hungarian Academy of Sciences
Aranysas Patikamúzeum
Batthyány-palota
Várszínház
Széchenyi lánchíd
Sziklakórház
Sándor-palota
Sikló
Royal Palace
Magyar Nemzeti Galéria
Hungarian National Gallery
Semmelweis Orvostörténeti Muz.
Szarvas-ház
TABÁN
Tabáni plébániatemplom
Erzsébet királyné szobra
Rác gyógyfürdő
Statue of St Gellért
Rudas gyógyfürdő
Gresham Palace
Földművelésügyi Minisztérium
Kossuth Lajos tér
KOSSUTH LAJOS TÉR
SZÉCHENYI ISTVÁN TÉR
CLARK ÁDÁM TÉR
DÍSZ TÉR
SZT. GYÖRGY TÉR
SZENTHÁROMSÁG TÉR
CORVIN TÉR
SZILÁGYI TÉR
MÁRIA TÉR
DÓZSA TÉR
NAPHEGY TÉR
YBL. M. TÉR
DÖBRENTEI TÉR
EÖTVÖS TÉR
BEM RAKPART
STEHLO GÁBOR
FRIEDRICH BORN RAKPART
LÁNCHÍD U.
SZÉCHENYI RAKPART
ID. ANTALL JÓZSEF RAKPART
JANE HANING RAKPART
HUNYADI JÁNOS ÚT
ATTILA ÚT
KRISZTINA KÖRÚT
HEGYALJA ÚT
ALAGÚT U.
PALOTA ÚT
SÁNC ÚT
FŐ U.
BATTHYÁNY U.
CZAKÓ U.

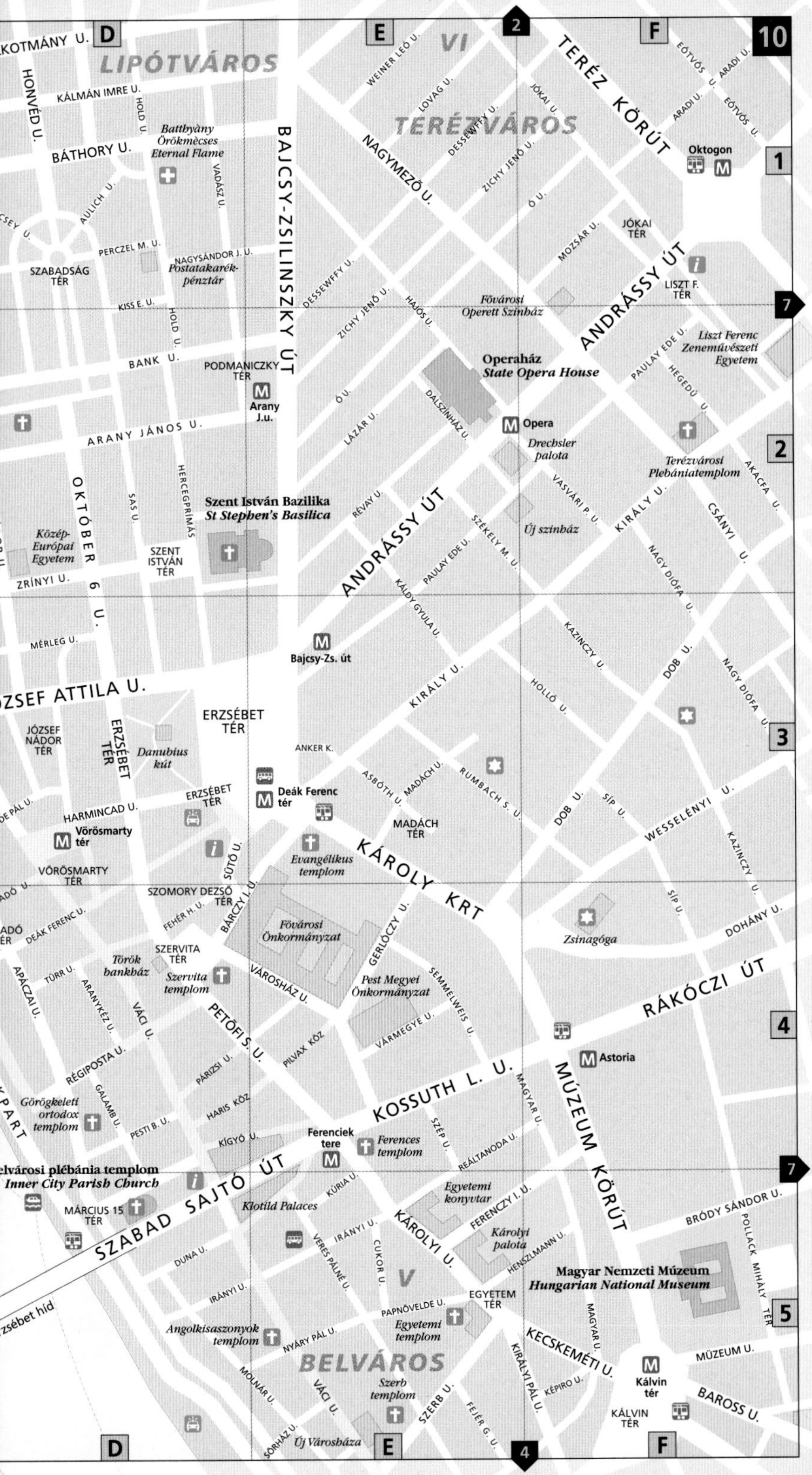

10
D
E
F
LIPÓTVÁROS
VI
TERÉZVÁROS
BELVÁROS
V
BAJCSY-ZSILINSZKY ÚT
TERÉZ KÖRÚT
ANDRÁSSY ÚT
NAGYMEZŐ U.
KÁROLY KRT
RÁKÓCZI ÚT
MÚZEUM KÖRÚT
KOSSUTH L. U.
SZABAD SAJTÓ ÚT
JÓZSEF ATTILA U.
OKTÓBER 6 U.
Batthyány Örökmècses Eternal Flame
Postatakarék-pénztár
SZABADSÁG TÉR
PODMANICZKY TÉR
Arany J.u.
Szent István Bazilika
St Stephen's Basilica
SZENT ISTVÁN TÉR
Közép-Európai Egyetem
Oktogon
JÓKAI TÉR
LISZT F. TÉR
Fővárosi Operett Színház
Liszt Ferenc Zeneművészeti Egyetem
Operaház
State Opera House
Opera
Drechsler palota
Terézvárosi Plebániatemplom
Új színház
Bajcsy-Zs. út
ERZSÉBET TÉR
JÓZSEF NÁDOR TÉR
Danubius kút
Deák Ferenc tér
Vörösmarty tér
VÖRÖSMARTY TÉR
MADÁCH TÉR
Evangélikus templom
Fővárosi Önkormányzat
Zsinagóga
SZERVITA TÉR
Török bankház
Szervita templom
Pest Megyei Önkormányzat
Astoria
Görögkeleti ortodox templom
Ferenciek tere
Ferences templom
Belvárosi plébánia templom
Inner City Parish Church
MÁRCIUS 15 TÉR
Klotild Palaces
Egyetemi konyvtar
Károlyi palota
Magyar Nemzeti Múzeum
Hungarian National Museum
EGYETEM TÉR
Egyetemi templom
Angolkisaszonyok templom
Szerb templom
Új Városháza
Kálvin tér
KÁLVIN TÉR
Erzsébet híd
KECSKEMÉTI U.
BAROSS U.
MÚZEUM U.
BRÓDY SÁNDOR U.
KÁROLYI U.
PETŐFI S. U.
VÁCI U.
KIRÁLY U.
DOB U.
WESSELÉNYI U.
DOHÁNY U.

Street Finder Index

P

R

S

T

U

Ú

Ü

V

W

Y

Z

Index

Page numbers in **bold** type refer to main entries.

Acknowledgments

Dorling Kindersley would like to thank the following people whose contributions and assistance have made this book possible.

Main Contributor

Tadeusz Olszanski was born in 1929 in Poland. During World War II, he fled with his parents to Hungary, where he attended a Polish school in Balatonboglar. He has since visited Hungary many times as a journalist and is the author of five books about the country. These include a volume of articles, Budapesztanskíe ABC. In addition, he has translated over 30 Hungarian novels and dramas into Polish. From 1986 to 1994, he lived in Hungary, working both as the manager of the Institute of Polish Culture and as a correspondent for Polish Radio and TV. In recognition of his activities in promoting Hungarian literature and culture, he was awarded the Pro-Hungarian Culture Award and the Tibor Derye Literary Prize.

Additional Contributors

Sławomir Fangrat, Mariusz Jarymowicz, Iza Mo cicka, Barbara Olszanska, Ágnes Ördög, Ewa Roguska, Craig Turp.

Editorial and Design

SENIOR MANAGING EDITOR Vivien Crump
DEPUTY ART DIRECTOR Gillian Allan
PRODUCTION Jo Blackmore, David Proffit
DTP DESIGNERS Lee Redmond, Ingrid Vienings
MAPS Elizabeth Atherton, Dariusz Osuch (D Osuch i Spółka), Maria Wojciechowska
REVISIONS TEAM Umesh Aggarwal, Emma Anacootee, Shruti Bahl, Claire Baranowski, Kate Berens, Arwen Burnett, Lucinda Cooke, Mariana Evmolpidou, Fay Franklin, Anna Freiberger, Rhiannon Furbear, Lydia Halliday, Krisztián R. Hildebrand, Vicki Ingle, Sumita Khatwani, Maite Lantaron, Jason LIttle, Darren Longley, Alison McGill, Rebecca Milner, Casper Morris, George Nimmo, Scarlett O'Hara, Agnes Ordog, Catherine Palmi, Helen Partington, Pure Content, Amir Reuveni, Ellen Root, Beverly Smart, Jaynan Spengler, Anna Streiffert, Rachel Symons, Andrew Szudek, Julie Thompson, Priyansha Tuli, Ros Walford, Sophie Warne, Márta Wessely, Scott Alexander Young.

Researchers

Julia Bennett, Javier Espinosa de los Monteros.

Indexer

Hilary Bird.

Additional Photography

Demetrio Carrasco, Roger Dixon, Martin Hladik, Ian O'Leary, Rough Guides/Eddie Gerald, Rough Guides/Michelle Grant, Scott Alexander Young.

Special Assistance

The Publisher would like to thank the staff at shops, museums, hotels, restaurants and other organizations in Budapest for their invaluable help. Particular thanks go to: the Ambassador for the Republic of Hungary in Warsaw; the Ambassador for the Republic of Poland in Budapest; Gábor Bányai; Katalin Bara and the rest of the staff at the Hungarian airline, Malév; Beatrix Basics, Tibor Kovács, Izabella Bősze and Péter Gaál at the Hungarian National Museum; Éva Benkő and Judit Füredi Hamvasné at the Museum of Fine Arts; Zoltan Fejős and Endre Stefana Szemkeő at the Ethnographical Museum; Béla Juszel and Éva Orosz at the Hungarian National Bank; the staff of the Kiscelli Museum; Imre Kiss, Zsuzsa Mátyus and Tivadar Mihalkovics at the State Opera House; Konrad Adenauer Stifung; the staff of the Franz Liszt Museum; Zsuzsa Lovag at the Museum of Applied Arts; the Meteorological Office of the Republic of Hungary; the staff at the Hungarian Post Office; Katalin Neray at the Ludwig Museum; Anita Obrotfa at the Budapesti Turisztikai Hivatal; Csilla Pataky at Cartographia Ltd; Géza Szabó; Mária Vida at the Semmelweis Museum of Medical History; Annamária Vigh at the Budapest History Museum. Ágnes Ördög and Judit Mihalcsik at the Tourism Office of Budapest, 1056 Március 15 tér 7, for sourcing pictures and providing new information.

Photography Permissions

Dorling Kindersley would like to thank the following for their kind permission to photograph at their establishments: Ágnes Bakos, Margit Bakos and Bence Tihanyi at the Budapest History Museum; the staff of the Budapesti Turisztikai Hivatal; Eszter Gordon; István Gordon at the Kurir Archive; Astoria Hotel; Dénes Józsa at the Museum of Fine Arts; Ágnes Kolozs at the Museum of Applied Arts; the Ludwig Museum; the Hungarian National Museum; the Hungarian Academy of Sciences; Tibor Mester at the Hungarian National Gallery; Béla Mezey; the Imre Varga Gallery; András Rázsó at the Museum of Fine Arts; the Semmelweis Museum of Medical History; Judit Szalatnyay at the Kiscelli Museum; Ágnes Szél; Ferenc Tobias and Erzsébet Winter at the Ethnographical Museum; Richard Wagner at the Museum of Applied Arts; the Hungarian airline, Malév.
Dorling Kindersley would also like to thank all the shops, restaurants, cafés, hotels, churches and public services who aided us with our photography. These are too numerous to mention individually.
Particular thanks are due to Marta Zámbó at the Gundel Étterem, who provided the Hungarian cuisine photographed for this guidebook.

Picture Credits

a=above; b=below/bottom; c=centre; f=far; l=left; r=right; t=top.

The publisher is grateful to the following individuals, companies and picture libraries for permission to reproduce their photographs:

21 Magyar Vendéglő: 197tr.

Airportshuttle.hu.zrt: 233cla, 233tr; **Alamy Images:** Tibor Bognar 179tl; Eye Ubiquitous/John Dakers 230tr; Peter Forsberg 127crb, 239crb; Kevin Foy 10cla; 49tr; hemis.fr/Ludovic Maisant 180–81; Don Klumpp 65cr; INSADCO Photography/Martin Bobrovski 193c; Jon Arnold Images/Doug Pearson 192cl; Joanne Moyes 84b; nagelestock.com 84r; Lou Oghi Travel 103cra; PBstock 230bl; Robert Pearson 60–61; Sergio Pitamitz

43bc, 83c; Jean-Yves Roure 231tr; Travelog Picture Library 11br; Westend61/Johannes Simon 178cla; **Aranyszarvas Vendéglő:** 197bc; **Auguszt cukrászda**: 200tc.

BFTK Budapest Festival and Tourism Centre Non-profit Limited Liability Company: 222cr, 222bl; **BKK Centre for Budapest Transport:** 238tr, 238cla, 241cra, 241cl, 241br; **Bock Bisztró:** 205bc; **Borssó Bistro:** 202br; **Boscolo Budapest:** 185cra, 189tr, 205tr; **Brody House Group:** 187tr; **Budapest Airport Zrt:** 232bl; 233bl; **www.bridgeman.co.uk:** Bibliotheque Polonaise, Paris, Aleksander Lesser (1814-84) *Grand Duke of Lithuania* (engraving) 27br; Magyar Nemzeti Galeria, Budapest 81tr; **Budapest Festival Centre:** 62ca; **Budapest History Museum**: 27cr, 34 - 5, 40cb, 40bl, 76tl; **Budapest Spa Llc:** 55tr, 147tc; **Budapesti Turisztikai Hivatal:** 52cb, 52bl, 53bc, 63bl, 64bl, 160b.

Cafe Bouchon: 199bc; **Cafe Pierrot:** 191bl, 196bl; **Cave Church (Sziklatemplom):** 96bl; **Corbis**: JAI/Doug Pearson 39ca; Barry Lewis 95tl, 193tl; Reuters/Laszlo Balogh 215tr; Sylvain Sonnet 90; Rob Tilley 13br; **Costes:** 204tr.

Dagaly Baths: 53tl; **Danube-Ipoly National Park Directorate:** 164tl; **Dreamstime.com:**Michal Bednarek 12bl; Artur Bogacki 48clb, 67cra, 72, 104tl; Emicristea 100, 108l, 220-1; Icononiac 12tr; Ladiras81 2-3; Laraclarence 172; Alexander Reitter 5cr, 112tr Sergey Rodionov 156; Scanrail 70-1; Jozef Sedmak 38; Shchipkova Elena 68crb, 95bl; Anna Todero 82clb.

Europress Fotougynokseg: 11tr, 27crb, 29crb, 53crb, 87cr, 126bl, 160cl, 170tl, 170tr, 214bl; Darnay Katalin 97tr.

Firkász Kávéház Étterem: 206tl; **First Strudel House of Pest:** 198tl; **Fotaxi Zrt:** 233clb; **Four Seasons Hotesl and Resorts Gresham Palace:** 199tr; Paul Thuysbaert 182cla, 186bc; **Fuji Étterem:** 207tl.

Gerbeaud Gasztronomia Kft.: 130br, 201tr, 204bl; **Gerlóczy Kávéház :** Peter Flanek 202tl; **Getty Images:** AFP/Attila Kisbenedek 224tl, 238bl.

Robert Harding Picture Library: age fotostock/Gunter Kirsch 13tl; Gavin Hellier 178bl; Ellen Rooney 124t, 144; **Hemingway Etterem:** 191tc; **Hilton Budapest:** 182br, 184br; **House of Terror:** 148tl; **Hungarian National Gallery**: 18, 25b, 26-7, 28cla, 40cla, 56cla, 58cl, 78-9 all, 80 -1 all; **Hungarian National Museum**: 8-9, 22cl, 22cb, 22bl, 22bc, 23tl, 23ca, 23c, 23crb, 23br, 24 -5, 24clb, 24br, 25tl, 25ca, 25c, 25cb, 25br, 26cb, 26cl, 26bl, 27tl, 28bc, 29tl, 29ca, 29cb, 30cl, 30-1, 30cb, 31tl, 31ca, 31cb, 32cl, 33tc, 34ca, 34cl, 34cb, 35ca 39clb, 134 -5, 136br, 137 all.

Jewish Museum: 41cra.

Kárpátia Étterem: 203tl; **KNRDY American Steakhouse and Bar:** Balazs Glodi 200br; **Kurir Archive:** 36bc, 37br; Eszter Gordon 37cla.

Labirintus: 89tr; **Liszt Academy:** Fejer Gabor 133br; Marjai Judit 215bl; **Ludwig Museum:** 42br.

MELLOW MOOD HOTELS: 183tl, 184tl, 188bl; **Museum of Applied Arts:** Ágnes Kolozs 5crb, 58tr, 59clb 140tr, 141 all; **Museum of Fine Arts:** 41tl, 150- 1 all, 152-3 all.

Office of the President of the Republic: 21tr.
ORFK Kommunikációs Szolgálat Sajtóügyelet: 226cra.

Palffy, Georgina: 48cla; **La Pampa Steakhouse:** 190bl.

Racz Hotel & Thermal Spa: Bujnovszky Tamás 53c, 99cl; **Red Dot, Budapest:** 52tr, Serenc Isza 53cra; **Remiz Étterem:** Joszef Mezodi 206br; **Rozmaring Kert Vendéglő**: 207br; **Reuters:**STR 63cr.

STA Travel Group: 224c; **Széchenyi National Gallery:** 40br; **Széchenyi National Library:** 26c, 27bc, 28-9, 76bc; **Ágnes Szél:** 39br, 110tr, 164br.

Tratorria Pomo D'Oro: Artamax Design Studio 198bc; **Tourism Office of Budapest:** 10br, 47tr, 69tl, 118tl, 131bc, 155tr, 179br, 215tr, 223tl, 236cra, 237bc, 240cla, 241bl.

Vigado Es Kultura Kft: 130tl.; **Vörös Postakocsi Étterem:** Serge Tregubov 203br.

courtesy of **Ms Márta Wessely (Perfectum Ltd):** 192br, 193bl; **Westend City Center:** 210cra.

Zwack Unicum: 195cb, 195br.

Front Endpaper: Corbis: Sylvain Sonnet Lbc; **Dreamstime.com:** Artur Bogacki Lcl; Emicristea Ltl Rtl; **Robert Harding Picture Library:** Ellen Rooney Rbc, Rcrb.

Map Cover.Robert Harding Picture Library: Neil Farrin.

Jacket Front and Spine top: Robert Harding Picture Library: Neil Farrin.

Phrase Book

Pronunciation

When reading the literal pronunciation given in the right-hand column of this phrase book, pronounce each syllable as if it formed part of an English word. Remember the points below, and your pronunciation will be even closer to correct Hungarian. The first syllable of each word should be stressed (and is shown in bold). When asking a question the pitch should be raised on the penultimate syllable. "R"s in Hungarian words are rolled.

a	**as the long 'a' in father**
ay	**as in 'pay'**
e	**as in 'Ted'**
ew	**similar to the sound in 'hew'**
g	**always as in 'goat'**
i	**as in 'bit'**
o	**as in the 'ou' in 'ought'**
u	**as in 'tuck'**
y	**always as in 'yes' (except as in** *ay* **above)**
yuh	**as the 'yo' in 'canyon'**
zh	**like the 's' in leisure**

In Emergency

Help!	**Segítség!**	**shege***etshayg*
Stop!	**Stop!**	*shtop*
Look out!	**Vigyázzon!**	**vig***yahzon*
Call a doctor	**Hívjon orvost!**	**heev***yon* **or***vosht*
Call an ambulance	**Hívjon mentőt!**	**heev***yon* **ment***urt*
Call the police	**Hívja a rendőrséget!**	**heev***ya a* **ren***dur* **shay***get*
Call the fire department	**Hívja a tűzoltókat!**	**heev***ya a* **tewz***oltowkot*
Where is the nearest telephone?	**Hol van a legközelebbi telefon?**	*hol von a* **leg***kurzelebbi* **tel***efon*
Where is the nearest hospital?	**Hol van a legközelebbi kórház?**	*hol von a* **leg***kurzelebbi* **koor***hahz*

Communications Essentials

Yes/No	**Igen/Nem**	**ig***en/nem*
Please (offering)	**Tessék**	**tesh***ayk*
Please (asking)	**Kérem**	**kay***rem*
Thank you	**Köszönöm**	**kurss***urnurm*
No, thank you	**Köszönöm nem**	**kurss***urnurm nem*
Excuse me, please	**Bocsánatot kérek**	**boch***anutot* **kay***rek*
Hello	**Jó napot**	*yow* **nop***ot*
Goodbye	**Viszontlátásra**	**viss***ontlatashruh*
Good night	**Jó éjszakát/jó éjt**	*yaw-***ayss***ukat/yaw-ayt*
morning (4-9 am)	**reggel**	**reg***gel*
morning (9am-noon)	**délelőtt**	**dayl***elurt*
morning (midnight-4am)	**éjjel**	**ay**-*ye l*
afternoon	**délután**	**day***lootan*
evening	**este**	**esh***teh*
yesterday	**tegnap**	**teg***nup*
today	**ma**	*muh*
tomorrow	**holnap**	**hol***nup*
here	**itt**	*it*
there	**ott**	*ot*
What?	**mi**	*mi*
When?	**mikor**	**mi***kor*
Why?	**miért**	**mia***yrt*
Where?	**hol**	*hol*

Useful Phrases

How are you?	**Hogy van?**	**hod**-*yuh vun*
Very well, thank you	**köszönöm nagyon jól**	**kurss***urnurm* **noj***jon yowl*
Pleased to meet you	**Örülök hogy megismerhettem**	**ur**-*rewlurk* **hod**-*yuh* **meg***ishmerhettem*
See you soon	**Szia!**	**see***yuh*
Excellent!	**Nagyszerű!**	**nud**-*yusserew*
Is there … here?	**Van itt … ?**	*vun itt*
Where can I get …?	**Hol kaphatok …-t?**	*hol* **kup***hutok …-t*
How do you get to?	**Hogy lehet …-ba eljutni?**	**hod**-*yuh* **leh***et …-buh* **el**-*yootni*
How far is …?	**milyen messze van …**	**mee***yen* **mes***seh van …*
Do you speak English?	**Beszél angolul?**	**bess***ayl* **ung***olool*
I can't speak Hungarian	**Nem beszélek magyarul**	*nem* **bess***aylek* **mud**-*yarool*
I don't understand	**Nem értem**	*nem* **ayr***tem*
Can you help me?	**Kérhetem a segítségét?**	**kayr***hetem uh* **shege***echaygayt*
Please speak slowly	**Tessék lassabban beszélni**	**tesh***ayk* **lush***ubbun* **bess***aylni*
Sorry!	**Elnézést!**	**el***nayzaysht*

Useful Words

big	**nagy**	*noj*
small	**kicsi**	**kich***i*
hot	**forró**	**mel***eg*
cold	**hideg**	**hid***eg*
good	**jó**	*yow*
bad	**rossz**	*ross*
enough	**elég**	**el***ayg*
open	**nyitva**	**nyit***va*
closed	**zárva**	**zar***va*
left	**bal**	*bol*
right	**jobb**	*yob*
straight on	**egyenesen**	**ej***eneshen*
near	**közel**	**kurz***el*
far	**messze**	**mes***seh*
up	**fel**	*fel*
down	**le**	*leh*
early	**korán**	**kor***an*
late	**késő**	**kaysh***ur*
entrance	**bejárat**	**beh**-*yarut*
exit	**kijárat**	**ki**-*yarut*
toilet	**WC**	*vaytsay*
free/unoccupied	**szabad**	**sobb***od*
free/no charge	**ingyen**	**in***jen*

Making a Telephone Call

Can I call abroad from here?	**Telefonálhatok innen külföldre?**	**tel***efonalhutok* **in***en* **kewl***furldreh*
I would like to call collect	**Szeretnék egy R-beszélgetést lebonyolítani**	**ser***etnayk ed-yuh* **er**-**bess***aylgetaysht* **le***bon-yoleetuni*
local call	**helyi beszélgetés**	**hay***ee* **bess***aylgetaysht*
I'll ring back later	**Visszahívom később**	**viss***uh-heevom* **kaysh***urb*
Could I leave a message?	**Hagyhatnék egy üzenetet?**	**hud**-*yuhutnayk ed-yuh* **ewz***enetet*
Hold on	**Várjon!**	**vahr**-*yon*
Could you speak up a little please?	**kicsit hangosabban, kérem!**	**kich***it* **hung***osh-shob-bon* **kay***rem*

Shopping

How much is this?	**Ez mennyibe kerül?**	*ez* **menn**-*yibeh* **ker***ewl*
I would like …	**Szeretnék egy …-t**	**ser***etnayk ed-yuh …-t*
Do you have …?	**Kapható önöknél …?**	**kup***hutaw* **urn***urknayl*
I'm just looking	**Csak körülnézek**	*chuk* **kur**-*rewlnayzek*
Do you take credit cards?	**Elfogadják a hitelkártyákat?**	**el***fogud-yak uh* **hi***telkart-yakut*
What time do you open?	**Hánykor nyitnak?**	**Hahn***kor* **nyit***nak?*
What time do you close?	**Hánykor zárnak??**	**Hahn***kor* **zár***nak*
this one	**ez**	*ez*
that one	**az**	*oz*
expensive	**drága**	**drah***ga*
cheap	**olcsó**	**ol***chow*
size	**méret**	**may***ret*
white	**fehér**	**fe***heer*
black	**fekete**	**fe***keteh*
red	**piros**	**pi***rosh*
yellow	**sárga**	**shar***ga*
green	**zöld**	*zurld*
blue	**kék**	*cake*
brown	**barna**	**bor***na*

Types of Shop

antique dealer	**régiségkereskedő**	**ray***geeshaygkerreshkedur*
baker's	**pékség**	**payk***shayg*
bank	**bank**	*bonk*
bookshop	**könyvesbolt**	**kurn**-*yuveshbolt*
cake shop	**cukrászda**	**tsook***rassduh*
chemist	**patika**	**pu***tikuh*
department store	**áruház**	**ar***oo-haz*
florist	**virágüzlet**	**vi** *rag-ewzlet*
greengrocer	**zöldséges**	**zurld**-*shaygesh*
market	**piac**	**pi**-*uts*
newsagent	**újságos**	**oo**-*yushagosh*
post office	**postahivatal**	**posh***ta-hivatal*
shoe shop	**cipőbolt**	**tsi***purbolt*
souvenir shop	**ajándékbolt**	**uy**-*yandaykbolt*
supermarket	**ábécé/ABC**	**a***baytsay*
travel agent	**utazási iroda**	**oot***uzashi iroduh*

Staying in a Hotel

Have you any vacancies?	**Van kiadó szobájuk?**	*vun* **ki**-*udaw* **sob***a-yook*
double room with double bed	**francia-ágyas szoba**	**front***sia*-**ah***josh* **sob***uh*
twin room	**kétágyas szoba**	**kaytad**-*yush* **sob***uh*
single room	**egyágyas szoba**	**ed-yad**-*yush* **sob***uh*
room with a bath/shower	**fürdőszobás/ zuhanyzós szoba**	**fewr***dur*-**sob***ahsh/* **zoo***honzahsh* **sob***a*
porter	**portás**	**por***tahsh*
key	**kulcs**	*koolch*
I have a reservation	**Foglaltam egy szobát**	**fog***lultum ed-yuh* **sob***at*

Sightseeing

bus	**autóbusz**	**ow***tawbooss*
tram	**villamos**	**vil***lumosh*
trolley bus	**troli(busz)**	**trol***i(booss)*
train	**vonat**	**von***ut*
underground	**metró**	**met***raw*
bus stop	**buszmegálló**	**boossmeg***allaw*
tram stop	**villamosmegálló**	**vil***lomosh*-**meg***ahllaw*
art gallery	**képcsarnok**	**kayp**-*chornok*
palace	**palota**	**pol***ola*
cathedral	**székesegyház**	**say***kesh-ejhajz*
church	**templom**	**temp***lom*
garden	**kert**	*kert*
library	**könyvtár**	**kurn***vtar*
museum	**múzeum**	**moo***zayoom*
tourist information	**turista információ**	**toor***ishta informatzeeo*
train station	**vasútállomás**	vashootallawmash
closed for public holiday	**ünnepnap zárva**	**ewn**-*nepnap* **zar***va*

Eating Out

A table for … please	**Egy asztalt szeretnék… személyre**	*ed-yuh* **usst***ult* **ser***et-nayk* … **sem***ayreh*
I want to reserve a table	**Szeretnék egy asztalt foglalni**	**ser***etnayk* **ed-***yuh* **usst***ult***fog***lolni*
The bill please	**Kérem a számlát**	**kay***rem uh* **sam***lat*
I am a vegetarian	**Vegetáriánus vagyok**	**veg***etari-ahnoosh* **voj***ok*
I'd like …	**Szeret nék egy …-t**	**ser***et nayk ed-yuh …-t*
waiter/waitress	**pincér/pincérnő**	**pints***ayr*/**pints***ayrnur*
menu	**étlap**	**ayt***lup*
wine list	**itallap**	**it***ullup*
chef's special	**konyhafőnök ajánlata**	**kon***ha*-**fur***nurt* **oy***ahu-lotta*
tip	**borravaló**	**bor***ovolo*
glass	**pohár**	*pohar*
bottle	**üveg**	**ew***veg*
knife	**kés**	*kaysh*
fork	**villa**	*villuh*
spoon	**kanál**	**kun***al*
breakfast	**reggeli**	**reg**-*geli*
lunch	**ebéd**	**eb***ayd*
dinner	**vacsora**	**voch***ora*
main courses	**főételek**	**fur**-*aytelek*
starters	**előételek**	**el***ur-aytelek*
vegetables	**zöldség**	**zurld**-*shayg*
desserts	**édességek**	**ayd***esh-shaydek*
rare	**angolosan**	**ongo***loshan*
well done	**átsütve**	**aht***shewtveh*

Numbers

0	**nulla**	**nool***luh*
1	**egy**	**ed**-*yuh*
2	**kettő, két**	**ket***tur, kayt*
3	**három**	**har***om*
4	**négy**	**nayd**-*yuh*
5	**öt**	*urt*
6	**hat**	*hut*
7	**hét**	*hayt*
8	**nyolc**	**n**-*yolts*
9	**kilenc**	**ki***lents*
10	**tíz**	*teez*
11	**tizenegy**	**tiz***ened-yuh*
12	**tizenkettő**	**tiz***enkettur*
13	**tizenhárom**	**tiz***enharom*
14	**tizennégy**	**tiz***en-nayd-yuh*
15	**tizenöt**	**tiz***enurt*
16	**tizenhat**	**tiz***enhut*
17	**tizenhét**	**tiz***enhayt*
18	**tizennyolc**	**tiz***enn-yolts*
19	**tizenkilenc**	**tiz***enkilents*
20	**húsz**	*hooss*
21	**huszonegy**	**hooss***oned-yuh*
22	**huszonkettő**	**hooss***onkettur*
30	**harminc**	**hur***mints*
31	**harmincegy**	**hur***mintsed-yuh*
32	**harminckettő**	**hur***mintskettur*
40	**negyven**	**ned**-*yuven*
50	**ötven**	**urt***ven*
60	**hatvan**	**hut***vun*
70	**hetven**	**het***ven*
80	**nyolcvan**	**n-yolts***vun*
90	**kilencven**	**ki***lentsven*
100	**száz**	*saz*
200	**kétszáz**	**kayt**-*saz*
300	**háromszáz**	**ha***romssaz*
1000	**ezer**	**ez***er*
10,000	**tízezer**	**teez***ezer*
1,000,000	**millió**	**mil***liaw*

Time

one minute	**egy perc**	**ed**-*yuh perts*
hour	**óra**	**aw***ruh*
half an hour	**félóra**	**fayl***awruh*
Sunday	**vasárnap**	**vush***arnup*
Monday	**hétfő**	**hayt***fur*
Tuesday	**kedd**	*kedd*
Wednesday	**szerda**	*serduh*
Thursday	**csütörtök**	**chew***turturk*
Friday	**péntek**	**payn***tek*
Saturday	**szombat**	**som***bat*

Menu Decoder

alma	**olma**	*apple*
ásványvíz	**ahshvahnveez**	*mineral water*
bab	**bob**	*beans*
banán	**bonahn**	*banana*
barack	**borotsk**	*apricot*
bárány	**bahrahn**	*lamb*
bors	**borsh**	*pepper*
csirke	**cheerkeh**	*chicken*
csokoládé	**chokolahday**	*chocolate*
cukor	**tsookor**	*sugar*
ecet	**etset**	*vinegar*
fagylalt	**fodyuhloot**	*ice cream*
fehérbor	**feheerbor**	*white wine*
fokhagyma	**fokhodyuhma**	*garlic*
főtt	**furt**	*boiled*
gomba	**gomba**	*mushrooms*
gulyás	**gooyahsh**	*goulash*
gyümölcs	**dyewmurlch**	*fruit*
gyümölcslé	**dyewmurlch-lay**	*fruit juice*
hagyma	**hojma**	*onions*
hal	**hol**	*fish*
hús	**hoosh**	*meat*
kávé	**kavay**	*coffee*
kenyér	**ken-yeer**	*bread*
krumpli	**kroompli**	*potatoes*
kolbász	**kolbahss**	*sausage*
leves	**levesh**	*soup*
máj	**my**	*liver*
marha	**marha**	*beef*
mustár	**mooshtahr**	*mustard*
narancs	**noronch**	*orange*
olaj	**oloy**	*oil*
paradicsom	**porodichom**	*tomatoes*
párolt	**pahrolt**	*steamed*
pite	**piteh**	*pie*
sertéshús	**shertaysh-hoosh**	*pork*
rántott	**rahntsott**	*fried in batter*
rizs	**rizh**	*rice*
roston	**roshton-**	*grilled*
sajt	**shoyt**	*cheese*
saláta	**sholahta**	*salad*
só	**shaw**	*salt*
sonka	**shonka**	*ham*
sör	**shur**	*beer*
sült	**shewlt**	*fried/roasted*
sült burgonya	**shewlt boorgonya**	*chips*
sütemény	**shewtemayn-yuh**	*cake, pastry*
szendvics	**sendvich**	*sandwich*
szósz	**sowss**	*sauce*
tea	**tay-uh**	*tea*
tej	**tay**	*milk*
tejszín	**taysseen**	*cream*
tengeri hal	**tengeri hol**	*sea fish*
tojás	**toyahsh**	*egg*
töltött	**turlturt**	*stuffed*
vörösbor	**vur-rurshbor**	*red wine*
zsemle	**zhemleh**	*roll*
zsemlegombóc	**zhemleh-gombowts**	*dumplings*

Budapest Transport Map
Key
Metro station
Metro terminal
Metro line under const. (inset)
Interchange station (inset)
Tram terminal
Tram route
Tram stop
Train station
Train line
Cogwheel railway
Hév station
Coach station
River boat boarding point
Tourist information office
Budapest-Üröm
Szentendre
Aquincum felső
VÁCI ÚT
Újpest-Városkapu
Újpest
Kaszásdűlő
Filatorigát
Gyöngyösi u.
Angyalf
ANGYALFÖLD
Duna (Danube)
Forgách u.
VÖRÖSVÁRI ÚT
Árpád híd
ÓBUDA
Árpád bridge
RÓBERT
KÁROLY
KÖRÚT
BÉKE ÚT
Tímár u.
Árpád híd
Szépvölgyi út
Dózsa György út
ÁRPÁD FEJEDELEM ÚTJA
PESTI ALSÓ RAKPART
LEHEL U.
Hűvösvölgy
Lehel tér
Széchenyi fürdő
Margit híd
Margit bridge
TERÉZVÁROS
ANDRÁSSY ÚT
Hősök tere
SZILÁGYI ERZSÉBET FASOR
Nyugati pu.
Esze Tamás iskola
Sz. János kórház
VÍZIVÁROS
Bajza Utca
Batthyány tér
Kodály körönd
Széll Kálmán tér
Városmajor
Orgonás
LIPÓTVÁROS
Vörösmarty u.
Adonis utca
KISSVÁBHEGY
Kossuth Lajos tér
Arany János u.
Oktogon
ERZSÉBETVÁR
Déli pu.
Opera
Keleti pu
Deák Ferenc tér
Bajcsy-Zs. út
Blaha Lujza tér
Astoria
Vörösmarty tér
Ferenciek tere
II. János Pál pápa tér
NÉMETVÖLGYI ÚT
ALKOTÁS U.
TABÁN
Kálvin tér
Rákóczi tér
Szabadság bridge
Fővám tér
JÓZSEFVÁR
Corvin-negyed
GELLÉRT
VILLÁNYI ÚT
Móricz Zs. körtér
Szent Gellért tér
SASHEGY
Klinikák
Boráros tér
Petőfi bridge
Nagyvárad tér
SASAD
BUDAÖRSI ÚT
GAZDAGRÉTI ÚT
Újbuda-központ
Közvágóhíd
Bikás park
Közvágóhíd
Kelenföld vasútállomás
KELENFÖLD
BUDAFOKI ÚT
Beöthy utca
SOROKSÁRI ÚT
Soroksári út
BALATONI ÚT
TÉTÉNYI ÚT
FEHÉRVÁRI ÚT
Kén utca
Szabadkikötő
Budaörs
Nagytétény-Érdliget, Nagytétény-Diósd
Savoya Park, Budafok, Városház tér
Csepel
Soroksár
1-1A
19-41-61
4-6-59A
18-56-59
18-56
59
4-6-61
4-6
2
14
19-41
18
59-59A
56-61
47-49
28-37 37A-62
28-37-37A
18-19-41
51-51A
6
56
24
18-19-49
4
49
1
2-24
18-19
41-47-61